高等学校经管类专业系列教材

国 际 会 计
International Accounting

主　编　吕久琴

副主编　寿　欣

西安电子科技大学出版社

内 容 简 介

国际会计是财务会计的延伸，产生于 20 世纪六七十年代。它是随着跨国公司的蓬勃兴起和国际经济的一体化发展起来的。本书采用英文的形式，介绍国际财务会计和国际管理会计的问题。

本书主要介绍了世界上主要国家的会计制度的差异及其形成原因以及世界范围内的会计模式；揭示了会计国际化协调的程度和进展情况，尤其关注国际会计准则理事会、国际会计师联合会、证券委员会等国际组织的动向和理念；分析了跨国公司经营中遇到的财务会计和管理会计问题，包括国际财务报告的编报和披露问题，外币折算，物价变动，国际财务报表分析，跨国公司治理，国际税收和转移价格，跨国公司成本核算、决策、控制、绩效评价和战略管理系统等。本书能够帮助学生了解主要发达国家和地区的会计业务特征，熟悉中国会计的特色，掌握国际会计协调或者趋同的动态；熟练地应对跨国公司的会计问题。

本书适合会计学的本科生、研究生以及其他经济管理类专业的本科生和研究生使用。

图书在版编目(CIP)数据

国际会计：International Accounting：英文/吕久琴主编. --西安：西安电子科技大学出版社，2015.11(2025.8 重印)

ISBN 978-7-5606-3917-8

Ⅰ. ① 国… Ⅱ. ① 吕… Ⅲ. ① 国际会计—高等学校—教材—英文 Ⅳ. ① F811.2

中国版本图书馆 CIP 数据核字(2015)第 259902 号

责任编辑 马武装 杨美慧
出版发行 西安电子科技大学出版社(西安市太白南路 2 号)
电 话 (029)88202421 88201467 邮 编 710071
网 址 www.xduph.com 电子邮箱 xdupfxb001@163.com
经 销 新华书店
印刷单位 西安日报社印务中心
版 次 2015 年 11 月第 1 版 2025 年 8 月第 3 次印刷
开 本 787 毫米×1092 毫米 1/16 印 张 20
字 数 468 千字
定 价 36.00 元

ISBN 978-7-5606-3917-8

XDUP 4209001-3

如有印装问题可调换

前　言

　　最早接触国际会计是在 20 世纪 90 年代后期，那也是第一次为会计学专业的本科生开设国际会计课程。国际会计对于我的吸引力主要在于其"国际性"，学习国际会计不仅仅要掌握中国会计，还要掌握跨国公司会计、西方主要发达国家的会计以及会计的国际协调或者趋同。中国会计是学好、教好国际会计的基础，没有丰富、娴熟的中国会计知识体系，是无法完全掌握国际会计精髓的。于是乎，怀揣对国际会计的憧憬，开始了漫长的探索过程。

　　最初阅读的国际会计教材是常勋在 2001 年编写的，书中关于国际会计的三大难题深深地吸引了我，为了弄懂合并财务报表、外币折算、物价变动会计等会计难题，我翻阅了很多的杂志、书籍。在阅读了 Frederick D. S. Choi、Carol Ann Frost 和 Gary K. Meek（2002）的《国际会计学》之后，我开始拓展思路，从国际的视角去理解、探索国际会计。Lee H. Radebaugh、Sidney J. Gray 和 Ervin L. Black（2008）的书增强了我对跨国公司会计的了解。跨国公司的会计有很多有趣而没有解决的难题，合并报表、外币折算、物价变动、跨国财务报告披露、国际财务报表分析只是其中的一部分，跨国公司治理、国际税务和转移价格、国际审计、国际管理会计等也是跨国公司会计中的重要问题。随着资本市场的国际化，国际会计发生了很多变化，交易越来越复杂，既影响了国家会计，也影响了国际会计。国际金融市场越来越动荡，导致资产负债表、利润表的数据发生了较大变化。商业增长的国际化推动了国际会计的复杂性。在这种背景下，国际会计准则或者国际财务报告准则的重要性就越来越明显。会计的趋同或者协调正在加速进行着，它不仅影响着国家会计，也影响着国际会计的未来走向。近几年来，国际会计准则理事会与美国财务会计准则委员会的协调框架、协调进程深刻地影响着国家会计的规范体系及其变化，比如中国会计准则体系及其变化。

　　2009 年，由我主讲的国际会计课程被列为学校的双语示范课程，在此后的五年时间内，我一直在思考如何将国际会计课程打造成符合要求的双语示范课程。在课程建设期间，我不断充实原有的教案，增加了近年来的国际会计发展内容和趋势分析；丰富和完善了课程网站内容；完成了课程录像，增加了音频教学内容；收集了美国、英国、日本、德国、荷兰、法国等国家关于会计的资源。在已有习题集的基础上，我根据当前国内外经济形势发展，不断增加新的习题；在原有案例的基础上，增加了许多中国公司的案例，尤其是到美国上市的中国公司案例，绝大部分的案例都是我自己开发的。

　　本书是在原有国际会计课程教案的基础上修改而成的，它是我们十多年来辛苦积累的成果。本人负责全书的设计、大纲撰写、校对、修改以及第1～9章的撰写，寿欣负责第10～13章的撰写。尽管已经修改了多次，限于我们的知识和文笔水平，书中不妥之处在所难免，真诚地欢迎各位读者批评指正，我们将虚心接受并潜心更正。

吕久琴

2015 年 7 月于杭州小和山

目　　录

Chapter 1 Introduction

Learning objective

After careful study of this chapter, students will be able to:

1. Understand international feature of accounting, including international business expansion and development of Multinational Enterprise (MNE).

2. Explain operation environment, and accounting problems confronted by MNE and solution to these problems.

3. Briefly explain history of international accounting.

4. Describe the definition, different phases of international accounting.

5. Show the content of international accounting.

6. Discuss accounting issues when MNEs raise capital in international capital market.

7. Know the major capital market around world.

8. Explain international accounting language.

9. Understand international development of double entry accounting system.

1.1 International Accounting Issues

1.1.1 Two examples

1. Introduction of two examples

(1) Sony Corporation

Sony Corporation (ソニー株式会社, TYO: 6758, NYSE: SNE, LSE: SON), or commonly referred to as Sony, is a Japanese multinational conglomerate corporation headquartered in Minato, Tokyo, Japan and the world's fifth largest media conglomerate with revenue exceeding ¥ 7,730.0 trillion, or US$77.20 billion (2010). It ranked 94 on the 2013 list of Fortune Global 500. Sony is one of the leading manufacturers of electronics products for the consumer and professional markets.[1]

As an electronics business unit, Sony Corporation is the parent company of the Sony Group, which is engaged in business through its eight operating segments— Consumer Products & Devices (CPD), Networked Products & Services (NPS), B2B &

---

[1] The corporation introduction is from Wikipedia, the free encyclopedia.

Disc Manufacturing (B2B & Disc), Pictures, Music, Financial Services, Sony Ericsson and All Other. Sony's principal business operations include Sony Corporation (Sony Electronics in the U.S.), Sony Pictures Entertainment, Sony Computer Entertainment, Sony Music Entertainment, Sony Ericsson, and Sony Financial. Its subsidiaries such as Sony EMCS Corporation (6 plants in Japan), Sony Semiconductor Corporation (7 plants in Japan) and its subsidiaries outside Japan (Brazil, China, England, India, Malaysia, Singapore, South Korea, Thailand, Ireland and the United States) are responsible for manufacturing as well as product engineering (Sony EMCS is also responsible for customer service operations). In 2012, Sony rolled most of its consumer content services (including video, music, and gaming) into the Sony Entertainment Network.

Its founders Akio Morita and Masaru Ibuka derived the name from sonus, the Latin word for sound, and also from the English slang word "sonny", since they considered themselves to be "sonny boys", a loan word into Japanese which in the early 1950s connoted smart and presentable young men.

Sony was founded in the wake of World War II. In 1946, Masaru Ibuka started an electronics shop in a bomb-damaged department store building in Tokyo. Originally, The company had $530 in capital and a total of eight employees. The next year, Akio Morita, his colleague, joined him, and they founded a company called Tokyo Tsushin Kogyo (Tokyo Telecommunications Engineering Corporation). The company built Japan's first tape recorder, called the Type-G. In the early 1950s, Ibuka convinced Bell Labs', who invented transistor, to license the transistor technology to his Japanese company, for use in communications. Then population of portable transistor radios in the United States helps to propel the fledgling industry from an estimated 100,000 units in 1955 to 5 million units by the end of 1968.

Akio Morita founded Sony Corporation of America in 1960. He encouraged experienced, middle-aged employees of other companies to reevaluate their careers and consider joining Sony. Moreover, Sony played a major role in the development of Japan as a powerful exporter during the 1960s, 70s, and 80s. To some extent, Sony had improved American perceptions of "made in Japan" products.

In 1971, Masaru Ibuka handed the position of president over to Akio Morita. Sony began a life insurance company in 1979, one of its many peripheral businesses. In the early 1980s, due to global recession, electronics sales decreased and Sony's profits fell sharply. After Norio Ohga took up the role of president, he encouraged to develop Compact Disc in the 1970s and 1980s, and the Play Station in the early 1990s. Ohga continued to purchased both CBS Records in 1988 and Columbia Pictures in 1989, greatly expanding Sony's media presence.

Under the vision of Akio Morita and his successors, the company had aggressively expanded into new businesses, in order to pursuit "convergence," linking film, music, and digital electronics via the Internet. This expansion threatened Sony's ability to charge a premium on its products as well as its brand name. In 2005, Howard Stringer, who replaced Nobuyuki Idei as chief executive officer, hoped to sell off peripheral business and focus the company again on electronics.

In a bid to provide a unified brand for its global operations, Sony introduced a slogan known as "make believe" in 2009. Despite some successes, the company faced continued struggles in the mid- to late-2000s. It became known for its stagnancy, with a fading brand name. In 2012 Kazuo Hirai began as CEO and president.[①]

For some reasons, Sony's financial result is decreasing these two years. Still Sony is one of Japan's largest corporations by revenue. It had revenues of ¥7,767.2 billion, with operating profit ¥26.5 billion, and net loss ¥124.9 billion in 2013. On 6 February 2014, Sony announced it would trim as many as 5,000 jobs as it attempts to sell its PC business and focus on mobile and tablets.

On June 4, 2015, Sony Corporation Sony's long-term vision is to achieve a "zero environmental footprint" throughout all stages of its product lifecycles and business activities by 2050. The Green Management 2020 mid-term plan has been backcasted (calculated backwards) in order to determine the necessary intermediate steps on the way to this long-term goal. Sony expects to achieve all of the targets set forth in its previous plan, "Green Management 2015," which covers the five-year period up to and including fiscal 2015. With Green Management 2020, Sony will further accelerate its various initiatives directed towards its ultimate goal of a "zero environmental footprint." Sony will also continue to participate in the WWF's Climate Savers Programme, which aims to achieve reductions in greenhouse gas emissions, from fiscal 2016 onwards. Climate change targets are verified by WWF and a third-party verification body for their degrees of difficulty and progress.[②]

(2) China Petroleum & Chemical Corporation.

China Petrochemical Corporation(中国石油化工总公司)was organized in 1983, being a state owned corporation. In July 1998, it was reorganized and renamed into China Petrochemical Corp., or Sinopec Group(中国石油化工集团公司). In the same year, it earned revenue 281.8 billion RMB, and gained profit 3.49 billion RMB, and listed 73 for Fortune Global 500.

Sinopec Group, Sinopec Limited's parent, is one of the major state owned petroleum energy and chemicals companies in China, headquartered in Chaoyang District, Beijing, China. Sinopec Group initiated the establishment of an exclusive China Petroleum & Chemical Corporation (中国石油化工股份有限公司), or Sinopec Limited (Sinopec) in February 2000. Sinopec is a Chinese oil and gas company as a

---

① The corporation introduction is from Wikipedia, the free encyclopedia.

② Data comes from the following website: http://www.sony.net/SonyInfo/News/Press/201506/15-051E/index.html

joint stock entity, with its shares listed in Hong Kong, New York, London, and Shanghai(SSE: 600028; SEHK:0386; NYSE: SNP; LSE: SNP). About 16.78 billion H shares were initial public offering, and raised capital 3.462 billion U.S. Dollar. Sinopec is the world's fourth biggest company by revenue according to list of Fortune Global 500, with sales revenue $428167.4 million as of 2013.

Sinopec's business includes oil and gas exploration, refining, and marketing; production and sales of petrochemicals, chemical fibers, chemical fertilizers, and other chemical products; storage and pipeline transportation of crude oil and natural gas; import, export and import/export agency business of crude oil, natural gas, refined oil products, petrochemicals, and other chemicals.[1]

As we know, Sinopec is a state owned corporation with its market inside China. With the development and mature of domestic market, Sinopec began to expand its international market. On April 13, 2010 the Company announced acquisition of Conoco Phillips's 9% stake in the Canadian oil sands firms, Syncrude, for $4.65 billion. The deal was granted regulatory approval from the Canadian government on June 25, 2010. In October 2011, the company offered C$2.2 billion ($2.1 billion) to acquire Canadian oil and gas firm Daylight Energy. Furthermore, on November 11, 2011 Sinopec announced that the company will invest $5.2 billion in buying a 30 percent stake in the Brazilian unit of Galp Energia SGPS SA which discovered biggest reserved in the western hemisphere since 1976. On 17 December 2012 Talisman Energy UK announced Sinopec has invested $1.5 billion in a 49 percent stake of Talisman's North Sea properties. In April 2013, Sinopec agreed to sell a stake of 30 percent in an oil and gas block in Myanmar to Taiwan's CPC Corp.[2] In March 2013, China Petroleum and Chemical Corp. agreed to pay $1.5 billion for Sinopec Group's overseas oil and gas-producing assets (Charlie, 2013). In August 2013, Sinopec acquired a 33% stake in Apache Corporation's oil and gas business in Egypt for $3.1 billion (Avik, 2013). We could forecast that expansion strategy for Sinopec would continue to occur in the future.

2. International accounting issues

From the above, we could see that Sony is a totally MNE, with many subsidies or branches located worldwide. Please go to Sony's official website[3] and download its 2014 annual report. When you skip the annual report, you could consider many international accounting related questions. For example, a potential investor or business partner outside Japan would need to consider many international accounting issues to effectively use the information in Sony's annual report.

---

① The corporation introduction is from Wikipedia, the free encyclopedia.

② The corporation introduction is from Wikipedia, the free encyclopedia.

③ http://www.sony.net/SonyInfo/CorporateInfo/

(1) From a potential investor or business partner aspect

When a MNE raises capital in international capital market, it faces many internationally related questions. The first issue is about accounting standard selection. For example, what accounting principles are used in Sony's annual report, Japanese accounting standard or international accounting standard? Should the financial statements be restated to a different set of accounting principles such as international accounting standard or Chinese accounting standard in order to provide information that is more useful for the reader?

The second issue is about information quality. As regard Sony, what types of information does Sony not disclose that one would expect to find in financial statements of companies from the United States, the United Kingdom, or China? How does one compensate for Sony's Limited disclosure? What are the related other financial statement disclosures? How does Sony account for marketable securities? Is this approach different from or similar to the accounting approach used in financial statements from the reader's home country?

The third issue is about auditing. What does the auditor's report reveal about the level of audit quality? What auditing standards were used in Sony's annual report? Are they acceptable? Does the auditor's opinion mean the same thing in Japan as it does in the reader's home country such as China?

Other issue covers many aspects. For example, how do national inflation difference, translation or home country language difference influence information content? How are transactions in foreign currencies and financial instruments accounted for? Does the financial reporting of these items provide useful information to managers for managing transactions in these areas? Does Sony's tax expense reflect domestic taxes only? What are the tax consequences to Sony of doing business worldwide?

Answer to the above questions need to understand deeply international accounting. In other words, investor outside home country makes his decision based on international accounting knowledge. A good understanding of international accounting could help investor make appropriate decision.

(2) From MNEs (Multinational Enterprise) respective

When a company lists its shares on stock exchanges outside its home country, it immediately faces additional requirements for reporting accounting information. This is one of the costs of being internationally listed and capital being raised that every international company must pay. Both Sony and Sinopec have to pay additional price for foreign shares listing. Beyond complying with additional requirements, the company faces the further issue of how best to communicate with foreign shareholders around the world. Foreign shareholders probably do not interpret or understand information with the same eyes and minds as the company's domestic shareholders.

Therefore, the message conveyed by the company's financial report may be misinterpreted or misunderstood by the foreign users. Miscommunication may occur. In practice, both misinterpretation and miscommunication actually happened very often in international capital market. Overcoming these barriers to communication is the challenge faced by the company's manager. Additional disclosures may be helpful, especially voluntary disclosure. Some companies have also found that using International Financial Reporting Standards (IFRSs) is beneficial. In general, internationally listed companies can expect to accommodate the information needs of their international shareholders (Choi, Frost, and Meek, 2002).

It is obvious that both Sony and Sinopec face international accounting problems when they raise capital in international market. However, they face different accounting questions, since their goals and strategies are completely different.

From above two examples, we could see that international accounting issues cover a broader range. Before we find the solution, we should know where international accounting problems exist. Firstly, it seems reasonable to say that the international accounting problem lies primarily in the area of financial accounting. Reporting and the attendant ramifications of terminology and disclosure no doubt lead an enumeration of problem topics. Both form and substance of accounting reports become key elements in international accounting. The fullest disclosure may still leave the report reader wanting unless reports have a significant degree of comparability. Secondly, accounting practice broadly describes a second problem group. Thirdly, there are problems in the auditing area.

1.1.2 Additional requirements

Large companies often list their equity shares outside domestic stock market. This practice usually arise many accounting issues. Issues such as additional requirements for reporting accounting information, hard communicate with an expanding base of shareholders worldwide, and language problems are all considered.

In general, a publicly traded company needs to disclose its information to the public. Mandatory information is required to disclose, while voluntary information is selective with manager's intent to communicate with outside users. When large companies become internationally listing, both mandatory and voluntary information's requirements are different from that with domestic listing. Communication with foreign users is great challenge for these large companies. Among additional requirements, language problem is the first for large company to face and deal with.

1.1.3 International accounting language

Language is a way for company to communicate with outside users. Then which language may be the international accounting language. Is it Latin, English, Spanish, Portuguese, Italian, or Chinese?

Technical accounting terms do not travel well internationally or worldwide. Understanding technical terms is critical with international business or trade. Since technical accounting terms often have attributed meanings, it is difficult or impossible to translate these terms into other languages and keep their original meanings at the same time. For example, generally accepted accounting principles are neither generally accepted nor principles. In other disciplines, such considerations have caused the establishment of Latin as the universal language for botanical classifications, Italian as the language for specifying the tempo (and other matters of interpretation) of musical compositions, and English as the language of electronic computing. Since accounting is used worldwide, a single worldwide language for accounting makes sense. English should be designated as the formal international accounting language.

Why should English be the worldwide language for accounting? First of all, English already has become the language of world commerce and multinational business or trade. If you recall the development history of MNEs and international organizations, you would see that English is very common or popular to convey information and communicate with each other. Sometimes it seems natural for a MNE to communicate with others in English. Thus, the universal use of English in accounting would parallel a well-established business practice.

Secondly, the accounting discipline was in many respects developed as an offshoot of Anglo-American economics, which means that many accounting terms and concepts come from English. For example, the view "Fair and Truth" comes from British originally. The Anglo-Saxons were the population in Britain partly descended from the Germanic tribes who migrated from continental Europe and settled the south and east of the island beginning in the early 5th century. The term Anglo-Saxon is also used for the language, today more correctly called Old English, that was spoken and written by the Anglo-Saxons in England (and parts of south-eastern Scotland) between at least the mid-5th century and the mid-12th century, after which it is known as Middle English. The term "Anglo-Saxon" is sometimes used to refer to peoples descended or associated in some way with the English ethnic group, but there is no universal definition for the term. Outside Anglophone countries, both in Europe and in the rest of the world, the term "Anglo-Saxon" and its direct translations are used to refer to the Anglophone peoples and societies of Britain, the United States, and other countries or areas which are sometimes referred to as the Anglosphere.The term "Anglo-Saxon" can be used in a variety of contexts, often to identify the English-speaking world's distinctive language, culture, technology, wealth, markets, economy, and legal systems. Five core English-speaking countries, who are Australia, Canada, New Zealand, the United Kingdom, and the United States, have a common socio-political heritage. All of the above except the United Kingdom were former colonies of the UK.[①]

Thirdly, among non-English speaking people, English is the most common second language. In his book named "The English Languages", Tom McArthur lists 113 "areas" (including country, dependent state, colony and so on) that he named taking English as actual official language, or the second language or common language. Furthermore, Tom McArthur presented 232 "areas" (including above 113 areas), in which English is used to some extent. English have been developed "global language."

Fourthly, the vast majority of the world's accounting literature is written in English. For example, the top five accounting journals in the world are all published in English, and nearly all international accounting conventions and conferences take English as the official language.

Fifthly, multinational corporations generally use English in their accounting and financial operating manuals, as well as for corporate communications, without regard to national domiciles.

Therefore, the worldwide benefits of adopting English as the universal language of accounting are likely to be greater than for any other language, and the worldwide costs are likely to be less (Choi, Frost, and Meek, 2002).

1.2 The International Development of Double Entry System

Accounting is a function of the business environment in which it operates, and it originated in order to record business transactions or international trade transactions. Although the recording of transactions is probably as old as the history of record keeping, we tend to think of the establishment of double entry accounting, the basis for modern accounting, as the key event.

Record keeping, the foundation of accounting, has been traced back as far as 3600 B.C., and historians know that mathematical concepts were understood in various ancient civilizations from China, India, and Mesopotamia—often referred to as the "Cradle of Civilization"—to some of the ancient native cultures of Central and South America (Radebaugh, Gray and Black, 2007).

Double entry accounting was probably developed in the Italian city between the thirteenth and fifteenth centuries. In the eleventh and twelfth centuries, early industry and commerce appeared in several cities along Mediterranean coast. Along with appearance of industry and commerce, there were some simple or occasional accounting practices. The most significant influences on accounting took place in Genoa, Florence, and Venice. There is no defining moment when double entry

---

① Data comes from Wikipedia, the free encyclopedia.

accounting was born, but it seems to have evolved independently in different places, responding to the changing nature of business transactions and the need to record them properly.

The Genoese system was probably a development of the ancient Roman system. The Genoese system assumed the concept of a business entity, distinguishing between capital and income. Florentine commerce also flourished in the thirteenth and fourteenth centuries, leading to the birth of double entry accounting there as well. Florentine accounts listed debits above credits rather than on separate pages. Separate columns for transactions were needed to record which monetary value was used. However, Venice was key in the spread of double entry accounting. Venice was key commercial city of the Renaissance because of its commercial empire and advantages as a port (Radebaugh, Gray, and Black, 2007). The Venetians may not have developed double entry accounting before the Genoese and Florentines, but Venice "developed it, perfected it, and made it her own, and it was under the name of the Venetian method that it became known the world over" (Peragallo,1988).

Luca Pacioli, who was born in San Sepolcro in the Tuscany region of Italy in 1447, was educated as a mathematician by Franciscans and actually became a Franciscans monk himself. In 1494 in Venice, he published the first significant work on accounting, Summa de Arithmetica, Geometria, Proportioni et Proportionalita, more commonly known as Summa de Arithmetica. His discussion of accounting comprises one of the chapters in the chapters in Summa de Arithmetica. According to Pacioli, accounting is an ad hoc ordering system devised by the merchant. Its regular use provides the merchant with continued information about his business, and allows him to evaluate how things are going and to act accordingly. Pacioli recommends the Venetian method of double-entry bookkeeping above all others. In that time, the Venetian method became the standard for not only the Italians but also the Dutch, German, and English authors on accounting. Later, years by years, Venetian method has been transferred to other countries.

In the first place, the Venetian method was transferred to its adjacent countries. Gradually, the method was brought into the British. Then the British transferred the method to its former colony countries such as Australia, New Zealand, Canada, South Africa, Singapore, and so on. To some extent, we could say that British played an very important role on bringing double entry system worldwide.

1.3 The Development History of International Accounting

There is no clear point when international accounting was born. From business point of view, international accounting appeared with the development of international business or trade. International business creates a need for international accounting to be born, as international accounting could help a company to expand business worldwide. There are many events that could prove history of international accounting.

Usually the birth of International Accounting Standards Committee (IASC) could be taken as a key point in the history of international accounting. Therefore, the history of international accounting development could be classified into two stages. The cut point is the year of 1972. Exhibit 1.1 displays the detail significant events in different year.

In 1962, the eighth international accountant conference was held in New York. After the conference, "International education and research center" was created in University of Illinois and the International Journal of Accounting Education and Research was initiated. In 1966, International Accounting course was proposed in University of Illinois. The book of International Accounting written by Muller was published in 1967.

Exhibit 1.1　significant events in international accounting development

	Year	Event	City or Country
Before 1972	1904	the first international accountant conference	St. Louis
	1949	the first Pan-American accounting conference	Porto Rico
	After 1949	international accountant conference every 3 years	
	1951	European accounting and finance specialist union created	France
	1957	EEC(European Economic Community)	Rome
	1957	the first Asian-Pacific accountant conference	Manila
	1962	the 8th international accountant conference	New York
1972 to Now	1972	the 10th international accountant conference,	Sydney
	1973	IASC (International Accounting Standard Committee)	London
	1977	IFAC(The International Federation of Accountants)	Munich

Note: data was collected and reorganized by the author.

1.4　Definition of International Accounting

Until now there is no clear definition for international accounting. From history phases, we could know how researcher recognize or understand International Accounting. At the first place, in 1962 Jennings thought that International accounting was an important step for practice of accounting and auditing to be standardized and regulated. In 1965, Kollaritsch and Mahon indicated that International accounting would research and analyze accounting principle, method and standard for whole countries.

Among different researchers, Gerhard Mueller is the most important pioneer who contribute the international accounting greatly. According to the book of Michael (2010), Gerhard G. Mueller is the Father of International Accounting Education. Mueller promoted international accounting in two related ways. First, he wrote extensively about the significance of international differences, stressing their importance to both the CPA (Certified Public Accounting) profession and corporations that engage in international trade. Second, he wrote and lectured about why accounting programs need to incorporate international topics in their curriculum. "I strongly feel that graduate accounting education is remiss when it confines itself to the limited scope of the single-country situation"(p. 46), he wrote in a 1965 Accounting Review article—a sentiment that today seems almost trite, as schools are falling over themselves to determine how best to integrate IFRS (International Financial Reporting Standard) into their courses, but this was certainly uncommon in the mid-1960s. It is apparent from the extraordinary length and breadth of Mueller's publications that international accounting incorporated almost anything that involved entities outside of the United States. Indeed, Mueller himself defined international accounting as "the producing, exchanging, using, and interpreting of accounting data across national borders."

In the late 1960s, International Accounting attracted many eyes. In 1968, Zimmerman showed that International Accounting was a highest level abstract in developing worldwide accounting theory, with its application in any country. At the same year, Fantl found three concepts of International Accounting. In 1971, Welrich, Avery and Anderson stated the same in International Accounting Journal. The first concept is International Accounting being world accounting. International Accounting would set up generally accepted accounting principle worldwide. The global principle could be accepted by all countries, as a world accounting with its principle and practice being applied and developed. The second concept is multinational accounting. International Accounting will explain and discuss accounting method and standard among different countries. The third concept is foreign subsidiaries. International Accounting deals with only special accounting practice issues for controlling company and its subsidiaries. In 1981, International Committee of American Accounting Association provided three research fields, which are accounting explanation and contrast for different countries, creating international accounting and putting it into practice, analyzing special accounting issues for multinational enterprise. After that, in 1996, Steve Lawrence thought that International Accounting is a process to provide useful financial information based on multination. Exhibit 1.2 shows parts of examples.

Exhibit 1.2　Definition of international accounting

Year	Author	Explanation
1962	Jennings	an important step
1965	Kollaritsch and Mahon	analysis on accounting principle, method and standard of all countries
1965	Muller	the producing, exchanging, using, and interpreting of accounting data across national borders
1968	Zimmerman	highest level abstract in developing worldwide accounting theory
1968	Fantl	three concepts: world accounting; multi-nations accounting;
1971	Welrich, Avery and Anderson	affiliate organizations abroad accounting
1979	Enthove	micro-accounting; macro-accounting
1981	American Accounting Association	three fields: comparison, IAS, specific MNE issues
1992	Choi and Mueller	International accounting extends general-purpose nationally orientated accounting in its broadest sense to: (1) international comparative analysis; (2) accounting measurement and reporting issue unique to multinational enterprise; (3) accounting needs of international financial markets, and (4) harmonization of worldwide accounting and financial reporting diversity via political, organizational, professional and standard-setting activities.
1996	Steve Lawrence	two fields: international, and accounting
1998	M.Zafar Iqbal, Trini U.Melcher, Amin A.Elmallah	Accounting for international transactions, comparisons of accounting principles in different countries, and harmonization of diverse accounting standards worldwide.
2005	Choi and Meek	International accounting is distinct because the information concerns a multinational enterprise with foreign operations and transactions, or the users of the information are in a different domicile than the reporting entity

Note: Author collects these definitions.

Choi and Meek (2005) thought accounting as consisting of three broad areas, which are measurement, disclosure and auditing. Accounting is a branch of applied economics that provides information about business and financial transactions for users of that information. International accounting is distinct because the information concerns a multinational enterprise with foreign operations and transactions, or the users of the information are in a different domicile than the reporting entity.

The definition of international accounting by Choi and Mueller might be criticized as being lengthy and complex. However, their definition has the advantage of being comprehensive. Other definitions might be more streamlined but less complete.

For example, one international accounting text's definition mentions neither the needs of global financial markets nor global accounting harmonization. Differences between general-purpose, nationally-oriented accounting and international accounting are narrowing. Many national standard setters are working with each other to facilitate global harmonization. These cooperative efforts affect both national and international accounting standards.

1.5 Content of International Accounting

1.5.1 Basic content

Radebaugh, Gray and Blank (2007) indicate that study of international accounting involves two major areas such as descriptive/comparative accounting and the accounting dimensions of international transactions/multinational enterprise.

As a discipline, international accounting covers a broader issue. As general, international accounting include comparison of accounting standards, accounting harmonization or convergence, international financial accounting, international managerial accounting and international auditing.

1.5.2 International accounting in recent years

According to Mueller (1965), four reasons contribute why international accounting is important. These reasons include increasing international business and international investments, emergence of the international corporation, furthering accounting research and development and alignment with other disciplines.

From the beginning of 21th century, international accounting has developed very fast. In recent decade, developments such as the growth and spread of multinational operations, internationalization of the world's capital markets, increased cross border mergers and acquisitions, the phenomenon of global competition and financial innovation have accelerated reader dependence on foreign financial statements. Under the globalization, more and more investors began to search investment chances in international markets, while companies take advantage of any opportunities to expand business. As an international business language, accounting builds a bridge among investor, company, business partner and policy regulator. An understanding of accounting differences and their effect on reported measures of profitability, efficiency, solvency and liquidity are critical if proper decisions are to be made.

International accounting issues have become more complex in recent decade for several reasons. These reasons are diversified and cover a broader range. Firstly, financial transactions are becoming more complex, affecting both national and international accounting respectively. For example, the use of complex financial instruments and developing accounting standards for these exotic instruments has been problematic. Accounting of financial instruments becomes worldwide tough issue. In many emerging markets, practice of derivative financial instruments is few. Even in some developed market, derivative instrument is still in early exploration.

Secondly, global financial markets also are becoming more volatile, leading to large changes in asset and balance sheet amounts (items related to investments) and major sources of income, revenue and expense. Unstable financial markets make company decision be short time, and change transaction types. Then the related accounting issues become more difficult than ever.

Thirdly, the growing internationalization of business also promotes complexity. Accounting issues of foreign currency transactions and translation have been troublesome for years. Accounting becomes more important as cross-border business and finance increase. Also, differences in national accounting principles potentially are more troublesome as business or transaction becomes more international. In a long run, accounting difference among different countries would exist, and it is impossible to cancel or delete these differences. However, as convergence efforts worldwide accelerate, and more and more companies from different countries adopt International Financial Reporting Standards (IFRS), complexity arising from differences in national accounting principles will decrease (Choi, Frost, and Meek, 2002).

1.6 The Growing Internationalization of Capital Markets

1.6.1 The growing internationalization of capital markets

Internationalization of capital markets is a trend. The reason for the growing internationalization of capital markets are as follows. First of all, the amount of capital being raised in international equity offerings has been increasing. Secondly, the value of foreign share trading in international financial markets has been rising. Thirdly, more and more companies worldwide are adopting international accounting principles or standards that will be accepted in global capital markets.

Accounting plays a critical role in the efficient functioning of capital markets. Lenders, investors, financial analysts, stock broker, regulators, and stock exchanges require information about the financial performance, position, and the future prospects of companies. In order to seek financing, company will try to meet need of information users through disclosure mechanism. Needs of capital market participants have strongly shaped the development of accounting practice, which includes preparation and disclosure.

The stock market facilitates the allocation of a scarce resource of capital to productive purposes. Securities markets, and their regulatory bodies, are the predominant influence in determining the quality and quantity of publicly available information in corporate reports. The stock market tends to have a major influence on company accounts in the Anglo-Saxon countries--especially the United States and the United Kingdom. Stock markets also have a strong influence on accounts in the Netherlands and Sweden and are becoming more important in some Germanic and Asian countries. The trend toward technological innovation and service economies requires faster adjustments in capital markets and higher quality disclosures (Radebaugh,Gray and Black, 2007).

1.6.2 The main international capital markets

1. The New York Stock Exchange (NYSE)

NYSE traces its origins to 1792, when 24 New York City stockbrokers and merchants signed the Buttonwood Agreement. In 1863, this name was shortened to its modern form, the New York Stock Exchange, which became known as the NYSE. Over one hundred years later, until the NYSE went both electronic and public in April 2006, the exchange was a membership-only organization. You could only join the NYSE by purchasing existing seats, which were limited to a total of 1,366.

The New York Stock Exchange (NYSE) is the largest equities marketplace in the world with total global market value of approximately $25 trillion, as of December 31, 2006. NYSE has a variety of company types. Non-U.S. issuers play an increasingly important role on the Exchange. Our approximately 526 non-U.S. companies are valued at over $10 trillion.

The historic combination of NYSE Group and Euronext in 2007 marked a milestone for global financial markets. It brought together major marketplaces across Europe and the United States whose histories stretch back more than four centuries. The combination was by far the largest of its kind and the first to create a truly global marketplace group. Merging with the already publicly-traded Archipelago electronic stock exchange, the new company was called the NYSE Group, Inc., and the seats of the NYSE translated into shares of stock which are now traded under the ticker symbol NYSE: NYX. In 2008, NYSE Euronext welcomed the historic American Stock Exchange into the world's largest and most liquid exchange group(Data is from NYSE official website).

NYSE Euronext (NYX) Profile include New York Stock Exchange, Euronext, NYSE Liffe, NYSE Arca, NYSE Arca Europe, NYSE Alternext, NYSE Amex, NYSE Liffe US,LLC (NYSE Liffe US), NYSE Technologies, Inc (NYSE Technologies), EasyNext, BlueNext, Free Market (Marché Libre) and SmartPool.

NYSE Arca (part of NYSE Euronext) is a fully electronic stock exchange, trading more than 8,000 exchange-listed (Nasdaq included) equity securities. NYSE Arca's trading platform links traders to multiple US market centers and provides customers with fast electronic execution and open, direct and anonymous market access.

NYSE Amex completed its acquisition of the American Stock Exchange (Amex) in October 2008. As of end of 2010, more than 550 companies are listed.

ArcaEdge is a fast, efficient and fair platform to trade over-the-counter (OTC) stocks. ArcaEdge offers best-price executions based on liquidity, transparency, speed and anonymity.

2. American Stock Exchange (AMEX)

The AMEX started out in 1842 as such a market at the curbstone on Broad Street near Exchange Place. In 1921 the market was moved indoors into the building at 86 Trinity Place, Manhattan, where it still resides. The building was declared a National Historic Landmark in 1978. In 1998, the American Stock Exchange merged with the National Association of Securities Dealers (operators of NASDAQ) to create "The Nasdaq-Amex Market Group" where AMEX is an independent entity of the NASD parent company. After tension between the NASD and AMEX members, the latter group bought out the NASD and acquired control of the AMEX in 2004. Out of the three major American stock exchanges, the AMEX is known to have the most liberal policies concerning company listing, as most of its companies are generally smaller compared to the NYSE and NASDAQ. The Amex also specialize in the trading of ETFs (exchange traded funds), and hybrid/structured securities. The majority of US listed ETF's are traded at the AMEX including the SPDR and most Powershares

Among stock exchanges in U.S.A, AMEX is the only one where stock, option and derivative instrument are traded at the same time, and also one easily neglected place serving for small and medium sized companies.There are three distinct lines of business. They are a wide variety of listed equities, an extensive options market, and an unrivaled listing of more than 200 exchange traded funds (ETFs).[1]

In January 16, 2009, NYSE Euronext group acquired AMEX, paying stock shares valuing $0.26 billion.

3. NASDAQ

NASDAQ was Established in 1971. Acronym for the National Association of Securities Dealers Automated Quotation system, is one of the largest markets in the world for the trading of stocks. The number of companies listed on NASDAQ (about 3200 companies) is more than that on any of the other stock exchanges in the United States, including the New York Stock Exchange (NYSE) and the American Stock Exchange (AMEX). The majority of companies listed on NASDAQ are smaller than

---

① Data is from former AMEX official website.

most of those on the NYSE and AMEX. NASDAQ has become known as the home of new technology companies, particularly computer and computer-related businesses.

As the world's first electronic stock market, NASDAQ long ago set a precedent for technological trading innovation that is unrivaled. Now poised to become the world's first truly global market, the NASDAQ Stock Market is the market of choice for business industry leaders worldwide. By providing an efficient environment for raising capital NASDAQ has helped thousands of companies achieve their desired growth and successfully make the leap into public ownership.[1]

In 2006, NASDAQ completed its separation from the NASD and began to operate as a national securities exchange. In 2007, NASDAQ combined with the powerful Scandinavian exchange group OMX and officially became The NASDAQ OMX Group, further demonstrating its commitment to technology and innovation across global markets.

Today, the NASDAQ OMX Group owns and operates 24 markets, 3 clearing houses, and 5 central securities depositories, spanning six continents-making us the world's largest exchange company. Eighteen of our 24 markets trade equities. The other six trade options, derivatives, fixed income, and commodities. We are the largest single liquidity pool for US equities and the power behind 1 in 10 of the world's securities transactions. Seventy exchanges in 50 countries trust our trading technology to power their markets, driving growth in emerging and developed economies. [2]

Now Nasdaq is a public company listed on The NASDAQ Global Select Market (NDAQ) and part of the S&P 500 since 2008.

4. Tokyo Stock Exchange (TSE)

There are three stock exchanges, named Tokyo, JASDAQ and Nagoya in Japan. Tokyo Stock Exchange Co., Ltd was established on May 15, 1878. It was dissolved in 1946. After World War Two, the market was reopened in 1949, changing its name from Tokyo Stock Exchange into Tokyo Securities Exchange. In April 30, 1999, exchange in Tokyo has been changed into electronic ones, and new TSE Arrows was used in May 9, 2000.

TSE is the second global stock exchange, but it is not a big international finance center. There are few oversea companies listing their share here. Japanese company dominates the market. There was 2414 listed corporations as if 2007, with 25 foreign corporations or so.

In October, 2012, total market value of both Tokyo and JASDA list globally the fourth. On November 20, 2012 both Tokyo Stock Exchange and Jasdaq Securities Exchange held the press conference media session and claimed they would merger into

---

① Data is from Nasdaq official website.

② Data is from Nasdaq official website.

"Japan Exchange Group, Inc.", a holding company, with Tokyo Stock Exchange, Jasdaq Securities Exchange, The Tokyo Stock Exchange Corporation self regulation and Japan securities clearing agencies in it. In February 28, 2014, there are 3416 listed companies in Tokyo Stock Exchange, with 12 foreign companies.

5. London Stock Exchange

London Stock Exchange is the world's oldest stock exchanges, with a history more than 300 years. Starting life in the coffee houses of 17th century London, the Exchange quickly grew to become the City's most important financial institution. Over the hundreds, London Stock Exchange developed to be a global, powerful and financial community.

In London, the earliest evidence of organized trading in marketable securities is that John Castaing begins to issue "at this Office in Jonathan's Coffee-house" a list of stock and commodity prices called "The Course of the Exchange and other things". In 1854, the Stock Exchange was rebuilt. In 1986, there is Deregulation of the market, known as "Big Bang". Then the London Stock Exchange involved great reform including changing fixed commission system, allowing big sized company to enter for trading, computing securities trading, achieving 24 hours transaction, and so on. In 2007, London Stock Exchange merges with Borsa Italiana, creating London Stock Exchange Group.

London Stock Exchange Group (LSE.L) is a diversified international exchange Group. The Group operates a broad range of international equity, bond and derivatives markets, including London Stock Exchange; Borsa Italiana; MTS, Europe's leading fixed income market; and the pan-European equities platform, Turquoise. Headquartered in London, the United Kingdom with significant operations in Italy, France, North America and Sri Lanka, the Group employs approximately 2,800 people.

6. Hong Kong Securities market

Reports of securities trading in Hong Kong date back to the mid-19th century. However, the first formal market, the Association of Stockbrokers in Hong Kong, was not established until 1891. The Association was re-named the Hong Kong Stock Exchange in 1914.

As the second exchange, the Hong Kong Stockbrokers' Association was incorporated in 1921. The two exchanges merged to form the Hong Kong Stock Exchange in 1947 and re-establish the stock market after the Second World War. Rapid growth of the Hong Kong economy led to the establishment of three other exchanges. They are the Far East Exchange in 1969, the Kam Ngan Stock Exchange in 1971, and the Kowloon Stock Exchange in 1972. Pressure to strengthen market regulation and to unify the four exchanges led to the incorporation of the Stock Exchange of Hong Kong Limited in 1980. The four exchanges ceased business on 27 March 1986 and the new exchange commenced trading through a computer-assisted system on 2 April 1986. Prior to the completion of the exchange merger in March 2000, the unified stock exchange had 570 participant organizations

HKEx is the holding company of the Stock Exchange of Hong Kong Limited, Hong Kong Futures Exchange Limited and Hong Kong Securities Clearing Company Limited. HKEx went public in June 2000 following the integration of the securities and futures market. As a listed company(HKEx: 0388), answerable to its shareholders, HKEx competes vigorously for opportunities in the region and around the world. It is a market-driven business, operating business-driven markets. HKEx is having an effective commercial business structure, geared to achieving growth and continuing success. Its operations are organized into focused and commercially driven business units, directly supervised and controlled by HKEx's management and board. The board, HKEx's highest decision-making body, shapes policies for major strategic and operational matters. HKEx provides a comprehensive range of pre- and post-trade investment services. Business units comprising the Exchange Division, Clearing Division, Business Development Division, Information Services Department and Information Technology Division are geared towards providing services which add value for investors, market intermediary and listed companies.

Established in 1976, Hong Kong Futures Exchange Limited is a derivatives leader in the Asia-Pacific region. It provides efficient and diversified markets for trading futures and options contracts by its more than 130 participant organizations, including many that are affiliated to international financial institutions. Derivatives market under HKEx operates futures and options markets on a broad range of products, including equity index, stock and interest rate. HKEx and its subsidiaries, HKFE Clearing Corporation Limited and SEHK Options Clearing House Limited, operate rigorous risk management system which enables participants and their clients to meet their investment and hedging needs in a liquid and well-regulated market place.

Hong Kong Securities Clearing Company Limited was incorporated in 1989. It created CCASS, the central clearing and settlement system, which started operating in 1992 and became the central counterparty for all CCASS participants. The clearing operation is based on the immobilisation of share certificates in a central depository. Share settlement is on a continuous net settlement basis by electronic book entry to participants' stock accounts in CCASS. Transactions between CCASS participants are settled on T+2, the second trading day following the transaction. The company also offers nominee service.

1.6.3 Chinese publicly traded company worldwide

As of June, 2012, there are about 900 companies listed outside China. Especially in recent decade, more and more Chinese company raises capital in international capital market. With development of international business, many companies begin to search outside capital source and increase their ability to survive in international market. The phenomenon shows Chinese company has grown and developed very fast.

However, since late 2010, China listing corporation suffered a credit crisis in the United States. The credit crisis makes us consider the problems deeply. Is it a good way for Chinese company to raise capital in international capital market? What is gain for these listed companies outside? Why most Chinese company faces the same problem? How to deal with the problems? How Chinese company does behave to do business internationally? Chinese companies need to consider these issues deeply in order to get out of the credit crisis and shape a good way to survive in international capital market.

Terms of the Chapter

accountability 责任
accounting model 会计模式
accounting practice 会计实务
acquisition 收购
adequate disclosure 充分披露
affiliated company 附属公司
alliance 联盟
Anglo-Saxon 盎格鲁-萨克森
auditing standards 审计准则
auditor report 审计报告
balance sheet 资产负债表
benchmark 标杆
bookkeeping 簿记
business partner 商业合作伙伴
cash flow statement 现金流量表
capitalization 资本化
capital market 资本市场
conferences 会议 研讨会
continental europe 大陆欧洲
consolidated financial statement 合并财务报表
convergence 趋同
derivative instrument 衍生金融工具
double-entry system 复式记账
external investor 外部投资者
events 事项

financial instrument　金融工具

Financial Reporting　财务报告

foreign currency translation　外币折算

framework　框架

Generally Accepted Accounting Principle (GAAP) (美国)公认会计原则

global equity markets　全球权益市场

Gross Domestic Product(GDP)　国内生产总值

harmonization　协调

home country　母国

income statement　收益表

internal manager　内部管理者

international accounting　国际会计

international accounting conventions　国际会计惯例

International Accounting Standards (IAS)国际会计准则

international capital market　国际资本市场

International Financial Reporting Standards (IFRS)国际财务报告准则

international financial statement analysis　国际财务报表分析

international taxation and transferring price　国际税收与转移价格

liquidity　流动性

listed company or publicly traded company　上市公司

managerial planning and control　管理计划与控制

marketable securities　可交易证券或短期投资

measurement　计量

multinational enterprise (mne)　跨国公司

options　期权

parent company　母公司

price to earning ratio　市盈率

portfolio　投资组合

quantity of information　信息量

recognition　确认

regulatory system　规范系统

reconciliations of shareholders' funds　股东权益调节表

return on equity　股东权益回报(率)

securities market　证券市场

segmental disclosure　分部披露

self-imposed restriction　自我限制

shareholder　股东

solvency　偿债能力

stock-based compensation　股票薪酬

stock exchanges　股票交易
stockbrokers　股票经纪人
subsidiary　子公司
synergy　融合
transactions　交易
trade barriers　贸易障碍

Discussion Questions

1．In your own opinion, when did the practice of accounting begin in Italy? Explain the background situation when early accounting practice occurred.

2．Based on the brief history of accounting provided in this chapter, list some of the key historical events that have shaped the accounting profession so far. For each event, briefly explain how the event affected the practice of accounting.

3．Explain definition, content of international accounting.

4．Identify the most important business, cultural, and political forces at work, and explain how these developments affect the accounting profession in China.

5．One of the environmental influences on accounting is the existence of a sound infrastructure of accounting education and research. Evaluate accounting education and research in China. How could they be improved to prepare Chinese company to compete in an increasingly global economy?

6. Evaluate the political, legal and economic systems in China. Do they support or hinder the establishment of MNEs? Why?

7．How important is the stock exchange or capital market in China? Try to explain motivation, development process, and orientation of Chinese capital market.

8．The chapter states that securities markets are crucial in promoting the development of external reporting systems. What role does accounting information play in securities markets? What is the role of accounting information in Chinese securities markets?

9．Do companies have a responsibility to disclose information for foreign information users when companies do business internationally? If they do, what kinds of extra information should companies disclose?

10．What extra accountability obligations come when a company decides to grow outside its home country? You could take a Chinese company as an example.

11．Suppose that you will someday work for a MNE. What accounting skills do you think you will need to prepare when you are a student?

12．From the history or development process of capital market in the United States, the United Kingdom, Japan, and Hong Kong, explain the role of international accounting.

True or False

1. Napoleon found the Italian system of accounting to be efficient and did work well, therefore he imported the system to France.

2. Venice's commerce was not driven by sea traffic or inflation.

3. Double entry accounting system has been practised several hundred years before it was introduced to other countries.

4. Double entry bookkeeping quickly had world-wide acceptance, as the British accepted it in the 1400s. Then British transferred double entry bookkeeping system to its former colony through its effect.

5. When hyperinflation exists, it is necessary for a alternative systems to replace historical cost based accounting system according to Italian double entry booking system.

6. The International Accounting Standards Board, an international organization dedicated to the diversity of accounting standards worldwide.

7. One trend in international securities markets is consolidation and standardization.

8. The continental accounting system is closely linked to the tax collection system.

9. The first step into international business is usually the creation of a foreign subsidiary or branch.

10. If a firm will not involve in international commercial transactions, knowledge of international business is unnecessary.

11. It is not necessary for him to know international accounting if an accountant works in a domestic company.

12. Luca Pacioli, who was born in San Sepolcro in the Tuscany region of Italy in 1447, was educated as a mathematician.

13. In 1495 in Venice, Luca Pacioli published the first significant work on accounting, Summa de Arithmetica.

14. Needs of capital market participants have strongly shaped the development of accounting practice.

15. International accounting is distinct because the information concerns a multinational enterprise only.

Multiple Choice

1. International accounting is
   a. not a branch of applied economics.
   b. not a independent discipline.

c. an independent discipline completely.

d. a branch of behavior economics

2. Luca Pacioli (or Paciolo) is best known for

    a. his famous mathematics book named "Summa de Arithmetica," which contains a chapter on double entry accounting.

    b. developing an accounting system based on the banks rather than non-bank commercial enterprises and after hundred years later, the system was transferred worldwide.

    c. developing the international trade or business in Italy.

    d. his political and academic ability, which resulted in the adoption of double entry accounting in Italy.

3. Which of the following is true about Luca Pacioli?

    a. He did claim that he developed Venetian double entry accounting in 1494.

    b. He created the first accounting program in Italy.

    c. He was a Franciscan monk.

    d. He was an accountant or bookkeeper.

4. According to Luca Pacioli, where a transaction would be first recorded?

    a. Journal.

    b. Memorandum book.

    c. Trial balance.

    d. Ledger.

5. Which of the following is a part of Pacioli's initial contributions to accounting?

    a. His objective was to publish a detailed, useful mathematical approach to accounting rather than a popular version of accounting that could be used in practice by all.

    b. He believed that all transactions required both a debit and a credit in order for transactions to remain in equilibrium.

    c. He introduced the memorandum book, trial balance, the journal, the ledger and financial statement.

    d. The key point for the accounting system was the financial statement.

6. The underlying reason for national differences in accounting systems is

    a. level of capital market development.

    b. globalization or internationalism.

    c. application of computer technology.

    d. institutional and environmental factors.

7. Which of the following accurately reflects institutional and environmental influences on accounting?

    a. employment system, social stabilization and population planning which is regulated by central government.

b. economic, political or military fluctuation.

c. taxation factor in situations where accounting systems are strongly influenced by state objectives.

d. accounting profession, no matter that centralized and uniform accounting systems, or judgmentally-based systems.

8. Securities markets influence financial reporting for public corporation

   a. by forcing companies to increase both the quantity and quality of their disclosures.

   b. by regulating mandatory disclosures.

   c. by requiring strict social responsibility disclosures due to pressure of warmer climate.

   d. in developed countries but not developing ones.

9. Which of the following is a true statement concerning MNEs?

   a. In developing country, MNEs tend to come from services and utilities sectors

   b. There are no MNEs from developing countries due to underdeveloped situation.

   c. There are no MNEs in developing country due to small and medium sized corporation.

   d. There are more and more MNEs appearing in Latin American and Asian in recent decades.

10. International accounting becomes more complex in recent years, because of

    a. natural resources' unfair consume and allocation.

    b. political force from the U.S.A.

    c. global financial markets' more volatile.

    d. effect from IASB (International Accounting Standards Board) or IFAC (International Federation of Accountant).

Case Analysis

Case 1   Sinopec's Global Expansion

中国石油化工股份有限公司
CHINA PETROLEUM & CHEMICAL CORPORATION

Company Profile

China Petroleum & Chemical Corporation (Sinopec Corp) is a China-based energy and chemical company, and also an old state-owned company. The Company engages in oil and gas and chemical operations through its subsidiaries in China. Oil and gas operations consist of exploring for, developing and producing crude oil and natural gas, transporting crude oil and natural gas by pipelines, refining crude oil into finished petroleum products, and marketing crude oil, natural gas and refined petroleum products. And chemical operations include the manufacture and marketing of a range of chemicals for industrial uses. In other words, the Company operates in four business segments or lines, including exploration and production, refining, marketing and distribution and chemicals.

History

China Petrochemical Corporation(中国石油化工总公司) was organized in 1983, In 1998, there was a great reform in the management of the petroleum and petrochemical industry in China. According to the principle of separating the government functions from enterprises management, Chinese government set up two major oil corporations, China Petroleum Corporation and China Petrochemical Industry Corporation (hereinafter referred to as "Sinopec Group"). At first, Chinese Government strived to turn these two oil corporations into a world-famous multinational corporation, support them with stronger competitiveness and higher prestige in the international market. As we know, these two corporations have continuously carried on a series of nationwide reform since 1998.

The Company was incorporated on 25th February, 2000 by China Petrochemical Corporation as the sole initiator, under the Company Law of the People's Republic of China. Sinopec issued 16.78 billion H shares in Hong Kong, New York and London Stock Exchanges on 18th and 19th October, 2000. One year later, the Company issued 2.3 billion A shares in Shanghai Stock Exchange on 16th July, 2001. As of end 2009, the Company's total numbers of shares were 86.7 billion, of which 75.84% were held by Sinopec Group, 19.35% overseas and 4.81% domestic public shares. Clearly, Sinopec is a state authorized investment and state owned controlling company. The total number of shareholders of Sinopec Corp. as at 31 December 2012 was 732,218 including 725,663 holders of domestic A Shares and 6,555 holders of overseas H Shares. As at 18 March 2013, the total number of shareholders of Sinopec Corp. was 699,189.

Table 1 contains the significant events about Sinopec Corp. from 2000 to 2013.

Table 1   Significant Event for Sinopec Corp.

February 28, 2000	As the sole initiator, China Petrochemical Corporation (Sinopec Group) incorporated China Petroleum & Chemical Corporation (Sinopec Corp.).
October 18, 2000	Sinopec Corp. made a successful global IPO at Hong Kong, New York and London Stock Exchanges with a total issuance of 16.78 billion H shares (including ADRs in the US).

July 16, 2001	On July 16, 2001, Sinopec Corp. issued 2.8 billion A shares in the PRC market. On August 8, 2001, Sinopec Corp. was successfully listed on the Shanghai Stock Exchange.
August 24, 2001	Sinopec Corp. acquired China's New Star Petroleum Company.
December 31, 2004	Sinopec Corp. acquired chemical assets, catalyst assets and service stations from Sinopec Group and sold down-hole operation assets as a swap.
November 2004	Sinopec officially joined the United Nations global compact organization.
October 10, 2006	Reform on share-split for A-share was implemented.
October 11, 2006	Capital was injected into Hainan Petrochemical Co., Ltd. to increase its registered capital. Upon the completion of the capital increase, Sinopec Corp. held 75% of the equity interests in Hainan Petrochemical Co., Ltd.
December 31, 2006	Sinopec Corp. acquired the oil production assets of Shengli Petroleum Administration Bureau from Sinopec Group.
April 17, 2007	Sinopec Corp. issued HK$11.7 billion convertible bonds overseas.
December 31, 2007	Sinopec Corp. acquired five refineries including Zhanjiang Dongxing from Sinopec Group.
February 20, 2008	On February 20, 2008, Sinopec Corp. issued RMB30 billion convertible bonds with warrants in PRC market. On March 4, 2008, bonds and warrants went public on Shanghai Stock Exchange.
2010	The company made quite a number of achievements in oil and gas exploration and production.
February 23, 2011	A Share convertible bonds of RMB 23 billion were issued by Sinopec Corp.
2012	Sinopec Corp. enhanced its corporate governance in 2012 through a number of initiatives.
February 28, 2013	a total of 4,006 shares was converted from the RMB 23 billion A share convertible bond

Shares and Bonds: Where They Come From and Where They Go

The Company was established on 25 February 2000 with a registered capital of 68.8 billion domestic state-owned shares with a par value of RMB 1.00 each. Such shares were issued to Sinopec Group Company in consideration for the assets and liabilities of the Predecessor Operations transferred to the Company.

Pursuant to the resolutions passed at an Extraordinary General Meeting held on 25 July 2000 and approvals from relevant government authorities, the Company is authorised to increase its share capital to a maximum of 88.3 billion shares with a par value of RMB 1.00 each and offer not more than 19.5 billion shares with a par value of RMB 1.00 each to investors outside the China. Sinopec Group Company is authorised to offer not more than 3.5 billion shares of its shareholdings in the Company to investors outside the China. The shares sold by Sinopec Group Company to investors outside the China would be converted into H shares.

In October 2000, the Company issued 15,102,439,000 H shares with a par value of RMB 1.00 each, representing 12,521,864,000 H shares and 25,805,750 American Depositary Shares ("ADSs", each representing 100 H shares), at prices of HK$ 1.59 per H share and US$ 20.645 per ADS, respectively, by way of a global initial public offering to Hong Kong and overseas investors. As part of the global initial public offering, 1,678,049,000 domestic state-owned ordinary shares of RMB 1.00 each owned by Sinopec Group Company were converted into H shares and sold to Hong Kong and overseas investors.

The proceeds from the issuance of H shares of Sinopec Corp in 2000 amounted to RMB 25.802 billion. After deducting the issuance expenses, the net proceeds from the issuance of H shares amounted to RMB 24.326 billion, of which RMB 4.5 billion was used in 2000 for repayment of loans, RMB 13.735 billion was used in 2001, RMB 2.818 billion was used in 2002. In the period convered by this report, RMB 3.273 billion was used, of which RMB 2.273 billion was used for exploration and development and building up production capacity, RMB 540 million was used for the BASF-Yangzi Integrated Site Project, whilst RMB 360 million for the Shanghai Secco Project. As at the date of 31 December 2003, the proceeds from the issuance of H shares were all used up.

In July 2001, the Company issued 2.8 billion domestic listed A shares with a par value of RMB 1.00 each at RMB 4.22 by way of a public offering to natural persons and institutional investors in the PRC.

On 25 September 2006, the shareholders of listed A shares accepted the proposal offered by the shareholders of state-owned A shares whereby the shareholders of state-owned A shares agreed to transfer 2.8 state-owned A shares to shareholders of listed A shares for every 10 listed A shares they held, in exchange for the approval for the listing of all state-owned A shares. In October 2006, the 67,121,951,000 domestic state-owned A shares became listed A shares.

In 2001, the proceeds from the issuance of A shares of Sinopec Corp. amounted to RMB 11.816 billion. Excluding issuance expenses, the net proceeds from the issuance of A shares amounted to RMB 11.648 billion, of which RMB 7.766 billion was used in 2001 mainly for the acquisition of Sinopec National Star and to supplement the Company's working capital. In 2002, RMB 696 million was used   mainly to cover the initial preparation costs of the southwest oil products pipeline project and to build the Ningbo-Shanghai-Nanjing crude oil pipeline. In 2003, RMB 1.514 billion was used, of which RMB 700 million was used for building the southwest oil products pipeline and RMB 814 million was used for building the Ningbo-Shanghai-Nanjing crude oil pipeline. RMB 1.061 billion was used in 2004 for the southwest oil products pipeline project. RMB 611 million was used during this reporting period for the southwest oil products pipeline project. As of 30 June 2005, the proceeds from issuance of A shares were exhausted.

On 10 May 2007, Sinopec Corp. issued RMB 5 billion 10-year term corporate bonds in the domestic market with a credit rating of AAA and a fixed coupon rate of 4.2% per annum. The proceeds from the issuance will be used to fund Tianjin 1 million tpa (tonnes per annum) ethylene project, Zhenhai 1 million tpa ethylene project, Guangzhou 800 thousand tpa ethylene expansion project, and Jinling 600 thousand tpa PX and aromatics project.

On 13 November 2007, Sinopec Corp. issued RMB 20 billion corporate bonds including RMB 11.5 billion 10-year term corporate bonds with a fixed coupon rate of 5.68% per annum and RMB 8.5 billion 5-year term corporate bonds with a fixed coupon rate of 5.40% per annum. The proceeds from the issuance will be used to fund the Sichuan-to- East China Gas Project.

At the first extraordinary general meeting of shareholders of Sinopec Corp. for 2007 held on 22 January 2007, the proposal relating to the issuance of corporate bonds convertible into overseas shares of Sinopec Corp. was approved. On 24 April 2007, Sinopec Corp. issued HK$11.7 billion zero coupon convertible bonds with a term of 7 years. The proceeds from the issuance were used to repay the foreign currency loans of Sinopec Corp. incurred in connection with the privatization of former Beijing Yanhua Petrochemical Company Limited and former Sinopec Zhenhai Refining & Chemical Company Limited, both of which were previously listed on the Hong Kong Stock Exchange.

Table 2　Number of Bonds held

Name of holder	As at 31 December 2008, Number of Bonds held(unit:10,000)
Euroclear	7,578,700
Clearst ream	4,121,300

On February 20, 2008, Sinope Corp. issued convertible bonds with warrants at amount of RMB 30 billion ("Bonds with Warrants"). The bonds were issued with a term of six years, fixed annual interest rate of 0.8% and 3.03 billion warrants. The warrants are valid for two years with an exercise ratio of 2:1 between warrants and A Share. On March 4, 2008, the bonds and warrants were listed in Shanghai Stock Exchange. The proceeds from issuing bonds will be used for Sichuan- East China Gas Project, Tianjin 1 million tonnes per annum (tpa) ethylene project, Zhenhai 1 million tpa ethylene project and repayment of bank loans. The proceeds from exercise of the warrants will be used for the projects of Tianjin 1 million tpa ethylene project, Zhenhai 1 million tpa ethylene project, Wuhan ethylene project, repayment of bank loans and replenishment of working capital of Sinopec Corp.

During 2008, the company issued short-term financing debentures at the amount of RMB 15 billion, which were issued on December 22, 2008. The term was six months and the interest rate was 2.30%. The debentures are targeted on institutional investors on the bond market among Chinese banks (excluding investors prohibited by the law and relevant regulations).

In 2011, in pursuit of the goal of building world-class energy trading position, the company continued to expand global trade and steadily boost our performance. Trade volume of crude oil reached a record high of over 200 million tonnes. Total revenue of petroleum trade in 2011 was USD 170.8 billion, exceeding 1 trillion yuan, for the first time, among which USD 75 billion was from external trade. While ensuring supply security, the company carried out strategic procurement with close cooperation with more than 700 companies worldwide and significantly lowered cost and increased profit.[1]

In 2013, the Company will continue to focus on quality and efficiency of development, enforce strict controls of its procedures for investment management and meticulously organize engineering construction. Total capital expenditure is budgeted at RMB 181.7 billion. Among which, E&P segment will account for RMB 89.1 billion, for the refining segment is RMB 33.8 billion, for the marketing and distribution segment is RMB 27 billion, and for the chemicals segment is RMB 25.9 billion. At the same time corporate and others capital expenditures is expected to be RMB 5.9 billion, mainly for scientific research and information-technology projects .[2]

Question:

1. Why did Sinopec Corp. choose to list in Hong Kong, London and New York in 2000 at the same time?

2. What are possible incentives behind that Sinopec Corp. listed on the Shanghai Stock Exchange in 2001 since it was listed on three Stock Exchanges oversea in 2000?

3. We know the company listed in Hong Kong London and New York in 2000, and in Shanghai in 2001. What do you think the possible reason for company not listing in Shanghai in 2000?

4. How much did Sinopec Corp. raise during 2000 to 2001 and where did the fund-raising go?

5. After company used up all the proceeds early from the issuance of H shares and A shares, We know the company has listed overseas, but why did Sinopec Corp. only issue bonds in the domestic market? Discuss.

6. What are international accounting issues faced by Sinopec Corp. when it raised capital in Hong Kong, London and New York stock exchange? And how are these international accounting issues different from those faced by Sony?

---

① Data comes from Sinopec official website.

② Data comes from Sinopec annual report in 2012.

Chapter 2　Development and Classification

Learning objective

After careful study of this chapter, students will be able to:

1. Explain the effect factors of accounting development in a country.

2. Discuss the relationship among factors affecting accounting development.

3. Discuss factors that affect development of Chinese accounting most importantly.

4. Examine the key dimensions of national culture and how they influence behavior in work situations.

5. Show how cultural values and accounting values relate to each other in the development of accounting standards and practices worldwide.

6. Describe four accounting values from Gray.

7. Describe four accounting comparative models.

8. Explain how accounting model develop with the environmental or institutional model of an economy.

9. Distinguish fair presentation and compliance accounting.

Both development and classification is a way to understand national and international accounting. There are many factors to affect development of accounting . National accounting originate, and develop in a certain political, economic and institutional situation. Why should we know how accounting develops? If we could identify what causes accounting to develop, we would be able to influence or anticipate its direction and rate of change, analyze its rule. Different countries have different development stages with specific country history. Then we can better understand a nation's accounting by knowing the underlying factors that influence its development.

Why should we classify national or regional financial accounting systems? Classification may refer to categorization, the process in which ideas and objects are recognized, differentiated, and understood (from Wikipedia). From accounting point of view, the goal of classification is to group countries according to the distinctive characteristics of their financial accounting systems. Also classification is a fundamental to understanding and analyzing why and how national accounting system differs. The classification process should help us describe and compare international accounting systems in a way that will promote improved understanding of the complex realities of accounting practice. By classification, we could know the extent to which nations in accounting are similar to or different from each other, the pattern of development individual national system and its change, and reasons that some national system dominates while others do not.

Furthermore, classification also has some practical benefits. The countries in a particular group are likely to react to new circumstances in similar ways. The differences among groups are barriers to the regional and worldwide harmonization efforts. Developing countries may be able to pattern their standards after existing standards. Communication problems are likely to be more severe when a company reports to financial statement users who are unfamiliar with the company's home-country accounting standards (Choi, Frost, and Meek, 2002).

2.1 Development

2.1.1 Factors influencing accounting development

Every nation's accounting standards and practices result from a complex interaction of political, economic, historical, institutional, and cultural factors. Diversity among nations is to be expected. The factors that influence national accounting development also help explain the accounting diversity among nations. In some countries such as France, Germany, and Japan, institutional factors are more important while in other countries such as the United States, and the United Kingdom, economic factors are more dominated.

The following eight factors have a significant influence on accounting development in all. The first seven are economic, socio-historical, and /or institutional in nature, and they have occupied most of the attention of accounting writers (Choi and Meek, 2008), while the last one is cultural.

1. Source of finance

Source of finance affects way which manager raise capital in stock market, then manager's behavior lead to change of accounting policy selection, information disclosure and quality. In some countries, manager in an enterprise tends to raise capital in an open equity market, while in other countries, manager like to borrow money from a bank. That means equity market dominate the source of finance in some countries, while bank is the main source of finance in other countries. For countries with strong equity markets, investor protection is more emphasized. Flexibility of accounting is ahead of compulsory regulation. Accounting focuses on how well management runs the profitability, and is designed to help investors assess future cash flows and related risks. Therefore, disclosures are extensive. In countries where bank dominates source of finance, regulation of accounting is priority to flexibility.

Accounting focuses on creditor protection through conservative accounting measurements. Thus, extensive public disclosures are not considered necessarily. Accounting is prone to meet the information need of bank mainly.

Exhibit 2.1　Initial classification based on corporate financing

Features	
A	B
Strong equity market	Weaker equity market
Many outside shareholders	Core inside shareholders
Large auditing profession	Small auditing profession
Accounting and tax rules separation	Tax rules dominates accounting system
Example of countries	
United States	France
United Kingdom	Italy
Australia	Germany
New Zealand	Japan
Canada	South Korea

2. Legal system

The legal system determines how individuals and institutions interact with each other. According to the WIKIPEDIA(the free encyclopedia), legal systems of the world are generally based on one of three basic systems: civil law, common law, and religious law – or combinations of these. However, the legal system of each country is shaped by its unique history and so incorporates individual variations.

Civil law is the most widespread system of law around the world. It is also sometimes known as Continental European law. The central source of law that is recognized as authoritative is codifications in a constitution or statute passed by legislature, to amend a code. While the concept of codification could trace back to the Code of Hammurabi in Babylon ca. 1790 BC, civil law systems derive from the Roman Empire and, more particularly, the Corpus Juris Civilis issued by the Emperor Justinian ca. AD 529. This was an extensive reform of the law in the Byzantine Empire, bringing it together into codified documents. Civil law was also partly influenced by religious laws such as Canon law and Islamic law (the free encyclopedia website). Some scholars classify civil law countries into four categories, including French civil law, German civil law, Scandinavian civil law and Chinese law.

Chinese civil law is a mixture of civil law and socialist law in use. In ancient China, the first comprehensive criminal code was the Tang Code, created in 624 AD in the Tang Dynasty. This, and subsequent imperial codes, formed the basis for the penal system of both China and other East Asian states under its cultural influence. The last and best preserved imperial code is the Great Qing Legal Code, created in 1644 upon the founding of the Qing Dynasty. This code was the exclusive and exhaustive statement of Chinese law between 1644 and 1912. Though it was in form a criminal code, large parts of the code dealt with civil law matters and the settlement of civil disputes. The Code ceased its operation upon the fall of the Qing dynasty in 1912, but significant provisions remained in operation in Hong Kong until well into the 1970s due to a peculiar interaction between it and the British common law system (the free encyclopedia website).

Common law is systems of law whose sources are the decisions in cases by judges. Every system will have a legislature that passes new laws and statutes. The relationships between statutes and judicial decisions can be complex. In some jurisdictions, such statutes may overrule judicial decisions or codify the topic covered by several contradictory or ambiguous decisions, while in other jurisdictions, judicial decisions may decide whether the jurisdiction's constitution allowed a particular statute or statutory provision to be made or what meaning is contained within the statutory provisions. Statutes were allowed to be made by the government. Common law developed in England, influenced by Anglo-Saxon law and to a much lesser extent by the Norman conquest of England which introduced legal concepts from Norman law, which had its origins in Salic law. Common law was later inherited by the Commonwealth of Nations, and almost every former colony of the British Empire has adopted it (Malta being an exception). The doctrine of stare decisis or precedent by courts is the major difference to codified civil law systems (the free encyclopedia website).

Religious law refers to the notion of a religious system or document being used as a legal source, though the methodology used varies. For example, the use of Jewish Halakha for public law has a static and unalterable quality, precluding amendment through legislative acts of government or development through judicial precedent; Christian Canon law is more similar to civil law in its use of civil codes; and Islamic Sharia law (and Fiqh jurisprudence) is based on legal precedent and reasoning by analogy (Qiyas), and is thus considered similar to common law. The main kinds of religious law are Sharia in Islam, Halakha in Judaism, and canon law in some Christian groups. In some cases these are intended purely as individual moral guidance, whereas in other cases they are intended and may be used as the basis for a country's legal system. The latter was particularly common during the Middle Ages. The Islamic legal system of Sharia (Islamic law) and Fiqh (Islamic jurisprudence) is the most widely used religious law (the free encyclopedia website).

In Civil Code law countries, laws are an all-embracing set of requirements and procedures. Accounting rules incorporated into national laws and tend to be highly prescriptive and procedural.

Common law develops on a case by case basis with no attempt to cover all cases in an all-encompassing code. Statute law does exist, but it tends to be less detailed and more flexible. Common law derives from English case law. Accounting rules are established by private sector professional organization. Except for broad statutory requirements, most accounting rules are not incorporated directly into statute law.

Exhibit 2.2　Legal systems

Common law countries (or area)	Civil law countries (or area)			
	French civil law	German civil law	Scandinavian civil law	Chinese law
Ireland	France	Germany	Denmark	the People's Republic of China
the United Kingdom	the Benelux countries	Austria	Norway	
Australia	Romania	Switzerland	Sweden	
New Zealand	Italy	Estonia	Finland	
Bangladesh	Spain	Latvia	Iceland	
India (excluding Goa)	former colonies of above countries	former Yugoslav republics		
Pakistan		Greece		
South Africa		Portugal and its former colonies		
Canada (excluding Quebec)		Japan		
Hong Kong		Turkey		
the United States (excluding Louisiana)		Taiwan area		

Note: data comes from the free encyclopedia website.

3. Taxation

It is indirect for taxation to affect accounting theory. Issue and enforcement of taxation is a way to protect new accounting methods to be practiced. It is helpful for taxation to enhance necessity and materiality of accounting work, and improve the continuity of accounting practice.

Tax legislation is a part of law system in a country. To what extent tax legislation related to accounting regulation depends on the law system in a specific country. In many countries, tax legislation effectively determines accounting standards because companies must record revenues and expenses in their accounts to claim them for tax purposes. For example, in Germany and Sweden, tax legislation determines accounting standards. Moreover, tax accounting and financial accounting is not separate in these countries.

But in other countries, tax legislation and accounting standard are two different systems and could be separated. Even where financial and tax accounting are separated with each other, tax legislation may occasionally require the application of certain accounting principles. For example, in Netherlands and U.S.A, tax legislation and accounting standard are separate, and tax legislation may occasionally require the application of accounting standards or principles. And in a certain extent, tax accounting is different from financial accounting.

4. Political and economic ties

Any country is not independent in the world. International trade makes a country more close to another one and shortens the distance between two countries. Political or economic agreement provides chances for a country to communicate or trade with another country. Accounting communication is a part of international communication. Accounting ideas and technologies could be transferred through conquest, commerce, and similar forces.

Double-entry bookkeeping was originated in Italy, but transferred to British Colonialism by the United Kingdom through conquest. In the early 1920s, under the political influence, American accounting is transferred to the British commonwealth of nations. Germany, who used political relation with Japan, Sweden, made accounting method export these countries. Another example is that German occupation during World War Two led France to adopt its Plan Comptable. The United States forced U S-style accounting regulatory regimes on Japan after World War Two. Both political and economic relationship between U.S.A. and Taiwan area makes accounting standard and auditing standard setting process similar with each other. Recent years, accounting methods in the European Union have influenced accounting in its member country through various Directives.

5. Inflation

Inflation will have a great effect on both accounting theory and practice. Firstly, inflation changes the assumption of monetary measurement. Under the inflation, accounting information based on historical cost make accounting information lost comparability and understandability. Historical, current and realizable costs are all usually used measurement ways. Many countries such as U.S.A., China, France, and Germany take historical cost as basic measurement, while both historical and current cost are used in British and Netherlands. If there is an inflation or deflation, relevance of accounting information could be influenced. Inflation distorts historical cost accounting and affects the tendency of a country to incorporate price changes into the accounts. The result is to reduce the relevance of accounting information. In the late 1970s, both U.K and U.S.A experimented with reporting the effects of changing prices. Israel, Mexico and certain countries of South America use general price level accounting because of hyperinflation.

Also inflation challenge basic principle of accounting records, and shake principle of historical cost and prudence. Furthermore, inflation has certain influence on matching principle.

In practice, inflation will distort basic accounting data, financial position and operating result. Under the inflation, capital in a company could not show its real situation. Finally, because of distortion of accounting data, and later financial statement, decision from information users will be affected.

6. Level of economic development

To some extent, there is a more developed economy, and accounting is more important. Developed economy provides base for accounting to improve, while complex business creates the necessity for accounting information.

The level of economic development affects the types of business transactions conducted in an economy. The higher level of economic development will bring new business activities, and complicated transaction, while lower level of economic development results in simple or regular business activities. In a developed economy, business transaction are complex, and challenged with new transaction or events happening, while in an undeveloped economy, business transactions are simple or unchallenged. The type of transactions determines the accounting issues that are faced. For example, stock based executive compensation or asset securitization makes little sense in economies with underdeveloped capital markets. New accounting changes, such as valuing intangibles and human resources, are emerging in industrial economy. Financial instrument accounting makes little sense in a very developing economy, while it is affused and challenged in a developed economy.

7. Education level

Education system is a part of institutional system. Education level reflects degree of social progress and civilization in a country. Education includes general educational degree and professional education situation. High educational level could help to train high degree accountant and promote accounting profession.

In different countries, there are different educational systems with a variety level. In countries with developed education, concern for accounting information is high. Highly sophisticated accounting standards and practices could be understood, while in a developing education, understanding of standards or regulation could be hard. Accounting regulations are useless if they are misunderstood and misused. Furthermore, education is a basis for development of accounting information system, and accounting profession. Education can train much more professional accountants and help them deal with complicated business activities.

8. Culture

Culture is an old and debating issue. Culture is a concept based on a term first used in classical antiquity by the Roman orator Cicero. In the 20th century, "culture" emerged as a central concept in anthropology, encompassing the range of human phenomena that cannot be directly attributed to genetic inheritance (from Wikipedia).

Generally speaking, culture means the values and attitudes shared by a society. Research on culture has a long history. Many researchers have great interest in culture. One of the best researches is Geert Hofstede, who comes from the Netherlands. Hofstede developed his original model as a result of using factor analysis to examine the results of a world-wide survey of employee values by IBM in the 1960s and 1970s. In 1980, Hofstede enunciated four national cultural dimensions or societal values. They are individualism versus collectivism, great versus small power distance, strong versus weak uncertainty avoidance and masculinity versus feminism. In 1988, Hofstede and Bond increased "Confucian Dynamism" or "Long-term orientation" based on the findings of Hofstede in 1980, to cover aspects of values not discussed in the original paradigm. In the 2010 edition of Cultures and Organizations: Software of the Mind, Hofstede added a sixth dimension, indulgence versus self-restraint, as a result of co-author Michael Minkov's analysis of data from the World Values Survey (Hofstede,2010). Further research has refined some of the original dimensions, and introduced the difference between country-level and individual-level data in analysis.

Hofstede's cultural dimensions theory is a framework for cross-cultural communication. It describes the effects of a society's culture on the values of its members, and how these values relate to behavior, using a structure derived from factor analysis. The theory has been widely used in several fields as a paradigm for research, particularly in cross-cultural psychology, international management, and cross-cultural communication. Hofstede's work established a major research tradition in cross-cultural psychology and has also been drawn upon by researchers and consultants in many fields relating to international business and communication. It continues to be a major resource in cross-cultural fields. It has inspired a number of other major cross-cultural studies of values, as well as research on other aspects of culture, such as social beliefs (from Wikipedia).

Gray proposed a framework linking culture and accounting, drawing on Hofsted's analysis. The theory of Gray (1988) leaves from a theoretical model to link the culture with the Accounting, on the understanding that the impact of culture on the values of Accounting, and the changes that occur in that context, can be evaluated. The values of Accounting, in turn, influence, in view of the author (Gray,1988), accounting practices, including how to report and disclose information, thus creating what the literature calls, in the study of international differences, Accounting Systems. Gray suggests four accounting value dimensions that affect a nation's financial reporting practices. They are professionalism versus statutory control, uniformity versus flexibility, conservatism versus optimism and secrecy versus transparency.

Professionalism versus statutory control: relates to the preference of each professional for the exercise of free judgment and for the maintenance of professional self-regulation, as opposed to compliance with legal and regulatory requirements in force and statutory control.

Uniformity versus flexibility: relates to the preference for the application of uniform accounting practices between enterprises and the consistent use of such practices over time, as opposed to a possible flexibility, i.e., to act according to circumstances inherent to each company.

Conservatism versus optimism: relates to the preference for a cautious approach in order to cope with the uncertainty of future events, as opposed to a more optimistic view, related to the taking of risks in the form of a less cautious approach.

Secrecy versus transparency: concerns to the preference for confidentiality and restriction of the disclosure of information on the business only to those who are intimately involved with the management and financing business, as opposed to an approach of greater transparency, openness and public responsibility.

Please see the Exhibit 2.3 for details.

Exhibit 2.3   Relationships between Gray's accounting values and Hofstede's cultural dimensions

Cultural dimension (Hofstede)	Accounting Values (Gray)			
	Professionalism	Uniformity	Conservatism	Secrecy
Individualism	+	−	−	−
Power distance	−	+	?	+
Uncertainty avoidance	−	+	+	+
Masculinity	?	?	−	−

Note: *"+" indicates a direct relationship between the variables; "−" indicates an inverse relationship. Question marks indicate that the nature of the relationship is indeterminate. Gray hypothesizes that individualism and uncertainty avoidance will influence accounting the most, followed by power distance, then masculinity.* The exhibit come from Choi(2008), page 32, exhibit2-2.

Baydoun and Willett (2005) proposed the theory of cultural relevance in Accounting, based on Gray (1988), which emphasizes the connection between the accounting values and the practices that materialize in form, content and the qualitative characteristics underlying financial reporting. According to De Albuquerque et al (2011), the results found strongly support for the accounting value of the statutory control and uniformity and reasonably support for the secrecy and conservatism, suggesting the reclassification of the country or a redefinition of such values. The results show further evidence of that conservatism is linked to issues related to the measurement based on market values and the reliability of fair value, while the secrecy in Portugal is less present in the amount of information instead of quality of information disclosed. It is intended that this paper help to consider the importance of subjective aspects related to the quality of information in the process of the financial reporting.

2.1.2 Related factors

Among the above eight factors, it is obvious that the first seven ones belong to institutional factors. We should know that several of the first seven variables are closely associated with each other. For example, the common law system originated in British and was exported to such countries as Australia, Canada, and the USA. The four countries all have highly developed capital markets, and financial and tax accounting system are separated. To some extent, taxation is a part of legal system. Or article of taxation rule is restricted by legal system. Besides, in a higher level of economic development, educational level is also higher. Higher level of economic development could lead to flourish capital market, while developed capital market would provide good chance of source of finance for business.

2.2 Classification

According to Wikipedia, classification may refer to categorization, the process in which ideas and objects are recognized, differentiated, and understood. From economic point of view, classification is a way of viewing the world. Briefly, classification is seen as a fundamental step in an organized and scientific study of a population; as a method to "sharpen description and analysis" (AAA, 1977, p.97), to reveal underlying structures, and to predict the behavior of a member of the population, and as a tool to assist in the analysis of the need for, means towards and progress of harmonization (Nobes, 1983).

In accounting, classifications provide the basic structure for understanding what is alike and what is different in accounting around the world. International classification in accounting had been discussed many times before the late 1970s, for example by Hatfield in 1911 (Hatfield, 1966) and Mueller (1967). However, from the late 1970s, a series of papers (e.g. da Costa et al., 1978; Frank, 1979; Nair and Frank, 1980; and Goodrich, 1982) have reported on a "scientific" approach to classification, which has moved away from the earlier "subjective" studies (Nobes, 1983).

There are two main forms of international classification of accounting systems. One is called deductive or judgmental approach, while the other is inductive or empirical approach. Judgmental classifications rely on knowledge, intuition, and experience. For the deductive or judgmental approach, relevant environmental factors need to be identified, and by linking these to national accounting practices, international groupings or development patterns are proposed. For the inductive or empirical approach, individual accounting practices are analyzed, development patterns or groupings are then identified, and finally explanations keyed to a variety of economic, social, political, and cultural factors are proposed.

2.2.1 Deductive approach

1. Comparative development patterns

In 1967, Gerhard Mueller, instead of difference of national accounting practice, and based indirectly on effect degree of economic, and political factors on accounting system, proposed four developmental patterns for accounting. There are Macroeconomic pattern, Microeconomic pattern, Independent discipline approach and the uniform accounting approach. The pattern is based on business operating background. Accounting is the language of business operation. The role of accounting is dependent whether accounting could apply properly into its operating environment. In a country, operating environment decides main features of accounting system. Through classification of business operation, it is certain to which model accounting system in a country belong.

Under the Macroeconomic pattern, corporate accounting practices are derived from and designed to enhance national macroeconomic goals. Also accounting is taken as an extra part of national economic policy. Value added statement, and social responsibility accounting are emphasized by a society. Under the pattern, financial accounting and tax accounting are not separated. Besides, accounting process of income smoothing is encouraged. The pattern is based on three propositions. The business enterprise is an essential unit in national economy. The business enterprise could accomplish its goals through close coordination of its activities with national economic policies. Public interest could be served best if business enterprise accounting is closely linked to national economic policies. Among the different countries, Sweden has followed the macroeconomic development pattern of accounting most completely.

Under the Microeconomic pattern, accounting is a branch of business economics, and develops from the principles of microeconomics. Private enterprise is dominated in the whole national economy. Individual firm focuses on its business activities. The main goal of a firm is to survive. A firm's best strategy for survival is its economic optimization. As a branch of business economics, accounting derives its concepts and applications from economic analysis. The central accounting concept here is that the accounting process must hold the amount invested in the firm constant in real terms. Due to influence of microeconomics, accounting tries to reflect economic practice in measurement. It is said that an accounting measurement system based on replacement costs fits this approach best, while historical cost measurement could not meet the need. Accounting in the Netherlands is the best example of the microeconomic approach.

The Independent discipline was developed independently outside political and economic theory. Theory is not emphasized by the discipline. Under the Independent discipline approach, accounting is viewed as a service function that derives its concepts and principles from the business process it serves. Accounting is an independent discipline that develops on an ad hoc, piecemeal basis from judgment and trial-and-error. The United Kingdom and the United States are countries where accounting has developed as an independent discipline. However, independent discipline approach has been changed a lot in recent decades. In both the United Kingdom and the United States, framework is developed to be the basis of accounting principles or standards.

Under the Uniform accounting approach, accounting is standardized and employed as a tool for administrative control by central government. Various definition, measurement, and statements listing are required be uniformed and standardized. Accounting is used by government to control economic activities. Uniformity in measurement, disclosure, and presentation makes it easier to use accounting information to control all types of businesses, evaluate performance, allocate capital, manage price, and envy tax by government. France, with its national uniform chart of accounts, is the leading exponent of the uniform approach.

The four patterns of accounting development was created by Gerhard Muller in 1967. Although the classification is simple, the pattern covers almost all accounting systems worldwide at that time. As a creative research, the achievement is logical, and taken as one of possible best classifications.

Later in 1968, Mueller wrote a paper published in Journal of International Accounting Education and Research, and proposed deep idea. He thought different business environment need different accounting systems to accompany, while this situation should be considered when accounting system has been changed or standardized. Furthermore, he indicated difference of business environment exist in economic development situation, business complex degree, political and social environment, and lawful system. These differences are the root of accounting difference and various models. Then Mueller classified into 10 business environment according to these difference. Although the deep classification is more detailed, the result is unsatisfactory.

With the time going, these four patterns, namely Macroeconomic pattern, Microeconomic pattern, Independent Discipline, and Uniformity, may have been changed. However, these patterns of accounting development are still valid today. The description of accounting in the chapter for the respective exemplar countries is still broadly true. The Netherlands is really the only country that can be described by the microeconomic pattern. There are also only a few countries like Sweden that follow the macroeconomic pattern. The independent discipline approach is not as ad hoc as it was in 1967 with the environmental change. Most of these countries now have conceptual frameworks to guide accounting policy formulation. Finally, we might predict that the uniform accounting approach may break down as more and more countries privatize their economies (Choi, Frost, and Meek, 2002).

2. Nobes' classification

Christopher Nobes is an accounting professor in Royal Holloway College, University of London. In Nobes' paper named "a judgemental international classification of financial reporting practices" (1983), he classify countries by the financial reporting practices of public companies. The countries chosen as a population are those of the developed Western world: the reporting practices will be those concerned with measurement and valuation. The date of the classification is 1980, before the enactments in EEC countries of the Fourth Directive on Company Law. The hypothetical classification was drawn up in 1979 and first published in 1980; it has been slightly amended since then. It is based on the evolution of accounting, and the suggestions of many academics interested in comparative accounting. The proposed classification which results from consideration of these background factors is designed as a "prediction" of how countries will be grouped together on consideration of their measurement practices. Through analysis of scoring, testing, and totaling, the final classification contains a hierarchy which borrows its labels from biology. The split between the two "classes" is very clear. The further split into sub-classes and then families (Nobes, 1983).

Nobes adapted and extended Mueller's environmental analysis. He based his hypothetical classification on an evolutionary approach to the identification of measurement practices in developed Western nations, adopting a hierarchical scheme of classification to lend more subtlety and discrimination the assessment of country differences. Nobes made distinction microeconomic and macroeconomic systems. Business economics and business practice orientations are disaggregated under the micro-based classification. Under the macro-uniform based classification, he made a disaggregation between a government/tax/legal orientation and a government/economics orientation.

Using a structural approach to accounting practices whereby he assessed major feature such as the importance of tax rules, the use of prudent/conservative valuation procedures, and the making of replacement cost adjustments, Nobes tested classification system by means of a judgmental analysis of measurement and valuation reporting practices in 14 developed countries. Then nine factors were identified.

In 1998, Nobes has updated his classification scheme to distinguish between strong and weak equity market and shareholder orientations (see exhibit 2.4). In his paper, after examining terminological problems, a preliminary parsimonious model is developed to explain the initial split of accounting systems into tow classes. The term "accounting system" is used to mean the financial reporting practices used by an enterprise. A country might exhibit the use of several such systems in any one year or over time. Consequently, it should be systems and not countries that are classified. The model proposes a two-way classification using two variables: the strengths of equity markets and the degree of cultural dominance. For culturally self-sufficient countries, it is suggested that the class of the predominant accounting system depends on the strength of the equity-outsider market. For culturally dominated countries, the class of the accounting system is determined by the cultural influence. However, sometimes an equity-outsider market may gradually develop, or certain companies may be interested in foreign equity markets. This will lead to the development of the appropriate accounting, and it is one of the reasons for the existence of more than one class of accounting in one country (Nobes,1998).

Exhibit 2.4   Reasons for international difference in financial reporting

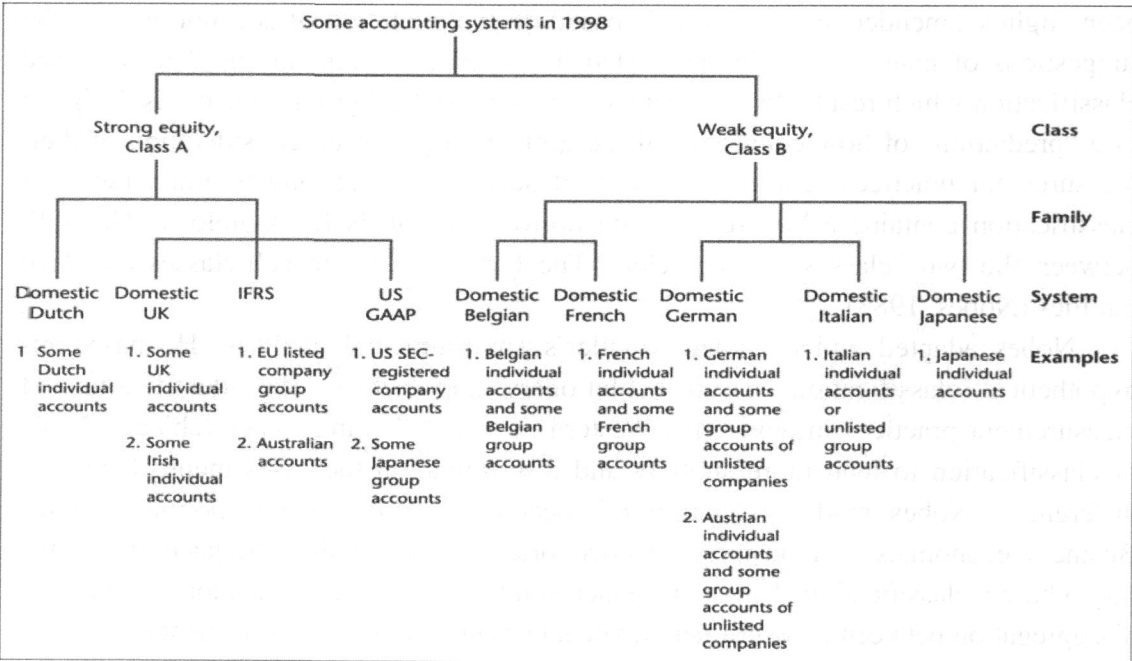

Note: The exhibit comes from International Accounting by Choi and Meek (the 5th edition)

3. Gray's classification

Having related societal values to international accounting values, Gray made a useful distinction between the authority for accounting systems and the measurement and disclosure characteristics of accounting systems.

The accounting values most relevant to the professional or statutory authority for accounting systems as well as their enforcement appear to be professionalism and uniformity. Both are concerned with regulation and the degree of enforcement or conformity. Accordingly, these can be combined and the classification of culture areas hypothesized on a judgmental basis (see Exhibit 2.1, it comes from Choi, Frost and Meek (2002), page52, exhibit 2.3). The accounting values most relevant to the measurement practices used and the extent of information disclosed is the conservatism and secrecy dimensions, respectively. These can therefore be combined and the classification of culture areas hypothesized on a judgmental basis.

Exhibit 2.1 Gray's classification

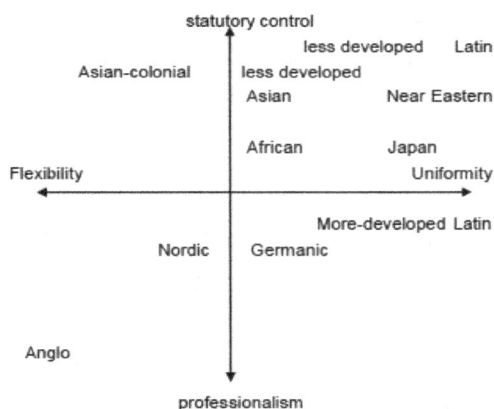
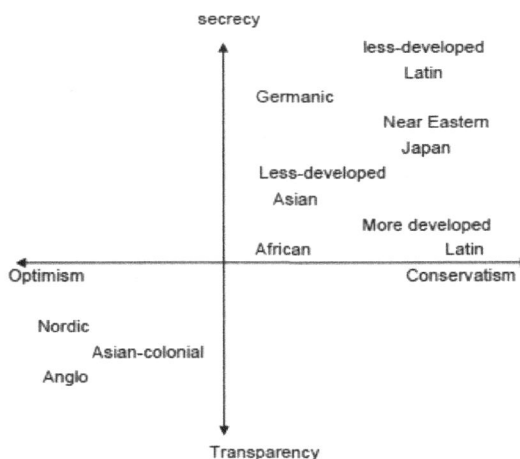

2.2.2 Inductive approach

In a number of subsequent studies, classifications were developed through statistical analysis of data on financial reporting practices compiled by Price Waterhouse (PW) International (1973, 1975, 1979) (e.g., Da Costa et al. (1978); Frank (1979); Nair and Frank (1980); Nair (1982)). Factor analysis was used to identify groups of countries with similar accounting practices (Doupnik and Salter,1993).

1. Berry

Nobes (1983) and Berry (1987) both have classified a variety of national accounting systems through hierarchical families. Berry's classification of thirty-seven capitalist countries represents a significant extension of Nobes's earlier work. Berry (1987) presented a hierarchical classification scheme for forty-eight countries. Berry's classification appears to be primarily inductive in nature with no explicit statement of any underlying theory. In addition to thirty-seven capitalist countries, Berry included eleven communist countries in his classification. The scope of the current study did not include the countries labeled by Berry as communist (other than Egypt) as it was not expected that reliable data on accounting practices could be obtained (Doupnik and Salter,1993).

For Berry (1987), each of Nobes's (1983) fourteen countries remain in their respective families. Most of the capitalist countries added by Berry are either Latin American or former members of the British empire. Other than Bermuda, the added British countries are hypothesized as being members of the micro class/U.K.-influence family. Thus, the U.K.'s influence is seen to extend beyond the more highly developed members of the British Commonwealth to countries as diverse as Malaysia, Nigeria, and Trinidad. Several added countries are hypothesized as being members of the U.S.-influence family. Berry suggests that due to geographical proximity, Mexican and Venezuelan accounting have been strongly influenced by the U.S. Presumably the Philippines is classified as a U.S.-influence country by virtue of its former colonial status (Doupnik and Salter,1993).

2. Nair and Frank

Inductive approach to identifying accounting patterns begins with an analysis of individual accounting practices. It is an empirical study. Empirically derived classifications apply statistical methods to databases of accounting principles and practices around the world. Frank, using 1973 Price Waterhouse data, derived empirically four groups: British Commonwealth, Latin American, Continental European and the United States. Nair and Frank extended the Frank study into two ways in 1975. Among the approaches, perhaps the most important contribution of the type was by Nair and Frank (1980), who carried out a statistical analysis of international accounting practices using the Price Waterhouse surveys of 1973 and 1975. They made an empirical distinction between measurement and disclosure practice because these were considered to have different patterns of development.

With respect to the Price Waterhouse (1973) data it was possible to identify four measurement groupings characterized broadly as the British Commonwealth, Latin American, Continental European and the United States. This result seems plausible and fits quite well with prior research on national accounting systems. Regarding disclosure, however, seven groupings were identified that could not be plausibly described, nor could any explanation be offered for the differences between them and the measurement groupings.

With respect to the Waterhouse (1973) data it was possible to identify four measurement groupings of countries, with Chile as a single-country "group". However the number of grouping increased to seven when disclosure practices were considered, the same number as in the results of the 1973 data analysis. The disclosure groupings, on the other hand, could not be similarly described, nor could any plausible description or explanation be offered.

Besides, Nair and Frank attempted to assess the relationship of these groupings with a number of explanatory variables. Although relationship were established with respect to some of the variables—which included language, various aspects of economic structure, and trading ties—it was clear that there were differences between the measurement and disclosure groupings.

One problem of the research is the lack of reliability and relevance in the data for the research problem under investigation. Data errors, misleading answers, swamping of important questions by trivial ones, and exaggeration of differences between the United States and the United Kingdom are all contributed to doubtful result.

3. Doupnik and Salter

In 1993, both Doupnik and Salter cooperated to finish a paper named "an empirical test of a judgmental international classification of financial reporting practices". They empirically classified current national financial reporting systems and tested the validity of a hierarchical classification proposed by Nobes (1983) and extended by Berry (1987). Data on accounting practices were obtained for fifty countries and used as input into a hierarchical cluster analysis. The resulting classification bears significant similarity to the aforementioned taxonomies and provides several additional insights (Doupnik and Salter,1993).

The two-cluster solution resulted in two groups of countries which generally correspond to Nobes's (1983) and Betty's (1987) "micro" and "macro" classes of countries. The micro group (A1) includes those countries that rely primarily on practitioners and other non-legislative sources to develop accounting principles. This group includes all British Commonwealth countries, the U.S., the Netherlands, and their related colonies and former colonies. It also includes Taiwan, which has strong U.S. ties, and Luxembourg, which is a close neighbor of the Netherlands. The macro group (A2) consists of countries that traditionally have relied on legislative fiat for accounting matters. This group includes all continental European countries (excluding Luxembourg and the Netherlands) and countries drawing their law from this continental base, namely countries in Latin America, the Arab world, and non-British

Asia (Doupnik and Salter,1993). Exhibit 2.5 shows the related result.

Exhibit 2.5   Doupnik – Salter accounting groups

	Number of cluster			Malaysia			
Country	Two	Six	Nine	S.Africa			
Japan		B5	C9	Zimbabwe			
Geramany		B5	C8	Hong Kong(area)			
Fintand		B4	C7	Singapore			
Sweden		B4	C7	Namibla			
Egypt				Ireland			
Saud Arabla				United Kingdom			
Belglum				Zambia			
UAE			C5	Australia			
Uberla				Papua N.Guinea			
Thalland				New Zealand	A1 Micro Based	B1	C2
Panama	A2 Macro Unitorm	B3		Trinidad			
Portugal				Nigeria			
Spaln				Stilanka			
Colombia				Botswana			
Italy			C5	Jamaica			
Korea				Philippines			
Denmark				Taiwan(area)			
Norway				Netheriands			
France				Neth. Antilles			
Argentina				Luxemboarg			
Medco				Bermuda			
Brazll		B2	C4	Istrael			C1
Chlle				Canada			
Costa Rica				United States			

Note: the exhibt comes from Choi, Frost and Meek(2002), page 56.

2.3 Conclusion

2.3.1 Stable classification of accounting systems

In this chapter, we discussed many classification models. With the change of political, economic and institutional environment, classification models may have changed gradually. This generalization that classification about accounting systems has been remarkably stable over time is only partly true. Situation about stable classification mainly apply to developed, western countries, but not developing countries. Furthermore, the generalization is true about measurement practices but not disclosure practices.

2.3.2 Accounting practice at the national level or transnational level

It is important to distinguish accounting practice at the national level from that at the transnational level. Financial statements include individual and consolidated financial statements. Two sets of financial statements are clearly distinguishable. However, in some countries such France, Germany, and Italy, consolidated financial statements are prepared according to IFRS or IASs, while individual financial statements are prepared according to domestic rule or regulation.

2.3.3 Many distinctions of accounting at the national level

The chapter contends that many distinctions of accounting at the national level are becoming blurred. As general, it is pressures of global capital market. Some code law countries where accounting is aimed at legal compliance are sanctioning dual reporting. Consolidated financial statements are aimed at fair presentation, while individual company financial statements continue to be aimed at legal compliance.

2.3.4 Fair presentation vs. legal compliance accounting

There are two major accounting models in the world. Fair presentation emphasizes substance over form and is oriented toward the decision needs of external investors. Fair presentation accounting is capital markets oriented. Financial statements help investor judge managerial performance and predict future cash flows and profitability. Extensive disclosures provide additional relevant information for these purposes.

Legal compliance accounting is designed to satisfy government-imposed requirements such as calculating taxable income or complying with the national government's macroeconomic plan. The income amount may also be the basis for dividends paid to shareholders and bonuses paid to employees. Conservative measurements ensure that prudent amounts are distributed and smooth income brings stable tax, dividend, and bonus payouts. Fair presentation accounting is associated with common law countries, while legal compliance accounting is associated with code law countries. However, many companies from code law countries now follow International Financial Reporting Standards in their consolidated financial statements. IFRS are based on the principles of fair presentation.

A third model is the inflation-adjusted model. It is essentially an add-on to one of the other two models in some countries with high inflation. For example, Mexico and

Israel follow fair presentation principles, but inflation-adjust their accounts. Some South American countries have legal compliance accounting, but with inflation adjustments.

Terms of the Chapter

account 账户

accounting practice 会计实务

administrative control 管理控制

amortized expense 分摊的费用

application of accounting principles 会计原则应用

balance sheet format 资产负债表格式

balance sheet items 资产负债表项目

central government 中央政府

Classification 分类

Code or Civil Law 成文法

Commercial Code 商典法

Common or Case Law 普通法

communication 交流

comparative development patterns 比较发展模式

conceptual frameworks 概念框架

Confucian Dynamism 儒家力本轮

conservatism vs. optimism 稳健主义对乐观主义

corporate financing 公司融资

deductive approach 演绎法

deferred tax 递延税

depreciation 折旧

derivative financial instruments 衍生金融工具

development 发展

directive 指令

disclosure 披露

education level 教育水平

emerging market economy 新兴市场经济

empirically derived classifications 实证性分类

equity market 权益市场

fair presentation 公允表述

finance lease 融资租赁

financial accounting system 财务会计系统

future economic benefit 未来经济利益

generalization 原则，原理

hedge 套期

independent discipline approach 独立学科模式

individual-company financial statements 单个公司财务报表

individualism vs. collectivism 个人主义对集体主义

inductive approach 归纳法

inflation 通货膨胀

inflation-adjusted model 通货膨胀调整模式

institutional factor 制度因素

International Financial Reporting Standards(IFRS) 国际财务报告准则

judgmental classifications 判断性分类

latest annual report 最新年度报告

leased asset 租赁资产

legal compliance 法规符合

legal system 法律体系

level of economic development 经济发展水平

liability 负债

long-term orientation 长期趋势

macroeconomic pattern 宏观经济模式

masculinity vs. feminism 刚性对柔性

measurement practice 计量实务

measurement 计量

microeconomic pattern 微观经济模式

pension 抚恤金

performance 业绩

political and economic ties 政治与经济联系

power distance 权力距离

professionalism vs. statutory control 职业化对法规化

profitability 盈利能力

prospect 前景

provision 条款

receivables and payables 应收和应付账款

relevance 相关性

relevant information 相关信息

reliability 可靠性

secrecy vs. transparency 保密与透明

shareholder 股东

smoothing income 平滑收益

source of finance 筹资来源

statutory authority　强制性的权威

substance over form　实质重于形式

tax accounting　税收会计

taxable income　应税收益

taxation　税收

taxonomy　分类法

the uniform accounting approach　统一会计模式

transnational level　跨国水平

transparent　透明的

treasury shares　库藏股

trial-and-error method　试错法

uncertainty avoidance　不确定性的避免

uniformity vs. flexibility　统一性对弹性

Discussion Questions

1．Why do we study development and classification of accounting?

2．The chapter discusses seven economic, social-historical, and institutional factors being believed to influence accounting development. Explain how each one affects accounting practice.

3．Which factor affects Chinese accounting development most importantly? Why?

4．Which of the factors affecting accounting development are likely to be the most serious obstacles to the EU harmonization effort? What factors indicate the EU harmonization effort can succeed?

5．What is the purpose of classifying accounting systems?

6．In 1967, Gerhard Mueller proposed four developmental patterns including Macroeconomic pattern, Microeconomic pattern, Independent discipline approach, and the uniform accounting approach. The four patterns of accounting development still are valid today? Why or why not?

7．To what extent, the distinction between strong and weak equity market is a useful way to identify different patterns of accounting development. Explain the reasoning.

8．Are cultural differences likely to have a larger impact on accounting measurement and disclosure practices?

9．Discuss the accounting values of both professionalism V.S statutory control and uniformity vs. flexibility in China.

10．Try to identify Chinese cultural dimension according to Hofstede's dimension. Then explain how these cultural dimensions relate to accounting values.

11．Identify Chinese accounting pattern in terms of Mueller's four developmental patterns.

12. Compare and contrast the empirically derived classifications of existing accounting practices by Nair and Frank, Doupnik and Salter.

13. Compare and contrast the judgmental classification of existing accounting practice by Nobes (1998) and Gary (1988).

14. Try to distinguish features between fair presentation and legal compliance accounting. How do these two patterns affect accounting measurement and disclosure practice?

True or False

1. International classification of accounting should improve the understanding why some national systems have a dominant influence while others do not have.

2. One of Hofstede's societal values is "power distance."

3. One of Hofstede's societal values is "uniformity specialization."

4. One of Gray's accounting values is "professionalism versus flexibility."

5. One of Gray's accounting values is "secrecy versus statutory control."

6. In code law countries, accounting are all legal compliance.

7. Conservatism can be linked most closely with uncertainty avoidance.

8. In Anglo-Saxson countries, source of finance is mainly from equity market while in France and Germany, bank dominates source of finance for enterprise.

9. Fair presentation accounting is capital markets oriented while legal compliance accounting is designed to satisfy government-imposed requirements.

10. IFRS are based on the principles of legal compliance accounting.

11. Developed economy provides base for accounting to improve, while complex business creates the necessity for accounting information.

12. Civil law develops on a case by case basis with no attempt to cover all cases in an all-encompassing code.

13. The United Kingdom and the United States are countries where accounting has developed as an independent discipline.

14. Nobes (1983) and Berry (1987) both have classified a variety of national accounting systems through hierarchical families.

15. High educational level could help to train high degree accountant and promote accounting profession.

Multiple Choice

1. The Mueller system of classifying countries based on their business and economic environments is an example of

a. deductive classification.

b. inductive classification.

c. comparative approach.

d. cultural relativism.

2. Christopher Nobes developed a hypothetical classification for financial reporting, which

a. is an inductive approach to classification.

b. is a hierarchical approach of classification that distinguishes countries according to microeconomic and macroeconomic systems.

c. based on cultural dimension.

d. based measurement and disclosure practices.

3. Which of the following is cultural value developed by Hofstede?

a. uniformity.

b. professionalism.

c. power distance.

d. secrecy.

4. Small power distance in Hofstede's cultural value implies that

a. people prefer a loosely knit social framework to hierarchical system in a society.

b. people accept a hierarchical order.

c. people strive for power equalization.

d. people maintain a nervous atmosphere in which practice counts more than principles and deviance is not easily tolerated.

5. Confucian dynamism is a cultural value which:

a. emphasizes a Confucian approach to business.

b. refers to a conservative versus transparent orientation to business.

c. a Chinese value adopted as is a Chinese accounting principle.

d. is associated with a religious order in China.

6. Flexibility is more compatible with which accounting value?

a. secrecy.

b. uniformity.

c. Individualism

d. collectivism.

7. Professionalism is more compatible with

a. individualism.

b. collectivism.

c. weak uncertainty avoidance.

d. optimism.

8. The concept of "true and fair view" of a company's financial reports depends

heavily upon

    a. professionalism.

    b. transparency .

    c. Confucian dynamism

    d. secrecy.

9. Anglo-Saxon countries, such as the United States, and the United Kingdom, would tend to reflect which of the following accounting values?

    a. transparency.

    b. secrecy.

    c. conservatism.

    d. uniformity.

10. In the United Kingdom,

    a. the Company Law contains all detailed accounting requirement.

    b. the SSAP is set up by government.

    c. due to the strength of the profession, there is no accounting standard setting board.

    d. the "true and fair view" is a basic accounting concept and represents a flexible approach.

11. Under the Microeconomic pattern, individual firm focus on

    a. financing activities.

    b. investing activities.

    c. business activities.

    d. deductible taxation.

12. Under the Independent Discipline, accounting principles develop from

    a. company law.

    b. operating activities.

    c. judgment and trial-and-error.

    d. conceptual framework.

13. From accounting pattern point of view, Netherlands is an example of

    a. Macroeconomic pattern.

    b. Microeconomic pattern.

    c. Independent discipline.

    d. Uniformity pattern.

Case Analysis

Case 2　China as Civil Code or Common Code?

China endured many years of political unrest, but major conflict ended in the fall of 1949. By that time, the Chinese Communists had established the People's Republic of China. Shortly after assuming leadership of the country, the Communist government began adopting the former Soviet Union's economic model. Its focus was centralized planning and uniformity in an economy where all major production was owned by the government. The Ministry of Finance was established to take charge of all accounting work in the country.

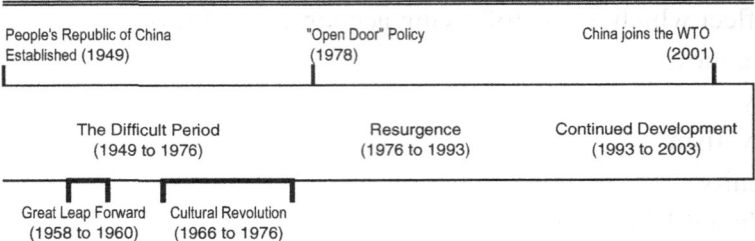

Figure 2-1   Periods to be explored

Under the pattern of Former Soviet Union, the most significant feature of the uniform accounting system was its rule-based approach. All the accounting rules were centrally devised and very detailed. The requirements were designed to cover all possible situations. Rules could be modified for individual cases only with special permission from the central authorities.

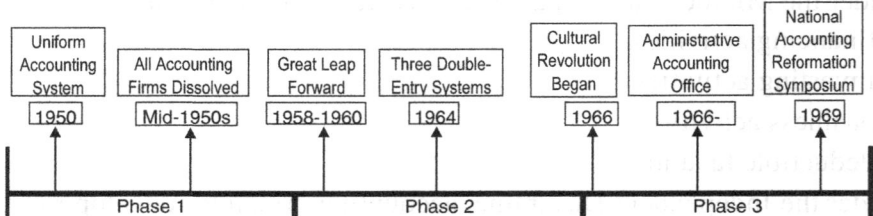

Figure 2-2   The Difficult Period

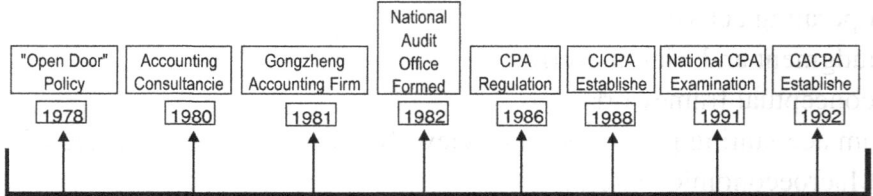

Figure 2-3   Resurgence

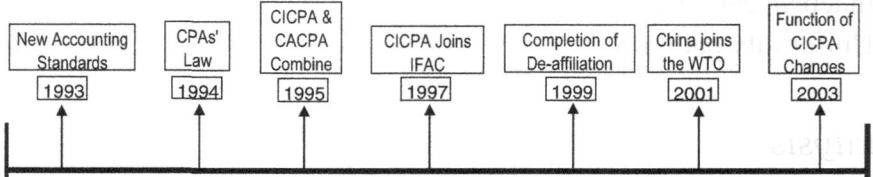

Figure 2-4   Continued Development

Beginning in 1949, however, the outlook for public accounting in China became grimmer and more uncertain. The profession entered its Difficult Period, and within just a few years, all accounting firms throughout China were dissolved.

Over the next twenty-five years, the People's Republic of China experienced several different cultural and economic phases. The "Great Leap Forward" and the Cultural Revolution brought about major changes for the Chinese people and the country's accounting profession as well. Over the years, the Chinese government implemented various approaches to economic development. As policies changed, the Chinese government modified the accounting information it required. Some periods called for simplification, while others expanded the complexity and number of financial statements and accounts.

It was not until the end of the Cultural Revolution in 1976 that the Chinese public accounting profession was resurrected. Adoption of an open door policy in 1978 marked a significant change in the way China would interact with other nations. The government's 1979 policy of "economic liberalization and reformation" resulted in major changes throughout China. Private ownership of businesses was again allowed, and the number of enterprises financed by stock exploded. In addition, during this time, the Ministry of Finance issued several regulations providing a foundation for the development and growth of the accounting profession.

After thirty years of extinction, China's public accounting profession was reborn. In 1981, the first accounting firm in this modern era was established. The profession matured during the 1980s and 1990s, as both its place in the country's economy and its governing regulations were established. Figure 2-5 provides an overview of the progress made and setbacks endured as China's public accounting profession evolved.

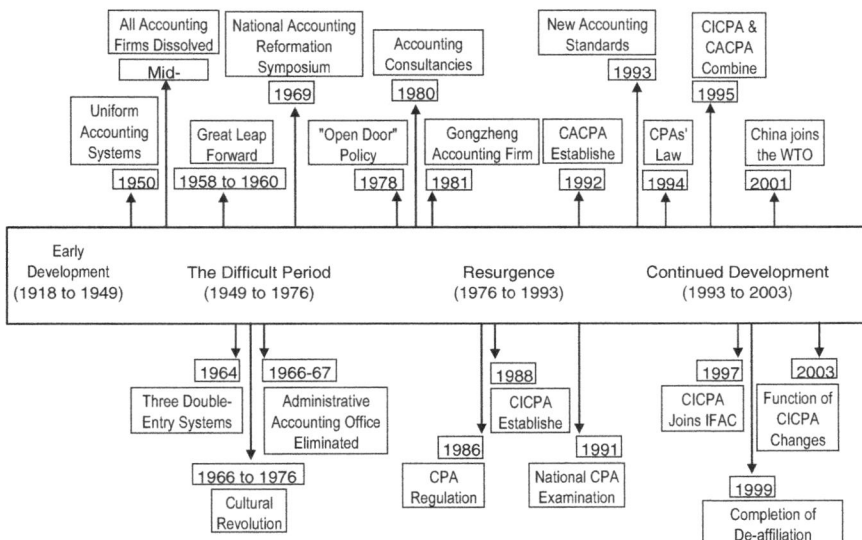

Figure 2-5　History of Public Accounting in China

Figure 2-5 also indicates that the profession has entered a new period in its development. In a decade or two, historians will look back and tell the story of this new chapter. At this point in time, we know that the Chinese public accounting profession is experiencing tremendous growth.

(Note: the data and document comes from working paper written by Jiuqin Lu, and Jean B. Price in 2005)

From the above, answer the following questions.

1. From the characteristics, discuss which code is adopted in China? Civil Code or Common Code? Which evidences support your idea?

2. Under the selected code, describe the accounting features in China from both the accounting system and accounting industry respectively.

3. Using the above document, explain the development stages of public accounting in China.

4. From the clue provided above, forecast the future development feature of public accounting in China.

Chapter 3   Accounting in Developed Countries

![image](Learning objective icon) *Learning objective*

After careful study of this chapter, students will be able to:

1. Explain what are accounting standard and accounting standards setting.

2. Understand the relationship between accounting standards and accounting practice.

3. Describe distinct accounting features of six countries.

4. Compare and contrast differences of financial reporting among six developed countries.

5. Compare and contrast differences of accounting practices among six developed countries.

6. Explain why standard setting sector was established in both France and Germany in late 1990s.

7. Depict changing situation in recent decades for Japanese accounting.

8. Distinguish the main differences of accounting practice between the U.K and the U.S.A.

9. State how the conceptual framework was created and what were included in the United States.

10. Depict the most novel feature of the Dutch accounting scene.

3.1   Basic concepts

Comparative accounting has a short term development history, and a lot of issues still are in debate. Comparative accounting deals with difference and similarity of accounting among developed and developing countries. In developed countries there is a completely different institutional background from that in developing countries. Specific knowledge of accounting in a country is needed to analyze institutional factor at the first, as accounting system is based on that background in a country. On one hand, accounting technique or method could be disseminated from one country to another. On the other hand, accounting in different countries could be affected, permeated, and carried forward with each other. All of these contribute to creation and development of comparative accounting. In this chapter, we will study accounting system of selected developed countries, while in the next chapter we will examine the accounting system of selected developing countries. Developed countries include France, Germany, Japan, the Netherlands, the United States, and the United Kingdom, while developing countries deal with four "emerging market" countries, such as the Czech Republic, China, Mexico, and Taiwan area.

3.1.1 Accounting standards

Accounting standards are the regulations or rules (often including laws and statutes) that govern the work of accountant such as regular record, measurement, preparation of financial statements and disclosure. From point of operational feature of preparer of view, there are two types for accounting standards, namely profit organization and non-profit organization. Furthermore, accounting standards setting is the process by which accounting standards are formulated. Therefore, accounting standards are the product of standards setting.

There are two sectors involved into the setting process around the world. They are private sector and public sector. The private sector includes the accounting profession organizations and other groups affected by the financial reporting process such as users and preparers of financial statements and employees. The public sector includes agencies such as tax authorities, ministries responsible for commercial law, or ministries of finance, and securities commissions. Stock exchanges may influence the process and may be in either the private or public sector, depending on the country in question. The roles and effect of these groups in setting accounting standard differ from one country to the other. These differences may help to explain why standards vary so much around the world.

3.1.2 Accounting standards and practices

Both in theory or in practice, many people argue the relationship between accounting standard and practice. The debate on relationship between accounting standards and accounting practice are never stopped. Generally speaking, the relationship is complexity. As we know, there is no doubt that actual accounting practice deviate from the standards required or vice verse. In routine cases, after standards are created, these standards need to be followed by people in practice in the next period. Then a lag is created accordingly. During the practice, the insufficient enforcement happens very often depending on how enforcement has been carried out. Mandatory enforcement does not lead definitely expected results. In many cases, company voluntarily discloses more information beyond what is required in response to the demand for information by investor, creditor and other users. Surely, voluntarily discloses are managers' discretionary response to users of financial statements. If the demand for information is strong enough, standards may be changed into mandatory disclosures. In order to represent a company's results and financial position better, many rules or regulation are required. However, more regulations could lead to standards' being overridden. For example, since 2005 two sets of accounting standards have been required in some European countries such as France, Germany, and Italy. In these countries, national accounting standards only apply to individual company accounts, not to the consolidated ones, while consolidated financial statements are prepared according to IFRSs or IASs. Two sets of accounting standards could make some companies confusion when both individual and consolidated financial statements are prepared at the same period.

3.1.3 Fair presentation and legal compliance accounting

In the chapter 2, two accounting orientations, fair presentation and legal compliance accounting are mentioned. Both fair presentation and legal compliance accounting orientation would affect preparation and disclosure of financial reporting. Both fairness and substance over form characterize so-called Anglo-Saxon accounting.

Anglo-Saxon accounting is practiced in English-speaking countries such as the United Kingdom, the United States, Canada, New Zealand, Australia and Ireland (From Wikipedia, the free encyclopedia). If we talk about accounting from law system point of view, it is obvious that Anglo-Saxon accounting systems are usually associated with a common law legal system. Within Anglo-Saxon accounting countries, shareholders usually take capital market as the principal source of finance. Some other countries with fair presentation feature in accounting may be strongly influenced by political and economic ties. For example, British influence its former Empire on Australia, Canada, Hong Kong, India, Ireland, Kenya, Malaysia, New Zealand, Nigeria, Singapore, and South Africa, while the United States influence on Canada, Mexico, and the Philippines.

Countries with legal compliance accounting are associated with Code law legal system. Code law is generally associated with greater government intervention in economic activity and weaker protection of private property than common law. Strony political influence occurs at the national and firm levels (Ronald, and Benedicte,2007).In Code law countries, companies usually rely on heavily on banks or the government as sources of finance. The group includes most of the countries in Continental Europe, their former colonies in Africa and Southeast Asia, and Japan. In these countries, measurement practices are relatively conservative. Also there is a close linkage between financial and tax accounting in countries with legal compliance accounting. Because company in these countries must record revenues and expenses in their accounts to claim for tax purpose, tax laws effectively determine the amounts reported in its financial statement. Moreover, to some extent, tax law dominates accounting regulation or rule.

The distinction between fair presentation and legal compliance accounting has pervasive effect on many accounting issues such as depreciation, leases, pension, standard setting, discretionary reserves, historical or other valuation for tangible and intangible assets, and auditing. In other words, different orientation would lead to different accounting practice. This view will be proved in both this chapter and next chapter.

3.2 France

3.2.1 Introduction

France is one of the largest countries in Europe. It is bordered by six countries: Belgium, Luxembourg and Germany to the north-east, Switzerland and Italy across the Alps to the south-east and Spain across the Pyrenees to the south-west. The UK is across the English Channel (La Manche). France is regarded by many people as the geographical gateway to Europe. France is divided into 22 official 'régions' each of which is subdivided into several administrative 'départements'. Many of the regions have very clearly defined and distinct regional identities (Data from website[①]).

In European countries, there has, at least to the present time, been a more definite effort made to regulate accounting practice by direct legislation. Bookkeeping methods, like so many other industrial activities, have been distinctly regulated by the government. Thus, it is almost universally the custom in countries all around the world to prescribe by law that merchants, as well as corporations, must keep accounts (Henry, 1966).

Corporate financial reporting has been changed substantially since world war Two in France (Nobes and Park, 2005). Colasse and Standish (1998) classified into four stages. The first stages (1946-1957) occurred in reconstruction after World War Two and economic planning. The Plan Comptable General (PCG) was set up in this period, and macro-economy dominates the society. At the same time, accounting profession has little voice. The second stage (1958-1973) was modernization and high speed economic development. During the period, PCG was applied deeply in different fields, and was related with taxation regulation. The third stage happened from 1958 to 1973, which economy fluctuates and accounting began to standardize. During the period, European Directive was inserted into accounting in France. The Fourth stage happened from 1984 to now, when there were globalization, little supervision and privatization. During the period, French approach faced to tough challenge. Then accounting association was reset up and profession's role was strengthened. IASs became

---

① http://www.frenchpropertylinks.com/essential/france-intro.html

competitive with domestic standard.

France is the world's leading advocate of national uniform accounting. The Ministry of National Economy approved the first formal Plan Comptable General (national accounting code) in September 1947. A revised plan came into effect in 1957. A further revision of the plan was enacted in 1982 under the influence of the Fourth Directive of the European Union. In 1986 the plan was extended to implement the requirements of the EU Seventh Directive on consolidated financial statements, and it was further revised in 1999. The content of the Plan Comptable General are extensive and include objectives and principles of financial accounting and reporting, definitions of assets, liabilities, shareholders' equity, revenue and expense, a detailed Chart of Accounts, with numberic coding for all the accounts, rules relating to valuation and profit measurement, models for financial statement presentation, consolidation requirements, and so on.

As in the Germanic countries, company law seems to be the predominant influence on accounting in France. The laws relating to accounting can be traced back to the original Code de Commerce of the early 1800s. The Code de Commerce has its roots in the 1673 and 1681 ordinances of Colbert, was enacted by Napoleon in 1807. French law reflects the classic position, dating from the French Revolution and the Code Napoleon, that engagement in commerce creates obligations to keep accounts and prepare financial statements. In France uniformity and its application through the standardized national code of accounting, the Plan Comptable General, is emphasized.

Apart from company law and the Plan Comptable General, taxation is another major influence on French accounting. The first income tax law was passed in 1914. The tax law tends to override the accounting rules to the extent. The charges deductible for tax purposes must be recorded in the accounts if the tax benefit is to be claimed. However, under the 1982 Plan Comptable General, the rules permit a distinction to be made between economic depreciation and exceptional depreciation, the latter being the excess of tax deductible over economic depreciation.

A feature of French accounting is the dichotomy between individual company financial statements and those for the consolidated group. Even though individual company accounts must follow statutory reporting requirement, the law permits companies to follow International Accounting Standards or even U.S. Generally Accepted Accounting Practices (GAAP) in their consolidated financial statements. The reason for this flexibility is that when the EU Seventh Directive was implemented in 1986, many French Multinationals were already preparing consolidated financial statements based on Anglo-Saxon principles for purposes of stock exchange listings abroad. French companies referring to IAS or U.S. GAAP often declare that their financial statements comply both with French standards and with international or U.S. standards. As European Union accounting initiatives converge with International

Accounting Standards, the U.S.GAAP option will likely be eliminated.

The accounting profession in France is relatively small. The roles of public accounting and auditing are carried out by separate institutions established by law. As regard to capital market, the stock market is still relatively small in France. That means the major sources of finance are banks, the government, and family interests. However, more emphasis on investor interest has been given in recent years following the establishment in 1967 of the Commission des Operations de Bourse (COB).

In recent years, the French accountancy market has grown slowly, with the exception of 2012 when marginal decline was seen. Further decline also happened in 2014 and the market will recover with low growth being projected through to 2019. Deloitte, Ernst & Young, KPMG, and PwC are the leading players and exercise great influence, particularly at the upper end of the market. It is expected for the French accountancy market to generate total revenues of $15.4bn in 2014, representing a compound annual growth rate (CAGR) of 1.3% between 2010 and 2014. In comparison, the German and UK markets will grow with CAGRs of 1.7% and 5.6% respectively, over the same period, to get respective values of $36.1bn and $36.8bn in 2014. The performance of the market will accelerate, with an anticipated CAGR of 1.5% for the five-year period 2014—2019, which is expected to drive the market to a value of $16.6bn by the end of 2019. Comparatively, the German and UK markets will grow with CAGRs of 1.5% and 4.7% respectively, over the same period, to reach respective values of $38.9bn and $46.3bn in 2019[①].

3.2.2　Accounting regulation and enforcement

In France and Germany, two model continental European systems of accounting, is much more recent, in confronting systems which have traditionally largely been determined within each government, using the law and legal regulations. However, since 1998, there have been fundamental reforms, embodied in a fundamental law of 2001. These reforms are almost complete (Rowan et al.,2013).

There are five major organizations involved in setting standards in France. The first organization is Conseil National de la Comptabilite or CNC (National Accounting Board). CNC issues rulings and recommendations on accounting issues. The second organization is Comite de la Reglementation Comptable or CRC (Accounting Regulation Committee). CRC was established in1998. CRC is responsible for converting CNC rulings and recommendations into binding regulations. Therefore, it has real regulatory power. The third party is Financial Markets Authority (FMA). Its predecessor is Commission des Operations de Bourse or COB (National Securities

---

① MarketLine industry profile Accountancy in France, 12 2014 , p1-27. 27p.www.marketline.com.

Commission). However, FMA has important but limited influence. The forth one is Ordre des Experts-Comptables or OEC (Institute of Public Accountants). OEC is Under the jurisdiction of the Ministry of Economy and Finance. The last one is Compagnie Nationale des Commissaires aux Comptes or CNCC (National Institute of Statutory Auditors). There are some overlap in both OEC and CNSS, while CNCC is Under the jurisdiction of the Ministry of Justice.

3.2.3 Financial reporting

The French National Accounting Council (Conseil National de la Comptabilite, CNC) issues the accounting code, plan Comptable General (PCG). French companies must report the following statements. The CNC is responsible for the establishment of a national accounting language acceptable to all parties using financial accounting information. However, some powerful groups such as large companies and tax administration have been involved in the CNC decisions. Their concerns about tax-deductible allowances for depreciation and other unamortized expenditures are said to have dominated many issues presented to the CNC (Choi and Meek, 2005; Nobes and Parker, 2006).

One of the central objective of the PCG is to provide standardized financial reports. The code prescribes regulations ranging from abstract principles, such as prudence, consistency, and faithful reckoning, to detailed procedures. The PCG fits into the structure of French commercial law. Its mandatory core chart of accounts forms the basis for operation of the accounting system, presentation of periodic accounts, and design of audit programs. Their goal is to produce a true and fair view of the position and operation of the enterprise (Ronald and Benedicte, 2007).

In France, financial report include Balance sheet, Income statement, Notes to financial statements, Directors' report and Auditor's report.

Large companies also must prepare documents relating to the prevention of business bankruptcies and a social report, both of which are unique to France. Although there is no requirement for cash flow statement or statement of changes in financial position, the CNC recommends a statement of cash flow and almost all large companies prepare one. Individual company and consolidated statement are both required. Small and medium-sized companies could prepare simplified financial statements in terms of the Code de Commerce.

Extensive and detailed footnote disclosures are required in France (Choi, Frost and Meek, 2002). Footnote has a complex content. Example include explanation of measurement rules employed, accounting treatment of foreign currency items, statement of changes in fixed assets and depreciation, details of provision, details of any revaluations, breakdown of receivables and liabilities by maturity, and list of subsidiaries and share holdings. Furthermore, mount of commitments for pension and other retirement benefits, details of the impact of taxes on the financial statements, average number of employees listed by category, and analysis of turnover by activity and geographically are all in it.

Besides, a social report is required for all companies with 300 or more employees. The report includes training, industrial relations, health and safety conditions, wage levels and other employment benefits, and many additional relevant work environment conditions. However, the report is required for individual company not consolidated groups.

3.2.4 Accounting measurement

Firstly, French accounting is characterized by duality. Individual companies must follow fixed regulations, while consolidated groups have more flexibility.

Secondly, tangible assets are normally valued at historical cost. Revaluations are allowed, but are seldom found in practice. Fixed assets are depreciated according to tax provisions, either straight line method or declining balance basis. Inventory must be valued at the lower of cost or realizable value using either First in, First out (FIFO), or weighted-average methods.

Thirdly, research and development costs are expensed as incurred, but may be capitalized in restricted circumstances. Capitalized research and development must be amortized over no more than five years. Leased asset are expensed. Furthermore, pension and other retirement benefits are normally expensed when paid and future commitments are seldom recognized as liabilities. As for deferred tax, company does not account for deferred taxed in individual company financial statements. Legal reserves must be created by appropriating 5 percent of income each year until the reserve equals 10 percent of legal capital.

Finally, the purchase method is used to account for business combinations. Goodwill is capitalized and amortized to income, but no maximum amortization period is specified. Proportional consolidation is used for joint ventures and the equity method is used to accounting for investments in nonconsolidated entities. As for foreign currency translation, both temporal and closing rate methods are permitted for foreign currency translation. It is recommended that the temporal method be used when operations are integrated with the parent and that the closing method be used when operations are independent of the parent.

3.3 Germany

3.3.1 Introduction

Located in Central Europe, Germany has common borders with Denmark, the

Netherlands, Belgium, Luxembourg, France, Switzerland, Austria, the Czech Republic and Poland[1]. After the Second World War, Germany was divided into American, French, British, and Soviet zones of occupation. Since reunification in October 1990, Germany has been a federal republic composed of 16 Lander (states): 10 from the former West, 5 from the former East, and Berlin, the capital city.

Traditionally the primary source of finance for German companies is bank loans, rather than equity being raised through the capital market. This determines to a larger extent the purpose for financial reporting by companies. Since reunification, German accounting has been greatly affected by the increasing internationalization of the German economy and the growing integration of the world's capital markets. An increasing number of German companies, such as DaimlerChrysler and Deutsche Telecom, have been raising capital on international markets, particularly the New York Stock Exchange.

Historically, Germany has had a considerable influence on the accounting systems in many countries, especially Japan, Austria, Switzerland, and some Nordic countries such as Denmark and Sweden. These countries adapted the idea and concepts developed in Germany to suit their conditions (Doupnik and Perera, 2007).

Accounting environment has changed continuously and remarkably since the end of World War Two. The 1965 Company Act moved the German financial reporting system toward British-American ideas (only for large corporation). Some practices such as more disclosure, limited consolidation, and a corporate management report were required. In order to integrate with other members in European Union, Germany try to adopt Directives through adjusting law or regulation. Among Directives in the European Union, the Fourth Directive covers public and private companies in all EU countries. Its articles include those referring to valuation rules, formats of published financial statements and disclosure requirements. The Seventh Directive concerns a number of matters connected with share capital, the difference between public and private companies and consolidated accounting. For the Eighth Directive, its main effect has been to decide on who is allowed to audit accounts in certain countries that have small numbers of accountants, such as Denmark and Germany. Some changes to auditor independence and audit firms also occurred (Nobes and Parker, 2010). The Fourth, Seventh, and Eighth EU Directives all entered German law through the Comprehensive Accounting Act of December.19, 1985. Compared with other European countries, German law provides further that the books of account must be bound with consecutively numbered pages, free from lacunae, erasures and alteration. German accounting's reliance on statutes and court decision is another fundamental characteristic.

---

[1] Data comes from the website: http://www1.american.edu/initeb/es0939a/germany.htm

Creditor protection is the fundamental concern in the Commercial Code. Conservative balance sheet valuations are central to creditor protection. With the revision of Commercial Code, two new provisions were passed in 1998. The first added a new paragraph in the German Commercial Code allowing parent companies to use internationally accepted accounting principles in their consolidated financial statements. The second allowed the establishment of a private sector organization to set accounting standards for consolidated financial statements.

As for relationship between tax law and commercial accounting, tax law largely determines commercial accounting. There is no distinction between financial statements prepared for tax purposes and those published in financial reports.

Auditing dominates the financial reporting related professional activities in Germany. The title for certified auditors, Wirtschaftsprufer (WP) was created by the Companies Act of 1931. The Institute der Wirtschaftsprufer (Institute of Auditors) is a private association of public auditors and public audit firms. It comprises approximately 10800 public auditors and over 900 public audit firms, and represents about 85 percent of the profession. However, the German auditing profession is much smaller than its counterpart in the United States (about 11000 WPs vs. over 250000 CPAs). The auditing profession is headed by the Wirtschaftspruferkammer (WPK) (Chamber of Auditors), an independent organization responsible for the supervision of its members and for the representation of the profession to other parties. It is a state supervised organization. All public accountants are mandatory members of the WPK. Another important organization is the Institute of Auditors, whose main task is to publish statements on accounting and auditing questions, which usually serve as accounting and auditing standards (Doupnik and Perera, 2007).

3.3.2 Accounting regulation and enforcement

National government has most significant influence on accounting in Germany. Financial reporting in Germany is dominated by commercial law, tax Law, and pronouncements issued by the profession. The Commercial Code contains most of the country's financial reporting principles. The German Stock Exchange listing requirements have much less influence on financial reporting compared to those in the United States.

In Germany, the predominance of the principle of prudence is clearly established in the law. The principle of prudence was incorporated in the 1937 Stock Corporation Law, which also specifically required that the compulsory audits of public corporations be performed by WPs.

In the mid 1960s, there were signs of a change in financial reporting in Germany from a creditor orientation towards a shareholder orientation. The Company Act of 1965 can be regarded as the initiator of this change. For two decades, the Company Act provided the primary source of accounting regulation for listed companies, supplemented by provisions in the Commercial Code and Income Tax Law.

More recently, German accounting regulation has been heavily influenced by the EU directives. The Accounting Act of 1985 implemented the EU Fourth, Seventh, and Eighth Directives, and transformed them into German Commercial Law.

Before 1998, there are not financial accounting standards setting function in Germany. In1998, law on control and transparency introduced the requirements for the Ministry of Justice to recognize a private national standard-setting body to sever as developing recommendation, advising for new accounting legislation, and representing Germany.

The German Accounting Standards Committee (GASC) was founded as standard setting authority. The GASC oversees the German Accounting Standards Board (GASB), who dose the technical work with issuing the accounting standards. GASB is a private sector body like the FASB (U.S), ASB (U.K) and IASB. The process for accounting standard establishing is similar with that in the U.S, the U.K. Working groups examine, discuss the issues and make recommendations to the Board. These groups represent a broad constituency including accounting profession, business, government agency, trade union, and general public. GASB deliberations follow a due process, which is similar with that in the United States, and meetings are open to the public.

In Germany, GASB's standards are only applied to consolidated financial statements. In 2003, the GASB aligned its work program with the IASB's effort to achieve a convergence of standards. The GASB was given the task of adapting German accounting principle to international norms by 2004. The establishment of this committee also provided a vehicle for the German accounting profession to participate formally in the activities of international bodies such as the IASB. The GASB is staffed by independent expert that includes three from industry, two auditors, one financial analyst, and one academic, modeled on the FASB (Doupnik and Perera, 2007).

3.3.3 Financial reporting

In Germany, the development of financial reporting largely has depended on the statute-particularly the Commercial Code, and the tax system, also the gains of creditors to a degree (Jones and Luther, 2005). Furthermore, the financial reporting in Germany is lack of enough detail disclosure for investors and accounting analysts to satisfy their information demands as the reason that tax avoidance policy has a strong impact on German reporting. Besides, German standards afford a lot of discretion to companies, which leads the company could conduct income applying large silent reserves (Leuz and Venecchia, 2000).

The 1985 Accounting Act specifies the content and format of financial statements according to company size. There are three size classes, small, medium and large, in terms of balance sheet totals, annual sales totals, and numbers of employees. The 1985 Accounting Act specifies that formal financial statement include Balance sheet, Income statement, Notes, Management report and Auditor's report.

Small companies are exempt from the audit requirement and may prepare an abbreviated balance sheet. Small and medium sized companies may prepare abbreviated income statements, and have few disclosure requirement for their notes. Publicly traded companies must provide a statement of cash flow.

Legislation enacted in 1998 allows listed companies to use internationally accepted standards such as IAS or U.S.GAAP in consolidated financial statements in lieu of the German Commercial Code.

3.3.4 Accounting measurement

The purchase or acquisition method is the primary consolidation method under German rules, though pooling of interests is acceptable in limited circumstance. Goodwill could either be offset against reserves in equity or amortized systematically over its economic life. The law states a four-year period as the regular amortization period, but ranges up to 20 years are also acceptable. The equity method must be used for nonconsolidated entities where 20 percent or more of the company is owned by another entity. No special requirements are for foreign currency translation and German companies use a number of methods.

Historical cost is the basis for valuing tangible assets. On the balance sheet, inventory is shown at the lower of cost or market. For valuation of inventory outflow, FIFO, average, and LIFO are all acceptable. As for depreciation, depreciable fixed assets are subject to tax depreciation rates.

Research and development costs are expensed when incurred. Financial leases typically are not capitalized, but pension obligations are occurred based on their actuarially deter present value consistent with tax laws. Deferred taxes do not normally arise in individual company accounts, because these are tax determined.

Provisions are estimate of future expenses or losses are used heavily due to prudence principle. Provisions must be set up for deferred maintenance expenses, product guarantees, potential losses from pending transaction, and other uncertain liabilities. It is obvious that provision gives German companies many opportunities to smooth income (Choi, Frost and Meek 2002).

3.4 Japan

3.4.1 Introduction

Japan is an island nation in East Asia. Located in the Pacific Ocean, it lies to the east of the Sea of Japan, China, North Korea, South Korea and Russia, stretching from the Sea of Okhotsk in the north to the East China Sea and Taiwan in the south. The Kanji that make up Japannese name mean "sun origin", and Japan is often called the "Land of the Rising Sun"[①].

As of 2012, Japan is the third largest national economy in the world, after the United States and China, in terms of nominal GDP, and the fourth largest national economy in the world, after the United States, China and India, in terms of purchasing power parity. As of December 2013, Japan's public debt was more than 200 percent of its annual gross domestic product, the second largest of any nation in the world. The service sector accounts for three quarters of the gross domestic product[②].

Prior to World War II, the Japanese economy was dominated by zaibatsu (family financial combines). Family financial combines derived their power from both economic strength and political affiliations. Zaibatsu get its capital source from bank mainly. Therefore banks are one major source of finance for the groups. During the postwar occupation of Japan by the allied forces, zaibatsu were dissolved by the Anti-Monopoly Law of 1947. However when the allied forces left Japan in 1952, the old conglomerates started to reappear under a different name, keiretsu.

In business world, cross-corporate ownership dominates Japanese business. About 70 percent of the equity shares of listed firms in Japan are cross-owned by corporate shareholders such as financial institutions and other companies, keiretsu control about a half of the top 200 firms in Japan through cross-corporate shareholdings, which amount to more than 25 percent of all the assets in Japan. This situation reflects cultural value of collectivism in Japan.

The ways of business finance affect financial reporting and attitudes of interested parties toward accounting information. Banks and cross-corporate ownership are main source of finance. Banks as an insider have access to their clients' financial information, therefore, there is less pressure for public disclosure. Extensive disclosure is not so necessary.

In the 1990s, economy in Japan is under the depressed situation. Japanese companies were compelled to search for abroad finance sources because of recessionary pressures in Japanese economy. In order to attract foreign investment, Japanese began to think about international finance sources. Japanese businesses and regulators found it very necessary to respond to the demands of the international capital markets. More recently, the effects of the IASB have been felt, and many change occurred with the establishment of a private sector standard setting organization in 2001.

---

① Data comes from website: http://en.wikipedia.org/wiki/Japan.

② Data comes from website: http://en.wikipedia.org/wiki/Japan.

3.4.2 Accounting regulation and enforcement

The national government has the most significant influence on the accounting in Japan. Accounting regulation is covered in three laws. They are the Commercial Code, the Securities and Exchange Law (SEL), and the corporate Income Tax Law. The Commercial Code was enacted in 1890, but not implemented until 1899 It is administered by the Ministry of Justice (MOJ) with being the center of accounting regulation. The Commercial Code has the most pervasive influence on accounting. All companies incorporated under the Commercial Code are required to meet its accounting provisions. The Securities and Exchange Law regulates publicly owned companies. The Ministry of Finance is responsible for SEL. The Business Accounting Deliberation Council (BADC) is a special advisory body within the Ministry of Finance being responsible for developing accounting standards under the SEL. The BADC could not issue a standard at variance with commercial law or tax law. Member of BADC are appointed by the Ministry of Finance and serve on a part-time basis. Furthermore, the BADC is supported by a research organization known as the Corporation Finance Research Institute.

The influence of the tax code is significant in Japan. Taxable income is based on the amount calculated under the Commercial Code. If the Commercial Code does not prescribe an accounting treatment, then Tax Law is often followed.

In July 2001, ASBJ (Accounting Standard Board in Japan) replaced BADC, similar to FASB. The Financial Accounting Standards Foundation (FASF) oversights ASBJ, and is responsible for funding and naming its members. Funding comes from companies and the accounting profession, not the government. As an independent private sectors organization, the ASBJ is stronger, and recommends reliability and transparency of information. ASBJ collaborates with the IASB in developing IFRS and in 2005 launched a joint project with the IASB to reduce difference between Japanese accounting standards and IFRS (Choi, and Meek,2011). In January 2005, both sides disclaim to formally use the plan.

The Japanese Institute of Certified Public Accountants (JICPA) represents professional organization of CPAs in Japan with establishment in 1949. In addition to providing guidance on the conduct of an audit, the JICPA publishes implementation guidelines on accounting matters, and consults with the BADC in developing accounting standards. Generally accepted auditing standards are promulgated by the BAC rather than the JICPA. In 2003 the Certified Public Accountant and Auditing Oversight Board was built. As a government agency, it is designed to monitor and oversee the auditing profession and improve the quality of Japanese audits. In 2004, the Certified Public Accountant and Auditing Oversight Board was put under the Financial Service Agency (FSA). The FSA is in charge of a reference document known a Business Accounting Principle, which was first issued in 1949 and is amended about once a decade. All companies that report under the Securities Law must comply with these Principles (Nobes, and Parker, 2010).

3.4.3 Financial reporting

The Ministry of Justice first issued regulations about the form and content of the financial statements in 1963. The regulation has been amended subsequently from time to time, including a major revision in 1982 (Nobes, and Parker, 2010). Companies incorporated under the Commercial Code are required to prepare and disclose the following financial statements: Balance sheet, Income statement, Business report, Proposal for appropriation of retained earnings, and Supporting schedules. Supplementary Schedules provided to the shareholders' meeting include details of changes to share capital and reserves, acquisitions and disposals of fixed assets, and transactions with directors and shareholders. The JICPA has published a specimen set of financial statements that conform to the disclosure requirements of the regulations under the Commercial Code.

The financial statements prepared under the Securities Law must include a balance sheet, an income statement, a statement of proposed appropriation of earnings, certain supplementary schedules and certain additional unaudited information. The supplementary schedules include details of share capital and reserves, long-term debt, fixed assets and intra-group transactions. The additional unaudited information includes details of the company's organizational structure, employees, production and cash flows (Nobes, and Parker, 2010).

Listed companies must prepare financial statements under the SEL, which generally require the same basic statements as the Company Law plus a statement of cash flows. Under the SEL, a cash flow statement is added besides one required by Commercial Code. Consolidated financial statements are also the main focus under the SEL. Additional footnotes and schedules are also required. Auditing by independent auditors is needed for financial statements and schedules under the SEL. From year of 2008, listed company must submit an annual assessment of the company's internal controls and a letter certifying the accuracy of the annual report. And internal control report must be audited (Choi, and Meek, 2011).

In Japan, the IFRSs have been permitted for a number of international companies since 2010. The decision about mandatory adoption of IFRS happened around 2012.

3.4.4 Accounting measurement

Though pooling is allowed, the purchase method for business combination is normally used in Japan. Goodwill is measured on the basis of the fair value of the net assets acquired and is amortized over a maximum of 20 years or less and is subject to an impairment test. The equity is used for investments in affiliated companies when the parent and subsidiary exert significant influence over their financial and operational policies (Choi, and Meek, 2011). The equity method is applied for investment, not only for associated companies in group accounts, but also for joint ventures.

From 1996, a modified temporal method is required to translate the financial statements of foreign subsidiaries for consolidation purposes. Since 1999, assets and liabilities of foreign subsidiaries are translated at the current exchange rate, revenue and expense at the average rate, and translation adjustments are in stockholders' equity.

Inventory may be valued at cost or the lower of cost or market. Cost is the basic valuation method. However inventory must be written down to market if there is a significant and permanent decline in value. FIFO, LIFO, and average are all acceptable, while the average is the most popular. Investments in securities are valued at market. In detail, marketable trading securities are valued at fair value with gains and losses going to income. In an investor's unconsolidated statement, investments in subsidies, joint ventures and associates are held at cost, while bonds held to maturity are valued at amortized cost. Other investments are valued at fair value with gains and losses going to equity.

Fixed assets are valued at cost and depreciation in accordance with the tax laws. The declining-balance method (reducing-balance method) is the most common depreciation method. As for intangible assets, the Commercial Code and the Business Accounting Principles generally permitted a company to deter both research and development costs. However, the BADC required R&D to be expensed from April 2000 onwards (Nobes, and Parker, 2010). Through some surveys of Japanese financial reporting, researchers such as Gray et al.(1984) and Cooke and Kikuya (1992) found that 80 percent of the companies wrote off development cost immediately as incurred.

For legal reserve, it is required (Choi, Frost and Meek, 2002). Under the Commercial Code, a company could transfer an amount equal to at least 10 percent of its dividends paid to a legal reserve, until the reserve equals 25 percent of the capital stock account. Furthermore, the legal reserve is undistributable but may be capitalized following the appropriate legal procedures. For other items, finance lease are capitalized while operating lease are expensed when incurred. Deferred taxes are provided for all timing difference using the liability method. Contingent losses are provided for when they can be probable and reasonable estimated. Pension and other employee retirement benefits are fully accrued as employee earn. Extraordinary items in the income statement are separated out from other and shown in a separated section before corporate taxes.

3.5 The Netherlands

3.5.1 Introduction

The Kingdom of the Netherlands, commonly known as the Netherlands, is a sovereign state and constitutional monarchy with territory in western Europe and in the Caribbean. The four parts of the Kingdom – Aruba, Curaçao, Sint Maarten and the Netherlands – are separate countries (landen in Dutch) and participate on a basis of equality as partners in the Kingdom. In practice, however, most of the Kingdom affairs are administered by the Netherlands – which comprises roughly 98% of the Kingdom's land area and population – on behalf of the entire Kingdom[①].

The Netherlands accounting is very famous for its "micro-economics model." To some extent, the Netherlands accounting is similar with that in the United States, and the United Kingdom. However, the Netherlands accounting show several interesting paradoxes. First of all, there is relatively permissive statutory accounting and financial reporting requirement, but high professional practice standards in the Netherlands. Secondly, the Netherlands is a code law country, but its accounting is oriented toward fair presentation. Thirdly, in the Netherland, there are two separate activities between financial reporting and tax accounting. Fourthly, its fairness orientation for accounting has been developed without a strong stock market influence in the Netherlands. Lastly, there is a strong accounting profession in the Netherlands, and its accounting profession has significant influence on standards and regulations.

How to open these paradoxes needs to understand Dutch institution and culture. The Netherland is famous for its business economic approach to accounting. Microeconomic thinking influences accounting deeply from time to time. Accounting in the Netherlands is a branch of business economics. Both of economic and academic thought have admitted and accepted the microeconomic view. Moreover, accountants in the Netherland like to receive foreign ideas. For example, the Netherlands is one country of the earliest proponents of IASs. Also the Netherlands is the home to several largest multinational enterprises such as Philips, Royal Dutch/Shell, and Unilever. These enterprises have been internationally listed since 1950s, and have been affected by American and British accounting. These multinational enterprises have influenced the financial reporting of other Dutch companies.

Whereas investors are pride of place as preferred users of accounts, the information demand of other users, especially employees are recognized on a voluntary basis. Since 1970s, the practice of social reporting has been established and involves

---

① Data comes from the website: http://en.wikipedia.org/wiki/Kingdom_of_the_Netherlands

disclosures mainly about employment and personnel policies in both annual reports and special reports.

Accounting in the Netherland is similar in many ways to that of the United Kingdom and the Anglo-American approach as a whole. Company law and the accounting profession are the major factors. Although size for listed company is comparatively small, their shares are of state owned ownership and international background (Radebaugh et at., 2008).

3.5.2 Accounting regulation and enforcement

Like other European continental countries, Company law in the Netherlands is incorporated into the Civil Code, which is based on Roman law. Civil Code has not traditionally provided a detailed framework for business activities. Dutch government has had a somewhat laissez-faire attitude toward commercial matters, much as in the United Kingdom. Before 1970, law for Dutch accounting model is short of, therefore, accounting regulation remained liberal. Statutory financial reporting requirements are included in Civil Code. However, in 1970 the Act on Annual Financial Statements was enacted in order to reflect the coming harmonization of company law within the EU. The Act on Annual Financial Statements set into motion and formation of the Tripartite Accounting Study Group (replaced in 1981 by the Council on Annual Reporting) and give birth to the Enterprise Chamber. The Act, incorporated into the civil code in 1975, was amended by legislation in 1983.The Council for Annual Reporting issues guidelines on generally acceptable (not accepted) accounting principles. Council on Annual Reporting is a private organization and financed by grants from the business community and the Netherlands Institute of Register accountants. The guidelines do not have the force of law, but are followed by most large companies and auditors.

The Enterprise Chamber is a specialist court connected with the High Court of Amsterdam with a unique feature of the Dutch system of enforcing compliance with accounting requirements. The Enterprise Chamber is composed of three judges and two expert accountants, no jury. Under the Civil Code, there is a specific provision. That is any party may complain to this chamber if he believes a company's statements do not conform to applicable law. Any party includes shareholders, employees, trade unions, public prosecutor, etc. Its decision may lead to modifications of financial statements or various penalties.

It is obvious that the most novel feature of the Dutch accounting scene is the Enterprise Chamber of the Court of Justice of Amsterdam. What is the mission of the Enterprise Chamber? How is this mission carried out?

The Enterprise Chamber carries out its mission by determining whether the allegations of deficient financial reporting are true and how material such deficiencies are. Depending upon the case, the Chamber may require that financial statements be modified or it may seek penalties through the Court of Justice. The Chamber is composed of three judges and two Dutch RAs. There is no jury within the Chamber. However, appeals of any of the Chambers' rulings are difficult, may only be lodged with the Dutch Supreme Court, and are restricted to points of law.

Financial reporting is very flexible in the Netherlands. For examples, Dutch financial statements can be in one of several languages such as English, French, Dutch, or German. For measurement, companies may use either historical cost or current costs. In the Netherlands, guidelines from the Council on Annual Reporting are recommendations only, not the required law.

The Netherlands Institute of Registeraccountants (NIvRA) is fully autonomous in setting auditing standards. Its strong professional code of conduct has statutory status and involves in everything that is accounting related in the Netherlands. Accountant participates in the Council for Annual Reporting and in commissions charged with revising the accounting statutes of the civil code. Member of NIvRA serves on the Enterprise Chamber, as accounting faculty at leading Dutch universities, and on the IASB, OECD, the UN, and IFAC. In the Netherlands, there are two kinds of auditors, i.e. register accountants (RAs, or chartered accountants) and administrative accountants (AAs). Administrative accountants are allowed to certify financial statements in 1993 if they undergo additional training.

3.5.3 Financial reporting

The quality of Dutch financial statements is uniformly high as there is few auditor sued cases in the Netherlands. Statutory financial statements should be filed in Dutch, but English, French, and German are also acceptable. The financial statements include as follows such as balance sheet, income statement, notes, Director's report, and other prescribed information. Statement of Cash Flow is recommended by a council guideline. Most Dutch companies provide Statement of Cash Flow voluntarily. For large and medium-sized companies, Statement of Cash Flow is required. Besides, annual financial reports must be presented on both a parent-company-only and a consolidated basis.

Consistent with EU Directives, reporting requirements vary by company size. Small, medium-sized, and large companies are defined in the Civil Code. Small companies are exempt from the requirements for an audit and for consolidated financial statements, and they may file an abbreviated balance sheet and income statement. Medium-sized companies must be audited, but many publish a condensed income statement. Listed Dutch companies must prepare consolidated financial statements according to IFRS. Their parent-company statements may also be prepared using IFRSs, Dutch accounting guidelines, or a mixture of the two. All Dutch companies are allowed to use IFRSs instead of Dutch guidelines (Choi and Meek, 2011).

3.5.4 Accounting measurement

The purchase method is the normal practice, while the pooling of interest method for business combination is allowed in limited circumstance, or is rarely used in the Netherlands. Goodwill can be treated in many ways, while most companies charge it to reserves. Or goodwill is capitalized and amortized over its estimated useful life, up to a maximum of 20 years. The equity method is required when investor exercises significant influence on business and financial policy (Choi and Meek, 2011). Joint venture could use either equity method or proportional consolidation. As for translation of foreign currency, the closing rate is used for balance sheet of a foreign entity that is independent of the parent, while the closing rate or average rate is used for income statement. Translation adjustments are charged to shareholders' equity. The temporal method is used for foreign entities that are not independent of the parent, with the translation adjustment charged to income.

Current values are used for tangible assets such as inventory and depreciable assets. Companies using current values should provide additional historical cost information on the notes. Historical cost is also acceptable. When historical cost is used for inventory, it is stated at the lower of cost or market, with cost determined by FIFO, LIFO, average, or even base stock methods. Research and development cost are capitalized only when the amounts are recoverable and sufficiently certain. Leases, contingencies, and pension costs are generally measured as they are in the United Kingdom and the United States. Deferred income taxes are recognized on the basis of the comprehensive allocation concept and measured according to the liability method. Sometimes, deferred income taxes could be also valued at discounted present value. Current values accounting is not acceptable for tax purpose. Once current value is applied for financial reporting, permanent rather than temporary difference occurs.

3 6 The United Kingdom

3.6.1 Introduction

The United Kingdom consists of four constituent regions which are England, Wales, Scotland, and Northern Ireland. The legislative authority lies with Parliament, which includes the House of Commons and the House of Lords. The main form of business organization is the limited liability company in the United Kingdom. The capital market provides the main source of funding for business. Therefore, facilitating the efficient working of the capital market is the primary purpose of accounting. There are approximately 15,000 private limited companies, of which about 2,500 are listed on the London Stock Exchange. The United Kingdom has by far the greatest number of companies listed on a regulated market in the European Union. Listed companies and other large companies file a full set of audited annual financial statements with the Registrar of Companies (Doupnik and Perera, 2007).

The securities markets of the United Kingdom have a significant influence on accounting practice. However, the market does not dominate the process of accounting regulation. Company Law in the United Kingdom has a much wider remit than the U.S securities laws as far as the provision of accounting information is concerned.

The United Kingdom is the first country to develop accountancy profession. Accounting in the United Kingdom was developed as an independent discipline. Although company law added structure and other requirements, it still allowed accountants considerable flexibility in professional judgment. Since the 1970s, the most significant source of development in company law has been the EU Directives such as the Fourth and Seventh Directives.

The United Kingdom contributes accounting profession development around the world a lot. For example, the concept of a fair presentation is of British origin. Professional accounting thinking and practice was exported to other countries and its former possessions: Australia, Canada, the United States, Hong Kong, India, Kenya, New Zealand, Nigeria, Singapore, South Africa (Choi and Meek, 2011).

3.6.2 Accounting regulation and enforcement

There are two major sources of financial accounting standards who are company law and accounting profession in the United Kingdom. Prior to the 1980s, company law was perceived as providing little more than a framework for accounting regulation, but the accounting profession could set more detailed accounting rules or standards. Later primarily to implement the EU Fourth Directive on company accounts and the Seventh Directive on consolidated accounts, in 1981 and 1989 respectively, there have been many revisions to U.K company law. The Company Law of 1985 consolidated all previous extant company acts, and it was passed in 1989. The Company Law includes accounting requirements for all limited liability companies, not just large companies or those listed on stock exchanges.

Accounting in the United Kingdom grows as an independent discipline with being significant influence on the development of accounting profession in many countries. The establishment of the first professional accounting body, the Society of Accountants in Edinburgh, in 1853 can be regarded as the beginning of the modern accounting profession. With the development of accounting profession, more and more accounting profession bodies were established. Now there are six national accountancy professional bodies linked together with each other through the Consultative Committee of Accountancy Bodies (CCAB, organized in 1970) in the United Kingdom.

They are the institute of Chartered Accountants in England and Wales (ICAEW), the Institute of Chartered Accountants in Ireland (ICAI), the Institute of Chartered Accountants in Scotland (ICAS), the Association of Chartered Certified Accountants (ACCA), the Chartered Institute of Management Accountants (CIMA), and the Chartered Institute of Public Finance and Accountancy (CIPFA).

Accounting principles issued by the Institute of Charted Accountants in England and Wales began at 1942. In 1970, to stave off government intervention and the creation of a U.S style SEC, the profession set up its own self-regulatory organization, the Accounting Standards Steering Committee (ASSC). Since 1971, ASSC has issued Statement on Standard Accounting Practice (SSAPs). In 1976, the Accounting Standards Committee (ASC) replaced the ASSC. SSAPs were issued and enforced by the six accounting bodies, any one of which could effectively veto the standard. However, the veto power of these six organizations often led to much more delays and compromises in developing SSAPs (Choi and Meek, 2011). Until July 1990, 25 SSAPs was issued, while 11 SSAPs still are valid today.

The Dearing Report, issued in 1988, expressed dissatisfaction with the existing standard-setting arrangement. A new structure for setting accounting standards was recommended. The Companies Act of 1989 was important not only for incorporating the EU Seventh Directive but also for enacting the recommendations of the Dearing Report. The Company Act of 1989 receipt recommendations of the Dearing Report. The Company Act of 1989 created a new Financial Reporting Council (FRC). There are three offshoots of FRC, which include the Accounting Standards Board (ASB), replaced the ASC in 1990, Urgent Issues Task Force (UITF), and Financial Reporting Review Panel (FRRP). ASB issues Financial Reporting Standards (FRSs). Until March 2006, 29 FRSs were issued. The ASB is one of several national standard setters that have a formal liaison relationship with the IASB. The ASB is committed to align UK accounting standards with IFRSs wherever practicable, by a phased replacement of existing UK standards with new UK standards based on IFRSs. Since FRS 20, ASB has taken IFRSs at its FRSs. (FRS 20 – FRS 29). Again the revision of Company Act came into effect in October 2004. Under the Companies Act of 2004, the authority of the FRRP would be extended to cover financial information, other than annual accounts, published by entities that have securities listed on a UK market and where mandatory accounting requirements may apply.

Auditing standards in the United Kingdom are issued by the Auditing Practices Board (APB). Auditing standards include Statement of Auditing Standards (SASs), Auditing Guidelines, and Statements of Investment Circular Reporting Standards (SIRs). The APB is funded by the CCAB (the Consultative Committee of Accountancy Bodies), and its membership consists of practicing auditors and others from business, academia, law, and the public sector (Doupnik and Perera, 2007). In 2003, the

Accountancy Foundation, which regulate and oversee the auditing profession, was dissolved and its function was transferred to the FRC. A newly established Professional Oversight Board (POB) oversee the regulation of the auditing profession by monitoring the activities of the professional accounting bodies. The APB was transferred from the Accountancy Foundation to the FRC. The Accountancy Investigation and Discipline Board (now the Accountancy and Actuarial Discipline Board, or AADB) was built as a mechanism to investigate and discipline accountants or accounting firms for professional misconduct. Therefore, the Financial Reporting Council is responsible for both accounting and auditing standards, and their enforcement (Choi and Meek, 2011).

3.6.3 Financial reporting

Financial statements in the United Kingdom are the most comprehensive in the world. Financial statements generally include directors' report, profit and loss account and balance sheet, cash flow statement, statement of total recognized gains and losses, statement of accounting policies, notes that are referenced to the financial statements and auditor's report.

Consolidated financial statements are required in addition to a parent-only balance sheet. In London Stock Exchange, listed companies must provide half-year interim reports besides annual report. Listed companies must also report earning per share, and the earning figure used in the calculation must be the one after tax and extraordinary items.

Under the Company Act of 2006, a company must prepare either a balance sheet and a profit and loss account that comply with the detailed regulations, or statements that comply with international accounting standards. Both the statement of total recognized gains and losses (STRGL) and cash flow statement are required by accounting standards, but not by company legislation. FRS 3 regulates the function of the STRGL, while cash flow statement is required by FRS 1, except for certain small companies. The Companies Act sets out size criteria. Small and medium sized companies are exempt from many financial reporting obligations, including exempt from preparing consolidated statements, and preparing abbreviated accounts with little information. For small companies, requirements in standards can be replaced by the FRSSE, which requires a STRGL but not a cash flow statement (Nobes and Parker, 2010).

3.6.4 Accounting measurement

Both acquisition and merger (pooling of interests in the United States) are allowed for business combination. But merger is seldom used. Goodwill is capitalized and amortized over 20 years or less. However a longer period or an indefinite period is possible if goodwill is subject to an annual impairment review. The equity method is applied for associated undertakings and for joint ventures. SSAP 20 deals with foreign currency translation and requires the closing rate (current rate) method for independent subsidiaries and the temporal method for integrated subsidiaries.

Assets may be valued at historical cost, current cost, or using a mixture of the two. Therefore, revaluation of land and buildings are permissible or allowable. Depreciation and amortization must correspond to the measurement basis used for the underlying asset. Research expenses are written off in the year of the expenditure, and development costs may be deferred under some specific circumstances. However, few British companies capitalize any development costs in practice. Inventory is valued at the lower of cost or net realizable value on a FIFO or average cost basis. LIFO is not acceptable in the United Kingdom (Choi and Meek, 2011).

Lease, which transfer the risks and rewards of ownership to the lessee, are capitalized and the lease obligation could be taken as a liability. The costs of providing pensions and other retirement benefits must be recognized systematically and rationally over the period during which the employees' services are provided. Deferred taxes are calculated by using the liability method, but only to the extent that it is probable that a tax asset or liability will materialize. In the United Kingdom, income smoothing opportunities actually exist in some asset valuation and other measurement areas (Choi, Frost, and Meek, 2002).

3.7 The United States

3.7.1 Introduction

Before 1930s, the United Kingdom accounting is the most developed in the world. After 1930s, there is the most developed accounting model in the world in the United States. Accounting in the United States is very similar to that in the United Kingdom, as two countries are closely related with history, culture and investment. Just as the language and legal system of the United States were an export from the United Kingdom, founding fathers of U.S accounting, including pioneers such as Arthur Yong (a Glasgow University graduate of the 1880s) and James Marwick (whose names are now incorporated in to the names of the accounting firms Ernst & Young and KPMG, respectively) were expatriate Briton. The other two big accounting firms in the US (i.e, Deloitte, Price, Waterhouse, and the Cooper brothers) are all British, showing the origins of the firms (Nobes and Parker, 2010). Nevertheless, the United States has adapted rather than adopted the United Kingdom's accounting tradition. Indeed, recent historical and environmental circumstances of the United States have given rise to some significant distinguishing features (Radebaugh, Gary, and Black, 2007).

In the United States, financial accounting objective is to protect investors, especially individual investors. The relevance of information to business decisions is paramount subject to the constraint of reliability. In the United States, there is the most developed securities market. The securities markets are the dominant influence on accounting regulations. Dealing in securities and investor protection are regulated and enforced at the federal government level under the Securities Act of 1933 and the Securities Exchange Act of 1934, which were passed in response to the stock market crash of 1929 and subsequent financial crises.

Based on the findings in these hearings, Congress—during the peak year of the Depression—passed the Securities Act of 1933. This law, together with the Securities Exchange Act of 1934, which created the Securities and Exchange Commission (SEC), was designed to restore investor confidence in US capital markets by providing investors and the markets with more reliable information and clear rules of honest dealing. The mission of the U.S. Securities and Exchange Commission is to protect investors, maintain fair, orderly, and efficient markets, and facilitate capital formation. The SEC oversees the key participants in the securities world, including securities exchanges, securities brokers and dealers, investment advisors, and mutual funds. Here the SEC is concerned primarily with promoting the disclosure of important market-related information, maintaining fair dealing, and protecting against fraud. As a legal authority SEC recognize and enforce accounting standards for listed company. Although accounting standard sector is Financial Accounting Standard Board (FASB), the SEC acts in a supervisory capacity only if it deems necessary to intervene. Sometimes the SEC issues instructions on how to do accounting in "Accounting Series Releases", "Financial Reporting Releases", and "Staff Accounting Bulletins". However, the SEC tends to limit its authority to a supervisory role, encouraging the FASB to keep leadership in the standard setting process.

In February 2001, the accounting scandals of Enron and WorldCom happened. Then the Big 5 accounting firm, Andersen, collapsed. Under the situation, Public Company Accounting Reform and Investor Protection Act of 2002 was issued by Congress in 25 July, 2002. It also is called Sarbanes-Oxley Act of 2002, which revised Securities Act of 1933, and Securities Exchange Act of 1934, enhanced independence of FASB, and required standards should be recognized by SEC, and cut relationship between AICPA and FASB. The SEC will oversee the PCAOB, while the PCAOB is an either non-profit sector or non-governmental sector(argued), with supervising CPA industry and being responsible for auditing standards.

3.7.2 Accounting regulation and enforcement

In the United States, the generally accepted accounting principle (GAAP) is issued by an independent Financial Accounting Standards Board (FASB), which was established in 1973 following criticism of the standard-setting procedures of the American Institute of Certified Public Accountants (AICPA). Before establishment of FASB, there are two former accounting setting sectors.

The first former standard setting sector is the Committee on Accounting Procedure (CAP), which belonged to the AICPA, and existed during the period from 1938 to 1958, and issued 51 Accounting Research Bulletins. The second sector is the Accounting Principle Board (APB), which replaced the CAP in 1959, also belonged to the AICPA, existed during the period from 1959 to 1973, and issued 31 Opinion with 4 Statements up to 1973. In 1971, growing dissatisfaction with the procedure for setting accounting standards led AICPA to build up two committees to review these procedures. In 1972, report named Establishing Financial Accounting Standards by the Wheat Committee, led to the creation of three new bodies which were the FASB, the FAF (Financial Accounting Foundation), and FASAC (Financial Accounting Standards Advisory Council). On the other hand, the Trueblood Committee was formed to prepare a report on the objectives of financial reporting—a first step in the development of the FASB's conceptual framework project (Nobes and Parker, 2010).

The FASB exists in the year from 1973 to now, issuing Statement of Financial Accounting Standards (SFASs), Statements of Financial Accounting Concepts, and Interpretation. Statements of Standards establish new standards or amend those previously issued, and Concepts Statements set up general concepts that guide the development of standards, and Interpretations clarify, explain or elaborate existing standards. Until March 2006, 158 statements of financial accounting standards, 47 statements of financial accounting concepts and interpretations, 52 technical statements, and 496 EITF (emerging issues task force) were issued. Since 1973, the FASB has been the designated organization in the private sector for establishing standards of financial accounting that governs the preparation of financial reports by nongovernmental entities. Those standards are officially recognized as authoritative by the SEC (Financial Reporting Release No. 1, Section 101, and reaffirmed in its April 2003 Policy Statement) and the AICPA (Rule 203, Rules of Professional Conduct, as amended May 1973 and May 1979)[1]. Corporation must follow FASB standards. Otherwise, the SEC will refuse registration and hence trading in their securities.

The mission of the FASB is to establish and improve standards of financial accounting and reporting that foster financial reporting by nongovernmental entities that provides decision-useful information to investors and other users of financial reports. The FASB accomplishes its mission through a comprehensive and independent process that encourages broad participation, objectively considers all stakeholder views, and is subject to oversight by the Financial Accounting Foundation's Board of Trustees.

---

[1] Data comes from website such as "www.iasb.org".

The FASB is part of a structure that is independent of all other business and professional organizations. That structure includes the Financial Accounting Foundation (FAF), the FASB, the Financial Accounting Standards Advisory Council (FASAC), the Governmental Accounting Standards Board (GASB), and the Governmental Accounting Standards Advisory Council (GASAC).The Foundation is the independent, private sector organization that is responsible for the oversight, administration, and finances of the FASB, the GASB, and their advisory councils FASAC and GASAC. The Foundation's primary duties include protecting the independence and integrity of the standards-setting process and appointing members of the FASB, GASB, FASAC, and GASAC. Consistent with that mission, the FASB maintains the FASB Accounting Standards Codification, which was introduced IN 2009, represented the source of authoritative standards of accounting and reporting, other than those issued by the SEC, recognized by the FASB to be applied by nongovernmental entities. The Accounting Standards Codification combines together all previously issued authoritative GAAP in one code (Nobes and Parker, 2010).

The FAF is made up of trustees appointed by several other bodies, which are the Financial Executives Institute (FEI), the Financial Analysts Foundation (FFA), American Accounting Association (AAA), AICPA, National Accountant Association (NAA), and Securities Institute Association (SIA). This body was established as a result of same Wheat Commission report in 1972 that resulted in the creation of the FASB, as what it was mentioned previously in this chapter.

The FASB's use of a conceptual framework is a significant feature of accounting standard setting in the United States. Statement of Financial Accounting Concepts set forth fundamentals on which financial accounting and reporting standards are based. The FASB's framework has been influential around the world. Both IASB's framework and the UK's Statement of Principles clearly are affected by the framework in the US.

Exhibit 3.1   Conceptual Framework in the United States

Issuance date	Name	Title	Notes
1978.11	SFAC No.1	Objectives of Financial Reporting by Business Enterprises	
1980.5,	SFAC No.2	Qualitative Characteristics of Accounting Information	
1980.12	SFAC No.3	Elements Of Financial Statements of Business Enterprises	
1980.12	SFAC No.4	Objectives of financial Reporting by Non-business Organizations	
1984.12	SFAC No.5	Recognition and Measurement in Financial Statements of Business Enterprises	
1985.12	SFAC No.6	Elements of Financial Statements	Replaced No.3, Revised No.2,
2000.2	SFAC No.7	Using Cash Flow Information and Present Value in Accounting Measurements	
2010.9	SFAC No.8	Conceptual Framework for Financial Reporting 2010	Replaced No.1 and No.2

The AICPA (American Institute of Certified Public Accountants), founded in 1887, is the world's largest association representing the accounting profession, with nearly 377,000 members in 128 countries. AICPA members represent many areas of practice, including business and industry, public practice, government, education and consulting. Membership is also available to accounting students and CPA candidates. The AICPA sets ethical standards for the profession. Before 2001, the AICPA was responsible for US auditing standards covering audits of private companies, non-profit organizations and federal, state and local governments. After scandals of Enron and WorldCom, auditing standard setting was transferred to the PCAOB.

Mission of the AICPA is to provide members with the resources, information, and leadership that enable them to provide valuable services in the highest professional manner to benefit the public as well as employers and clients. Its objectivity is advocacy, certification and licensing, communications, recruiting and education, standards and performance. Also the AICPA develops and grades the uniform CPA examination.

3.7.3 Financial reporting

Generally speaking, the financial reporting is intended to provide information that is useful in making business economic decision. In detail, there are three aspects. The first is a general objective, which financial reporting should provide information that is useful to present and potential investors, creditors and other users in making rational investment, credit and similar decision. The second is specific objective, which financial reporting should provide information to help present and potential investors and creditors and other users in assessing the amounts, timing and uncertainty of prospective cash receipts from dividends or interest and the proceeds from the sale, redemption, or maturity of securities or loans. The third is more specific objective, which financial reporting should provide information about the economic resources of an enterprise, the claims to those resources, and the effects of transactions, events and circumstances that change its resources and claims to those resources (Nobes and Parker, 2011).

A typical annual financial report of a large U.S corporation is as follows.

Exhibit 3.2   Annual financial report

Sequence number	Name	Detail
1	report of management	
2	report of independent auditors	
3	primary financial statements	income statement, balance sheet, statement of cash flows, statement of comprehensive income, statement of stockholders' equity

Sequence number	Name	Detail
4	management discussion and analysis of results of operations and financial condition	
5	disclosure of accounting policies with the most critical impact on financial statements	
6	notes to financial statements	
7	five-or ten-year comparison of selected financial data	
8	selected quarterly data	

Consolidated financial statements are required, while published U.S. financial reporting typically do not contain parent-company-only statements. Two further US reporting practices bear great intention. The first is segment reporting which is required for all publicly traded companies. The second concerns earning per share disclosures. Both basic earning per share and diluted earning per share need to be computed and disclosed in income statement. This treatment is substantially the same as IAS 33 (Choi, Frost, and Meek,2002).

3.7.4 Accounting measurement

Both purchase and pooling of interests are used for business combination. Pooling of interest must be used when the combination meets the criteria specified in GAAP. Under the purchase, goodwill is capitalized and amortized on a straight line basis over a maximum of 40 years and the amortization amount is included in current period income. Under no circumstance can it be charged against shareholders' equity. The APB Opinion 17 regulated goodwill treatment until 2001. In 2001, SFAS 142 was issued, which abolished amortization, requiring instead annual impairment tests.

Foreign currency translation follows the requirements of SFAS No.52, which introduces a concept named functional currency, and relies on the foreign subsidiary's functional currency to determine translation methodology.

Historical cost is used to value tangible and intangible asset. Revaluation is permitted only after a business combination accounted for as a purchase. Both accelerated and straight line depreciation methods are permissible. The financial statement carrying values of property, plant and equipment or intangible assets are not increased on the basis of upward appraisals of changes in prices. In other word, revaluation is not allowed. All research and development costs are expensed as incurred, there are special capitalization rules for computer software costs.

LIFO, FIFO, and average cost methods are permissible and widely used for inventory pricing, while LIFO is more popular. When financial leases are in substance the purchase of property, the value of the property is capitalized and a corresponding liability is booked. The cost of pensions and other postretirement benefits are accrued over the periods in which employees earn their benefit and unfunded obligations are reported as a liability. Both pension benefit and post-retirement medical benefit must be accounted for at the discounted value of expected payments. Contingent losses/liabilities are accrued when they are probable and the amount can be reasonably estimated. Furthermore, income smoothing is not allowed in the United States.

Income taxes are accounted for using the liability method. Deferred taxes are accrued for the tax effects of temporary differences between financial and tax accounting methods, and are measured based on the future tax rates that will apply when these items reverse. Comprehensive income tax allocation is also required (Choi, Frost and Meek, 2002).

3.8 Comparison of Accounting Measurement

As we see, there are different accounting measurements existing in six developed countries even treating the same transaction or event. Comparison of accounting measurement in the six developed countries is show in Exhibit 3.2 (Exhibit mainly comes from Choi, and Meek (2005), page 75).

It is obvious that there are much more similar practice between France and Germany. Although accounting practice in Japan was affected by Germany, a lot of changes occurred in recent decades in Japan. Accounting practice in the Netherlands raise much more interesting issues, which are worth research in the future.

Given the common accounting tradition, the strong investor orientation and the highly developed stock markets in London and New York, it would seem unlikely that major differences should exist between the two countries. Furthermore, the UK and US have been closely linked in a number of international classification studies, which suggest that accounting in the both countries is pragmatic and derived from business practice. Still there are some both similarities and difference. Similarities between two countries include many aspects such as business combination, use of equity method, foreign currency translation, depreciation charge, capital lease, and deferred tax. However, many differences exist apparently. The accounting practice of goodwill, asset valuation, LIFO, reserve for income smoothing, and long term liability are all treated in different ways.

Weetman and Gray (1990) show that US companies are likely to report systematically more conservative or understated measure of earning, with UK earning being up to 25% higher on average than US earning . The most frequently occurring adjustments were found to be those dealing with amortization of goodwill and with provision for deferred taxation. Of the two, the amortization of goodwill is the dominant effect when measured as a percentage of US reported earnings. With an average of 18% of US earnings in 1987 being taken by a charge for goodwill which is not found in UK income statements, this is clearly an item of material effect on reported earnings. Deferred taxation was also a cause of material differences between UK and US reported profit when UK corporation tax rates and capital allowances were relatively high. It became progressively less material over the period 1985 to 1987 insofar as UK partial provision differs from US full provision. Now that both countries are using the liability method, one source of difference has been eliminated. There remain the potentially complicated effects of differing treatments of tax losses and unrecovered Advance Corporate Tax. In a word, the difference between the UK and the US accounting practices show that in the case of both adjustments the UK treatment is less conservative, or the US more conservative, in its effect on the income statement. Both areas are covered by UK accounting standards which have been subject to a considerable element of corporate pressure during their development, more so than is possible in the US standard setting process.

Exhibit 3.2   Summary of significant accounting practices among six countries

	France	Germany	Japan	The Netherlands	The U.K	The U.S
Business combination	purchase	purchase	purchase	purchase	purchase	purchase
Goodwill	Capitalize & amortize	Capitalize & amortize	Capitalize & amortize	Capitalize & amortize	Capitalize & amortize	Capitalize & impairment tested
Affiliated companies	Equity method	Equity method	Equity method	Equity method	Equity method	Equity method
Foreign currency translation: currency rate method,	Autonomous subsidiaries	Autonomous subsidiaries	All subsidiaries	Autonomous subsidiaries	Autonomous subsidiaries	Autonomous subsidiaries
temporal method	Integrated subsidiaries	Integrated subsidiaries	Not used	Integrated subsidiaries	Integrated subsidiaries	Integrated subsidiaries
Asset valuation	Historical cost	Historical cost	Historical cost	Historical & current cost	Historical & current cost	Historical cost
Depreciation charges	Economic based	Tax based	Tax based	Economic based	Economic based	Economic based
LIFO	Not used	Not used	Not used	Not used	Not acceptable	used
Finance leases	Not capitalized	Not capitalized	capitalized	capitalized	capitalized	capitalized
Deferred taxes	accrued	accrued	accrued	accrued	accrued	accrued
Reserves for income smoothing	used	used	no	some	some	no

Terms of the Chapter

accounting standard 会计准则

accounting profession 会计职业

accounting practice 会计实务

Anglo-Saxon accounting 盎格鲁撒克什会计

Accounting Regulation and Enforcement 会计规范与实施

Accounting Research Bulletin 会计研究公告

Accounting Series Releases 会计系列公告

AICPA (American Institute of Certified Public Accountants) 美国注册会计师

Accounting Standards Steering Committee (ASSC) 会计准则指导或筹划委员会

accounting regulation 会计规范

accounting policy 会计政策

accrual basis accounting 应计制会计

accounting measurement 会计计量

arm's length 公平独立

book value 账面价值

bubble economy 高风险经济

big bang 大爆炸

conceptual framework 概念框架

consolidated financial statement 合并财务报表

capitalization and amortization 资本化和摊销

commercial legislation 商法

creditor protection 债权人保护

conglomerate 财团

certified public accountant 注册会计师

cash flow forecast 现金流预测

common stock and preferred stock 普通股和优先股

depreciable fixed assets 可折旧固定资产

expense 费用

director's report 董事会报告

disclosure 披露

deferred tax 递延税

declining balance method 余额递减法(折旧方法)

due process procedure 适当的(职业)程序

draft 草稿

diluted earning 稀释收益

discretionary reserves 自由准备金

earning per share 每股收益

Elements of Financial Statements 财务报表要素

equity method 权益法

fairness orientation 公允导向

federal income tax 联邦所得税

Financial Accounting Standard Board (FASB) 财务会计准则委员会(美国)

financial position 财务状况

financial performance 财务经营结果

footnotes 脚注

industry 行业

intangible asset 无形资产

inventory 存货

independent audit 独立审计

income tax 所得税

investment decision making 投资决策

lag 时滞

leases 租赁

legal reserve 法定准备

legal capital 法定资本

low of cost or net realizable value 成本或可变现净值孰低法

losses and gains 损失和利得

liability method 债务法(所得税会计的处理方法)

measurement rules 计量规则

medium sized company 中型企业

minority interest 少数股东权益

notes to financial statements 财务报表附注

national uniform accounting 国家统一会计

national uniform chart of accounts 国家统一会计科目表

nationalization and internationalization 国家化和国际化

opinion (美国)意见书

public sector and private sector 公立团体和私人团体

preparation of financial statements 财务报表编制

pension 抚恤金

parent company 母公司

post-balance sheet events 资产负债表后事项

periodicity 会计分期

proportional consolidation 按比例合并

Present Value 现行价值

public hearings 公共听证会

Public Company Accounting Reform and Investor Protection Act of 2002 公共公司会计改革与投资者保护的 2002 法案

    professional association　职业协会

    provision　备付款或准备金

    pension and retirement benefits　抚恤金和退休利益

    quality of information　信息质量

    recognition and measurement　确认与计量

    realization　实现

    revenue　收入

    retained earning　留存收益

    revaluation　重新计价

    replacement value　重置价值

    realized income　已实现收益

    standard setting　准则制定

    substance over form　实质重于形式

    securities market　证券市场

    stock exchange　股票交易

    supervise　监管

    shareholders' equity　股东权益

    statutory requirement　强制性要求

    social report　社会报告

    statutory auditors　法定审计师

    supporting schedule　附表

    subsidiaries　子公司(或明细账户)

    segmental reporting　分部报告

    tax authorities　税务部门

    taxable income　应税收益

    tangible asset　有形资产

    the Securities and Exchange Commission (SEC)　证监会

    transaction　会计交易或事项

    transparency　透明

    to raise capital　筹集资本

Discussion Questions

1. Explain the distinction between fair presentation orientation and legal compliance accounting by using some examples of each orientation.

2. Describe the relationship between accounting standards and accounting practice through some examples.

3. Other than the United States, which country appears to have the most effective accounting and financial reporting supervision mechanism for companies whose securities are traded in public financial markets?

4. Is it necessary for a country, who has a stock exchange (or a public financial market), to have a regulatory agency that enforces accounting and financial reporting rules? Why or why not?

5. The U.K and the U.S have some common accounting heritages and are linked by history and language. Anglo-American accounting is a term sometimes used to denote their accounting styles being similar in orientation, purpose, and approach. Yet accounting differences still exist between these two countries. Please identify the major differences and similarities between U.K and U.S accounting discussed in this chapter.

6. In most countries, published financial accounting standards differ from those actually used in practice. What causes such differences?

7. Large companies often list their equity shares on different stock exchange around the world, especially in international capital markets such as NYEX, AMEX, and Nasdaq, London and Tokyo, what accounting issues does this practice raise?

8. The most novel feature of the Dutch accounting scene is the Enterprise Chamber of the Court of Justice of Amsterdam. What is the mission of the Enterprise Chamber? How is this mission carried out?

9. How does the Keiretsu form of bushiness organization affect accounting in Japan?

10. Compare and contrast Japanese accounting to Anglo-American accounting by using some examples.

11. If an accounting system is concerned primarily with collecting taxes, how will it differ from an accounting system concerned with providing relevant and reliable information to investors? Which countries mentioned in this chapter have traditionally had a focus on tax? Why?

12. In the United States, some private and /or small public companies are exempt from compliance with certain specified SFASs. This exemption may eventually lead to different sets of GAAP for large and small companies. Is this development desirable from an international vantage point? Why or why not?

13. Describe the role of conceptual framework for accounting in the United States. And how does the conceptual framework in the United States affect the accounting system in other countries or IASB?

14. Compare and contrast both differences and similarities of accounting practices among six developed countries.

15. Analyze and conclude features existing in Anglo-American accounting model.

True or False

1. Accounting standards are the regulations or rules while accounting standards setting is the process by which accounting standards are formulated.

2. The securities markets influence on accounting regulation or GAAP greatly in the United States.

3. The reliability of information to business decisions is paramount subject constraint in both the United States, the United Kingdom.

4. In the Netherlands business economics or microeconomics is very famous and popular, and affect accounting development deeply.

5. In both Germany and France, the financial statement accounts form the basis for the tax accounts.

6. In French accounting, an underlying objective of more effective national economic planning is required.

7. In the United Kingdom, EU directives has been quickly adopted in order to support major state-owned enterprises.

8. A major business Japanese feature that influences accounting is the keiretsu.

9. Japanese companies listed their share in international capital markets often prepare an additional set of financial statement in English.

10. In the Netherlands, both historical and current cost measurements are acceptable.

11. In the United States, LIFO is very popular, while FIFO, average methods could not be acceptable.

12. In the United States, the generally accepted accounting principle (GAAP) is issued by an independent Financial Accounting Standards Board (FASB).

13. After the Enron crisis, Public Company Act was issued by Congress in 25 July, 2002.

14. In both the United Kingdom and the United States, current cost is used as measurement.

15. Economic based depreciation charges are applied in both France and Germany.

16. The equity method is applied in the United States, and the United Kingdom, but not used in France, Germany, and Japan.

Multiple Choice

1. In which of the following countries, do reserves for income smoothing exist to some extent?

a. The United States.

b. Japan.

c. Germany.

d. Mexico.

2. Which of the following pair of countries has similar accounting systems?

    a. The United States and France.

    b. France and Germany.

    c. The United Kingdom and Japan.

    d. Germany and the United Kingdom.

3. In the United States, the SEC acts in a supervisory capacity over FASB

    a. frequently.

    b. rarely.

    c. never.

    d. casual.

4. The British accounting system

    a. does not follow European Directives.

    b. has its rules created by Ministry of Finance.

    c. is not going to adopt the IFRS because of the British pound.

    d. has its rules created by a self-regulatory organization or professional organization.

5. The British accounting system

    a. is based on a uniformity justification.

    b. takes a flexible approach.

    c. does not separate tax accounting and financial accounting.

    d. takes a conservative accounting approach.

6. Which of the following accurately characterize Dutch accounting?

    a. Accounting standards are set up by government.

    b. A true and fair view concept is not acceptable.

    c. Micro-economic thinking is deeply accepted in the society.

    d. There is little social reporting for employees since tax law dominates.

7. Which of the following accurately reflects German accounting?

    a. There is fairly significant professional influence on accounting.

    b. The focus is on creditor protection.

    c. Tax accounting is separated with financial accounting.

    d. The current cost valuation has been adopted as the primary method in accounting measurement.

8. Which of the following accurately reflects French accounting?

    a. Professional organization has strong influence on accounting.

    b. Tax accounting is separated with financial accounting.

c. According to the measurement and disclosure scales in Gray's model, the French would lean to secrecy and conservatism.

d. The true and fair view was accepted as a part of French tradition.

9. Which of the following countries prepares statements according to US GAAP?

a. Germany.

b. Japan.

c. The Netherlands.

d. France.

10. Which of the following accurately characterize Japanese accounting?

a. Accounting standards are set by accounting profession organization .

b. Accounting standards are established by a government body.

c. The true and fair view was accepted as a part of tradition.

d. Smoothing income is an accounting issue.

11. Which of the following accurately reflects Japanese accounting?

a. The current cost valuation has been adopted as the primary method in accounting measurement.

b. There is little social reporting for employees since tax law dominates.

c. There is a tendency to follow a micro-economics approach to valuation.

d. Tax law is a major influence as corporate tax returns must be based on the annual accounts approved by shareholders.

12. Which of the following countries seems to have a higher accounting reporting quality?

a. The Netherlands.

b. France.

c. Germany.

d. Japan.

13. LIFO is used in which of the following countries?

a. the United Kingdom.

b. the United States.

c. the Netherlands.

d. Japan.

Case Analysis

Case 3   Rule based or principle based accounting

The following paragraphs came from Mike Ng(2004). Please read it carefully and answer the questions.

During the past decade companies have created increasingly complex transactions that often fall outside the scope of accounting standards. This has lead to an increase in corporate fraud, as evident by recent scandals such as Enron, WorldCom, Adelphia, and Global Crossing.

Additionally, energy companies, such as Dynegy, Reliant Resources and CMS (http://www.cmsenergy.com), have engaged in "swap" or "round trip" transactions, which involved one company selling power to the other and purchasing the same amount in return. The transactions did not result in the companies obtaining any economic benefits. Nevertheless, each company recognized revenues on the transaction, which boosted earnings and gave the perception that there was a high demand for these services. These events have led many critics to question whether a principles-based approach to standards setting might produce more transparent financial statement.

Required

1. What is the difference between rules-based and principle-based accounting standards and what are the advantages and disadvantages of each?

2. Why has US GAAP evolved into a rule-based approach? Would principles-based standards be effective in the United States? Why or why not?

3. What needs to change in the United States to make principles-based standards effective?

4. Are investors and analysts better served by rules-based or principles-based accounting standards? Why or why not?

Chapter 4   Accounting in Emerging Market Countries

Learning objective

After careful study of this chapter, students will be able to:

1. Show some observations about the four countries or areas.

2. Compare accounting standard setting in developed countries and developing countries.

3. Identify how 7 socioeconomic and institutional factors discussed in Chapter 2 affect accounting in these four countries or areas.

4. Describe the relationship between accounting standard and practice.

5. Describe special features from a point of view such as Chinese accounting standard setting, regulation and enforcement, financial reporting, and measurement.

6. Show briefly the history or development period of Chinese accounting.

7. Compare the accounting characteristics between China and Czech Republic.

8. Explain the similarities and differences of standard setting in the Taiwan and the United States.

9. Discuss accounting feature in Mexico. Explain how accounting in the United States affects Mexican accounting.

10. Explain difference of government role on accounting setting and intervention in China, Czech Republic, Mexico and Taiwan Area.

4.1 Introduction

There are many accounting differences between developed and developing countries or emerging market countries. For some emerging market countries, accounting has been changed a lot with the development of international accounting. In this chapter, we will discuss accounting in some emerging market countries. Choi, Frost and Meek (2002) explained some reasons for choosing these four countries.

China, officially the People's Republic of China(PRC), is the world's most populous country, with a population of over 1.35 billion. The PRC exercises jurisdiction over 22 provinces, five autonomous regions, four direct-controlled municipalities and two mostly self-governing special administrative regions, with capital located in Beijing. Covering approximately 9.6 million square kilometers, China is the world's second-largest country by land area, and either the third or fourth-largest by total area, depending on the method of measurement. China is a member of the WTO and is the world's largest trading power, with a total international trade value of US$3.87 trillion in 2012[①]. There are so huge people in China that more and more multinational enterprises (MNEs) are eager to do business and expend sales market in China. The phenomenon pushes economic development to some extent.

Czech Republic is Soviet bloc country, possessing a developed, high-income economy with a per capita GDP rate that is 82% of the European Union average. As one of the most stable and prosperous of the post-Communist states, the Czech Republic saw growth of over 6% annually in the three years before the outbreak of the recent global economic crisis. Growth has been caused by exports to the European Union, especially Germany, and foreign investment, while domestic demand is reviving. Most of the economy has been privatized, including the banks and telecommunications. A 2009 survey in cooperation with the Czech Economic Association found that the majority of Czech economists favor continued liberalization in most sectors of the economy.[②]

Taiwan has 23 million people with a combined area of approximately 36,000 square km, making it slightly smaller than the Netherlands. It comprises the main island of Taiwan, the archipelagoes of Penghu, Kinmen and Matsu, and a number of other islands. Taiwan has become one of Asia's big traders. It is considered to have achieved an economic miracle, becoming one of the world's top producers of computer technology. Also Taiwan's historical and cultural connection to Mainland adds interest because of the very different directions that accounting has taken in these two economies.

As regard to Mexico, we want to include a Latin American country. We choose Mexico because the 1994 North American Free Trade Agreement created many challenge and opportunities in Mexican accounting. Mexico is a federal republic in North America. It is bordered on the north by the United States, on the south and west by the Pacific Ocean, on the southeast by Guatemala, Belize, and the Caribbean Sea, and on the east by the Gulf of Mexico. Covering almost two million square kilometres, Mexico is the fifth largest country in the Americas by total area and the 13th largest independent nation in the world. With a population of over 113 million, it is the eleventh most populous and the most populous Spanish-speaking country in the world and the second most populous country in Latin America. Mexico is a federation comprising thirty-one states and a Federal District, its capital and largest city[③].

If you compare with these four countries or area, some observations will be felt. In China, import and export is low compared with its population, with significantly

---

① Data comes from the website: http://en.wikipedia.org/wiki/China
② Data comes from the following website, http://en.wikipedia.org/wiki/Czech_Republic
③ Data comes from the following website,, http://en.wikipedia.org/wiki/Mexico

poorer than the other three. Chinese national economy is much more agricultural to some extent. In recent decade, more and more listed companies raise capital in foreign capital market. Czech Republic has relatively low standard of living. Most of its trading has been done with neighboring countries. For Taiwan area, Per capita GDP is the highest of the three. China and the U.S.A represents Taiwan's largest trading partner. However, more companies are listed their shares in London Stock Exchange. As regard to Mexico, much influence comes from the U.S.A. Among the four countries or areas, service is the most important part of the economy of the Czech Republic, Taiwan area, and Mexico.

In Chapter 2, eight factors affecting national accounting development are discussed. The eight factors still explain accounting in developing countries or emerging market countries or areas. The relative importance of certain factors may be quite different in developing countries as in developed ones. The influence may appear in different ways. It is worth to mention that the effect of the type of legal system is less important in these four countries or area. Mexico has a civil law legal system, yet accounting is oriented toward fairness. Political and economic ties are arguably more important for the four countries or areas.

4.2 Czech Republic

4.2.1 Introduction

Czech Republic (CR) is a landlocked country, located in Central Europe with Germany to the west and northwest, Austria to the South, the Slovak Republic to the east, and Poland to the north.

It is a pluralist multi-party parliamentary representative democracy, a member of the European Union, North Atlantic Treaty Organization (NATO), the Organization for Economic Co-operation and Development (OECD), the Organization for Security and Co-operation in Europe (OSCE), the Council of Europe and the Visegrád Group.

The Czech state, formerly known as Bohemia, was formed in the late 9th century as a small duchy around Prague. It was under dominance of the powerful Great Moravian Empire (Which reached its greatest territorial extent during the reign of Svatopluk I from the House of Mojmír) at that time. After the fall of the Empire in 907, the centre of power was transferred from Moravia to Bohemia, under the Přemyslids. During the rule and governance of Přemyslid dukes/kings and their successors, the Luxembourgs, the country reached its greatest territorial extent (at about 13th–14th century). Life in the country was significantly influenced by the Hussite wars, during which it faced economic embargo and crusades from all over Europe. Following the

Battle of Mohács in 1526, the Crown of Bohemia was gradually integrated into the Habsburg monarchy as one of its three principal parts alongside the Archduchy of Austria and the Kingdom of Hungary. The Bohemian Revolt (1618—1620) led to the further centralization of the monarchy including forced recatholization and Germanization. During radical reforms in the 18th century the Bohemian Crown was even de facto abolished (1749). In the 19th century the Czech lands became the industrial powerhouse of the monarchy and the center of the Republic of Czechoslovakia. It is known that the Republic of Czechoslovakiawhich was formed in 1918, following the collapse or breakdown of the Austro-Hungarian empire after World War I.

After the Munich Agreement, which was a settlement permitting Nazi Germany's annexation of portions of Czechoslovakia along the country's borders mainly inhabited by German speakers, Czechoslovakia experienced Polish annexation of Zaolzie and German occupation and the consequent disillusion with the Western response. Czechoslovakia had gratitude for the liberation of the major portion in the country by the Red Army. In the 1946 elections, the Communist Party of Czechoslovakia won the majority. In the 1948, Czechoslovakia became a communist-ruled state. In 1968, the increasing dissatisfaction culminated in attempts to reform the communist regime. The events, known as the Prague Spring of 1968, ended with an invasion by the armies of the Warsaw Pact countries (with the exception of Romania). The troops remained in the country until the 1989 Velvet Revolution, when the communist regime collapsed. On 1 January 1993, Czechoslovakia split into two nations peacefully, the Czech Republic and the Slovak Republic.

The Czech Republic is the first former member of the Comecon to achieve the status of a developed country according to the World Bank (Velinge,2007). In addition, the country has the highest human development in Central and Eastern Europe, ranking as a "Very High Human Development" nation. It is also ranked as the third most peaceful country in Europe and most democratic and healthy (by infant mortality) country in the region[1].

Accounting has changed direction several times in the twentieth century, reflecting its political history. Accounting practice and principles reflected those of the German-speaking countries of Europe until the end of World War Two. Then accounting practice was based on the Soviet Union. After 1989 Czechoslovakia moved quickly toward a market-oriented economy.

In 1993, the Prague Stock Exchange began regular operation. Czech had a fully privatizations process. In 1995, the Czech Republic became the first post Communist member of the OECD, joined NATO in 1999, Achieving full membership in EU in May, 2004.

---

[1] Data from Wikipedia, the free encyclopedia, http://en.wikipedia.org/wiki/Czech_Republic - cite_note-hdi09-8

After the "velvet divorce" from Slovakia on 1 January 1993, the Czech Republic

became one of the most stable and prosperous countries of Central and Eastern Europe. Building upon a rich industrial heritage, the primary industrial commodities exported and imported by the Czech Republic are still machinery and transport equipment and other manufactured goods. However, while the major trading partners of the former Czechoslovakia were the other East European countries and the Soviet Union, since 1989 there has been a shift towards the European Union (EU) and the United States. By 2000 Germany became the Czech Republic's most significant trading partner, followed by Austria, France, Italy, Poland, the United Kingdom, the United States and the Russian Federation (László Kónya, 2009).

4.2.2 Accounting regulation and enforcement

In 1952, the Czech accounting system had been influenced by the German accounting system, however it was not chosen as a basis for the recent accounting reform. Instead the French system was selected. As there was a relatively high proportion of the French economy had been nationalized, the plan comptable general had been introduced. The former Czechoslovak Federal Ministry of Finance was responsible for the preparation of the new accounting system. The Union of Accountants (Svazucetnich, a professional institution) and the Chamber of Auditors of the Czech Republic are proposing to create, together with the Ministry of Finance, a broader committee somewhat like the French Conseil National de la comptabilite.

Under the centrally planned economy, accounting in the Czech was required to fulfill the needs of the central institution of the planned economy, such as the State Planning Commission Central Statistical Office, Ministry of Finance. The financial statements were required to provide information for the use of the central authorities in the administration of the planned economy. Also the financial statements fulfilled d dual role but the roles were on the contradiction. On the one hand, the financial statements were used as an instrument of control over the fulfillment of the planned targets for the current period. On the other hand, financial statements provided information serving as a basis for fixing the planned targets for the next period. Furthermore, the accounting data was considered to be secret and the financial statements were not published.[1]

After the transitional period (1990—1992), a new accounting system was introduced on 1 January 1993. It has been conceived as a system suited to the market economy. A feature of the new system is that only when subject to transfer from the cost accounting records to the financial accounting records. Also Act on Auditor was passed in 1992.

---

① Data comes from website: http://www.doc88.com/p-146874051810.html.

The Czech Republic implemented the stock therapy model in an effort to convert to a market economy. Though highly successful for the first few years, the Czech Republic ran into problems with its currency in1996, which required it to make tight monetary policy decisions. However, many feel that the Czech Republic transition to a market economy is complete, signified by its entrance into the EU in 2004.

The new Commercial Code was enacted by Parliament in 1991 and became effective on Jan. 1, 1992. The Commercial Code influenced by the Austrian roots of the old commercial code and modeled on German commercial law, and introduced a large amount of legislations relating to business. Czech law is based on the civil code law system of Continental Europe.

The Accountancy Act was established in 1991, and became effective in Jan. 1 1993, which regulated the basic accounting principles. Under the Accountancy Act, provision of the "true and fair view" was declared. Three basic charts of accounts have been published that include entrepreneurs, non-profit seeking organizations, and other organizations. Also there is a special chart of accounts for banks and insurance companies. Moreover, the obligatory methodology for recording current transactions in the financial accounting records is regulated. Current accounting refers to the compilation of the accounting record from the prime entry through to the entries in the ledger accounts. Sometimes alternative accounting treatments could be permitted. Besides, the system of financial statements was determined. A new regulation on the contents of the cash flow statement and the appendix to the financial statements has been issued recently. The cash flow statement is based on the standard proposed by the International Accounting Standards Board (IASB).

The Czech Republic introduced a new tax and accounting system in 1993. And this marked a shift away from a heavy tax orientation. Standards are still created by the Ministry of Finance, but they now focus more on standards for a market driven economy. The Czech Republic is currently working toward eliminating differences between Czech Republic accounting rules and IFRS. The revised Accounting Act of 2002 allows Czech Republic companies to opt for using IFRS over Czech rules.

Czech Republic's admission to the EU marks a huge step for the country. This indicates the country's success in becoming a market economy, even though economic struggles may still exist. Furthermore, the Czech Republic adopted IFRS in 2005. The Czech Republic's challenge now is to continue with its rapid pace of change without senior management disregarding the change as a nuisance (Radebaugh, Gray and Black, 2007).

In its general conception the Czech accounting system is based on French experience. Later, the Czech accounting incorporated the Fourth and Seventh Directive in it. Also The accounting in the Czech Republic is influenced by the Commercial Code, Accountancy Act, and the Ministry of Finance.

4.2.3 Financial reporting

Financial statements must be comparative, consisting of balance sheet, profit and loss accounts and notes. The Notes must also include a cash flow statement besides accounting policies, and other relevant information for assessing the financial statements.

Consolidated financial statements are required for groups with equity in excess of CZK300 million or revenues in excess of CZK600 million, adapting EU Seventh Directive in the Czech Republic. Small and other companies not subject to audit have abbreviated disclosure requirements. Financial statements are approved at the annual meeting of shareholders. Listed companies are also required to present quarterly financial statements and audited annual financial statements according to IASs or IFRSs (Choi, Frost and Meek, 2002).

4.2.4 Accounting measurement

In the Czech Republic, the purchase method is used to account for business combination. Goodwill is written off in the first year of consolidation or capitalized and amortized over 5 years. The equity method is used for associated companies and for joint ventures. The closing exchange rate or current exchange rate is used to translate both the income statement and the balance sheet of foreign subsidiaries. However, there is no guideline for reporting translation adjustments.

Historical cost is used to value tangible and intangible assets. Assets are written off over their expected economic lives, with a 5 year maximum for intangibles. FIFO, and weighted average are allowable for inventory measurement, while LIFO is not allowable. Research and development cost may be capitalized if they relate to projects completed successfully and capable of generating future income. Leased assets are not capitalized. Deferred income taxes are only recognized for the difference between accounting and tax depreciation. Contingent losses are recorded when they are probable and can be reliably measured. Besides, legal reserves are also required (Choi, Frost and Meek, 2002).

4.3 Taiwan Area

4.3.1 Introduction

Taiwan is an area in East Asia. Taiwan (formerly known as Formosa) makes up over 99% of its current area, as well as Penghu, Kinmen, Matsu, and other minor islands. Neighbors include the mainland to the west, Japan to the east and northeast, and the Philippines to the south.

The earliest evidence of Taiwan being inhabited is from the late Paleolithic era. The island of Taiwan was mainly inhabited by Taiwanese aborigines before being colonized in the 17th century by the Dutch as Dutch Formosa in 1624 and the Spanish as Spanish Formosa in 1626. The Spanish were expelled from the island in 1644 by the Dutch. The first Han Chinese polity on Taiwan began when Koxinga's troops defeated Dutch forces and established the Kingdom of Tungning. The island was subsequently ruled by the Qing Dynasty after the kingdom's defeat in the Battle of Penghu in 1683, a period that lasted for over 200 years. Following Japan's victory over the Qing Dynasty in the first Sino-Japanese war, Taiwan was ceded to Japan under the Treaty of Shimonoseki in 1895.

In the 1980s and early 1990s, Taiwan evolved into a multi-party democracy with universal suffrage. Building on the infrastructure and education improvements that was initiated during the Japanese era, Taiwan has experienced rapid economic growth and industrialization during the latter half of the 20th century. And Taiwan now is an advanced industrial economy. It is one of the Four Asian Tigers. As one of the 19th-largest economy in the world, its advanced technology industry plays a key role in the global economy[1].

Over four decades, Taiwan transformed itself from an underdeveloped, agricultural island to an economic power, being a leading producer of high-technology goods. There are three phases for Taiwan's development. During the 1950s, agricultural and import substituting industries dominated economic growth. The second phase began in the 1960s and focused on export expansion, propelled by the assembly of imported component parts for consumer goods and low technology, light industry. The most recent phase involves high technology and capital intensive industries.

In Taiwan, early growth was fueled by substantial economic aid from the U.S.A. Also Taiwan is an aid donor and major investor, especially in Asia, with dynamic capitalist economy. Small, family owned businesses are the basis of the economy. In 2000, the U.S is Taiwan's largest trading partner, taking 25% of its export and supplying 17% of its imports, but in 2003, China supplanted the United States as Taiwan's largest trade partner.(U.S. Department of State, "Background Notes: Taiwan", October 2000, p.12).

Taiwan Stock Exchange (hereinafter referred to as TWSE) was established in 1961, and began operating as a stock exchange on 9 February 1962. Taiwan Stock Exchange is a privately held corporation with 15 directors and 3 supervisors. At least five of the directors and one supervisor are appointed by the government. TWSE's primary business activities are listing, trading, clearing, and market surveillance. Specifically, these activities include helping businesses navigate the listing application

---

① Data comes from Wikipedia, the free encyclopedia.

process, continually enhancing trading mechanisms, and maintaining an orderly market[①]. It is regulated by the Financial Supervisory Commission. As of 31 December 2013, the Taiwan Stock Exchange had 809 listed companies with a combined market capitalization of NT$ 24,519,622 million.

4.3.2 Accounting regulation and enforcement

The Commercial Accounting Law, amended in 1987, regulates accounting records and financial statement in Taiwan. Accounting standards are set by the Financial Accounting Standards Committee (FASC) of the Accounting Research and Development Foundation (ARDF). The ARDF was established in 1984, modeled on the FAF in the U.S, supervised by the Ministry of Finance. The FASC was established in 1984, followed a due process like FASB.

Another committee of the ARDF, the Auditing Standard Committee (ASC), issues auditing standards. The National Federation of CPA Association (NFCPAA) represents the accounting profession. Coordinating with government regulatory authorities, the NFCPAA issue statements on professional ethics, and provide continuing professional education.

Before the establishment of ARDF, the NFCPAA issued accounting and auditing standards. The examination and licensing of CPAs is a government responsibility in Taiwan. Both the examination and CPA certificate are administrated and issued by the Ministry of Finance.

4.3.3 Financial reporting

Under the Law of Stock Exchange in Taiwan, publicly traded company should prepare annual, semi-annual, and quarterly financial report. Moreover, the Company Act regulates that Board of Directors in a company must provide list of statements, and other specific information.

The commercial accounting law requires the following financial statements, including balance sheet, income statement, statement of changes in owner's equity, statement of cash flow and notes.

Financial statements must be comparative and the fiscal period must be the calendar year. Financial statements by publicly traded companies, and nonpublic companies with capital in excess of NT$30 million or outstanding bank loans of more than NT$30 million are required to audit. Banks, insurance companies, and securities firms must have their financial statements audited by CPAs. State-run government enterprises are audited by government auditors. Listed companies need to provide audited semiannual financial statements, while their quarterly financial statements need

---

① Data comes from the website: http://wwwc.twse.com.tw/en/about/company/download/annual/2013/P2.pdf

to be reviewed by a CPA. A monthly sales report is also needed to provide.

For example, for a public company in Taiwan, a concise financial statement includes consolidated concise balance sheet, consolidated concise statement of comprehensive income, parent company concise balance sheet, parent company concise statement of comprehensive income, besides providing information about corporate social responsibility, future perspective.

4.3.4 Accounting measurement

The purchase method is used for business combination, while pooling of interest method is not used. Goodwill is normally capitalized and amortized over 20 years or less. The equity method is used when there is 20 percent or more ownership in another company. Foreign currency translation is consistent with the International Standards 21 and the U.S SFAS No.52.

Fixed assets, including land and natural resources, and intangible assets may be revalued. The government announces values for land each year. When prices rise by more than 25 percent since purchase or previous revaluation other assets may be revalued. Capital reserves are credited when assets are revalued. Intangible assets are amortized over a maximum period of 20 years. Depreciation and amortization of revalued assets are based on their carrying values after revaluation.

Inventory is stated at the lower of cost or market. FIFO, LIFO, and average are acceptable. Research and development are charged to expense when incurred. Lease, contingencies, and deferred taxes accounting are consistent with international and U.S approaches. Companies in Taiwan must also set up legal reserve in shareholders' equity. 10 percent of net income is appropriated each year until the reserve equals the total authorized capital stock of the company (Choi, Frost and Meek, 2002).

4.4 Mexico

4.4.1 Introduction

Mexico, officially the United Mexican States, is a federal constitutional republic in North America. It border shows on the north by the United States of America, on the south and west by the Pacific Ocean, on the southeast by Guatemala, Belize, and the Caribbean Sea, and on the east by the Gulf of Mexico. Covering almost two million square kilometers (over 760,000 square miles), Mexico is the fifth largest country in the Americas by total area and the thirteenth largest independent nation in the world. With an estimated population of over 113 million, it is the eleventh most populous country and the most populous Spanish-speaking country. Furthermore, Mexico is a federation with thirty-one states and a Federal District, the capital city.

In the Pre-Columbian Mexico, many cultures matured into advanced civilizations such as the Olmec, the Toltec, the Teotihuacan, the Zapotec, the Maya and the Aztec before the first contact with Europeans. In 1521, Spain conquered and colonized the territory from its base in México-Tenochtitlan, which was administered as the Viceroyalty of New Spain. This territory would eventually become Mexico, while the colony's independence was recognized or admitted in 1821. The post-independence period was characterized by economic instability, meaning that Mexico experiencing the Mexican-American War and territorial cession to the United States, a civil war, two empires and a domestic dictatorship. The domestic dictatorship finally led to the Mexican Revolution in 1910, which culminated with the promulgation of the 1917 Constitution and the emergence of the country's current political system. Election was held in July 2000, marking the first time that an opposition party won the presidency from the Institutional Revolutionary Party.

About several decades ago, a substantial proportion of the Mexican business sector was government controlled, and a large number of business enterprises were government owned. From the mid-1970s to the late 1980s, Mexico faced persistent balance-of –payments problems resulting from the government's efforts to defend the overvalued peso while incurring massive external debt. These and other problems were attributed largely to government acquisition and control of private enterprises. In recent years, something has been done by the government to change the situation. As part of reform, there has been a major effort to privatize state-owned enterprises by the government. This new economic program was designed to accelerate long-term economic growth in Mexico.

Mexico has one of the world's largest economies, and is considered both a regional power and middle power. In addition, Mexico was considered the first Latin American member of the Organisation for Economic Co-operation and Development OECD since 1994, and taken an upper-middle income country by the World Bank. Mexico is considered a newly industrialized country and an emerging economy. It has the thirteenth largest nominal GDP and the eleventh largest by purchasing power parity. The Mexican economy is strongly linked to those of its North American Free Trade Agreement (NAFTA) partners, especially the United States. Mexico ranks sixth in the world and first in the Americas by number of UNESCO (United Nations Educational, Scientific and Cultural Organization) World Heritage Sites with 31, and in 2007 was the tenth most visited country in the world with about 21.4 million international arrivals or visitors per year[1].

Mexico has one stock exchange, the Bolsa Mexiacana de Valores (BMV), located

---

[1] Data comes from Wikipedia, the free encyclopedia.

in Mexico City. The Mexican Stock Exchange is the second largest stock exchange by market capitalization in Latin America. BMV originally started in 1886 as the Bolsa Mercantil de Mexico (Mexican Mercantile Exchange). It changed its name in 1975 to its current name, Bolsa Mexicana de Valores, and acquired smaller exchanges in Monterrey and Guadalajara. Historically, the Mexican business sector has been predominantly family-owned. The influx of foreign capital and the return of Mexican capital previously invested abroad in the late 1980s and early 1990s have stimulated the growth of the Mexican stock market. For its first 114 years of existence, the stock exchange was a private institution jointly owned by 32 brokerage houses, most recently by a group of Mexican banks and brokerages. BMV itself is now a public company which is listed on its own stock exchange following a 2008 IPO. Prior approval of the National Banking and Securities Commission (NBSC) is required for listing on the stock exchange. Besides, the National Banking and Securities Commission regulates the Mexican Stock Exchange.

The first professional organization of public accountants in Mexico, the Association de Contadores Publicos, was established in 1917. The organization was replaced by the Mexican Institute of Public Accountants (MIPA) in 1964. The MIPA was officially recognized in 1977 as a federation of state and local associations of registered public accountants in Mexico. As an independent, nongovernmental professional association, the MIPA is governed by three bodies, the General Conference of Members, the Government Group, and the National Executive Committee (NEC). The first two bodies perform sponsoring and oversight function, while the NEC oversees the day-to-day activities of MIPA. The MIPA is designed to establish and communicate the accounting principles to be followed in preparing financial information for external users and to promote principles' acceptance.

4.4.2 Accounting regulation and enforcement

The Mexican Commercial Code and income tax laws contain requirements for keeping certain summary accounting records and preparing financial statements, but their influence on financial reporting is generally minimal (Choi, and Meek, 2011). The Mexican Institute of Public Accountants issues accounting and auditing standards (also called IMCP, Institute Mexicano De Contadores Publicos, Mexican self-regulated institution overseeing the accounting profession). The MIPA is an independent non-government professional association, representing the overwhelming majority of public accountants. Accounting standards are developed by the Institute's Accounting Principles Commission, which is under the MIPA. Auditing standards are the responsibility of its Auditing Standards and Procedures Commission, which is also under the MIPA. Despite a legal system based on civil law, accounting standard setting takes a British-American, or Anglo-Saxon approach.

The MIPA issues four kinds of pronouncements, known as bulletins. Series A bulletins deal with the basic accounting principles that define the framework of accounting principles. Series B bulletins consider the accounting principles that are pervasive to all financial statements. Series C bulletins provide guidance with respect to specific balance sheet and income statement accounts. Series D bulletins show specific topics that are key to determining the net income of an enterprise.

More recently in 2001, the MIPA formed the Mexican Council for Research and Development of Financial Reporting Standards (CINIF). This institution is responsible for creating accounting standards in line with IFRS. Actual GAAP will remain effective until modified or replaced, but rights to analyze, evaluate, modify, and issue GAAP have been transferred to the CINIF. On May 1 2004, the standards issued by the IMCP were passed to CINIF, which currently is the new institution in charge of reviewing and issuing new Mexican GAAP. As of the beginning of 2005, Mexican GAAP was approximately 70 percent in line with international standards.

Mexican accounting principles do not distinguish between large and small companies, and are applicable to all business entities. Requirement for preparing financial statements and having them audited vary by type and size of company. All companies incorporated under Mexican law should provide at least one statutory auditor to sign on annual financial statements. Statutory auditors do not have to be public accountants, but when a firm uses independent auditors, a member of the auditing firm frequently acts as statutory auditor.

Since 2012, all companies listing their shares on the Mexican Stock Exchange should provide financial statements according to IFRSs. Surely, listed companies have rights to choose either IFRS or Mexican GAAP, while non-listing company could use Mexican GAAP, which is developed by CINIF.

4.4.3　Financial reporting

Under the requirement of Mexican tax agency under the Ministry of Finance, all public companies and other companies whose employees or asset is over 300 or US$5 million should provide audited financial reporting before 30 June in each year. Although both IFRS and Mexican GAAP could be selected freely, it is encouraged that IFRS is the best choice.

In Mexico, comparative consolidated financial statements should include the following items such as balance sheet, income statement, statement of change in stockholders' equity, statement of changes in financial position and notes. Notes are emphasized including accounting policy, material contingencies, commitments for substantial purchases of assets or under lease contracts, details of long term debt and foreign currency exposure, limitations on dividends, guarantees, employees' pension plans, transactions with related parties, and income taxes (Choi, and Meek, 2011).

Since 2008, financial statement in Mexico must be adjusted for inflation, and general price level accounting is applied accordingly. Under the general price level accounting, historical costs of nonmonetary assets, and components of stockholders' equity were restated into pesos of current purchasing power. The gain or loss from holding monetary assets and liabilities were included in current income statement, however the effects of other restatement could put into the stockholders' equity in the balance sheet. Furthermore, a statement of changes in financial position, and statement of cash flows, should be presented too. As regards when to use inflation accounting, Mexican Financial Reporting Standards B-10 shows that under the condition of 3-year cumulative inflation rate equaling or exceeding 26 percent, a company must provide general price level accounting.

4.4.4 Accounting measurement

When a parent controls another company, consolidated financial statements are required. Control normally happens when more than 50 percent of a company' common stock is owned. There are many ways for a parent to exercise control power. The equity method could be used when a company has a great influence but not control on another company. Normally, great influence means an ownership level exists between 10 and 50 percent. In Mexico, both the purchase and pooling of interests methods for business combination are used. Goodwill is amortized to income over the expected benefit period, which is limited to 20 years.

General price level accounting is used in Mexico. The historical costs of nonmonetary assets are restated in pesos of current purchasing power by applying factors derived from the National Consumer Price Index (NCPI). The components of stockholders' equity are also restated using the NCPI. The gain or loss forms holding monetary items are included in current period income, but the effects of other restatements are in stockholders' equity. Costs of sales and depreciation expense are expressed in constant pesos on the income statement.

Research and development cost is expensed when incurred. Finance lease are capitalized, while operating lease's rent is expensed. Contingent losses are accrued when they are possible and measureable. However, general contingency reserves are not acceptable in Mexico. The partial liability method is used for deferred taxes. The costs of employee pensions, seniority premium, and termination pay are accrued currently when they can be reasonably estimated. Statutory reserves are created by allocating 5 percent of income each year until the reserves equals 20 percent of the value of the outstanding capital stock.

4.5 China

4.5.1 Introduction

China, officially the People's Republic of China (PRC), is the world's most-populous country, with a population of over 1.3 billion. Covering approximately 9.6 million square kilometer, China is the world's second-largest country by land area, and the third- or fourth-largest in total area, depending on the definition of total area.

The People's Republic of China exercises jurisdiction over 22 provinces, five autonomous regions, four directly controlled municipalities (Beijing, Tianjin, Shanghai, and Chongqing), and two mostly self-governing special administrative regions (Hong Kong and Macau).

China has had numerous historical incarnations. The ancient Chinese civilization—one of the world's earliest—flourished in the fertile basin of the Yellow River in the North China Plain.

Since 1949, Communist Party has built up a new Chinese country by introducing economic model of former Soviet Union, which was called planned economy. Under the planned economic model, accounts were uniformity and financial statements were provided for tool of government controlling whole national economy. Public information disclosure was not necessary in that time. Under the planned economy model, China was relatively conservative. However situation or circumstance changes later. In 1971, the PRC gained admission to the United Nations and took the Chinese seat as a permanent member of the U.N. Security Council. China is also a member of numerous formal and informal multilateral organizations, including the WTO (World Trade Organization), APEC (Asia-Pacific Economic Cooperation), BRICS (Brazil、 Russia 、 India 、 China), the Shanghai Cooperation Organisation, the BCIM (Bangladesh-China-India-Myanmar Regional Economic Cooperation) and the G-20[1].

The market-based economic reform system was introduced in 1978. Since then, China has become the world's fastest-growing major economy. Many reform policies result in economic development quickly. As of 2012, China is the world's second-largest economy, after the United States, by both nominal GDP (Gross Domestic Product) and purchasing power parity (PPP). Furthermore, China is also the world's largest exporter and second-largest importer of goods. On a per capita income

---

[1] The Group of Twenty (also known as the G-20 or G20) is an international forum for the governments and central bank governors from 20 major economies. The members include 19 individual countries such as Argentina, Australia, Brazil, Canada, China, France, Germany, India, Indonesia, Italy, Japan, Mexico, Russia, Saudi Arabia, South Africa, South Korea, Turkey, the United Kingdom and the United States, and European Union. The G-20 was founded in 1999 with the aim of studying, reviewing, and promoting high-level discussion of policy issues pertaining to the promotion of international financial stability.

basis, China ranked 90th by nominal GDP and 91st by GDP (PPP) in 2011, according to the IMF (International Monetary Fund). Therefore, China has been characterized as a potential superpower by a number of academics, military analysts, and public policy and economics analysts[①].

4.5.2 Accounting regulation and enforcement

Accounting Regulation has changed along the progress of Chinese political and economic reform and development. Though accounting history in China could track back more than three thousand years, the country's public accounting profession is relatively young. By the end of the 19th century, China was experiencing a large influx of foreign investments and taking the first steps toward its new commodity-based economy. These changes brought about an increase in commerce and a growing need for accounting services. In 1918, China's public accounting profession was officially established. From that point, the profession grew steadily for thirty years.

Beginning in 1949, however, the outlook for public accounting in China became grimmer and more uncertain. The profession entered its Difficult Period, and within just a few years, all accounting firms throughout China were dissolved.

Over the next twenty-five years, the People's Republic of China experienced several different cultural and economic phases. The "Great Leap Forward" and the Cultural Revolution brought about major changes for the Chinese people and the country's accounting profession as well. Over the years, the Chinese government implemented various approaches to economic development. As policies changed, the Chinese government modified the accounting information it required. Some periods called for simplification, while others expanded the complexity and number of financial statements and accounts.

It was not until the end of the "Cultural Revolution" in 1976 that the Chinese public accounting profession was resurrected. Adoption of an open door policy in 1978 marked a significant change in the way China would interact with other nations. The government's 1979 policy of "economic liberalization and reformation" resulted in major changes throughout China. Private ownership of businesses was again allowed, and the number of enterprises financed by stock exploded. In addition, during this time, the Ministry of Finance issued several regulations providing a foundation for the development and growth of the accounting profession.

After thirty years of extinction, China's public accounting profession was reborn. In 1981, the first accounting firm was established, marking the new development phase for public accounting. The profession matured during the 1980s and 1990s, as both its place in the country's economy and its governing regulations were established.

---

① Data comes from Wikipedia, the free encyclopedia.

The year 1993 was a significant milestone in the maturation of Chinese public accounting. It marked the start of a new era in the reformation of the profession. On July 1 of that year, the Accounting Standards for Business Enterprise, Financial Standards for Business Enterprise, and 13 new industry-specific accounting regulations were enacted. Chinese accounting's entire process of recording, measuring, and reporting business activities has been changed. Once these standards were in place, the Chinese accounting system had completed its transformation. Instead of serving a centrally-planned economy, the new system would be serving China's new market-based economy.

In 1994, in order to protect CPAs' legal interest and further regulate the accounting profession, the Law of the People's Republic of China on Certified Public Accountants (CPAs' Law) was issued. The issuance of this set of guidelines was another milestone for the profession, because it gave Chinese CPAs a means of self-regulation and a legal basis for enforcing rules (Xu, Xie, & Hu, 1997). The CPAs' Law specifically permits and encourages the forming of private, independent accounting firms with partnerships and limited liability corporations being two types of approved organizational structures (Yang & Yang, 1997). The CPAs' Law also contains some additions and changes that affected the requirements for obtaining the CPA designation. The CPA examination had been administered and organized annually since 1991, and hundreds of thousands of candidates had taken it. Obtaining the CPA license required both a passing grade on the CPA examination and two years of auditing experience (Tang, 2000). The CICPA was given responsibility for checking applications and issuing CPA certificates to those candidates meeting all requirements. As outlined in the CPAs' Law, the Ministry of Finance retained the right to direct the CICPA to withdraw the certification of anyone it did not consider suitable. The Ministry of Finance supervises whole public accounting profession.

During 1995, the public accounting profession in China underwent two major changes. Although government officials hadn't been allowed to be CPAs since 1986, they were still allowed to establish and operate accounting firms. These officials were called affiliated firms. These affiliated firms were plagued with the appearance of conflicts of interest, and their independence was often in question. In order to eliminate problems caused by affiliated firms, the Ministry of Finance issued Certified Public Accountant Practice Rules. Rule 25 of the regulations clearly states that effective from the issuance date, no affiliated accounting firm may be established. Affiliated accounting firms established prior to issuance of the Rules were required to be "de-affiliated" within the next three years. We can see that the process was slow and difficult, but by the end of 1999, the elimination of affiliated firms throughout China was complete finally.

The second major change occurred in 1995, requiring the collaboration of the National Audit Office and the Ministry of Finance. The two organizations worked together to forge an agreement between the Chinese Institute of Certified Public Accountants (CICPA) and the China Association of Certified Public Auditors (CACPA). In June 1995, the new organization, called simply the CICPA, became the single governing body over both major sectors of the Chinese accounting profession. After three years of overlapping operations, this change was a major improvement for the profession (Lu and Gary, 2006).

During the late 1990s, the accounting profession in China experienced another significant growth. Other two related fields appeared accordingly. The assets evaluation profession expanded significantly during the 1990s, and it became another group regulated by the CICPA in 2000. In 2002, the China Institute of Certified Public Tax Agents also joined the CICPA. With a larger portion of business professionals as members, the CICPA was in a better position to formulate and enforce the quality standards and professional ethics for all public accounting and tax practitioners across the country.

At the same time, the CICPA sought to communicate with international accounting organization. At the May 8, 1997 Council Meeting of the International Federation of Accountants (IFAC), the CICPA became a formal member of the Federation, and on December 11 2001, China became the 143rd member of the World Trade Organization (WTO). As China continues to hold its doors open to outside investors and international commerce, its public accounting profession continues to grow by leaps and bounds. As domestic CPA firms continue to increase in number, a recent surge of foreign CPAs in China was also evident. By May 2003, eleven foreign accounting firms had established seventeen offices throughout China (Feng, 2003). It is obvious that joining in by foreign accounting firm will push Chinese accounting profession to increase service quality and conduct qualified ethical behavior.

Over the years, the CICPA has had to change its role in order to adapt to the changing environment. In early 2003, the CICPA made a major change by returning some of its functions to the Ministry of Finance. The CICPA would no longer approve CPA firms for practice, punish CPAs and accounting firms for violations, or approve foreigners to open offices or branches in China. The Ministry of Finance also assumed responsibility for developing professional standards, and for developing content and rules for the CPA examination. In fact, the actual certification process to become a CPA requires final approval from the Ministry of Finance. These changes allowed the CICPA to concentrate on its service function. Primarily, the CICPA is responsible for submitting proposals for rules and regulations affecting the professions of its members. The organization also conducts the actual CPA examinations and maintains records of applicants and their payments (Lu, and Jean, 2005).

With the economic reform and development, Chinese accounting enter a new phase. More and more Chinese company raised capital in international capital market. Globalization of economy requires accounting to provide better service. As a international business language, accounting also change its rule or standards for harmonization or convergence. Then In the 2006, a set of new accounting standards were issued, including 1 revised basic standards, 38 specific standards in China. Since then, Chinese accounting came into a period of converging with IFRSs (International Financial Reporting Standard). At the beginning of 2014, the Ministry of Finance issued revised 6 standards, and 2 new standards, covering employee compensation, presentation of financial statement, consolidated financial statements, long-term equity investment, equity disclosure in other business entities, presentation of financial tools, and partnership arrangement, fair value measurement. These amended or new standards show that Chinese accounting is still at a process of converging with IFRS or IAS (International Accounting Standard).

4.5.3 Financial reporting

Basically, financial statements in China are as follows. Balance sheet, Income statement, Cash flow statement, Statement of owner's equity change and Notes are all parts of financial reporting. For publicly traded companies in Chinese capital markets, China Securities Regulatory Commission (CSRC) supervises their presentation and disclosure behavior. Although disclosure standard changed several times, a recently issued one appeared in September 2012, and effective in January 1, 2013, which was named No.2 Standard of Information Disclosure Contend and Format for Publicly Traded Company---Annual Report. The 2012 annual report required listed company to provide a complete set of financial reporting, with including 11 chapters as follows.

Exhibit 3.1   Annual report content for public company in China

Order Number	Chapter
1	Important announcement and content list
2	Brief introduction of the company
3	Major accounting and performance data
4	Directors' Board report
5	Material events
6	Capital change and stockholder's situation
7	Information about directors, supervisor, top managers and employees
8	Corporation governance
9	Internal control
10	Financial accounting reporting
11	Other issues

Note: Author translated according to regulation named No.2 Standard of Information Disclosure Contend and Format for Publicly Traded Company-Annual Report, which was issued by the CSRC.

4.5.4 Accounting measurement

The purchase method must be used to account for business combination in China. Goodwill is written off over the period benefited. The equity method is used by the acquirer when the ownership of acquiring another company exceeds 20 percent. Once the ownership exceeds 50 percent, the accounts of subsidiaries should be consolidated. For foreign currency translation, the current rate method is recommended. In other words, the year-end exchange rate is used for balance sheet, the average exchange rate is used for income statements, while translation adjustment is show as part of equity.

Historical cost is the basis for valuing tangible assets. FIFO, the average method and specific identification could be used for inventory valuation, while LIFO has not been used since 2006. Research and development could be classified into two stages including research and development phases. While research expenditure is expensed when incurred, development expenditure is capitalized when happened. Finance leases are capitalized and deferred taxes are explained by liability method. Contingent obligations could be recognized when they are both probable and reliable, or estimation can be made of their amount.

Terms of the Chapter

accounting policy 会计政策
accounting record 会计记录
appraisal 评估
asset impairment 资产贬值
auction 拍卖
audit practice 审计实务
audited annual financial statement 经过审计的年度财务报表
business entity 会计主体
balance sheet 资产负债表
centrally planned economy 集中计划经济
capital lease 资本性租赁
capital market 资本市场
Chinese Institute of Certified Public Accountant (CICPA) 中国注册会计师
code of professional ethics 职业道德标准(规范)
Commercial Code 商法
contingency 或有事项
conceptual framework 概念构架
conflict of interest 利益冲突

confucius 孔子

cost flow assumption 成本流转假设

Continental European Countries 欧洲大陆国家

coupon voucher system 订购凭单制度

credit based financial system 以信用为基础的财务制度

debt restructuring 债务重组

deferred income tax 递延所得税

depreciation 折旧

distribution of profit 利润分配

directives 指令(欧盟)

direct foreign investment 直接外国投资

due process procedure 适当程序

emerging market country 新兴市场国家

economic life 经济使用年限(寿命)

economic substance 经济实质

exposure draft 披露草案

fair trading 公允交易

family owned business 家族企业

financial accounting system 财务会计系统或制度

financial position and result 财务状况与结果

fiscal report 年度报告

foundation 基金会或联合会

general price level accounting 一般价格水平会计

global economy 全球经济

going concern 持续经营

harmonization 协调

hybrid economy 混合经济

historical cost accounting 历史成本会计

import substituting 进口替代

income statement 利润表

inflation 通货膨胀

initial public offers (初始)公开发行股票

institutional factor 制度因素

intangible asset 无形资产

International Federation of Accountant (IFAC) 国际会计师联合会

investment fund 投资基金

legal reserves 法定准备金

limited liability company 有限公司

listed company 上市公司

liquidity　流动性

light manufacturing　轻工业

lower of cost or market value　成本与市价孰低法

market orientation　市场导向

material events　重要事项

Ministry of Finance　财政部

monetary assets and liability　货币性资产和负债

North American Free Trade Agreement (NAFTA)　北美自由贸易协定

nominal price　名义价格

non-monetary transaction　非货币性交易

operating lease　经营性租赁

parent company　母公司

privatization　私有化

private-sector enterprise　私营企业

profitability　盈利能力

professional accounting body　职业会计团体

post-communist member　后共产主义成员(泛指部分欧洲及亚洲的前共产国家，在经济及政治上的一段过渡时期)

post-balance sheet events　资产负债表日后事项

purchase and pooling method　购买法和权益集合法

real estate　不动产

receipt and disbursement　收入和支付

related party transaction　关联交易

registration　注册

Securities Act　证券法

segment information　分部信息

self-regulated professional body　自律职业团体

small scale enterprise　小规模企业

State Council　国务院

statutory auditor　法定审计师

stewardship　委托关系

state owned company　国有公司

statement of cash flow　现金流量表

stockholder's equity　股东权益

soviet style central planning　苏联模式的计划经济

soviet bloc countries　(前)苏联集团国家

socialist market economy　社会主义市场经济

solvency　偿债能力

subsidiary　子公司

supremacy 霸权地位

tangible asset 有形资产

The Accounting Act 会计法

translation adjustment 折算调整

trading partners 贸易伙伴

to write off 注销

outstanding capital stock 已公开发行的股票

uniform chart of accounts 统一账户表

weighted average method 加权平均

Discussion Questions

1. Compare the different effect of eight factors, mentioned in Chapter 2, between developed and developing countries or areas.

2. Chapter 2 discussed 7 socioeconomic and institutional factors that affect accounting development. Please answer the following two questions.

(1) Identify the factor that you think is the most important influence on accounting in these four countries or area. Explain the significance of the factor and why you think it is the most important.

(2) Identify the factor that you think is the least influence on accounting in these four countries or area. Explain why you think it is the least important.

3. The Czech Republic is developing a body of accounting requirement consistent with EU Directives. What evidence does demonstrate that Czech accounting requirements comply with these Directives?

4. How might the liberalization of accounting and auditing services in China result in an improved level of investor protection? Give some examples.

5. How have economic reforms affected the demand for accounting services in China? Is it really necessary to enhance accounting service quality in Chinese capital market?

6. Do you think in what way are the development of accounting and auditing in China different from other countries?

7. Both China and the Czech Republic are restructuring their economies from central planning to more of a market orientation. Do you think what are the similarities and differences in the approaches each country is taking in embracing market reforms?

8. Take some examples to explain the major pressure for accounting regulation in China in recent year.

9. Explain the main external factors that have influenced financial reporting in Mexico in recent years.

10. Do you think what is an important contribution that Mexican accounting has

made to international accounting?

11. The chapter states that accounting and auditing standard setting in Taiwan is patterned after that in the U.S.A. What are the similarities and differences in standard setting in the two?

12. Show some evidence of similar accounting practices between Taiwan area and the U.S.A.

13. Government plays a role in developing accounting and auditing standards in all four countries or area. Please explain them carefully.

14. Does the development of accounting lead or lag behind the development of a nation's economy? Cite evidence from this chapter to support your idea.

True or False

1. The German origin of Mexico's legal system is a factor in its current accounting system values.

2. The cures for the "Asian flu" problem were to decrease conservatism and individualism.

3. Chinese government controls the accounting and auditing standards setting.

4. Czech Republic's admission to the EU indicates the country's success in becoming a market economy, even though some economic struggles may still exist.

5. Financial reports are approved at the annual meeting of shareholders in Czech Republic.

6. In China, Ministry of Finance is responsible for accounting and auditing standards setting.

7. Mexico is a code law country, so the accounting is a legal compliance orientation.

8. Mexican accounting principles do not distinguish between large and small companies, and are applicable to all business entities.

9. In Taiwan, both the examination and CPA certificate are administrated and issued by the Ministry of Finance.

10. Process of accounting standards setting in Taiwan is similar with that in the United States.

11. Historical cost is used to value tangible and intangible assets in Czech Republic.

12. The Czech Repulic implemented the stock therapy model in an effort to convert to a market economy.

13. Both the purchase and pooling of interests methods for business combination could be used in China.

14. In Taiwan area, accounting principles are applicable to all business entities no

matter how big a company size is.

15. Fixed assets, including land and natural resources, and intangible assets may not be revalued in Taiwan.

Multiple Choice

1. Which of the following accurately reflects Taiwan's accounting?
   a. British accounting convey a great influence on Taiwan's accounting.
   b. Setting of accounting standards models the American accounting.
   c. Government controls the setting of accounting and auditing standards.
   d. There is a powerful accounting profession, and accounting standards is set by private sector.
2. Which of the following accurately reflects Chinese accounting?
   a. Soviet-style exercised a strong influence on accounting.
   b. The accounting system has been changed to conform with U.S. principles since reform began.
   c. A more micro-oriented decision-making approach is being encouraged.
   d. The French system of accounting has been adopted.
3. Which of the following accurately reflects Chinese accounting?
   a. The accounting equation has replaced the communist fund accounting approach in the standard setting process.
   b. Accounting is fair presentation orientation.
   c. The only purpose of accounting is for national macroeconomic control.
   d. Due to previous state control, there is an abundance of accountants and auditors.
4. Which of the following has a significant impact on Czech Republic accounting?
   a. The accession to the EU.
   b. A micro-economics approach to accounting in the Czech Republic has resulted in widespread use of inflation-adjusted accounting.
   c. The effect of tax law is minimal, because tax and book accounting are not allowed to be the same.
   d. The Nordic legal tradition has had a strong impact on accounting standards and practices.
5. Information disclosure is constrained in developing countries where:
   a. shareholders are the most important user group.
   b. taxation rules influence accounting substantially.
   c. companies are financed mainly by banks, family members and government agencies.
   d. the accounting profession is not well developed with limited influence.

6. In China, CICPA mission are:

    a. to issue accounting standards.

    b. to issue auditing standards.

    c. to organize CPA exam and supervise CPA profession.

    d. to organize continuous education.

7. In Taiwan, accounting standards is issued by:

    a. The Ministry of Finance.

    b. the Accounting Research and Development Foundation (ARDF).

    c. the Financial Accounting Standards Committee (FASC).

    d. the Auditing Standards Committee (ASC).

8. Mexican business is dominated by:

    a. state-owned enterprise.

    b. private-owned enterprise.

    c. both state-owned and private-owned enterprise.

    d. family-owned enterprise.

9. In Mexico, converging with international accounting happen in recent years. The ways to convergence with international accounting are:

    a. Mexico takes IAS or IFRS completely without any change.

    b. Mexico takes IAS or IFRS as the basis for national accounting standards.

    c. CINIF issued Mexican GAAP in line with international accounting standards.

    d. After Mexico CINIF revised the international accounting, the international accounting became the Mexican accounting standards.

10. The evidences that indicate Chinese accounting is in line with the international accounting are:

    a. LIFO.

    b. Pooling of interest.

    c. finances lease is expensed.

    d. substance over form.

11. Which of the following explanation is right?

    a. China is a code law country and accounting is legal compliance orientation.

    b. Taiwan area is code law but accounting is orientated toward fair presentation.

    c. Mexico is common law, and accounting is orientated toward fair presentation.

    d. Czech Republic is common law and accounting is orientated toward fair presentation.

12. In Taiwan, accounting standard is set up by

    a. FASC.

b. ARDF.

c. NFCPAA.

d. NAFTA.

Case Analysis

Case 4   Raising Capital in International Market: an example for Sinopec

China Petroleum and Chemical Corporation (Sinopec Corp.) is one of growing Chinese companies that has crossly listed stock on foreign stock exchanges. You could go back to Chapter 1 and see case 1.1 for detail information. In October 2000, China petrochemical industry Corporation succeeded in being listed in Hong Kong, London, and New York stock exchange market at the same time after two years of reshuffle and preparation. In August 2001, Sinopec Corp. was successfully listed on the Shanghai Stock Exchange. China Petrochemical Industry was on the way to international capital market from then on.

To provide information that might be useful for a wide audience of readers outside China, Sinopec provides a reconciliation of income and stockholders' equity from Chinese GAAP to IFRSs. Furthermore, in order to provide information specifically for its North American shareholders, the company also provides a reconciliation of net income and stockholders' equity from IFRSs to U.S. GAAP. Please go to the Shanghai Stock Exchange (Stock code: 600028) or other website (www.cninfo.com.cn) to find Sinopec 2014 annual reporting, and answer the following questions.

1. Critically comment on the results reported by Sinopec under PRC GAAP, IFRSs, and U.S GAAP.

2. Compare and contrast the cost and benefit for Sinopec reconciliation.

3. Is Sinopec's reconciliation enough for foreign investors?

4. Identify the main areas of difference for Sinopec between:

a. PRC GAAP and IFRSs.

b. IFRSs and U.S GAAP.

5. Among the PRC GAAP, IFRSs, and U.S GAAP, which one seems to have conservative net income? Why?

Chapter 5   Reporting and Disclosure

Learning objective

After careful study of this chapter, students will be able to:

1. Describe the distinction between measurement and disclosure.

2. Explain the relationship between voluntary and regulatory disclosure.

3. Understand the ways how to avoid managers' negative effect if managers have incentives to disclose information voluntarily.

4. Know some debate on U.S. SEC financial reporting's requirement for non-domestic corporations.

5. Depict the content and current situation of forward looking information.

6. Explain segment disclosures' content and its role.

7. Explain the current situation and future improvement of Cash Flow and Funds Flow Statement around the world.

8. Describe the necessity of social responsibility disclosures in China.

9. Understand principles of corporate governance issued by OECD.

10. Explain the future development of internet business reporting and disclosure practice around the world.

5.1 Accounting Measurement and Disclosure

In chapter 3 and 4, we talk about national accounting from a measurement point of view. Now we turn to the disclosure in this chapter. Let us think about the following two questions: What is the distinction between accounting measurement and accounting disclosure? Which of the two reporting processes do you think promises substantial innovative advances during the next 10 years? Why?

The International Accounting Standards Board (IASB) and the U.S. Financial Accounting Standards Board (FASB) strive to base their financial accounting standards decisions on the concepts underlying financial reporting as specified in their Conceptual Frameworks. However, the framework does not include concepts relating to accounting measurement. This lack of concepts relating to measurement is a glaring hole in the framework that impedes progress on financial reporting standards involving measurement, which comprise much of the boards' work (Mary,2014). Regarding the definition of accounting measurement, the IASB's framework (IASB 2010a,4.54) defines measurement as the process of determining the monetary amounts that are any number can be an accounting measurement, regardless of whether it reflects an economic construct, such as a price, or simply results from a prescribed calculation with no specified objective of measurement (Baker 2013). This definition is not based on any measurement concepts or theory. A number of different measurement bases are employed to different degrees and in varying combinations in financial statements. They include Historical cost, Current cost, Realizable (settlement) value, and Present value. The measurement basis most commonly adopted by business entities in preparing their financial statements is historical cost. This is usually combined with other measurement bases.

Most accounting measurements are imprecise and provide, at best, a noisy representation of a firm's operations and underlying events. Intuitively, it may seem that such imprecision is always undesirable and should be eliminated to the extent possible. Accounting measurements of investment depend on many subjective judgments, estimates, and simplistic conventions that are necessitated by the inherent difficulty of separating investments (tangible and intangible) from operating cash flows. These judgments and conventions introduce random error into accounting measurements (Chandra, Rajdeep and Andrew, 2005). Mary (2014) concludes that fair value measurement is more consistent with existing concepts than either modified or unmodified historical cost. Although unmodified historical cost is consistent with some concepts, modified historical cost—which is widely used today—largely is not. Also, aggregate amounts, such as total assets and total liabilities based on modified or unmodified historical cost, lack meaning. Because financial statements include such aggregate amounts and changes in amounts of individual assets and liabilities determine comprehensive income, measurement concepts also need to contemplate these measurements.

FASB expanded those requirements by issuing Accounting Standards Update (ASU) No. 2010-06: Improving Disclosures About Fair Value Measurements. The update was issued in January 2010 to provide new and improved disclosure requirements and to increase transparency for entities that are required to disclose fair-value measurements in their financial statements.The overall objective of the update is to provide increased transparency for the users of financial statements that require assets and liabilities be measured at fair value. Fair value has been, and will always be, a sensitive area to investors and other users of financial statements. For many investment firms, the effort associated with compliance with the update will be offset by increased industry asset flows associated with restored investor confidence, particularly among institutional investors who typically rely on a greater level of disclosure (Del Core, Tom, Barbagallo, and John, 2010).

Accounting measurement is the process of assigning numerical symbols to events or objects. Disclosure, on the other hand, is the communication of accounting measurements to intended users. Advances in financial disclosure are likely to outpace those related to accounting measurement for a number of reasons.

First of all, many would argue that financial disclosure is a less controversial area than accounting measurement. Actually, when we talk about national accounting difference, we usually refer to measurement difference in most of time. People argue very often measurement difference in different countries. Some researchers argue that given efficient capital markets, those disclosure practices dealing with format are much less substantive than most measurement practices (Nair and Frank, 1980).

Second, changes in disclosure requirements are more rapidly implemented than changes in accounting measurement rules. Compared with measurement, disclosure is very easily changed. When regulator add some new disclosure requirements, it is relatively easy for a company to apply immediately without considering other company's reflection.

Finally, whereas a single set of accounting measurement rules may not serve users equally well under different social, economic, and legal systems, a company can disclose without necessarily sacrificing its accounting measurement system.

5.2 Development and Disclosure

In recent years, the amount of information disclosed by MNEs has expended considerably. The major pressure for increased disclosure comes from the financial and investment community. Both MNEs and standard-setting bodies in developed countries such as the United States, the United Kingdom, France, Germany and Japan, have been concerned primarily in response to pressures from this direction. Other bodies including government, trade unions, employees, and general public also need the information.

There is no doubt that information disclosure is important. The importance of information disclosed in financial statements and accompanying reports is being increasingly recognized by multinational corporations. The information could provide a way to evaluate the quality of earnings and financial position. A particularly important motivation for voluntary information disclosure by MNEs is that corporate reports provide the opportunity to communicate more policy and future oriented information for the corporation(Radebaugh, Gray and Black,2007).

From a national point of view, the development of disclosure systems closely parallels the development of accounting discussed in chapter 2. To some extent, national differences in disclosure are driven largely by differences in corporate governance and finance.

Governance means the responsibilities, accountability, and relationships among shareholders, board members, and managers to meet corporate objectives. Governance issues include rights and treatment of shareholders, responsibilities of the board, disclosure and transparency, role of stakeholders. There are actually many definitions of corporate governance, but they all concerns the systems of controls with the company, relationships between the company's board/shareholders/stakeholders, the company being managed in the interests of the stakeholders, and greater transparency and accountability to enable users of corporate information to determine whether the business is being managed in a way that they consider appropriate. A system of corporate government needs a good level of disclosure and adequate information to eliminate information asymmetries between all parties, making corporate insiders accountable for their actions. Management recognizes that there are economic benefits to be gained from a well managed disclosure policy. For management of firms, financial reporting and disclosure are potentially important means to communicate firm's performance and governance to outside investors. Therefore, good corporate governance is a key drive of sustainable corporate growth and long term competitive advantage. It focuses on a company's structure and processes to ensure fair, responsible, transparent, and accountable corporate behavior (Pankaj, 2014).

In the U.S. UK, and other Anglo-American countries, equity market have provided most corporate financing and have become highly developed. There is a great and strong need for accounting information. Therefore, disclosure has developed. In France, Germany Japan and numerous emerging market countries, shareholding remains highly concentrated and banks have been the primary source of finance. The need for accounting information comes mainly from banks. Therefore, disclosure is less developed

5.2.1 Voluntary disclosure

Voluntary disclosures are purely discretionary in nature. Why do managers have incentives to disclose information voluntarily? There may be incentives for the management of an MNE to disclose information voluntarily if it perceives to be in its own interests and those of the corporation to respond to the information demands of users and participant groups. Meek and Gray (1989) and others professors have shown that voluntary disclosure are forthcoming when corporations are competing for finance from investors, especially in a cross-border context. Besides, voluntary disclosures have many other benefits for the corporation. For example, Voluntary disclosures could lower transaction costs in the trading of the firm's securities, are attracted greater interest by financial analysts and investors, increase share liquidity, and lower cost of capital.

On the other hand, if management decides that the information demands are unreasonable or inimical to their interests or those of the MNE, they must either achieve some compromise or accept the consequences. There are many evidences strongly indicate that corporate managers often have strong incentives to delay the disclosure of adverse news, "manage" their financial reports to convey a more positive image of the firm, and overstate their firms' financial performance and prospects.

Avoiding managers' negative effect needs regulation such as accounting and disclosure regulation and third-party certificate such as auditing. Managers' disclosure choices reflect the combined effects of disclosure requirements and their incentives to disclose information voluntarily.

Voluntary disclosure level is different in developed countries and new emerging market countries. In many emerging market countries, equity markets are relatively developing, resulting in total lower demand for company information by investor and creditor. Most source of finance is provided by banks or family groups or insiders. Therefore this situation would lead to less demand for timely, credible, and relevant accounting information disclosure. In these emerging markets, increased disclosure may have limited benefits. But for developed markets, source of finance comes mainly from equity market. Investor and creditor want to understand timely, credible and relevant information disclosure. Here the demand for information is great. Thus, it is necessary to provide much more voluntary information for decision making of investor and creditor. Therefore, enhanced disclosure has much more benefit in developed capital market.

5.2.2 Mandatory disclosure

Mandatory disclosure is a requirement for a company to provide information. A majority of managers chooses disclosure rules with which all firms must comply. Disclosure rules are asymmetric with greater levels of disclosure over adverse events. This asymmetry is positively associated with the informativeness of the measurement and increasing in the level of verifiability and ex-ante uncertainty of the information(Bertomeu and Magee, 2015). Sometimes mandatory disclosure is a response to a public policy. The policy is issued by government or standard setting sector, with covering a great range. For example, mandatory information disclosure regulations seek to create institutional pressure to spur performance improvement. By examining how organizational characteristics moderate establishments' responses to a prominent environmental information disclosure program, Doshi, Dowell and Toffel (2013) find particularly rapid improvement among establishments located close to their headquarters and among establishments with proximate siblings, especially when the proximate siblings are in the same industry. Large establishments improve more slowly than small establishments in sparse regions, but both groups perform similarly in dense regions, suggesting that density mitigates the power of large establishments to resist institutional pressures.

In a developed capital market, more and more non-domestic corporations come here to seek capital and acceptance of investor. For example, in NYEX (New York Stock Exchange), over 500 foreign registrants raised capital here. To protect investors, most securities exchanges impose reporting and disclosure requirements on domestic and foreign companies that seek access to their markets. Mandatory disclosures are corporate disclosures made in response to regulatory requirements. For example, rules are issued by national regulators or stock exchanges commission.

Are there any different disclosure requirement for domestic companies and foreign listed firms? It depends on the countries.

Twin objectives of investor oriented markets exist (Frost and Lang 1996). One is investor protection while the other is market quality. Investor protection means investors are provided with material information, and are protected through monitoring and enforcement. Market quality means markets are fair, orderly, and efficient, and free from abuse and misconduct.

Both of the investor protection and market quality are very important. In absence of investor protection, investors will not be willing to participate in a market. In absence of market quality, markets will not function satisfactorily. Therefore, many would consider the objectives equally important and treat them in the same way.

5.2.3 Voluntary vs. mandatory disclosure

Voluntary disclosure is a managers' discretionary behavior while mandatory disclosure is a required behavior by regulations or rules. They are completely different. However, distinction between mandatory and voluntary disclosures can be ambiguous in some settings. Disclosure theory provides testable predictions of the interaction between a one-time mandated disclosure and future voluntary disclosure. For example, the requirement that U.S. companies must file Form 10-Ks is straightforward. However, measurement and disclosure approaches for some of the items in the Form 10-K are selective. Similarly, there are widely divergent views concerning what types of press announcements are mandatory versus voluntary.

In theory there are many papers discussing economic consequence of voluntary or mandatory disclosure. Healy and Palepu (2001) state that board of directors and investors hold managers accountable for current stock performance. Given the risk of job loss accompanying poor stock and earnings performance, managers use corporate disclosures to reduce the likelihood of undervaluation and to explain away poor earnings performance. Stephen, Sarah and Sean (2013) find that the voluntary forward looking disclosures issued during proxy contests provide more positive (or less negative) news relative to the pre-contest period. They suggest that voluntary disclosures contain more negative news after the proxy contest ends, which suggests the more positive (or less negative) disclosure news during proxy contests is temporary.

Elizabeth (2013) examined the economic consequences of the mandated disclosure of pension asset composition required under SFAS 132R. He found that under pension accounting rules, the composition of pension assets is a key determinate of the assumed expected rate of return (ERR) on pension assets. When firm disclose asset composition for the first time under SFAS 132R, firms that were previously using upward biased ERR response by increasing asset allocation to high risk securities and or reducing the ERR assumption. While disclosure requirements arguably create less powerful incentives to alter firm decisions than recognition requirements, these findings offer evidence that firms alter behavior in response to disclosure standards.

Eti (2005) studies the interaction between firms' mandatory and voluntary disclosures, demonstrating the key role that firm's mandatory disclosures play in determining their voluntary disclosure policies. By analyzing how various features of the disclosure regulation affect firms' incentives for making voluntary disclosures, he provides accounting policymakers with useful knowledge for designing disclosure rules in light of their overall impact on the level of disclosure in the market. The likelihood of voluntary disclosures are provided by firms in independent of the content of their mandatory disclosures, nonmonotonically related to the informational quality of their mandatory disclosures, negatively related to the level of discretion in mandatory reporting, and positively related to the scope of disclosure requirement.

5.2.4 U.S. SEC financial reporting debate

According to SEC requirement, foreign registrants must furnish financial information substantially similar to that required of domestic companies. They must reconcile net income and stockholders' equity and earning per share to U.S. GAAP if the registrant uses another GAAP. The requirement causes great argument, both in theory and practice. We could see that there is a tough discussion on SEC's requirement. During the discussion, two questions are always mentioned. Do SEC requirements deter foreign companies from listing their securities in the U.S.? Or do the requirements protect investors and ensure the quality of U.S. capital markets?

Whether the reconciliation requirement helps or hinders the SEC in meeting its regulatory objectives is widely debated. The SEC's requirement is generally consistent with the objectives of investor protection and market quality. However, too stringent reporting requirements may push some corporations to seek market in which there is a lower required reporting. For example, many Taiwan's companies go to London capital market for raising capital as condition of listing in London market is easier than that in NYEX. Therefore some commentators argue that the SEC's financial reporting requirements for foreign companies deter foreign companies from making their securities available in the United States. As a result, it is claimed that U.S. investors are more likely to trade in markets such as the U.S. Over-the-Counter (OTC) markets or overseas markets where liquidity may be relatively low, transaction costs relatively high, and investor protection less important. On the other hand, others counter that the current accounting and disclosure system both protects investors and ensures the quality of U.S. capital markets. Both foreign and domestic issuer should treat equal. It is also argued that the SEC's reporting requirements are not the primary obstacles for foreign companies to desire listing securities in the United States (Choi, Frost and Meek, 2002).

After year of 2000, Sarbanes-Oxley requirements, which listed company must prepare audited internal control report, are also believed to deter foreign companies from listing in the U.S. In many countries, the internal control reporting is hardly required and less practice. It will take time for companies to conduct the internal control practice. Thus, it is obvious that the debate has been never stopped.

While voluntary disclosure is discretionary in nature regulatory disclosure is a response to regulation or rules. In theory, company must disclose financial reporting according to mandatory requirements. From the perspective of a securities market regulator, more required disclosure may not be always better. There is no doubt that increased mandatory disclosure will further encourage investor participation in capital markets by providing more and better information on which to base investment decisions. Results of increased investor participation include increased liquidity, reduced transaction costs, and more accurate and efficient market pricing. However, it can be argued. In some situations disclosure requirements are excessive. In markets where disclosure requirements are considered too stringent, companies may be deterred from publicly listing their shares, and may choose to use secondary markets (such as the over-the-counter market in the United States). Some other companies may give up their chance of listing shares publicly. Thus, more required disclosure is not necessarily better than less.

How to evaluate financial reporting from disclosure point of view? Or what do companies around the world actually disclose in their annual reports? Generally speaking, annual report disclosure practices reflect manager's responses to regulatory disclosure requirements and their incentives to provide information to financial statement users voluntarily. In many parts of the world, disclosure rules mean little and monitoring and enforcement are largely absent. In a word, the whole disclosure level is low around the world. For disclosure practice, it is important to clearly distinguish between required disclosure and actual disclosure. During the disclosure, managerial discretion plays an important role. And disclosure rules vary dramatically worldwide.

5.3 Reporting and Disclosure Practice

5.3.1 Forward looking information

Forward looking information is very important and useful for users to make decision. Forward looking information includes many aspects with a wide range. According to Choi, Frost and Meek (2002), forward looking information involves three aspects. The first aspect involves forecasts of revenues, income (loss), earnings (loss) per share (EPS), capital expenditures and other financial items; The second is about prospective information about future economic performance or position that is less definite than forecasts in terms of projected item, fiscal period, and projected amount; The third concerns statements of management's plans and objectives for future operations.

The SEC encourages forward looking information in circumstances such as known material trends, events, commitments, and uncertainties. However, these requirements are not set in objective terms, as they allow for management discretion. Whether the disclosure of forward looking information is required depends cumulatively on management's assessment of (1) whether a circumstance is "presently known," (2) whether such a circumstance is "reasonably likely," and (3) whether "material effects" are to be expected. However, neither the term "reasonably likely " nor the term "material "are clearly defined. Therefore, management's discretion is given considerable leeway (Li, 2010).

In the United States, in order to encourage companies to provide forward looking information, any predictive information is explicitly covered by the safe-harbor rule for projections (Regulaiton S-K Item 303 (a) Instr.7). However, companies may be reluctant because of their uncertainty regarding judicial interpretation of the safe harbor provisions and because of dears regarding state court litigation where no such safe harbor is available. (Grundfest and Perino, 1997)

Forward looking information involved into estimate of future situation. The estimate is of subjective idea to some extent. Because of uncertainty situation in the future, forward looking information is an estimated with risk of not achieving its goal. That means forecasts are inherently unreliable and company disclosing forward looking information will face legal repercussions if forecasts aren't met. Once forward looking information is far from the actual situation, misled investors will lose confidence on the company in the future. Therefore, in order to avoid sue or future trouble, most companies provide soft information with special reminding of users' attention. Thus, softer information about future prospects is more common than precise forecasts.

Examples of forward looking information disclosure by BASF AG (a German firm) are as follows. In BASF AG 2006 annual report, the information includes four paragraph.

Exhibit 5.1   Forward looking information for BASF AG 2006 annual report

Economic trends	Expect : Global gross domestic product
	Anticipate
	Main factor affecting the overall economic climate
	Up to 2007, we forecast that gross domestic product will grow or slow by x%
Trends in the chemical industry	In the medium term, chemical industry is expected to grow faster than gross national product
	This positive outlook for the industry can be attributed to----
	Growth in global chemical production is expected to fall by x%
	In North American,---; In western Europe,---
	From 2007-2009, we again expect to see -----
Sales forecast	In the chemicals segment, we are planning to achieve ----
	In the plastics and fibers segment, sales did decline in 2006, due to---
	In the colorants and finishing products segment, we intend to increase sales,---
	In the health and nutrition segment, ---
	In oil and gas segment, we expect further growth in sales despite---
Earnings forecast	We expect a significant increase in income from operations in 2007, since---
	Different segments income forecast

Note: Author got the information from 2006 annual report of BASF AG.

Another example is for Schering AG (a German firm). The 2000 annual report shows as follows. In the 2001 financial year, the company will continue implementation of our growth strategy and move forward to next goals. The company will again be looking for double-digit sales growth to over 5 bn (based on last year's currency exchange rates). We expect an increase of more than 10% in net income despite the likely high marketing cost of introducing our new products.

"Safe Harbor for Forward Looking Statements" in the Annual Report 2000 of UniSource Energy Corp., (a U.S company) is very attractive. This annual report contains forward looking statements as defined by the Private Securities Litigation and Reform Act of 1995. Forward looking statements involve risks and uncertainties that cause actual results to differ from expected ones. By providing the disclosure, UniSource Energy is able to take advantage of the safe harbor provisions (certain protections form litigation) of the Private Securities Litigation and Reform Act of 1995 for forward looking statement. The safe harbor disclosure includes many cautionary statements.

In China, there is no specific regulation for forward looking information. But managers in a company tend to disclose forward looking information for many reasons. Disclosure of forward looking information for Chinese Listed company is listed in Managers discussion and analysis, Board of Directors Report (chapter 8 of annual report). The forward looking information type and content vary substantially from a company to another.

5.3.2 Segment disclosures

Consolidated financial statements, in spite of their obvious advantages, have a major drawback. The aggregation of all segments of the business into one overall economic entity makes it impossible for the users to assess the company's dependencies on individual business segments. Segment information is needed to identify trends of growth, profitability, and risks associated with each segment. Segment information is important to users of financial statements.

What is segment? Unfortunately, there is no easy answer to this question because the term is defined in many different ways worldwide. According to the U.S. GAAP, any foreign operation meeting either one of the two criteria below is a segment. The first is that foreign operations whose revenue from sales to unaffiliated customers is 10 percent or more of the consolidated revenue. The second is that the identifiable assets of foreign operations are 10 percent or more of consolidated assets, combined sales to unaffiliated customers in all reportable segments should be at least 75% of the total sales to unaffiliated customers by the company as a whole.

The FASB requires companies to disclose revenue, operating profit or loss, and identifiable assets for their foreign operations in the annual financial reporting if the above criteria are met. The U.S. SEC has conformed its earlier lines of business reporting requirements to the segment reporting guidelines specified by the FASB.

According to IAS 14, financial reporting by segment requires that companies whose securities are publicly traded and other "economically significant" enterprises present certain information for each significant industry segment and geographic area of operation. The required information is similar to those of SFAS No.14. One distinguishing difference between the two standards is that FASB disclosures are optional for nonpublic companies, whereas IASC disclosures are required for economically significant nonpublic companies. IAS 14 does not include specific definitions of an industry or geographic segment. Manager can judge to determine the segment of reporting. Namely, segment information requirement under the IAS 14 is more flexible than that in SFAS No.14.

At present, segment reporting is still at an experimental stage. Lacking of uniformity in reporting makes that aggregation of operations in broad geographical segments is prevalent among multinationals. Basically, the disaggregated information about a firm's industry and geographic operations and results includes information on revenue, income, depreciation and amortization, capital expenditures, assets and liabilities, and so on. Many multinationals exercised practice in segment information disclosure.

There is no doubt that segment information could help users understand how the parts make up the whole as product lines and areas of the world vary in terms of risks, returns, and opportunities. Many users of financial statement like to read segment information. More and more countries began to realize the importance of segment information regulation.

Still the final result about how a company to disclose segmental information or its economic consequence is on the way. Bugeja, Czernkowski, and Moran (2015) study how management approach for segment reporting impacted the number of reported segments and the extent of line item disclosures when Australia adopted IAS 14 (revised) and IFRS 8. An examination of the motives behind the non-disclosure of segments suggests that segment information was withheld for agency cost reasons. They find only limited support for the proprietary cost motive for non-reporting of segments. They also document that IFRS 8 led to a reduction in the amount of line item disclosure. Consistent with a proprietary cost explanation, the decrease in disclosure is greatest for firms with a higher number of profitable segments. Their results indicate that the change to the management approach to segment identification is not associated with the properties of analyst forecasts, nor did it lead to increased analyst following.

Blanco, Garcia, and Tribo (2014) find a positive relation between earnings quality and the quantity of segment disclosures, using a US sample for the period 2001–2006. They use lead-lag tests to examine the flow of causality, and results show that current segment disclosure is positively related to prior levels of earnings quality, while current earnings quality scores are not related to prior levels of segment disclosure. Thus, the causality flows from earnings quality to segment disclosure. Furthermore, Blanco, Garcia, and Tribo (2015) investigate whether segment disclosure influences cost of capital. Improved segment reporting is expected to decrease cost of capital by reducing estimation risk. However, in a competitive environment segment disclosure may also generate uncertainties about future prospects and lead to a larger cost of capital. Asset-pricing tests confirm that segment disclosure is a priced risk factor. Also, segment disclosure reduces ex-ante estimates of cost of equity capital and other measures connected to risk. These results suggest a negative relation between segment disclosure and cost of capital.

As for segmental practice in different countries, accounting rules in Japan, France, and Germany now require disclosure of business segment financial results. However, managers in these countries traditionally have been opposed to disclosing detailed segment information. Why have managers chosen to disclose relatively little information about the business segments of their companies, and why have accounting rules become more stringent despite their opposition?

Compared with the Anglo-Saxon countries, managers in Continental Europe and in Japan have for many years strongly objected to disclosing information about business segment financial results. These managers have argued that the information may be used by their competitors. Segment information used by competitor will make companies disclosing information stand in a disadvantage competition situation. In addition, Continental Europe and Japan have had strong traditions of low disclosure. Requirements for disclosure about segment results have become more stringent in Japan, France, and Germany in response to strong investor and analyst demand for the information. More generally, the three countries are striving to improve the quality of their financial reporting standards in order to improve the reputation and credibility of their capital markets (Iqbal, Melcher, and Elmallah, 1998).

5.3.3 Cash flow information

There is variation in content, format, and terminology of cash flow statements in different countries. Terminology such as cash flows, capital flows, funds, and liquidity all may be used in different countries. Cash flow statements show how much cash a company is generating from operations, and obtaining from (or distributing to) other sources.

Cash flow information can be used to forecast financial stress or liquidity problems. A company needs cash to survive, and emerging liquidity problems can be obscured when accrual-based income statements are the sole focus. A cash flow statement might be especially useful to a non-domestic financial statement user in situations where large differences in accounting standards cause difficulties in financial statement interpretation.

Habib (2008) examines the relative and incremental information content of earnings and cash flows and the role of firm-specific contextual factors in moderating information content in New Zealand. Accounting earnings are considered to be the premier information source for decision making and a substantial volume of literature, primarily in the United States, shows that earnings provide superior information to that of cash flows. However, significant reporting differences in New Zealand warrant and investigation of the role of earnings and cash flows to explain security returns. Results show that (a) earnings have higher explanatory power than cash flows, although the difference is not statistically significant, and (b) both earnings and cash flows have incremental information content for stock returns. Further analysis shows that the valuation role of earnings and cash flows is moderated by firm-specific factors.

5.3.4 Social responsibility disclosure

Social responsibility is not a new issue. The term social accounting traditionally means accounting for the economic performance of an entire nation. Here we use the term to refer to the measurement and communication of information about a firm's effects on employee welfare, the local community, and environment. That mean social accounting embraces non-financial as well as financial measures of performance. Reporting to "stakeholders" includes employees, customers, suppliers, governments, activist groups, and the general public. In addition to investors, social responsibility disclosure is a way to demonstrate corporate citizenship. Sustainability reports integrate economic, social, and environmental performance while triple-bottom line reporting should consider profits, people, and planet.

The phrase, triple-bottom line, was coined by John Elkington, co-founder of the business consultancy Sustainability, in his 1997 book *Cannibals with Forks: the triple-bottom line of 21st Century Business*. Triple Bottom Line Reporting concerns measuring environmental, social and economic performance. The triple bottom line captures an expanded spectrum of values and criteria for measuring organizational (and societal) success-economic, environmental and social. In practical terms, "triple bottom line accounting" usually means expanding the traditional company reporting framework to take into account not just financial outcomes but also environmental and social performance.

Recently, there is an increasingly being audited to avoid the charge of "green-washing". More and more companies began to care about their social responsibility. In order to attract investor's eyes, companies especially public companies, try to disclose social responsibility information. Pinto, DE Villiers, and Samkin (2014) investigates trends in the prevalence and volume of corporate social responsibility (CSR) disclosure by New Zealand's top 50 listed companies from 2005 to 2010, i.e., the period running up to and immediately after the initial impact of the global financial crisis (GFC). The results reveal a general upward trend in CSR disclosures over the six-year period. Companies operating within industries more prone to public scrutiny or those industries more sensitive to the social and environmental impacts of corporate operations, increased their CSR disclosures, whereas other companies decreased their disclosures. Jocelynhusser, Evraert-Bardinet, and Frederique (2014) study the relationship between market value, accounting fundamentals and companies' Corporate Social Responsibility (CSR) and Sustainable Development (SD) disclosures for the years 2007-2008. They use social and environmental scores derived from a structural analysis chart based on 120 companies' reports. The results show that investors measure a company's short-term performance using information about the quality of the company's environmental management. At the same time, a company's social disclosure concerning the quality of employee management influences short and long-term performance. Drobetz, Merikas, Merika and Tsionas (2014) use Markov Chain Monte Carlo (MCMC) techniques for Bayesian inference, and estimate the marginal effects of firm characteristics on CSR disclosure for each firm show a positive relationship between CSR disclosure and financial performance for each firm in their international sample. Firm size, financial leverage, and ownership structure are also associated with CSR disclosure. The findings suggest that a majority of listed shipping companies have integrated CSR practices into their strategic planning and operations.

In practice, there are many examples for social responsibility disclosure. The following is one of them. Employee reporting includes employment levels and personnel costs by division and region of the world, management development, compensation, diversity, and human rights. Environmental reporting concerns impact of production processes, products, and services on air, water, land, biodiversity and human health, water, raw material, and energy consumption, activities to reduce pollution, and spending on all of the above.

5.3.5 Special disclosures for non-domestic financial statement users

For non-domestic financial statements users, there are many issues for thinking about. For example, a MNE could consider issues about language translations and currency restatements, discussion of GAAP differences, limited restatement of income and stockholders' equity to another GAAP, and complete financial statements using another GAAP such as IFRS.

Internet business reporting and disclosure may help a lot for non-domestic financial statement users. World Wide Web is increasingly used as an information dissemination channel. Furthermore, XBRL (eXtensible Business Reporting Language) will allow users to easily manipulate companies' financial statement data. In the near future, XBRL will become a easy way to get accounting information.

Wang and Seng (2014) investigates the association between the mandatory adoption of the eXtensible Business Reporting Language (XBRL) in China and foreign institutional investors' interest. Based on a sample from the Shanghai Stock Exchange and the Shenzhen Stock Exchange in the period from 2004 to 2009, their results demonstrate that the adoption of XBRL is positively related to foreign institutional investors' holdings. In addition, although state-owned enterprises (SOEs), compared to non-SOEs, have fewer foreign institutional investors' holdings in their sample period, the adoption of XBRL reduces such differences for non-tradable shares. As China is one of the world's largest and growing economic entities and an early adopter of XBRL, their findings shed light on the role played by XBRL as a global standard and how it facilitates business information exchange around the world.

However, the adoption of XBRL in the United States is voluntary in nature. Boritz and Timoshenko (2015) attempts to overcome some of some limitations existing in prior literature by using a more comprehensive sample, employing a more effective matching procedure, and a more complete set of variables suggested by both voluntary disclosure and organization theories. Consistent with the theory, higher voluntary disclosure propensity, stronger corporate governance, and better profitability are found to be robustly significant factors associated with voluntary XBRL adoption in the U.S. Innovativeness is a distinguishing characteristic for non-high-tech VFP participants. Analyst following, auditor quality, and earnings quality are less robust characteristics.

5.3.6 Corporate governance disclosure

According to OECD(Organization for Economic Co-operation and Development) fifth principle of corporate governance disclosure and transparency, the corporate governance framework should ensure that timely and accurate disclosure is made on all material matters regarding the corporation, including the financial situation, performance, ownership and governance of the company. The corporate governance framework should be complemented by an effective approach that addresses and promotes the provision of analysis or advice by analysts, brokers, rating agencies and others, that is relevant to decisions by investors, free from material conflicts of interest that might compromise the integrity of their analysis or advice.[①]

Corporate governance disclosure practices are receiving increasing attention from regulators, investors and analysts. The governance framework (Dallas, 2004)[②] includes four parts. The first is market infrastructure, which concerns ownership patterns, extent to which companies are publicly listed, ownership rights, market for corporate control, board structure. The second is legal environment, which includes type of legal system shareholder/stakeholder rights and company/securities laws. The third part is regulatory environment, which includes regulatory bodies and their purview, regulatory gaps/overlap, information and timing requirements and effectiveness of enforcement. The fourth part is informational infrastructure, which includes accounting standards, auditing standards, and structure of the accounting/auditing profession. Governance mechanisms and disclosures are improving around the world in recent decades. OECD issued its revised Principles of Corporate Governance in 2004. Disclosure is a key element of any good system of corporate governance.

In theory, the discussion about corporate governance disclosure is not yet ended. There are many published papers, and here are some examples. Yousuf and Craig

---

① OECD Principles of Corporate Governance (2004):22-23 (www.oecd.org/dataoecd/32/18/31557724.pdf)
② The framework comes from Choi, Frost and Meek (2002), the fifth edition.

(2013) find that the disclosure of governance information lags behind general corporate social responsibility disclosures, and the textile and garment companies of Bangladesh disclose information about their governance practices in order to secure/maintain legitimacy and/or to meet community expectations, using content analysis. However, the governance disclosures still fall short of what would appear to be expected by the international community, and despite ongoing international concerns about workplace conditions and associated safety, the results suggest limited accountability and transparency in relation to social and environment-related governance practices within a developing country context.

Peter and Sue (2005) examine the relationship between the voluntary disclosure of information about corporate governance practices and the intention to raise external finance. This relationship is examined by using corporate governance disclosures in the annual reports of Australian companies in 1994. Data from this year are used because in subsequent years Australian Stock Exchange regulations influenced listed companies to make disclosures about their corporate governance practices. Regression analysis indicates that the voluntary disclosure of corporate governance information is positively associated with the intention to raise equity capital, but not with the intention to raise debt capital.

Pankaj (2014) discusses evolution of public sector corporate governance reforms and provides legal and institutional framework for corporate governance practices in Indian public sector. Corporate governance and disclosure practices of private sector and public sector firms listed in S&P BSE sectoral indices have been studied. The sample firms represent different sectors viz. Metal, Oil & Gas, Power, FMCG, Health Care, Consumer Durables, Capital Goods, Auto and IT. There is no significant difference in the corporate governance and disclosure practices of Indian firms across public and private sector firms. Hence, this research emphasizes that public sector reforms have lessened the differences between the two sectors, particularly with regard to corporate governance.

In addition, we should mention that in China publicly traded company provides their governance information in a separate part in annual report.

Terms of the Chapter

abbreviated reporting requirements 简化的报告要求
accounting measurement 会计计量
accounting principle 会计原则
accounting regulation 会计规范
accrual-basis income statement 应计制利润表(权责发生制收益表)
annual report disclosure 年度报告披露

audit committee 审计委员会

business segment 经营分部

cash and fund flow statement 现金流量表

capitalized start-up costs 资本化开办费用

credibility 可靠性

comprehensive income 综合收益

comparability 可比性

corporate governance 公司管制(治理)

cost effectiveness 成本有效性

cross-jurisdictional conformity of disclosure 跨管辖权的披露一致性

deferred tax 递延税

disclosure 披露

disclosure requirement 披露要求

diluted earning 稀释收益

earning forecast 收益预测

electronic information 电子信息

emerging market economy 新兴市场经济

fair value 公允价值

financial analyst 财务分析家

financial measurement of performance 财务业绩衡量

financial position 财务状况

financial reporting 财务报告

flexibility 弹性

footnotes 脚注

foreign listed firm 在外国上市的公司

forward-looking information 前景信息

funds flow statements 现金流量表

hedge accounting 套期会计

geographic and industry segment 地区和行业分部

governance structure 治理结构

government regulator 政府规范者

interest of shareholder 股东利益

investor protect 投资者保护

investor-oriented equity market 投资者导向权益市场

investor confidence 投资者信心

interpretation 解释

leasing contract 租赁合同

liquidity 流动性

market quality 市场质量

managers' incentives 管理者动机
material information 重要信息
managerial discretion 管理的意愿
mandatory disclosure 强制性披露
multinational company 跨国公司
operating segment 经营分部
operating result 经营结果
opacity 不透明性
over-the counter market 店头交易市场
privatization 私有化
prospectuses 计划书
prospective information 预测信息
publicly traded company 上市公司
reconciliation 调节表
regulatory disclosure 强制披露
related party transaction 关联方交易
revenue recognition 收入确认
reportable segments 可报告分部
special disclosure 特殊披露
social responsibility 社会责任
segment disclosure 分部信息披露
social accounting 社会会计
stakeholder 利益相关者
stock option 股票期权
stock exchange 股票交易
sustainable development 可持续发展
transaction cost 交易成本
transparency 透明度
unrealized gain or loss 未实现的利得或损失
voluntary disclosure 自愿披露
voting right 投票权
weighted average 加权平均
working capital 营运资本

Discussion Questions

1. What is the distinction between accounting measurement and accounting disclosure? Which of the two reporting processes do you think promises substantial innovative advances during the next 10 years? Why?

2. Taking some examples to explain the factors that drive national accounting disclosure development.

3. What is voluntary disclosure? Why do managers have incentives to disclose information voluntarily? How to avoid managers' negative effect?

4. Analyze the relationship between mandatory and voluntary disclosures.

5. How to evaluate the debate on requirement by SEC for financial reporting of non domestic registrants.

6. From the perspective of a securities market regulator, is more required disclosure always better than less? Why or why not?

7. What do companies around the world actually disclose in their annual reports?

8. What are the benefits of disclosing detailed financial reports to users as compared to providing simplified reports?

9. To what extent are information disclosures in directors' annual reports, as opposed to the financial statement, likely to be useful to financial analysts and investors?

10. What are possible costs and benefits for MNEs to make additional voluntary disclosures?

11. Are stocks exchange disclosure regulations more stringent in developed countries or developing countries?

12. How to use forward looking information for investor or creditor to make decision? Give some example.

13. Is segmental information useful for users of financial statements? Why or why not?

14. To what extent the information of cash flow are more useful for foreign investors?

15. Accounting rules in Japan, France, and Germany now require disclosure of business segment financial results. However, managers in these countries traditionally have been opposed to disclosing detailed segment information. Explain the change driver and future development in segment information disclosure.

16. Do you think what should be included in social responsibility reports for listed company in China? How about Chinese company listed in foreign capital market?

17. What kind of information is provided by corporate governance disclosure according to Chinese accounting regulation for listed companies?

True or False

1. Accounting measurement is the process of assigning numerical symbols to events or objects.

2. In order to attract customer, companies, especially public companies, try to disclose more social responsibility information.

3. After year of 2000, Sarbanes-Oxley requirements are also believed to help foreign companies from listing in the U.S.A capital market.

4. Nonconsolidation can be highly misleading as to overall financial performance with complex and high risk foreign operations.

5. No company uses the pooling-of interest consolidation method because it is now prohibited throughout in the European countries by standards.

6. Acquisition accounting in both the United States and United Kingdom generally requires assets to be adjusted to fair value or purchase price.

7. Segment information is more useful for investors to combine company-specific information with external information.

8. Internationally accepted yardsticks for performance evaluation are available for most diversified MNEs.

9. Gaming can occur if the users of financial reporting perceive the information contained in them to be a bad.

10. Forecasts of earnings studies have all concluded that prediction is less accurate and useless if they are based on line-of-business segmental data rather than consolidated earnings.

11. Many MNEs strongly opposed to disseminating more information because of a competitive disadvantage.

12. Excessive costs of preparing and disclosing segmental information may have doubtful validity.

13. Forward looking information is full of risk and uncertainty.

14. A cash flow statement might be especially useful to a domestic financial statement user in situations where large differences in accounting standards cause difficulties in financial statement interpretation.

15. Distinction between mandatory and voluntary disclosures can be clear in some settings.

Multiple Choice

1. The best means of accounting for business combinations around the world is
    a. by disaggregating data by industry area.
    b. by equity method.
    c. consolidation of financial information, combining parent with integrated subsidies information.
    d. through parent company statements only, not consolidated statements.
2. Which of the following accurately reflect voluntary information disclosure?

a. Voluntary disclosures could increase company's share price.

b. Voluntary disclosures are required information.

c. Manager likes to disclose voluntary information.

d. Voluntary information could lower cost of capital.

3. Proportional consolidation involves

a. including a proportion of the firm's income, assets, liabilities and equity.

b. using the cost method.

c. consolidating the ownership share of assets and liabilities on a pro-rata basis.

d. using the equity method.

4. Parent company balance sheets

a. are not permitted for French companies.

b. are not permitted in the United States.

c. are always provided by U.K. companies in addition to a consolidated balance sheet and profit and loss account.

d. are not permitted in the Germany companies.

5. For users, a major value of segment information is that

a. it focuses on cash flows information.

b. it focuses on industrial information.

c. it provides information to investors that might forecast company's future financial results.

d. it allows users to get industrial or geographic information that might be of use to them.

6. Voluntary information is

a. managers' discretionary behavior.

b. good news in most of time.

c. neither managers' discretionary behavior or good news in most of time.

d. both managers' discretionary behavior and good news in most of time

7. The looking forward information could help investors

a. to understand managers' perception in future results and financial situation.

b. to know exactly what will happen in the future.

c. to forecast company's geographic investment planning.

d. to know different industrial market shares.

8. Social responsibility information is

a. very easy for MNEs to compute.

b. useful because it indicate company's citizenship to some extent.

c. necessary for company to show its contribution to society.

d. useless for company to increase net income.

9. Mandatory information is typically provided for

a. responding to required disclosure regulations.

b. managers' behavior to attract investors.

c. managers' intent.

d. responding to governmental requirement.

10. Which of the following does not belong to forward looking information most possibly?

a. earning per share.

b. sale growth.

c. economic trends.

d. current net income.

11. Social responsibility disclosures could include financial and nonfinancial data. Indicate which of the following is of social responsibility information.

a. shareholder meeting reporting.

b. employee reporting.

c. Directors' report.

d. CEO's report.

12. Which of the following correctly reflect difference between measurement and disclosure?

a. financial disclosure is more controversial.

b. financial measurement is easily to harmonize worldwide.

c. financial disclosure is a less controversial area than accounting measurement.

d. financial disclosure is a more complex area than accounting measurement.

Case Analysis

The following paragraph comes from the SEC website:

http://www.sec.gov/news/press/2012/2012-146.htm

Please read it and answer the questions

Case 5.1   FOR IMMEDIATE RELEASE

2012-146

Washington, D.C., July 30, 2012 – The Securities and Exchange Commission today charged New York-based investment manager Peter Siris and two of his firms with a host of securities law violations mostly related to his activities with a Chinese reverse merger company, China Yingxia International Inc.

The SEC alleges that Siris, an active investor in Chinese companies and former newspaper money columnist, misled investors in his two hedge funds through which he invested $1.5 million in China Yingxia. Siris understated his involvement with the company particularly after it went out of business, and used his insider status to make iLegal trades based on nonpublic information as he received it. In an attempt to circumvent the registration provisions of the securities laws, Siris also received shares from the China Yingxia CEO's father and improperly sold them without any registration statement in effect. Siris further engaged in insider trading ahead of 10 confidentially solicited offerings for other Chinese issuers.

Siris and his firms agreed to pay more than $1.1 million to settle the SEC's charges. The SEC also separately charged five individuals and one firm for securities law violations related to China Yingxia.

"Siris operated by his own set of rules in his dealings with China Yingxia and other Chinese issuers," said Andrew M. Calamari, Acting Director of the SEC's New York Regional Office. "He was the go-to person when Chinese reverse merger companies wanted to raise capital or needed advice about operations, but he used his prominence and reputation in this area to illegally game the system to his advantage."

According to the SEC's complaint filed in U.S. District Court for the Southern District of New York, Siris and his firms Guerrilla Capital Management LLC and Hua Mei 21st Century LLC became involved with China Yingxia in 2007 and their misconduct continued until 2010. Along with being one of three "consultants" that improperly raised money for China Yingxia, Siris and Hua Mei acted as advisers to the purported nutritional foods company.

Insider Trading and Illegal Short Selling

The SEC alleges that in February and March 2009, Siris sold China Yingxia stock while in possession of material, nonpublic information about problems at China Yingxia that he learned directly from the CEO. This confidential information included that she had engaged in illegal fundraising activities in China and that a company factory had shut down. Siris immediately began selling hundreds of thousands of shares of China Yingxia stock prior to any public disclosure by China Yingxia about these issues. Siris learned additional material, nonpublic information during the late afternoon of March 3, 2009, when he received a draft press release and notice that China Yingxia planned to publicly disclose the problems. Siris increased his orders to sell over the next couple of days before China Yingxia issued its press release publicly on March 6. Siris, through his funds, sold 1,143,660 China Yingxia shares in a matter of weeks for ill-gotten gains of approximately $172,000.

According to the SEC's complaint, Siris and Guerrilla Capital Management also engaged in illegal insider trading ahead of 10 offering announcements for other Chinese issuers and made approximately $162,000 in ill-gotten gains. After expressly agreeing to go "over-the-wall," which included a prohibition on trading, Siris traded ahead of the offering announcements in breach of his duty not to trade on such information.

The SEC further alleges that Siris sold short the securities of two Chinese companies prior to participating in firm-commitment offerings.

Fraudulent Representations in a Securities Purchase Agreement

The SEC alleges that in order to induce at least one issuer to sell securities to his funds, Siris falsely represented in a securities purchase agreement that his funds had not engaged in any trading after being contacted in confidence about a particular deal, when in fact his funds had effected sales in that issuer's securities. Siris directed short sales of a Chinese issuer on Dec. 9, 2009, despite going "over-the-wall" in original solicitation discussions, and nevertheless Siris signed a securities purchase agreement later that afternoon that misrepresented he had not traded in those securities. The following morning, Siris directed additional sales of the company's shares before the public announcement of the offering. Siris realized illegal insider trading gains.

Materially Misleading Disclosures to Fund Investors

The SEC alleges that Siris generally disclosed that he and his consulting firm Hua Mei, may provide services to Chinese issuers, but he did not disclose the depth of his involvement in China Yingxia. Investors were not informed that Siris and his firm provided drafting assistance for press releases and SEC filings, translation services, management preparation in advance of conference calls, and officer recommendations. By omitting key facts and making misrepresentations about his role with the company, Siris deprived his investors of material information that could have impacted their continued investment decisions with his funds. Furthermore, when China Yingxia later collapsed, Siris wrote to his investors and placed blame on others he claimed were responsible for the SEC filings and key hiring decisions while omitting his significant role in these very same tasks.

Acting as an Unregistered Securities Broker

The SEC alleges that Siris, who was not registered as a broker or dealer nor associated with a registered broker-dealer, acted as an unregistered broker during China Yingxia's second securities offering, as he raised more than $2 million worth of investments. In a backdated consulting agreement, Siris through Hua Mei in fact received transaction-based fees for leading fundraising efforts for China Yingxia and not for providing consulting services. No disclosures were made to potential or actual investors concerning payments to three so-called consultants including Siris, who sold China Yingxia securities.

Improper Unregistered Sale of Securities

The SEC alleges that Siris and Hua Mei improperly sold securities that Hua Mei received from China Yingxia in a sham agreement intended to hide the fact that they were shares from a person controlled by the company. China Yingxia agreed to pay Siris for due diligence he conducted in connection with his lead investment in the company's July 2007 PIPE offering. The company transferred shares to Siris with the appearance that they came from a shareholder to reimburse him for services performed for that shareholder. In fact, the sham agreement was simply a means for China Yingxia to provide Hua Mei with shares believed to be immediately eligible for sale, because had the company issued the shares directly to Hua Mei, they would have been restricted stock subject to holding period and other requirements for resale. The shareholder and source of the shares was later revealed to be the father of China Yingxia's CEO—someone who was in fact a person directly or indirectly controlled by the issuer.

The SEC's complaint against Siris and his entities alleges violations of Sections 5(a), 5(c), and 17(a) of the Securities Act of 1933, Sections 10(b) and 15(a) of the Securities Exchange Act of 1934, Rule 10b-5 thereunder, Rule 105 of Regulation M, and Section 206(4) of the Investment Advisers Act of 1940, and Rule 206(4)-8 thereunder. Without admitting or denying the allegations, Siris and his firms agreed to pay $592,942.39 in disgorgement and $70,488.83 prejudgment interest. Siris agreed to pay a penalty of $464,011.93. They also consented to the entry of a judgment enjoining them from violations of the respective provisions of the Securities Act, Exchange Act, and Advisers Act. The settlement is subject to court approval.

Also charged for securities law violations related to China Yingxia

Ren Hu – the former CFO of China Yingxia made fraudulent representations in Sarbanes-Oxley (SOX) certifications, lied to auditors, failed to implement internal accounting controls, and aided and abetted China Yingxia's failure to implement internal controls.

Peter Dong Zhou – engaged in insider trading and unregistered sales of securities and aided and abetted unregistered broker-dealer activity while assisting China Yingxia with its reverse merger and virtually all of its public company tasks. Without admitting or denying the charges, Zhou agreed to pay $20,900 in disgorgement, $2,463.39 in prejudgment interest, and a penalty $50,000. He agreed to a three-year collateral bar, penny stock bar, and investment company bar.

Alan Sheinwald and his investor relations firm Alliance Advisors LLC, were retained as "consultants" to China Yingxia and acted as unregistered securities brokers while raising money for China Yingxia and at least one other issuer.

Steve Mazur, acted as an unregistered securities broker while selling away from his firm the securities of China Yingxia and one other issuer. Without admitting or denying the charges, Mazur agreed to pay $126,800 in disgorgement, $25,550.01 in prejudgment interest, and a penalty of $25,000. He agreed to a two-year collateral bar, penny stock bar, and investment company bar.

James Fuld, Jr., involved in the unregistered sales of securities. Without admitting or denying the charges, he agreed to pay $178,594.85 in disgorgement and $38,096.70 in prejudgment interest.

Mr. Calamari said, "With these charges, the SEC continues to make good on its commitment to hold accountable those who enable some Chinese reverse merger firms to take unfair advantage of investors in the U.S. capital markets."

The SEC's investigation, which is continuing, was conducted in the New York Regional Office by Celeste Chase, Eduardo A. Santiago-Acevedo, and Osman Nawaz, with assistance from Frank Milewski. Paul Gizzi and Osman Nawaz will lead the SEC's litigation team. The SEC acknowledges the assistance of the Financial Industry Regulatory Authority (FINRA) in this matter.

Questions:

1. Explain the reasons for SEC Charges N.Y.-Based Fund Manager and Others.

2. What regulation should be improved or provided if these violations could be avoided both in China and USA?

3. What could be learned from SEC's regulation for China Securities Regulation Commission and Chinese companies planned to raise capital in U.S.A capital markets?

4. From the case, analyze why and how confidence crises happen for Chinese company listed in the USA. capital market. From disclosure point of view, how to improve the disclosure practice and communicate with foreign users better?

Case 5.2   Social responsibility disclosure for China Mengniu Dairy Co. Ltd

Go to the Hang Kong Stock Exchange (www.hkex.com.hk) or Mengniu Dairy's official website (www.mengniuir.com;www.mengniu.com.cn), to get Mengniu Dairy's 2014 annual report, read it carefully, and discuss the following questions as a group.

1. What is the social responsibility for a company? And what is social responsibility of Mengniu Dairy?

2. How to demonstrate social responsibility for a company? How Mengniu Dairy to indicate its social responsibility?

3. Do you think what should be included in social responsibility report? Why or why not? From social responsibility Mengniu Dairy 2014 annual report, do you find how Mengniu Dairy exercises its social responsibility as a dairy product company?

4. How to improve information of social responsibility? And How to improve Mengniu Dairy information of social responsibility?

5. Why scandal of foodstuff occurred very often in recent years in China?

Chapter 6   International Accounting Harmonization or Convergence

![image](learning objective icon) *Learning objective*

After careful study of this chapter, students will be able to:

1. Explain the survey of international harmonization or convergence.

2. Discuss the objectives of International accounting standards board (IASB), and its mission.

3. Discuss the objectives of International federation of accountants (IFAC), and its mission.

4. Describe the contribution of European Union (EU) to improve international accounting harmonization or convergence.

5. Explain the objectives of International Organization of Securities Commissions (IOSCO), and its mission.

6. Depict the advantages and disadvantages of international harmonization.

7. Evaluate international accounting harmonization or convergence.

8. List some evidences that International Accounting Standard (IAS) or International Financial Reporting Standard (IFRS) are becoming widely accepted around the world.

9. Identify how multinational enterprises with different pressures lead to accounting harmonization and disclosure.

10. Argue the harmonization or convergence process of IASB and FASB, and describe some future prospect for accounting harmonization or convergence.

6.1 A survey of International Harmonization

6.1.1 Harmonization

Harmonization is a process of increasing the compatibility of accounting practices by setting limits on how much they can vary. The process of harmonization is described in a way that identifies departures from equiprobable accounting policy choice as either: (a) the systematic effects of harmonization, or (b) the effects of systematic divergence from international harmony where the frequency of adoption of differing accounting methods vary across countries, or (c) the effects of company-specific accounting policy choices. The understanding of harmony that underlies previous attempts to measure harmonization is such that, with respect to a particular financial statement item. a situation of maximum harmony is reached when all companies in all countries use the same accounting method. This notion ignores the possibility that companies may be subject to different circumstances which arguably justify the use of correspondingly different accounting methods in respect of that item (Simon, Pascale and Stuart,1996).

International harmonization of financial accounting standards has been the goal of many professional and academic accountants during the last 40 years. As of January 1, 2005, international accounting harmonization entered a new and perhaps decisive phase. From that date, all companies domiciled in the European Union with shares listed on securities exchanges are required to prepare their consolidated accounts in accordance with International Financial Reporting Standards (IFRS). This landmark event presents an opportunity for accounting researchers to assess the status of research on international accounting harmonization (Richard and Elena,2007).

People occasionally use the terms harmonization and standardization interchangeably, but in contrast to harmonization, standardization generally means the imposition of a rigid and narrow set of rules, and may even apply a single standard or rule to all situations. Generally speaking, accounting Harmonization includes accounting standards, which deal with measurement and disclosure, and auditing standards.

Compared with auditing harmonization, measurement and disclosure harmonization is harder and is discussed usually. Both of measurement and disclosure are two processes of accounting treatment. Therefore, they should be treated equally. Discrepancies in international measurement may produce accounting amounts that are vastly different even where financial transactions and position are identical. Difference of accounting amounts could lead to incorrect comparisons, which would mislead investors. Here it doesn't matter what is disclosed; No reliable comparisons are possibly anyway. As regard to disclosure, if companies do not disclose complete information, they can hide losses or future problems from financial statement users. For example, losses can be hidden by offsetting them against gains. Expected future problems related to loss contingencies can be hidden simply by not disclosing them. Thus, if disclosure is incomplete, even the application of similar measurement principles will also lead to incorrect comparisons. Clearly, international accounting harmonization requires that both measurement and disclosure be made comparable.

Harmonization of international accounting involves in a broad fields. A thoughtful approach to assessing the desirability of international harmonization recognizes that the cost and benefit vary from case to case.

6.1.2 Criticism and evaluation of international harmonization

According to Cairns (1997), among the most significant achievements of the IASC is its successful effort to build relationships with national standard setting bodies during the 1980s and 1990s. Lúcia Lima and Russell (2007) apply an innovative approach to explore the processes, effects and likely future progress of the convergence of national accounting standards with International Financial Reporting Standards (IFRS). They conclude by highlighting four matters that are thought likely to enhance understanding of the process of international accounting standards harmonization; and by averring that the international harmonization process is a dialectical process influenced by belief systems that are constructed in a context of isomorphism and decoupling.

Although international accounting harmonization is gradually accepted around the world, there exists still much criticism. First of all, critics doubt that international standards can be flexible enough to handle differences in national backgrounds, traditions, and economic environments, and may be a politically unacceptable challenge to sovereignty. International accounting standards contain many choices for the same transaction or event, however these choices are not enough to deal with national environment difference. Secondly, it is said that international accounting standard setting is a tactic for the large international accounting service firms to expand their markets. If the international standards are used by the international accounting firms, it will be helpful for the accounting firms to broaden their services. Thirdly, a well-developed international capital market has grown without international accounting standards. Before 1929 world economy crisis, there was no accounting rules or regulations. However, there has had a well-developed capital market in the United States. Fourthly, international standards may create overload for companies that do business internationally. Several standards will make accountant not to apply correctly when financial statements are prepared. Finally, too many national groups have vested interests in maintaining their own standards and practices. No nations would like to abandon their national rights, even if it is in the accounting field.

The international business community has thus been forced to commit to and undertake the daunting task of reconciling the accounting practices of different nations in an effort to improve the comparability of financial information. There are three feasible approaches to achieve this objective: mutual recognition of accounts, reconciliation with national standards, or harmonization (Cairns 1995). The current focus is on achieving harmonization.

Reconciliation, mutual recognition and IFRSs or IASs are all the ways to harmonize accounting. For reconciliation, foreign firms can prepare financial statements using the accounting standards of their home country, but also must provide reconciliation between accounting measures of the home country and the country where the financial statements are being filed. For example, U.S.A SEC requires foreign registrants to provide at least reconciliation of both net income and shareholders' equity if foreign registrants prepare its financial reporting according to foreign standards. It is obvious that reconciliations are less costly than preparing a full set of financial statements under a different set of accounting principles. Certainly, reconciliation provides only a summary, not the full picture of the enterprise.

Reciprocity, or mutual recognition, exists when regulators outside of the home country accept a foreign firm's financial statements based on the home country's principles. For example, in the London Stock Exchange U.S GAAP-based financial statements in filings are accepted or vice versa. Reciprocity does not reduce cross-country comparability of financial statements. On the contrary reciprocity could create an unlevel playing field. When foreign companies may be allowed to apply standards less rigorous than those applied to domestic companies, unlevel playing field will exist.

International standards are used as a result of either international or political agreement or voluntary (or professionally encouraged) compliance. When accounting standards are applied through political, legal, or regulatory procedures, statutory rules typically govern the process. The application of the EU accounting-related directives results from an international political agreement. There are different ways in which national standard setters use IFRS. Some nations take directly IFRS as national standards, while other nations use IFRS with creating some topics that IFRS do not cover. In some cases, IFRSs are used as national standards but are modified for local conditions or circumstances. In addition, national standards are separately developed but are based on and similar to the relevant IFRS. Or national standards generally provide additional explanatory material only. Sometimes, national accounting standards are separately developed but are based on and similar to IFRS in most cases. For some specific countries, national standards make no reference to IFRS. Same as above, only each standard includes a statement that compares the national standard with the relevant IFRS.

Surely, there are some advantages and disadvantages for each approach. One of the main problems with mutual recognition is to make financial statements within the home market non-comparable. For reconciliation, the United States SEC considers it to be a cost-effective means. Significant differences between domestic and foreign accounting principles can increase the burdens. Reconciliations do not provide a full picture of the enterprise. The use of International Financial Reporting Standards would provide many benefits for cross-border listings.

Different entities would like to choose different approaches according to their cost-benefit principles. Investors might prefer international standards in order to reduce decision cost. Company management might prefer mutual recognition due to preparing and disclosing convenience. Regulatory authorities might prefer reconciliation for supervising reasons. Stock exchanges might prefer harmonization for regulating benefit or market operation smoothly. Professional associations will take positions according to their constituents.

Some researcher such as Hoarau's (Christian Hoarau) preferred route to harmonization is mutual recognition accompanied by reconciliations to international benchmarks established by an international committee of standard setters. However, Nobes (1995) thought there are several problems with this. First, an international committee of standard setters would presumably have to include representatives from governmental bodies for such countries as France, Germany and Japan where the government is in charge of accounting rules. Secondly, there is no guarantee that such a committee would not also be biased towards US practices, since the US is 'ahead' on most issues. The third problem is that, since companies would have to reconcile from national practice to the benchmark for each of many issues, the resulting notes would be complex. Fourthly, this would not, in substance, be mutual recognition (Nobes, 1995).

The harmonization debate may never be completely settled. Increasing evidence shows that the goal of international harmonization of accounting, disclosure, and auditing has been so widely accepted that the trend towards international harmonization will continue or accelerate. Akwasi and Robert (2005) examine the main differences between U.S. Generally Accepted Accounting Principles (GAAP) and International Accounting Standards (IAS). They found that the impact of accounting differences between IASs and US GAAP is narrowing, and suggest that the IASB standards should be accepted without condition. The exact content of IASs may not be the same as U.S. GAAP, but in many ways the approach and degree of detail are similar. Given the IASB's international focus and the range of cultures it has to deal with, the degree of detail in the IASs may need to be even greater. This may not be a pleasant prospect, but without it, IASs may not succeed in achieving genuine harmonization. Their findings did not support widespread claims that U.S. GAAP produce financial statements of higher informational quality than IAS. Recommendation and acceptance of the IAS without regard to the complexity of business environments, culture, political, legal, and economics of the U.S. is premature. Research scientists concluded there was de facto harmonization even in countries where IAS was not necessarily the basis of accounting standards.

6.2 International Accounting Standards Board

6.2.1 Before IASB and IASC's work

In 1959, Jacob Kraayenhof, founding partner of a major European firm of independent accountants, urges that work on international accounting standards bargain. In 1961,Group d'Egudes, consisting of practicing accounting professionals, is established in Europe to advise European Union authorities on matters concerning accounting.

Numerous accountancy bodies, including those in the UK, US, Australia and Canada, have recently arrived at the conclusion that a large majority of accounting problems could be better resolved at an international, rather than a national, level (Carsberg 1996). A critical first step towards attaining some degree of similarity in accounting standards at the international level was taken in 1966 when the Accountants' International Study Group was formed through the cooperative efforts of professional accountancy bodies in the US, the UK, and Canada. Significant progress toward the development of a set of international accounting standards (lASs) began to be made in 1972 when an agreement was formed to establish the IASC at the World Congress of Accountants. In 1973, International Accounting Standards Committee (IASC) is established by 16 professional institutes from 9 countries, which include Australia, Canada, France, Germany, Japan, Mexico, the Netherlands, the United Kingdom, the United States. Its headquarter was located in London in that time. The IASC was founded with two stated objectives. The first objective is to formulate and publish in the public interest accounting standards to be observed in the presentation of financial statements and to promote their worldwide acceptance and observance. The second objective is to work generally for the improvement and harmonization of regulations, accounting standards, and procedures relating to the presentation of financial statements.

In its first 15 years, the IASC's main activity was the issuance of 26 generic International Accounting Standards (IASs), many of which allowed multiple options. Therefore, IASs was described as a lowest-common-denominator approach. In 1989, the Framework for the Preparation and Presentation of Financial Statements (Framework) was published. Framework is about the objectives of financial statements, the qualitative characteristics of information, definitions of the elements of financial statements, and the criteria for recognition of financial statement elements. In order to eliminate the choices of accounting treatment, the Comparability Project, 10 revised IASs were approved in 1993 and became effective in 1995.

In total, the IASC has passed through three distinct stages (Epstein and Mirza 1997). Stage one encompassed the early years, from 1973 through 1982, when the IASC attempted to promulgate a common body of standards through the examination and evaluation of the treatments used for all the major accounting issues. Essentially, the IASC ended up endorsing practically all of the conventional methods used by the major nations. As a result, the lASs produced during this period generally permitted numerous alternatives with no obvious conceptual basis. During stage two, which began in 1983, the IASC decided to obtain a first hand view of the accounting standard processes in place throughout the world. The IASC established a goal of visiting the standard setting bodies in each board member's country. By the time the IASC had embarked on its Comparability and Improvements project with the issuance of Exposure Draft (E) 32 in 1989 (Cairns 1997). Via the Comparability Project, the IASC reduced the number of alternatives allowed in ten IASs to facilitate comparability and promote harmonization. The third stage is marked by the pursuit of harmonization objectives and the endorsement of major stakeholders, such as the International Organization of Securities Commissions (IOSCO). (Donna and Kimberley, 1998).

International organization of securities commissions is called or abbreviated as IOSCO, which is an international regulator agency of capital markets. IOSCO became a member of the IASC's Consultative Group in 1987 and supported the IASC's comparability Project. In 1993, IOSCO and the IASC agreed on a list of 30 core standards that the IASC wanted to develop. In 1995, the IOSCO and the IASC agreed on a work program for the IASC to develop the set of core international standards. After completion of core standards, OSCO promises to evaluate the standards for possible endorsement for cross board purposes upon their completion (Doupnik and Perera, 2007).

In December 1998, the IASC completed its work program and the set of 30 core standards was developed. In May 2000, IOSCO's Technical Committee recommended that securities regulators permit foreign issuers to use the core standards. The Technical Committee consisted of securities regulators representing the 14 largest and most developed capital markets, such as the United States, the United Kingdom, Australia, France, Germany, Japan, and so on. Of the 14 countries members, only Canada and the United States do not allow foreign companies to use IASs without reconciliation to local GAAP for listing purposes. In 1996, the U.S SEC announced that IASC must meet three criteria for being accepted for cross listing purposes. Three criteria contains the IASC would have to constitute a comprehensive, generally accepted basis of accounting, be of high quality, resulting in comparability and transparency, and providing for full disclosure, and be rigorously interpreted and applied.

Then, the IASC created a Standing Interpretations Committee (SIC) to provide guidance. In 1999, the SEC began to assess the IASC's core standards. In 2000, SEC issued a concept release soliciting comments on whether it should modify it requirement that all financial statements be reconciled to U.S GAAP.

As a global standard setter, IASC faced problems of legitimacy with regard to constituent support, independence, and technical expertise. In order to response to these concerns, the IASC appointed a Strategy Working Party in 1996, which issued a discussion document in December 1998 entitled "Shaping IASC for the Future". The document proposed a vastly different structure and process for the development of

IASC.

On April 1,2000, the newly created International Accounting Standard Board (IASB) took over from the IACS as the creator of IASs. The process took over five years.

6.2.2 IASB's work

In March 2001, the International Accounting Standards Committee (IASC) Foundation was formed as a not-for-profit corporation incorporated in the State of Delaware, US. The IASC Foundation is the parent entity of the International Accounting Standards Board (IASB), an independent accounting standard-setter based in London, UK.

On 1 April 2001, the International Accounting Standards Board (IASB) assumed accounting standard-setting responsibilities from its predecessor body, the International Accounting Standards Committee. This was the culmination of a restructuring based on the recommendations of the report Recommendations on Shaping IASC for the Future. The IASB structure has the following main features with completely differing from its predecessor: the IASC Foundation is an independent organization having two main bodies, the Trustees and the IASB, as well as a Standards Advisory Council and the International Financial Reporting Interpretations Committee. The IASC Foundation Trustees appoint the IASB members, exercise oversight and raise the funds needed, but the IASB has sole responsibility for setting accounting standards.

The International Accounting Standards Board is an independent, privately-funded accounting standard-setter based in London, UK. The Board members come from nine countries and have a variety of functional backgrounds.

The IASB is committed to meet following three objectives. The first objective is to developing, in the public interest, a single set of high quality, understandable, and enforceable global accounting standards that require high quality, transparent and comparable information in financial statements and other financial reporting to help participants in the world's capital markets and other users make economic decisions. The second is to promote the use and rigorous application of those standards. The third is to bring about convergence of national accounting standards and International Accounting Standards to high quality solutions.

There are 14 Board members, each with one vote. The Trustees appoint the Board members. The IASC Foundation Constitution provides that the Trustees shall elect members of the IASB so that it will comprise a group of people representing, within that group, the best available combination of technical skills and background experience of relevant international business and market conditions in order to contribute to the development of high quality, global accounting standards.

As it develops International Financial Reporting Standards (IFRSs), the IASB follows a rigorous, open due process. IASB's has Due Process Handbook. The Handbook describes the consultative arrangements of the International Accounting Standards Board (IASB). It is based on the existing framework of the due process laid out in the Constitution of the International Accounting Standards Committee Foundation and the Preface to International Financial Reporting Standards issued by the IASB. It reflects the public consultation conducted by the IASB in 2004 and 2005.

The Trustees of the IASC Foundation have set up a committee-the Trustees' Procedures Committee-with the task of regularly reviewing and, if necessary, amending the procedures of due process in the light of experience and comments from the IASB and constituents. The Committee reviews proposed procedures for the IASB's due process on new projects and the composition of working groups and ensures that their membership reflects a diversity of views and expertise. The Trustees approved this Handbook on 23 March 2006, following two rounds of public consultations, review by the Standards Advisory Council, and public debate by the Trustees. Questions or comments regarding the IASB's Due Process should in the first instance be addressed to Director of Operations, IASC Foundation[1].

As of March 2005, 41 IASs and 6 IFRSs had been issued. A conceptual framework also has been created. Several IASs have been revised one or more times since original issuance.

6.2.3 IASB's harmonization or convergence effort

Since 2001, over 120 countries have required or permitted the use of IFRSs. Remaining major economies have time lines to converge with or adopt IFRSs in the near future.

Since financial crisis of 1998, both the IASB and the FASB have worked together to promote accounting harmonization. Now more than 100 countries adopted IASs or IFRSs to a different degree.

In October 2002, the FASB and IASB agreed on "Norwalk Agreement", where the two regulatory bodies committed to develop a set of high quality "compatible" standards. As we know the EU adopted the IFRS in 2004 and made IFRS compulsory for the consolidated accounts of listed companies as of 2005, The convergence process did not produce a common set of "European" accounting standards across EU state members but rather the cohabitation between a set of "international" standards and a variety of "national" standards.

In February, 2006, the FASB and the IASB issued an A Roadmap for Convergence between IFRSs and US GAAP-2006-2008, and hope to build up a bridge for foreign registrants listing their shares in capital markets in the U.S.A. At the same

---

[1] Data comes from IASB official website.

year, the IASB and FASB signed up a "Memorandum of Understanding" (MoU) which enhanced their commitment from a "compatible" to a "common" set of high quality standards. The MoU, which constituted a definite step forward in the convergence process, listed 11 topics that were deemed critical to convergence: business combinations, consolidation, fair value measurement guidance, liabilities and equities distinction, performance reporting, post-retirement benefits, derecognition, financial instruments, revenue recognition, intangible assets, and leases.

In 2007, the Securities and Exchange Commission (SEC) removed the reconciliation requirement for non U.S. companies reporting under IAS/IFRS in order to register in the U.S. The SEC granted operations of IAS/IFRS in the U.S., even if only for non-U.S. companies.

In September 2008, the IASB and the FASB issued an updated memorandum called Completing the February 2006 Memorandum of Understanding: A Progress Report and Timetable for Completion. The memorandum detailed convergence items for IFRSs and U.S GAAP. At the peak of the current financial crisis, the IASB and the FASB updated the MoU of 2006. In the new document, the two regulatory bodies reaffirmed the list of 11 fundamental topics that would lead to accounting convergence and stated 2011 as deadline.

In November 2009, the IASB and FASB issued a Joint Statement that restated the convergence process and confirmed 2011 as a deadline. The Joint Statement comprised a detailed status of the convergence process and identified two particularly controversial topics (i) accounting for financial instruments, and (ii) derecognition of assets and liabilities[1].

On 15 June 2011, the IASB and the FASB agreed to re-expose their revised proposals for a common revenue recognition standard. Re-exposing the revised proposals will provide interested parties with an opportunity to comment on revisions the boards have undertaken since the publication of an exposure draft on revenue recognition in June 2010[2].

On 13 June 2012, the IASB and the FASB agreed on an approach for accounting for lease expenses as part of a project to revise lease accounting in International Financial Reporting Standards (IFRSs) and the U.S. Generally Accepted Accounting Principles (U.S. GAAP). The boards undertook the leases project to address the widespread concern that many lease obligations currently are not recorded on the balance sheet and that the current accounting for lease transactions does not represent the economics of all lease transaction. Decisions on the leasing project reached to date

---

① Salvador Carmona, Marco Trombetta. The IASB and FASB Convergence Process and the Need for 'Concept-based' Accounting Teaching.
   http://bb.shufe.edu.cn/webapps/bb-silkIII-bb_bb60/case-foreign/case-foreign10.html
② Source comes from FASB official website.

are preliminary[1].

6.3 International Federation of Accountants (IFAC)

According to the Swiss Civil Code, International Federation of Accountants (IFAC) was created on October 7, 1977 in Munich, Germany, at the 11th World Congress of Accountants. At the first meeting of the IFAC Assembly and Council in October 1977, a 12-point work program[2] was developed to guide IFAC committees and staff through the first five years of activities. Many elements of this work program are still relevant today. The IFAC is to develop international standards of auditing, ethics, education, and training. IFAC has established a number of boards and committees to develop international standards and guidance and to focus on specific sectors of the profession.

In 1999, IFAC launched the International Forum on Accountancy Development (IFAD) in response to criticism from the World Bank that accounting profession was not doing well to increase accounting capacity and capabilities in emgering economy. The main aim of the forum is to promote transparent financial reporting, duly audited to high standards by a strong accounting and auditing profession.

As a global organization for the accountancy profession, IFAC's normal management institute is the International Congresses, organized by member who is selected by group member. It works with its 175 members and associates in 130 countries to protect the public interest by encouraging high quality practices by the world's accountants. IFAC members and associates, which are primarily national professional accountancy bodies, represent 2.84 million accountants employed in public practice, industry and commerce, government, and academia.

Through its independent standard-setting boards, IFAC develops international standards on ethics, auditing and assurance, education, and public sector accounting standards. It also issues guidance to support professional accountants in business, small and medium practices, and developing nations.

To serve the public interest, IFAC will continue to strengthen the worldwide accountancy profession and contribute to the development of strong international economies by establishing and promoting adherence to high-quality professional standards, facilitating the adoption and implementation of high-quality standards and guidance, furthering the international convergence of such standards and speaking out on public interest issues where the profession's expertise is most relevant.

---

[1] Source comes from IFRS official website.

[2] The 12-point work program was established at the inaugural meetings of the IFAC Assembly and of the Council in Munich, Germany in October 1977. These 12 points guided IFAC committees and staff through the first five years of operation. Many elements of this work program are still relevant today.

On 8 May 1997, a conference was held in Dominica. Through vote, CICPA got whole approval votes and became a normal member of IFAC. According to constitute of IFAC, CICPA also became a normal member of IASB.

6.4 International Organization of Securities Commissions (IOSCO)

Established in 1974, International Organization of Securities Commissions (IOSCO) was initially limited to providing a framework in which securities regulatory agencies in the America could exchange information and providing advice and assistance to those agencies supervising emerging markets. The International Organization of Securities Commissions (IOSCO) was transformed in 1983 from an inter-American regional association of securities regulators into an international body. In 1986, IOSCO opened its membership to regulatory agencies in other parts of the world, thus giving it the potential to become a truly international organization. Today, IOSCO is a leading organization for securities regulators around the world, with about 135 ordinary, associate, and affiliate members from about 100 countries (Doupnik and Perera, 2007). In 1995, China's Securities Regulatory Commission (CSRC) became the normal member of IOSCO.

IOSCO's aim is to ensure a better regulation of the markets on both the domestic and international levels, with providing assistance to guarantee integrity of markets. Another aim of IOSCO is to facilitate cross-board securities offering and listing by multinational issues. Thus, IOSCO advocate a set of high quality accounting standards for cross border listings. IOSCO's disclosure harmonization work is important because it has established a set of high quality disclosure standards, globally recognized, that serves as a model for nations around the world. Being the model, IOSCO develops national requirements for cross-border offerings and initial listings.

IOSCO has established two specialized working committees. One is called the Technical Committee while the other is called Emerging Markets Committee. The Technical Committee is made up of 15 agencies that regulate some of the world's larger, more developed and internationalized markets. The committee's goals are to review major regulatory issues related to international securities and futures transactions and to coordinate practical responses to these concerns. The second specialized committee, the Emerging Markets Committee, seeks to promote the development and improvement of efficiency of emerging securities markets.

The IOSCO principles report of June 2010 sets forth three objectives of securities regulation. These objectives include: protecting investors (including customers or other consumers of financial services); ensuring that markets are fair, efficient, and transparent; and reducing systemic risk. The 38 IOSCO principles are grouped into nine categories: regulators; self-regulation; securities regulation enforcement; cooperation in regulation; issuers; auditors, credit rating agencies, and other information providers; collective investment schemes; market intermediaries; and secondary markets. The first four relate to the organization, powers, and functioning of regulatory agencies (Karmel, 2012).

Although many agencies are involved in international harmonization of financial regulation, the IOSCO is the only organization specifically devoted to securities regulation. Also it is the only organization that includes all or virtually all of the world's securities commissions. IOSCO is devoted to establishing harmonized international standards for the regulation of securities issuances and trading, but because it includes both developed and emerging marketplaces in its constituency, it is able to formulate only very general standards for all of its members (Karmel, 2012).

6.5 European Union (EU)

6.5.1 EU directive

EU law is divided into primary and secondary legislation. The treaties (primary legislation) are the basis or ground rules for all EU action. Secondary legislation – which includes regulations, directives and decisions—are derived from the principles and objectives set out in the treaties .The EU's standard decision-making procedure is known as 'Ordinary Legislative Procedure' (ex "codecision"). This means that the directly elected European Parliament has to approve EU legislation together with the Council (the governments of the 28 EU countries)[1].

The EU attempted to harmonize company law and financial services through two main instruments. One is the Directives, which must be incorporated into the law of member states. The other is regulations, which become law throughout the EU without the need to pass through national legislatures. It is obvious that accounting harmonization in the EU is just one element of the overall project of harmonizing the legal and economic systems of the member states, and is part of the process of harmonizing company law. Among the Directives, the company law Directives of most relevance are the Fourth Seventh and Eighth.

The Fourth Directive, issued in 1978, illustrates the concept of harmonization, and specifies many accounting measurement and disclosure requirements. The Fourth Directive sets out valuation rules based upon historical cost but with alternative rules allowing current values. It also decrees that the true and fair view prevails over specific

---

① Data come from the following website: http://europa.eu/eu-law/decision-making/legal-acts/index_en.htm

provisions where circumstances justify it, and does so for footnote disclosures as well as for financial statements. Also, the Fourth Directive lists financial statement elements that must be stated in accordance with certain fundamental accounting concepts, including historical cost, going concern, prudence, accrual accounting, and consistency. It requires certain specific practices and alternatives dealing with such topics as incorporate investments, intangible assets and inventories.

The Seventh Directive, issued in 1983, addresses consolidated financial statements. It requires consolidation where either the parent or a subsidiary is a limited liability company. The principle of legal power of control determines the consolidation obligation. The Seventh Directive also sets out the conditions allowing exclusion from the consolidation obligation.

The Eighth Directive, issued in 1984, addresses various aspects of the qualifications of professionals authorized to carry out legally required (statutory) audits, and essentially sets out minimum standards. The Eighth Directive was amended in 2006, and is referred to as the Statutory Audit Directive. The Eighth Directive includes requirements for the appointment and removal of auditors, audit standards, continuing professional education, auditor rotation and public oversight (Choi and Meek, 2011).

The Fourth and Seventh Directives were incomplete and essentially remained as they were issued. Improvements to them proved difficult to achieve and the directives did not achieve the comparability expected. However, the Fourth and Seventh Directives had a dramatic impact on financial reporting throughout the EU, bringing accounting in all the member states up to a good and reasonable uniform level. These Directives harmonized the presentation of the profit and loss accounting and balance sheet and added minimum supplementary information in the notes (Choi and Meek, 2011). The evaluation on EU harmonization has not reached a certain answer. Some saw a set of Europe-wide standards as an unnecessary redundancy given the emergence of comprehensive IFRS. Others saw U.SGAAP as a rival to IFRS. The EU cannot influence U.S GAAP, but can influence IFRS. By putting its weight behind the IASB, the EU could serve as a counterweight to U.S GAAP.

6.5.2 EU's standard-setting procedures

Accounting and auditing requirements have been established under EU company law directives. The EU company law directives are legal instruments. Member countries must implement EU directives; thus, all accounting and auditing standards in EU directives become legally enforceable. The EU comprises several key organizations that need to be understood in order to understand how EU directives come into being.

Briefly, the European Commission initiates EU policy and acts in the community's general interest. Commissioners are completely independent and may not seek or take instructions from governments or interest groups.

The Council of the European Commission is the EU's decision maker. Here, the member states legislate for the EU, deciding some matters by majority vote and others unanimously.

The European Parliament represents the EU's citizens. Its main functions are to enact legislation and to scrutinize and control the use of executive power. The Treaty of European Union of 1993 strengthened the European Parliament's responsibilities.

Only the Commission can propose new directives. Proposals typically undergo many drafts. Proposed directives are submitted to the Council of the European Commission, which first seeks opinions of the Economic and Social Committee and the European Parliament. Next, a working party set up by the Council discusses the proposal. Member countries typically are allowed several years to implement a new directive after its final adoption (Choi, and Meek, 2005).

Terms of the Chapter

advisory council 咨询委员会
approach 方法
applicability 适应性
capitalization 资本化
commentator 评论家
comparability 可比性
compatibility 互换性/相容性
consistency 一致性原则
consolidated financial statement 合并财务报表
consultative group 咨询组
contingency 或有事项
convergence 趋同
deferred income taxes 递延所得税
derivative 衍生品，期权
directive 指令(欧盟)
discontinued operation 非持续经营
draft 草案
economic efficiency 经济效益
European Union 欧盟
extraordinary operation 意外营运
federation 联合会
flexibility 弹性
financial instrument 财务工具

framework 框架
going concern 持续经营
harmonization 协调
hedging 套期保值
high-quality standard 高质量准则
impairment 损坏
industrialized country 工业化国家
interim financial report 中期财务报告
internationalization 国际化
International Accounting Standard Board (IASB) 国际会计准则理事会
International Accounting Standard Committee (IASC) 国际会计准则委员会
International Foundation of Accountant (IFAC) 国际会计师联合会
International Financial Reporting Standard (IFRS) 国际财务报告准则
International Organization of Securities Commission(IOSCO) 证券委员会国际组织
Interpretation Committee 解释委员会
inventory 存货
jurisdiction 司法权
lease 租赁
lessee 承租者
lessor 租赁者
mutual recognition 相互确认
option plan 期权计划
political agreement 政治协定
post balance sheet events 资产负债表后事项
provision 条款
prudence 稳健性
public interest 公共利益
reconciliation 调节
registrant 注册者
related party 关联方
replacement cost 重置成本
restructure 重构
securities 证券
segment report 分部报告
social security 社会保障
standardization 标准化
statutory rule 强制性规范
taxation 税收
transparent information 透明信息

trustee 受托人，基金会

True or False

1. Discrepancies in international measurement may produce accounting amounts that are vastly different even where financial transactions and position are identical.

2. Pressures for harmonization of international accounting are the means to achieve comparability.

3. Governments or other governmental agencies are not major participant groups influencing MNE information disclosure.

4. IASB was formed to deal with the information overload from MNEs.

5. IFAC is an international accounting organization, representing interest of international accountancy profession.

6. IFAC is responsible for international auditing standards.

7. In the European Union, among the Directives, the Fourth, Seventh and Eighth Directives are related closely to accounting.

8. International accounting firms are not active in application of international accounting standards.

9. In the United States, the SEC does not now require the reconciliation of IFRS financial statements to US GAAP but require completely use of US GAAP for foreign registrants.

10. IASs or IFRSs are required to apply by EU in preparing consolidated financial statement for publicly trades companies.

11. Recent years, harmonization or convergence between IASB and FASB developed very fast and SEC agree to apply IFRS or IAS in U.S capital markets.

12. The International Accounting Standards Board is an independent, privately-funded accounting standard-setter based in London, UK.

13. Critics do not doubt that international standards can be flexible enough to handle differences in national backgrounds, traditions, and economic environments.

14. IOSCO's aim is not to ensure a better regulation of the markets on both the domestic and international levels.

15. Accounting and auditing requirements have been established under EU company law directives.

Multiple Choice

1. Which of the following accurately reflects international harmonization?

   a. Harmonization is a process of increasing the comparability of accounting practices by setting limits on how much they can vary.

  b. Harmonization is a process of decreasing difference of national accounting.

  c. Harmonization is a process of standardization.

  d. Harmonization is to develop a set of international accounting standards worldwide.

2. As a result of the international accounting harmonization,

  a. global investors are now able to compare information, which comes from different countries.

  b. governments are better able to regulate and monitor activities of MNEs.

  c. different information needs between and within groups may lead to conflicting and diversified demands for information.

  d. more and more MNEs could raise capital in an international market.

3. Pressures for information disclosure comes mainly from

  a. increasing sophistication of information systems.

  b. the internationalization of capital markets

  c. more and more MNEs.

  d. the simplification of information.

4. As regard to information disclosure levels,

  a. disclosure in the Japan is among the highest.

  b. disclosure levels in the U.K ranks among the highest.

  c. French disclosure levels are the highest in the world.

  d. German disclosure levels are higher than that in the U.S.A.

5. Which of the following organization is more active in international accounting harmonization?

  a. The IASB.

  b. MNEs.

  c. The OECD.

  d. The SEC.

6. Which of the following organizations has been the most effective government organization at harmonizing accounting practices?

  a. The United Nations.

  b. The IFAC.

  c. The IASB.

  d. The European Union.

7. Which of the following is true concerning the impact of SEC on accounting?

  a. SEC represents government to provide issues for standard setting.

  b. SEC has been more effective at monitoring accounting practices than at setting accounting standards.

  c. SEC represents accounting profession.

d. SEC set accounting standards rather than regulating or monitoring markets.

8. The European Union differs from the Organization for Economic Cooperation and Development for accounting harmonization efforts in that

    a. the OECD represents primarily developing countries, whereas the EU represents developed countries.

    b. the EU has the force of law behind it, whereas the OECD can only recommend disclosure practices.

    c. the EU is involved only in disclosure, whereas the OECD is only interested in measurement.

    d. the OECD represents governments, whereas the EU represents the profession.

9. According to the Fourth Directive of the EU,

    a. the "true and fair view" concept are not required for EU members.

    b. accounting directives are not necessary to be included in national law.

    c. Consolidated financial statements is required for EU members.

    d. EU companies must now adopt more similar approaches to record, measure, and report accounting information for similar transaction.

10. According to the Fourth Directive of the EU,

    a. historical cost measurement must be used.

    b. current cost measurement must be used.

    c. accumulated amortization is considered a liability.

    d. valuation rules could be historical cost but with alternative rules following current cost.

11. According to the Seventh Directive of the EU,

    a. worldwide consolidation is required.

    b. companies are not required to consolidate domestic but required foreign subsidiaries.

    c. auditor is of certain qualification.

    d. the pooling of interest method cannot be used for accounting for affiliates.

12. Which of the following accurately reflects international accounting standards?

    a. International accounting standard is strategy of international firm to expand business.

    b. International standards are used as a result of either international or political agreement or voluntary compliance.

    c. International accounting standard is strategy of multinational enterprise to expand business.

    d. International standards are voluntary in nature.

Case Analysis

Case 6.1   Why Not Allow FASB and IASB Standards to Compete in the U.S.?

Ronald A. Dye and Shyam Sunder published their paper titled "Why Not Allow FASB and IASB Standards to Compete in the U.S.?" in Accounting Horizons, Vol. 15 No.3, September 2001, pp.257-271.

This paper discusses arguments for and against introducing competition into the accounting standard-setting process in the U.S. by allowing individual corporations to issue financial reports prepared in accordance with either FASB or IASB rules. The paper examines several arguments supporting the status quo, including (1) the FASB's experience and world leadership in making accounting rules; (2) the increased risk of a "race to the bottom" under regulatory competition; (3) the inability of most users of financial reports to understand the complex technical issues underlying accounting standards; (4) the possibility that lASs or IFRSs will be diluted to gain international acceptance, allowing additional opportunities for earnings management; (5) the risks of the IASB being deadlocked or captured by interests hostile to business; (6) the costs of experimentation in standard setting; and (7) economies from network externalities.

Arguments examined on the other side include how competition will (1) help meet the needs of globalized businesses; (2) increase the likelihood that the accounting standards will be efficient; (3) help protect standard setters from undue pressure from interest groups; (4) allow different standards to develop for different corporate clienteles; (5) allow corporations to send more informative signals by their choice of accounting standards; (6) protect corporations against capture of regulatory body by narrow interests; and (7) not affect network externalities at national or global scales.

Instruction: please read the paper carefully, and answer the following questions.

1. What are the authors try to convey to reader through the discussion?

2. What is the motivation for the discussion?

3. Do you agree to put "competition" into standards setting process? Why or why not?

4. How the authors explain their idea about the competition in standards setting process?

Case 6.2   IASB and US FASB Complete First Stage of Conceptual Framework

The following paragraph comes from the FASB website:

Norwalk, CT, September 28, 2010—The International Accounting Standards Board (IASB) and the US Financial Accounting Standards Board (FASB) today announced the completion of the first phase of their joint project to develop an improved conceptual framework for International Financial Reporting Standards (IFRSs) and US generally accepted accounting practices (GAAP).

The objective of the conceptual framework project is to create a sound foundation for future accounting standards that are principles-based, internally consistent and internationally converged. The new framework builds on existing IASB and FASB frameworks. The IASB has revised portions of its framework; while the FASB has issued 'Concepts Statement 8' to replace 'Concepts Statements 1 and 2'.

This first phase of the conceptual framework deals with the objective and qualitative characteristics of financial reporting. As part of the consultation process, the IASB and FASB jointly published a discussion paper and exposure draft that resulted in more than 320 responses.

A feedback statement providing an overview of how the IASB responded to comments received through the consultation process is available for download. An IASB webcast introducing this first phase of the conceptual framework project will be held at 10am London time on Thursday 30 September, and repeated for the convenience of interested parties in different time zones at 3pm London time on the same day.

An IASB podcast summary of the project is available for download in individual mp3 files or from iTunes. On Friday 1 October, a podcast will be posted by the FASB on www.fasb.org that will examine and explain the purpose of a concepts statement.

Instruction:

1. Please go the FASB and IASB website and find the detailed cooperation work between IASB and FASB, and describe its development until today.

2. What is the Conceptual Framework? How is it important for standards setting and enforcement?

3. What is the similarity and difference of Conceptual Framework between the IASB and FASB? What looks like for future Conceptual Framework after convergence?

4. What is principles-based accounting standards? How do the FASB and IASB make convergence progress when U.S.GAAP is rule-based, and IASs or IFRSs are principles-based?

5. Try to forecast the future convergence progress for IASB and FASB.

Chapter 7   Foreign Currency Translation

Learning objective

After careful study of this chapter, students will be able to:

1. Describe the definition of translation and its reason.

2. Explain the current and noncurrent method.

3. Explain the monetary and nonmonetary method.

4. Explain the current rate method.

5. Explain the temporal method.

6. Compare and contrast four translation methods.

7. Explain the way to deal with translation gain or loss.

8. Depict the features of FASB 52.

9. Distinguish foreign currency conversion from translation.

10. Illustrate how companies account for foreign exchange.

11. Describe the requirements of applicable International Financial Reporting Standards (IFRSs).

12. Highlight translation procedures used internationally.

7.1 Translation and Its Reasons

Today in global business environment, many companies operate in foreign countries with subsidiary or branch office. Most operations located in foreign countries keep their accounting records and prepare financial statements in the local currency using local accounting principles. Then, how to deal with these different operations located worldwide in terms of consolidated financial statements involved into translation.

There are two translation definitions. One is that translation is a process of restatement. The local (functional) currency is kept as the unit of measure; that is, the translation process multiplies the financial results and relationships in the local currency accounts by a constant, the current rate. The other is that translation is a process of re-measurement. Re-measurement translates local currency results as if the underlying transactions had taken place in the reporting (functional) currency of the parent company. For example, it changes the unit of measure of a foreign subsidiary from its local (foreign) currency to the U.S. dollar.

Translation presents problems as exchange rates are not fixed. The fact that exchange rates are not fixed creates two problems for the accountant. The first problem concerns what is the appropriate rate to use when translating an asset or liability denominated in a foreign currency. Selection of exchange rates concerns the value to be placed on asset or liabilities of a company. This affects not only the balance sheet but also the calculation of income. The second involves how to account for translation gain or loss when exchange rates change. This problem is largely concerned with presentation. In other words, the problem shows how the gain or loss should be described, and where should be placed in the financial statement. The treatment to be accorded to the loss or gain in the financial statements will affect many important accounting variables such as net profit and earnings per share (Nobes and Parker, 2010) .

There are many reasons for translation. The first reason comes from need of consolidated financial statement. To prepare consolidated financial statements, parent companies must restate their foreign subsidiaries' financial statement in terms of the parent's reporting currency. If all subsidiaries use the same currency measurement, it is not necessary for a company to translate. Therefore, foreign currency translation is needed whenever to prepare consolidated financial statements. The second is to record foreign currency transactions. The translation of transaction concerns essentially the treatment of foreign currency transactions in the books of account and the financial statements of the individual company. The third is to measure a firm's exposure to the effects of currency gyrations. As exchange rate is not fixed, firm's exposure to the effects of currency gyrations is certain. Under different translation methods, measurement of exposure is different. The fourth is to communicate with foreign audiences of interest, when companies list their shares on a foreign stock exchange. For company wanted to raise capital in international market, translation is needed for it to communicate with foreign investors. The last one is to contemplate a foreign acquisition or joint venture. With the globalization, more and more company experience merger or acquisition, even joint venture, then translation would become a regular assistance to help both sides to achieve their goals.

7.2 Translation of Transactions vs. Translation of Financial Statement

Translation of transactions refers to the recording of transactions denominated in foreign currency in the books of account of an individual company, and the subsequent preparation of the financial statements of that company from these books of account. Before a transaction that is denominated in a foreign currency could be recorded in the books of account, it must be translated at first (Nobes and Parker, 2010).

Translation of financial statements refers to the preparation of the consolidated financial statements of a group of companies, where the financial statements of the parent company and those of one or more of its subsidiaries are not denominated in the same currency. Problem of translation of financial statements occurs when a parent company owns an interest in an entity, which keeps its books of account and draws up its financial statements in a foreign currency. Usually the business entity is located in a foreign currency and operates there. When the foreign currency financial statements are incorporated into the consolidated financial statements at the end of period, there exist problem of translation (Nobes and Parker, 2010).

In addition, there are differences between translation and conversion. With conversion, the asset is actually changed from one currency to another, as when dollars are exchanged for pounds in a bureau de change. With translation, the asset remains unchanged. The dollar bill itself remains the same, while the basis of measurement is changed (Nobes and Parker, 2010). Translation involves the bookkeeping while conversion will deal with practical currency change.

7.3 Selecting Foreign Currency Rate

There are three exchange rates that could be used to translate foreign currency balances to domestic currency. They are current rate, historical rate and average rate respectively. The current rate is the exchange rate at the company's fiscal year end. It is sometimes called the year-end or closing rate. The historical rate is the exchange rate at the time of the underlying transaction. The average rate is the average of various exchange rates during a fiscal period. Since the average rate normally is used to translate income statement items, it is often weighted to reflect any seasonal changes in the volume of transactions during the period.

Translation gains and losses do not occur if exchange rates do not change. However, if exchange rates change, the use of current and average rates causes translation gains and losses. These do not occur when the historical rate is used because the same (constant) rate is used for each period.

Using historical as opposed to current rates of exchange as foreign currency translation coefficients will affect presentation of financial statements. Historical exchange rates generally preserve the original cost equivalent of a foreign currency item in the domestic currency statements. The use of historical exchange rates would shield financial statements from foreign currency translation gain or loss. Under the historical exchange rate, there is no increase or decreases in the dollar equivalents of foreign currency balances due to fluctuations in the translation rate between reporting periods. However, the use of current rates may cause translation gains or losses. When the current exchange rate is different from the historical rate, a translation difference arises, which is generally taken as a gain or loss in the income statement.

Translation gains and losses definitely differ from transaction gains and losses. Both of which fall under the label exchange gains or losses. Foreign currency transactions occur whenever an enterprise purchases or sells goods for which payment is made in a foreign currency or when it borrows or lends foreign currency. Translation is necessary to maintain the accounting records in the currency of the reporting enterprise.

7.4 Translation Methods

There are four translation methods, which are current-noncurrent, monetary-nonmonetary, temporal and current rate method. Among the four methods, current rate method is called the single rate method while other three methods are called multiple rate methods. Under the single exchange rate, the current rate is used to translate all foreign currency assets and liabilities. Under the multiple rate methods, current and historical rates or some combination are used to translate foreign currency balances. The current rate method introduces multiple units of measure into a calculation that requires a single unit of measure. However, the temporal and current rate methods typify the flaws in translation (Paul, 1987).

7.4.1 Current-noncurrent method

Current-noncurrent method is the first method for translation practice around the world. This method was generally accepted in the United States from the early 1930s until FASB Statement No.8 was issued in October 1975. In December 1939, the CAP (Committee on Accounting Procedure) issued Foreign Operations and Foreign Exchange, which regulated current-noncurrent method as the generally accepted principle. Although it is predominant method, the method has been unacceptable in the United States since 1975. Furthermore, the method has never been allowed under International Financial Reporting Standards, and is seldom used in other countries (Doupnik and Perera, 2007).

The rules for the current-noncurrent method are as follows. For current asset and liabilities, current exchange rate is used for translation. For noncurrent asset and liabilities, and stockholders' equity, historical exchange rate is used. Retailed earning is calculated according to balance sheet equality relationship.

Under the current-noncurrent method, revenues and expenses(excluding depreciation and amortization) are translated at average rates. Depreciation and amortization charge are translated at historical rates in effect when related assets are acquired.

However, there is no theoretical basis underlying this method. The current-noncurrent method is based on the assumption that accounts should be grouped according to maturity. Anything due to mature in one year or less or within the normal business cycle should be translated at the current rate, whereas everything else should be carried at the rate in effect when the translation was originally recorded (Radebaugh, Gray and Black, 2007).

7.4.2 Monetary–nonmonetary method

To remedy the lack of theoretical justification for the current-noncurrent method, Hepworth (Samuel R.Hepworth) advised the monetary-nonmonetary method in his book "presentation for foreign operation" in 1956. Later APB (Accounting Principle Board) recommended the method in its Opinion No.6. Under monetary-nonmonetary method, monetary assets and liabilities accounts are translated at current exchange rate, while nonmonetary assets, liabilities and stockholders' equity accounts are translated at historical exchange rate. Monetary assets are those assets whose value does not fluctuate over time-primarily cash and receivables. Nonmonetary assets are those whose monetary value can fluctuate. They mainly consist of marketable securities, inventory, prepaid expenses, investments, fixed assets, and intangible assets. Monetary liabilities are those whose monetary value cannot fluctuate over time, which is true for most payables (Doupnik and Perera, 2007).

Under the monetary-nonmonetary method, for income statements accounts, translation way is the same as that in current-noncurrent method.

Under the monetary-nonmonetary method, the assumption is that monetary or financial assets and liabilities have similar attributes in that their value represents a fixed amount of money whose reporting currency equivalent changes each time the exchange rate changes. Monetary accounts should therefore be translated at the current exchange rate. In the current-noncurrent method, some current assets are monetary and others are nonmonetary, and yet all are translated at the current exchange rate. The proponents of the monetary-nonmonetary method consider it more meaningful to translate assets and liabilities on the basis of attributes instead of time (Radebaugh, Gray and Black, 2007).

7.4.3 Temporal method

In 1971, a researcher named Leonard Lorensen advised the temporal method in his book "Using dollar to present foreign operation for U.S company". Temporal method was originally proposed in Accounting Research Study 12 by the AICPA and formally required in Statement No.8. Foreign currency translation has been one of the most frequently discussed accounting issues. The Financial Accounting Standards Board (FASB) attempted to resolve this problem in 1975 with the issuance of Statement of Financial Accounting Standards (SFAS) No. 8, (Accounting for the Translation of Foreign Currency Transactions and Foreign Currency Financial Statements). The first objective of the temporal method is to change information stated in the kind of money in which the domestic money financial statements of a foreign operation are stated to information stated in the kind of money in which the consolidated financial statements are stated. The second of the temporal method is to present information on a foreign operation in consolidated financial statements the same as would have been presented had it been measured originally in the money in which those statements are stated. The third objective of the temporal method is to retain in the consolidated financial statements the accounting bases in the domestic money financial statements. The fourth objective is to derive consolidated financial statements that reflect one perspective—that of the users of the consolidated statements (Paul, 1987).

Under the Temporal method, monetary assets and liabilities are translated at the current exchange rate. Nonmonetary items are translated at rates that preserve their original measurement bases. Foreign currency balances carried at historical cost are translated at historical rates. Foreign currency balances carried at current cost or market value are translated at the current rate (Radebaugh, Gray and Black, 2007).

Under the temporal method, revenues and expenses, including cost of sales if inventories are carried at market, at average rates. Depreciation, amortization charges, and cost of sales when inventories are carried at cost, at historical rates in effect when related assets are acquired.

The attractiveness of the temporal method lies in its theory. The branches and subsidiaries of a parent company would be translated into the parent currency in such a way that the parent currency would be the single unit of measures. Another attractiveness of the method is its flexibility. If a company's measurement changes from historical cost accounting to current value accounting, its assets and liabilities will be translated at current exchange rate. SFAS No.8 presents the beneficial and detrimental effects of a change in a foreign exchange rate in different income statements. The managements that had to apply the method justifiably complained that keeping score that way was unfair to them and misled financial statements users (Paul, 1987).

7.4.4 Current rate method

The first objective of the current method is to produce amounts that all conform with generally accepted accounting principles; for example, inventories should be stated at the low of acquisition cost and market after translation. The second objective of the current method is to retain in the consolidated financial statements the results and relationships in the domestic money financial statements of the foreign operation. The third objective is to produce information that is compatible with the expected effects on the parent company's cash flows and equity of the change in the foreign exchange rate between the money the foreign operation uses and the money in which consolidated financial statements are stated.

Under the current rate method, for balance sheet items, all assets and liabilities are translated at current exchange rate. Capital stock is translated at historical rate, and retained earning is calculated by balance sheet relationship.

Under the current (single) rate method, for income statement items, all revenues and expenses are translated by an appropriately weighted average of current exchange rates for the period. Foreign currency revenues and expenses are generally translated at exchange rate prevailing when these items are recognized.

Current rate method is the easiest way to apply. Under the method, the fundamental concept is that a parent's entire investment in a foreign operation is exposed to foreign exchange risk and translation of the foreign operation's financial statements should reflect this risk. Moreover, the current rate approach results in translated statements that retain the same ratios and relationships that exist in the local currency.

7.4.5 Compare and contrast the features of four methods

Each method has its advantages and disadvantages. Under the current-noncurrent method, there are two advantages. First of all, some distortions in translated gross margins are reduced as inventories are translated at the current rate. Secondly, reported earnings are shielded from the distorting effects of currency fluctuations as excess translation gains are deferred and used to offset future translation losses. Still the method has some limitations. Using balance sheet classification as basis for translation has no theory support. Assuming that all current assets are exposed to exchange risk regardless of their form and long-term debt is sheltered from exchange rate risk does not conform to practical situation.

Under the monetary-nonmonetary method, translation result reflects changes in domestic currency equivalent of long-term debt on a timely basis. However, assuming that only monetary assets and liabilities are subject to exchange rate risk does not conform with practical situation. Exchange rate changes distort profit margins as sales transacted at current prices are matched against cost of sales measured at historical prices. Furthermore, using balance sheet classification as basis for translation has no theory to support. Nonmonetary items stated at current market values but translated at historical rates seem to make little sense.

Under the temporal method, the most attractiveness is theoretically valid, that is, compatible with any accounting measurement method. The method has the effect of translating foreign subsidiaries operations as if they were originally transacted in the home currency, which is desirable for foreign operations that are extensions of the parent's activities. However, a company could increase its earnings volatility by recognizing translation gains and losses currently. Some managers do not like the method while others have interest in it because the method could be used to smooth income. In addition, under the temporal method, a loss is reported when a change in a foreign exchange rate has a beneficial effect (Paul, 1987). Besides, the objectives of the temporal method are unhelpful as objectives of accounting for foreign operations, because they require the information to incorporate accounting for domestic operations. They are also unneeded. Information on foreign operations should be measured directly in the reporting money of the consolidated financial statements. Only one of the temporal methods, which is to derive consolidated financial statements that reflect one perspective, is helpful for accounting for foreign operations (Paul, 1987).

Under the current rate method, there are two advantages. Firstly, initial relationships in the foreign currency statements have been retained. Secondly, it is simple to apply. However, the method violates the basic purpose of consolidation, which is to present the results of a parent and its subsidiaries as if they were a single entity and is inconsistent with historical cost. The method presumes that all local assets and liabilities are subject to exchange risk. The assumption does not conform to actual situation. While stockholders' equity adjustments shield an MNE's bottom line from translation gains and losses, such adjustments could distort certain financial ratios and be confusing (Choi, Frost and Meek, 2002). In addition, the current rate method violates the rule of arithmetic that, to get an answer that means something more than just a number, all the numbers to be added or subtracted must have the same unit of measure. Furthermore, the current rate method's flaw is that it introduces multiple units of measure (multiple perspectives) into a calculation that requires a single unit of measure (a single perspective). Also some of the objective is unhelpful because they require presenting foreign operations incorporating accounting for domestic operations (Paul, 1987).

There is probably no one translation method that is appropriate for all circumstances in which translations occur and for all purposes that translation serves. As circumstance differ widely and translation purposes vary from case to case. It is probably more fruitful to identify circumstances in which they think one translation method is more appropriate than another.

7.5 Translation Gain or Loss

Translation adjustments arise when US multinational firms restate their foreign domiciled assets and liabilities, denominated in local currency units, into dollar equivalents at the balance sheet data. The translation adjustment itself is a function of the net foreign assets controlled by a firm and the change in the exchange rate from the prior balance sheet data. However, this accounting measure of exchange rate exposure may not adequately reflect the true, economic exposure to exchange rate movements at the firm level (Pinto, 2006).

Translation adjustment could be put into income statement or balance sheet, depending on standard requirement. There are several ways to deal with translation gain or loss. Deferral means the exclusion of translation adjustment in current income. Deferral of translation gain or loss is generally advocated because the adjustments merely result from a restatement process. Under the deferral approach, translation gain or loss should be accumulated separately as a part of consolidated equity in balance sheet. Deferral way may be opposed on the grounds that exchange rates may not reverse themselves.

Deferral and amortization approach refer to deferring translation gain or loss and amortizing these adjustments over the life of related balance sheet items. Such approaches can be criticized on theoretical and practical grounds.

Partial deferral is to recognize losses as soon as it occurs, but to recognize gains only as it is realized. Although the partial deferral gives conservative results, deferring a translation gain denies that a rate change has occurred, and is logically inconsistent. In practice, the method could result in "washing out" translation gain or loss in the long run. This approach also lacks any explicit criteria to determine when to recognize a translation gain.

No deferral means the translation gain or loss is put into income statement immediately. However including translation gains and losses in current income introduces a random element to earning that could result in significant earning fluctuations whenever exchange rates change. No deferral also could mislead information users as translation adjustment increases or decreases net income amount (Choi, and Meek, 2005).

7.6 Translation Accounting Development and U.S.A Standards No.52

7.6.1 International accounting standards

In July 1983, Accounting for the Effects of Changes in Foreign Exchange Rates (IAS 21) was issued by the International Accounting Standards Committee. The standard was later revised in 1993 as part of the comparability of financial statements project, with an effective date of January 1, 1995. It was revised again in 2003 as part of the convergence project with an effective date of January 1, 2005.

IAS 21 contains provisions for both transactions and translations of financial statements. The closing rate and temporal method are used depending on the operating characteristics of the foreign operations. If the foreign operations are integral to the operations of the reporting enterprise, the temporal method is used. If the foreign operations are considered to be a foreign entity, the closing rate is used.

7.6.2 Translation accounting development and U.S.A Standard No.52

Before 1965, current-noncurrent method was used. The related regulation was Accounting Research Bulletin (ARB) No.4, later was Chapter 12 of ARB No.43. Under the regulation, net translation losses were recognized in current income, while net translation gains were deferred in a balance sheet suspense account and used to offset translation losses in future period. In 1965, Accounting Principle Board (APB) issued Opinion No.6. Translating all foreign currency payables and receivables at the current rate was allowed.

In 1975, the SFAS No.8 was issued. The temporal method was required. Translation gains and losses had to be recognized in income during the period of the rate change. Reaction to the SFAS No.8 was mixed. This pronouncement required that monetary items and items carried at current money prices be translated al the current rate, that nonmonetary items be translated at the historic rate, and that the exchange gains and losses produced by the translation process be reflected in earnings. Changes in foreign currency exchange rates caused significant fluctuations in companies' earnings, especially interim earnings, and the accounting rules were widely criticized as a poor mirror of corporate economic performance. In May 1978, the FASB invited public comment on its first twelve pronouncements. A major weakness, according to Ruland and Doupnik (1988), was that a temporal rate method failed to reliably measure foreign currency translation gains and losses. Similarly, FASB believed that SFAS No. 8 produced results that did not reflect the underlying economic reality of many foreign operations [FASB, 1981, SFAS No. 52, paragraph 63]. This failure was evident in two respects: the volatility of reported earnings and the abnormality of financial results and relationships (Stephen and Brian, 1996).

Due to the adverse reaction to SFAS No. 8, after over 200 letters received related to SFAS No.8, the FASB issued SFAS No. 52 (Foreign Currency Translation) in December 1981. Under the new rules, the translation adjustments of many foreign entities are made directly to stockholders' equity on the balance sheet instead of being included in income (Benjamin, Grossman and Wiggins, 1986).

In contrast to SFAS No. 8, SFAS No. 52 requires that, "All (emphasis added) elements of financial statements be restated using a current exchange rate...If an entity's functional currency is a foreign currency, translation adjustments result from the process of translating the entity's financial statements into the reporting currency. Any resulting translation adjustment should not (emphasis added) be included in determining net income but shall be reported separately and accumulated in a separate component of equity" [FASB, 1981, paragraphs 12, 13] (Stephen and Brian, 1996).

The objective of translation under SFAS No.52 differs substantially from those of SFAS No.8. SFAS No.52 introduces a concept of functional currency. Its rule is to reflect, in consolidated statements, the financial results and relationships measured in the primary currency in which each consolidated entity does business (its functional currency), to provide information that is generally compatible with the expected economic effects of an exchange rate change on an enterprise's cash flows and equity. That is, the translation procedures required by SFAS No. 52 are designed to reliably measure the economic effect of exchange rate changes across a broad range of business conditions.

Under the SFAS No. 52, a company must identify the functional currency of the foreign operations. Functional currency is defined in SFAS No. 52 as the currency of the primary economic environment in which the entity operates, which is normally the currency in which an entity primarily generates and expends cash. It is commonly the local currency of the country in which the foreign entity operates. It may, however, be the parent's currency if the foreign operation is an integral component of the parent's operations, or it may be another currency (Susan and Donald, 2008). For example, the functional currency of a U.S. subsidiary doing business in Germany would be the German Mark. If the functional currency of the subsidiary is different than the currency of the U.S. parent (i.e., the reporting currency), translation from subsidiary to parent must be performed in accordance with SFAS No. 52 (Stephen and Brian, 1996).

Under the SFAS No. 52, when the parent currency is functional, foreign currency financial statements should be remeasured to reporting currency using the temporal method. Translation gains and losses resulting from the translation process are included in current income. When the local currency is functional, foreign currency financial statements should be translated to reporting currency using the current rate method. Translation gains and losses would be disclosed as a separate component of consolidated equity.

Exhibit 7.1 Functional Currency Criteria

Economic factors	Circumstances favoring local currency as functional currency	Circumstances favoring parent currency as functional currency
Cash flows	Primarily in the local currency and do not impact parent's cash flow	Directly impact parent's cash flows and are currently remittable to the parent
Sale price	Largely irresponsive to exchange rate change and governed primarily by local competition	Responsive to change in exchange rates and determined by worldwide competition
Sales market	Largely in the host country and denominated in local currency	Largely in the parent country and denominated in parent currency
Expense	Incurred primarily in the local environment	Primarily related to productive factors imported from the parent company
Financing	Primarily denominated in local currency and serviced by local operations	Primarily from the parent or reliance on parent company to meet debt obligations
Intercompany transactions	Infrequent, not extensive	Frequent and extensive

Source: Financial Accounting Standards Board, Statement of Financial Accounting Standards No.52, Stanford, CT: FASB,1981. Appendix A.

7.6.3 Relationship between foreign currency translation and inflation

The external value of a country's currency is inversely related to its rate of inflation. IAS 21 permits restatement for local inflation prior to currency translation. FAS No.52 requires use of the parent currency as the functional currency for foreign operations located in hyperinflationary environments (i.e., countries where the cumulative rate of inflation exceeds 100% over a three-year period).

Under the SFAS No. 52, two different translation procedures are allowed, depending on the country's inflation rate. If the cumulative three-year inflation rate is less than 100 percent, then the functional currency is the local currency, and the current rate method (also known as the net investment approach) is employed. The current rate method translates all assets and liabilities using the current exchange rate. The current rate method is the basis for SFAS No. 52 (Stephen and Brian, 1996).

If the cumulative three-year inflation rate is greater than or equal to 100 percent, then according to SFAS No. 52, the functional currency is the reporting currency and the temporal rate method [SFAS No. 8, FASB, 1975] is the basis for translation. The temporal rate method applies two different exchange rates in the translation process. Monetary assets and liabilities (primarily accounts receivable and accounts payable) are translated at the current exchange rate. Nonmonetary items (primarily inventory and fixed assets), on the other hand, are translated at the historical exchange rate (Gray, 1994).

Terms of the Chapter

affiliated company 附属公司
attribute 计量属性
alternative translation rate 可选择折算率
amortization 摊销
average rate 平均汇率
credibility 可信赖性
conversion 转换
current exchange rate (closing rate) 现行汇率
current noncurrent method 流动非流动法
deferral 递延
depreciation expense 折旧费用

dividend remittance rate 股利汇款汇率

domestic currency equivalent 本国货币等值

exposure 暴露

foreign currency assets 外币资产

foreign subsidiary 外国子公司

foreign currency translation 外币折算

foreign currency transaction 外币交易

foreign exchange rate 外汇汇率

forward market 远期市场

forward exchange contract 远期合约

foreign operation 外国经营

fluctuating exchange rate 变动的汇率

foreign currency financial statement 外币财务报表

free market rate 自由市场汇率

functional currency 功能货币

gains and losses 利得和损失

hedging strategy 套期策略

historical exchange rate 历史汇率

home currency 本国货币

hyperinflation 恶性通货膨胀

inflation adjustment 通货膨胀调整

local currency 当地货币

monetary items 货币性项目

multiple rate method 多种汇率法

monetary-nonmonetary method 货币非货币法

multinational corporation (Multinational Enterprise, MNE) 跨国公司

nonmonetary items 非货币性项目

parent company 母公司

parent country 母公司所在国

profitability 赢利能力

preference rate 优先汇率

profit margins 毛利或边际利润

reporting currency 报告货币

restatement 重新表述

remeasurement 重新计量

replacement cost 重置成本

rationale 基本理论

settled transaction 已结算交易

settlement date　结算日
single rate method　单一汇率法
spot market　即期市场
swap market　互换市场
temporal method　时态法
translation adjustment　折算调整额
translation gain or loss　折算利得或者损失
unsettled transaction　未结算交易

Discussion Questions

1. Define the foreign currency translation. Why foreign currency translation is needed?

2. What is the difference between translation and conversion, please give an example.

3. What is foreign exchange rate and its types? Which exchange rates can be used to translate foreign currency balances to domestic currency?

4. What are the financial statement effects of using historical as opposed to current rates of exchange as foreign currency translation coefficients?

5. What is difference between translation gains or losses and transaction gains or losses?

6. There are four translation methods, what are they? How to translate balance sheet and income statement in each of the four methods?

7. To compare and contrast features of the major foreign currency translation methods introduced in this chapter.

8. Which translation method do you think is best? Why or why not?

9. How to deal with translation gain or loss under different methods?

10. Describe briefly the history of foreign currency translation.

11. Explain why the FASB issued the SFAS No.52.

12. What are the features of SFAS No. 52 comparing with SFAS No.8?

13. What is functional currency, and how to choose functional currency?

14. Describe the future development for foreign currency translation.

15. A trial balance consists of following accounts for a100 percent foreign-owned subsidiary. There are three exchange rates, which include current, historical and average rate, being used to translate these accounts. Which rates would be used if the U.S. dollar were the functional currency? Which rates would be applied if the local currency were the functional currency?

Exhibit 7.2 Balance sheet

	Translation Rate	
	Local Currency is Functional Currency	Dollar is Functional Currency
Cash		
Marketable securities (cost)		(Fixed income securities intended to be held to maturity)
Accounts receivable		
Note receivable		
Inventory (market)		
Equipment		
Building		
Land		
Accumulated depreciation		
Patent		
Trademark		
Prepaid expenses		
Goodwill		
Accounts payable		
Note payable		
Salary payable		
Interest payable		
Bonds payable		
Income taxes payable		
Deferred income taxes		
Common stock		
Premium on common stock		
Preferred stock		
Premium on preferred stock		
Retained Earnings		

Exhibit 7.3 Income statement

	Local Currency is Functional Currency	Dollar is Functional Currency
Sales		
Purchases		
Cost of Sales		
General and administrative expenses		
Selling expenses		
Interest expense		
Salary expense		
Utilities expense		
Depreciation		
Amortization of goodwill		
Income tax expense		
Inter-company interest expense		

Note: The original idea comes from Choi and Meek (2005).

True or False

1. No foreign exchange accounting problem or no translation adjustment arises as long as the transactions are denominated in domestic currency.

2. IAS 21 and SFAS 52 are similar in translation adjustment record, measurement and report.

3. The functional currency is the currency of the primary economic environment in which the company operates.

4. The local currency and the reporting currency are always the same, both of them do not change with each other.

5. The current rate method would most likely have a translation adjustment with translation adjustment putting into the balance sheet.

6. Remeasurement does not require the temporal rate method but require the current exchange rate.

7. In the current rate method the assets are translated at market on the balance sheet date.

8. Current exchange rate is current spot rate.

9. Temporal method is the best translation one among the four methods.

10. Current exchange rate could result in translation gain or loss while historical exchange rate could not generate translation gain or loss.

11. In Chinese regulation, only current rate method is allowed.

12. Under the SFAS No.52, if local currency is functional currency, the temporal method should be used to translate foreign financial statements.

13. Under the SFAS No.52, if current rate method is used, the translation gain or loss should be put into consolidated balance sheet as part of equity.

14. US SFAS No.52 is the best regulation around the world for translation of foreign operation.

15. No deferral means the translation gain or loss is put into income statement immediately.

Multiple Choice

1. The process by which one currency is changed into another is known as
   a. translation.
   b. conversion.
   c. restatement.
   d. remeasurement.

2. The process by which one currency is expressed or restated in terms of another is known as

  a. translation.

  b. conversion.

  c. mark-to-market.

  d. equity method.

3. Which of the following describe translating local currency results as if the underlying transactions had taken place in the reporting (functional) currency of the parent company?

  a. remeasurement.

  b. restatement.

  c. replacement cost.

  d. temporal method.

4. From the standpoint of the parent company, a foreign currency is

  a. the currency in which the foreign subsidiary prepares its financial statements.

  b. any currency other than the parent country currency.

  c. the currency of the primary economic environment in which the firm operates.

  d. the currency in the country where the foreign firm is operating.

5. The currency of the primary economic environment in which the firm operates is the

  a. functional currency.

  b. reporting currency.

  c. parent currency.

  d. base currency.

6. The currency in which the parent company prepares its financial statements is the

  a. functional currency.

  b. reporting currency.

  c. subsidiary country currency.

  d. base currency.

7. The currency of the country where the foreign company is operating is the

  a. reporting currency.

  b. parent currency.

  c. local currency.

  d. functional currency.

8. If a Japan-based company has a subsidiary in China, and the Chinese subsidiary imports components from Britain, the British pound would most likely be considered (from the standpoint of the Chinese subsidiary)

  a. the reporting currency.

b. a foreign currency.

c. the functional currency.

d. the historical currency.

9. The reporting currency is

a. the currency in which the parent company prepares its financial statements.

b. any currency other than the parent currency.

c. the currency of the primary economic environment in which the firm operates.

d. the currency in the country where the foreign subsidiary is operating.

10. The local currency is

a. the currency in which the parent company prepares its financial statements.

b. any currency other than the parent currency.

c. the currency of the primary economic environment in which the firm operates.

d. the currency of the country where the foreign firm is operating.

11. The translation method in which monetary assets and liabilities are translated at current exchange rates and nonmonetary assets, liabilities and owner's equity are translated at historical exchange rates is known as the

a. current-noncurrent method.

b. monetary-nonmonetary method.

c. temporal method.

d. current rate method.

12. If parent currency is the functional currency, foreign currency financial statements should be remeasured to reporting currency using

a. current rate.

b. monetary nonmonetary method.

c. current noncurrent method.

d. temporal method

13. Which of the following translation method is the best one?

a. current rate.

b. temporal method.

c. monetary nonmonetary method.

d. no best method.

14. When the local currency is functional, foreign currency financial statements should be translated to reporting currency using the current rate method. Translation gains and losses would be disclosed as a

a. part of profit.

b. component of asset.

c. separate component of consolidated equity.

d. part of net income.

Case Analysis

Case 7.1　Foreign currency translation

Sunny Corporation is a recently acquired U.S manufacturing subsidiary located on the outskirts of Shanghai. The company produces plastic and colorful toys. Its products are marketed principally in the Shanghai with sales invoiced in RMB and prices determined by competitive conditions in Shanghai. To produce toy needs a lot of direct materials such as polyethylene, methyl methacrylate, polyvinyl chloride and so on. Most expenses including labor, direct material, and other production costs happened locally, but a significant quantity of components and parts is now imported from the U.S. parent. As a subsidiary, Sunny raised capital or operational fund primarily from its parent.

Following presents comparative balance sheets for Sunny Corporation at December 31, 2013 and 2014 and a statement of income for the year ended December 31,2014. The statements conform with U.S. generally accepted accounting principles prior translation to dollars.

Exchange rate information and additional data are as follows.

① exchange rates:

December 31, 2013	$1=RMB 6.5
December 31, 2014	$1= RMB6.8
Average during 2014	$1= RMB6.25
Average during fourth quarter 2013	$1= RMB6.05
Average during fourth quarter 2014	$1= RMB6.65

② Common stock was acquired, long term debt issued, and original fixed assets purchased when the exchange rate was $1= RMB7.0

③ Exchange rate prevailing when the intangible asset (patent) was acquired and additional fixed assets purchased was $1= RMB6.85

④ Purchases and dividends occurred evenly during 2014.

⑤ Of the RMB 100 (million)　depreciation expense for 2014, RMB 60 relates to fixed assets purchased during 2014.

⑥ Inventory represents approximately 3 months of production.

⑦ If current rate method was used, the Cumulative Translation Adjustment was 480 at 31, Dec. 2013.

Instruction: Headquarters management in the U.S.A must decide on the functional currency for its Shanghai operation. Should it be the U.S dollar or the RMB? You are asked to advise management on the appropriate currency designation and prepare its translation of financial statement.

Exhibit 7.4   Comparative balance sheet Year ended 12/31/2013 or 2014

	2013	2014
Assets		
Cash	340	190
Marketable securities	2700	3000
Accounts receivable	3159	3339
Inventory (FIFO)	2300	2256
Office supply	100	105
Long term investment	2400	2400
Fixed assets	1500	1747
Accumulated depreciation	100	200
Intangible asset (patent)		300
Total	12399	13137
Liabilities and stockholder's equity		
Short term loan	450	429
Accounts payable	3300	2500
Salary payable	120	120
Income tax payable	55	89
Interest payable	12	39
Deferred income tax		250
Long term debt	162	600
Common stock	5000	5000
Retained earnings	3300	4110
Total	12399	13137

Note: monetary unit is RMB million.

Exhibit 7.5   Income statement Year ended 12/31/2014

Sale		1500
Cost of sales	992	
General and administrative expense	102	
Sale expense	105	
Interest expense	45	
Impairment loss	20	
Depreciation expense	100	
Transaction gain (loss)		76
Income tax	75	
Net income		137

Note: monetary unit is RMB million.

Chapter 8   Changing Prices Accounting

![Learning objective icon] *Learning objective*

After careful study of this chapter, students will be able to:

1. Describe the effect of historical cost measurement on financial position and operating results in a inflation environment.

2. Understand price changing and its measurement.

3. Explain two types of price change and their calculation of price level index.

4. Discuss the reasons to recognize inflation's effect on financial statements.

5. Understand the general price-level adjustment and its process.

6. Master the current cost adjustment and its process.

7. Argue the difference between general price level adjustment and current cost adjustment.

8. Discuss the international perspective on inflation accounting.

8.1 Pricing Changing

8.1.1 Price change

Inflation accounting theory is conventionally structured around two apparent needs. The first is the issue of maintaining capital, usually on either a proprietary or an entity basis. The second is the valuation of assets. Both issues themselves fundamentally revolve around the role of money as a representation of value. Money is assumed to be the phenomenal form of otherwise unknown value (Robson 1994).

Substantial and sustained inflation is bad because it amounts to throwing a monkey wrench into the intricate fabric of the economy, thus producing distortions and unsound relationships. There is a jarring impact on business decision making, the plans and actions of those engaged in the processes of production and distribution throughout the economic pipeline. Assuming that at a given moment a structure of workable relationships exists in the field of business enterprise, the introduction of a substantial change in the size of the economic measuring unit may be a seriously disturbing factor. A major change in the financial measuring unit may not possibly be dealt with immediately and fully, produces new strains, distortions, and uncertainties. Severe inflation distorts the financial reporting of business, giving the illusion of soaring profits when, in fact, real profits—profits stripped of their inflationary increments—have failed to keep pace with the rising costs of replacing buildings, machinery and equipment, maintaining inventories, and supporting research and development (Webster, Largay III, and Stickney,1980).Business owners and executives are well aware of the fact that they are subject to criticism and complaint in political circles, and in the public eye, and they tend to become hesitant and less effective in the face of dollar devaluation, with its pressure on the price structure (Paton, 1968). In other words, a management made cognizant of the impact of inflation on reported sales and income figures undoubtedly will begin to evaluate decisions related to products, customer selection, pricing, service, credit and accounts receivable, promotion, distribution, and inventory policies in the new light shed by these inflation adjusted figures (Webster, Largay III, and Stickney,1980).A material change in the monetary unit poses serious problems of financial measurement for business corporations and other business enterprises (Paton, 1968).

There are two ways to evaluate price changing. One is general price level change, which refers to a movement in the prices of all goods and services in an economy on average. Positive price movement is termed inflation, while a negative price movement is called deflation. The other is specific price change, which refers to the movement in the price of a specific asset. For example, there exists specific price change such as inventory, plant, or equipment and machine.

General price level changes are measured by the use of a general price level index (GPL). GPL is a cost ratio that compares the cost of a basket of goods in the current period with the cost of that same basket in a prior or base period. The reciprocal of the GPL is a measure of the general purchasing power of the monetary unit. Specific price changes are measured by a specific price index (SPL). SPL is a cost ratio that compares the cost of a specific item with its cost in a prior or base period. The object of accounting for specific price changes is to preserve a company's productive capacity or operating capability.

8.1.2 Effect of historical cost measurement in an inflation environment

Conventional financial statements report all activities in terms of the nominal number of dollars expensed at the time asset were acquired, or "acquisition cost." If there is inflation or deflation, historical cost accounting fails to recognize two important, but different, effects of inflation. First, no recognition is given to the fact that the dollar does not represent a constant, or stable, measuring unit over time. The second deficiency of historical cost accounting is that, prior to sale, no recognition is given to changes in the prices of the specific assets held by a firm. Whereas the concern with the stability of the measuring unit is with changes in the general purchasing power of the dollar, the concern in this second case is with changes in the specific prices of particular assets (Webster, Largay III, and Stickney,1980).

Effect of historical cost on performance data is great. During periods of inflation, revenues are based on the general purchasing power of the current period. Expenses, such as depreciation and amortization, may be based on currency of higher general purchasing power because their related assets were typically acquired in the past when GPLs were lower. Deducting expenses based on historical purchasing power from revenues that expressed in currency of current purchasing power yields a nonsensical index of performance. During a period of specific price changes, assets recorded at their original acquisition costs or historical cost seldom reflect the assets' current (higher) value resulting in an overstatement in reported income. In a period of rising prices, traditional accounting practice tends to overstate the profitability of most enterprises by understanding the current cost of replacing inventory items sold and plant and equipment used (Webster, Largay III, and Stickney,1980).

Persistent inflation causes firm profits to be overstated by traditional, generally accepted accounting principles. Large publicly held firms are now being required to disclose a combination of constant dollar and current replacement cost adjustments to historical cost accounting data. Corporate managements are likely to make increased use of inflation adjusted financial data in their decision making as these data become the generally accepted measures of performance used by investors and stockholders in evaluating management (Webster, Largay III, and Stickney,1980). This, in turn, may lead to higher taxes, dividends, wages and other expenses. Use of historical cost accounting for tax purpose may amount to de facto industrial policy during a period of rising prices, to the detriment of manufacturing firms with substantial investments in depreciable assets. Identification of reported earning in excess of taxable earnings as a tax preference seems unfair. From a managerial perspective, accounting numbers unadjusted for changing prices could distort financial projections, budget comparisons and performance data.

From a user's perspective, there is the inherent problem in attempting to analyze historical cost-based financial statements of a company domiciled in an inflationary, devaluation-prone country. Historical-based financial statements may be misleading during periods of significant inflation. Many resources may have been acquired in periods when the purchasing power of the monetary unit was much higher. These expenses then typically are deducted from revenues that reflect current purchasing power. The resulting income number is unintelligible and makes little sense.

Another problem for statement readers is that the value of assets recorded at their historical acquisition cost is typically understated as a result of inflation. Understated asset values produce understated expenses and overstated earnings. Thus, financial trends are also difficult to interpret, as trend statistics generally include monetary units of different purchasing power. A positive trend in sales may be due to price changes, not real increases in sales. A negative trend in income may be due to higher acquired assets or expenses (Choi, and Meek, 2005).

Reliance on historical cost accounting is potentially dangerous. Users of financial statements are forced to develop ad hoc corrections to infer value from historical cost. During period of accelerating inflation, firms that utilize historical cost accounting need to widen their profit margins, and during periods of decelerating inflation, such firms need to narrow their profit margins. Lags in the recognition of change in the rate of inflation mean that the use of historical cost accounting will result in mispricing.

In practice, it is important to examine financial analysis based on historical cost ratios. Although the biases in historical cost accounting are well known, it was not known until now the extent these biases differ across firms. Accordingly, it is not known if rankings based on historical cost ratios are reflective of rankings based on replacement cost ratios. Financial analysis of firms based on historical cost based ratios, may result in arbitrary and possibly incorrect decisions in loan approval, bond rating, and stock analysis (Thies and Sturrock, 1987).

8.1.3 Reasons to recognize inflation's effect

Choi, Frost and Meek (2002) mention several reasons for recognizing inflation's effect. They are as follows. Firstly, the effects of changing prices depend partially on the transactions and circumstances of an enterprise. Users do not have detailed information about these factors. Secondly, managing the problems caused by changing prices depends on an accurate understanding of the problems. An accurate understanding requires that business performance be reported in terms that allow for the effects of changing prices. Thirdly, statements by managers about the problems caused by changing prices are easier to believe when businesses publish financial information that addresses those problems.

Although it is generally conceded in principle that price level-adjusted financial statements are more useful than conventional accounting statements during periods of significant inflation, it is a judgment call to identify exactly when price level-adjusted statements become more meaningful. For different countries, there are different judgment criteria. As a rule of thumb, executives in Brazil use an inflation rate greater than 10 % per month. Investors in Germany or Switzerland may believe that 5 % inflation per year is alarming. Unfortunately, no one has yet developed a formal, rigorous, easy-to-apply definition of meaningfulness.

As regard to cost and benefit of inflation adjustment, to a great extent, it is hard to evaluate. While the costs to generate such information can be measured, it is much harder to quantify the benefits. Measurement of the benefits of price level-adjusted information must cover all user groups in an economy. Multiple user groups such as investors, creditors, government agency, tax agency and so on, uneven distributions of benefits (both within and between groups), and favorable economy-wide spillover effects of price level information complicate the task. Adding international dimensions makes the problem even worse.

Ways of inflation adjustment involve cost and/or purchasing power change. There exist ways such as historical cost-nominal dollar accounting, historical cost-constant dollar accounting, current cost-nominal dollar accounting and current cost-constant dollar accounting.

8.2 General Price–level Adjustment

There are two basic models for price changing adjustment. One is called the historical cost-constant dollar model. The other is called the current cost model. The historical cost-constant dollar model measures the impact of *general* price level changes on a firm's reported performance and financial position. The current cost model examines the impact of *specific* price changes on enterprise income and wealth. The two measurement frameworks are similar in that both attempt to clarify the distinction between capital and income. They differ in reporting objectives. Whereas the historical cost-constant dollar model attempts to preserve the general purchasing power of a firm's original money capital, the current cost model attempts to preserve an entity's physical capital or productive capacity.

The general philosophy supporting general purchasing power (GPP) accounting is to report assets, liabilities, revenues, and expenses in units of the same purchasing power. The approach is that measure of monetary item should be uniform while retaining the basis of measurement used in the financial statement.

Under the GPP, the nonfinancial items in the financial statements (inventory, plant, and equipment) are restated to reflect a common purchasing power, usually at the balance sheet date. For the year-end financial statements, the financial assets and liabilities including cash, receivables, payables would not be adjusted because they are already stated in terms of purchasing power in December 31, but all other assets (including inventory, plant, equipment, and machine), liabilities, revenues, and expenses (including depreciation) would be adjusted.

It has been suggested that GPP accounting should be applied to financial assets and liabilities as well. For example, cash will lose purchasing power during an inflationary period. Borrower will benefit during inflation while creditor will lose purchasing power. Therefore, a company that has increased its net financial asset position during an inflationary period suffers a loss in purchasing power while a company has increased its net financial liabilities position enjoys a gain in purchasing power. The GPP accounts would reflect this loss or gain in a separate monetary items adjustment (Radebaugh, Gray and Black, 2007).

Most useful piece of information generated by constant dollar accounting is the purchasing power gain or loss on monetary items. It provides a rough measure of the direct effect of inflation on the value of net monetary items owned or owed by firms (Webster, Largay III, and Stickney,1980).

8.3 Current Value Accounting

Compared with the general price adjustment, current value accounting is concerned with the rise or fall in the cost or value of specific assets, not with the overall loss of purchasing power of a currency. Under the cost value accounting, purchasing is kept constant while historical cost should be changed into current cost. Here, historical cost means the replacement cost , selling price,   net realizable value or fair market value. With the concept, income is not considered to be earned until the company has maintained its capital in current value terms. As the most widely accepted method, current cost accounting is used for more classes of nonmonetary assets. Under the method, assets are valued at what it would cost to replace them or would be sold.

Current cost value accounting results in holding gains and losses when nonmonetary assets are revalued. When company holds monetary items, there is no holding gains or losses under the current cost value accounting. The gains or losses could involve either being taken into the income statement or on the balance sheet as a capital adjustment account. The key issue for current value accounting is to determine current value. There is no doubt that current cost, especially in undeveloped market, is hard to determine. Thus, current value accounting is obviously more complex to administer because it requires a mixture of actual prices, estimates, appraisal values, and indices for homogeneous groups of assets.

8.4 International Perspective on Inflation Accounting

8.4.1 IAS

In November 1981, the IASC issued IAS No.15, "Information Reflecting the Effects of Changing prices."The IAS 15 recommends that large publicly traded company disclose effect of changing price using any method, typically in supplementary form. Disclosure includes the amount of the adjustment to, or the adjusted amount of, depreciation of property, plant and equipment, cost of sales, a financing adjustment, and results related to the adjustments.

In 1990, IAS 29, "Financial Reporting in Hyperinflationary Economies", was in effective and reorganized in 1994. It is the inflation accounting model required in International Financial Reporting Standards implemented in 174 countries. For a hyperinflationary environment, the IAS 29 requires that restatement of primary financial statement information. A company that reports in a currency of a hyperinflationary economy, whether based on historical or current cost accounting framework, should be reexpressed in terms of constant purchasing power as of the balance sheet date. Purchasing power gain or loss related to a net monetary liabilities or asset position are to be included in current income.

Under the IAS 29, if the cumulative inflation rate over three years is approaching, or exceeds, 100%, companies are required to restate their historical cost financial reports in terms of the period end hyperinflation rate in order to make these financial reports more meaningful. The restatement of historical cost financial statements does not signify the abolishment of the historical cost model. IAS 29 requires the implementation of financial capital maintenance in units of constant purchasing power in terms of the monthly published CPI. That requirement does not result in actual capital maintenance in units of constant purchasing power since that can only be achieved with following all changes in the general price level; i.e., at least daily changes.

8.4.2 The United States

In September, 1979, the FASB issued SFAS No.33, "Financial Reporting and Changing Prices," requires U.S company with inventories and property, plant, and equipment of more than $125 million, or total assets of more than $1 billion, to experiment for 5 years with disclosing both historical cost-constant purchasing power and current cost-constant purchasing power. The SFAS No.33 required supplemental disclosures of the effects of inflation on the financial statements of most large publicly held firms beginning with the 1979 annual reports (FASB 1979). Those 1979 annual reports leave little doubt that these changes in financial reporting requirements will have a direct impact on the management decision.

After issuance, many complaints appeared for SFAS No. 33 including dual disclosure, excessive cost, less usefulness of historical cost-constant purchasing power disclosure. Then FASB decided to encourage, but no longer require disclosing either historical cost-constant purchasing power or current cost-constant purchasing power information. FASB published guidelines (SFAS No. 89) to assist company to report for effects of changing prices. SFAS No. 89, Financial Reporting and Changing Prices, was issued in December 1986.

U.S SFAS No. 89 encourages but does not mandate the following disclosures for each of the five most recent years.

Exhibit 8.1   Items recommended disclosure by SFAS No. 89

Order NO.	Items
1	Net sales
2	Income from continuing operations on a current-cost basis
3	Monetary gains or losses on net monetary items
4	Increases or decreases in the current cost or lower recoverable amount of inventory or plant, property and equipment, net of inflation
5	Aggregate foreign currency translation adjustment, on a current cost basis
6	Net assets at year-end on a current cost basis
7	Earnings per share on a current cost basis
8	Dividends per share of common stock
9	Level of the Consumer Price Index used to measure income from continuing operations

For foreign operations, two following requirements were included in the consolidated statements. One is to translate foreign accounts to dollars, then restate for U.S. inflation, if the dollar is the functional currency. The other is to restate for foreign inflation, then translate to U.S. dollars if the local currency is functional.

8.4.3 The United Kingdom

In March 1980, the U.K Accounting Standards Committee (ASC) issued Statement of Standard Accounting Practice No.16 (SSAP No.16), "Current Cost Accounting," on a three-year experimental basis. In 1988, SSAP No.16 was withdrawn. However, its methodology is recommended for companies that voluntary produce inflation adjusted accounts.

In the U.K, the SSAP 16 recommends one of three reporting options, seeing Exhibit 8.2.

Exhibit 8.2   Three reporting options from SSAP 16

Order NO.	Options
1	Present current-cost accounts as the basic financial statements with supplementary historical cost accounts
2	Present historical-cost accounts as the basic statements with supplementary current-cost accounts
3	Present current-cost accounts as the only accounts accompanied by adequate historical-cost information

The foregoing options must include a monetary working capital adjustment that captures the monetary gains or losses from holding net monetary assets. This adjustment, however, employs specific price indexes as opposed to general price level indexes. Also required is a gearing adjustment that offsets inflation-adjusted cost of sales, depreciation, and the monetary working capital adjustment for monetary gains resulting from the use of debt.

When consolidating the accounts of subsidiaries located in inflationary environments, management should choose one of the following methods, based on a dividend discount valuation framework. The first method is to restate these accounts for foreign inflation, then translate to parent currency. The second method is to translate unadjusted accounts to parent currency, then restate for parent country inflation.

Exhibit 8.3   Methods for consolidating the accounts of subsidiaries located in inflationary environments

Order NO.	Items
1	Restate statements to be consolidated for specific price changes.
2	Translate to parent currency using the current rate
3	Use specific price indexes to calculate monetary gains and losses

8.4.4 Some comments

The current inflation is a worldwide problem, and accountants in a number of countries have been struggling with its consequences. Accountants in the United Kingdom and the United States have discussed the effect of inflation on financial statements since the early 1900s, beginning with index number theory and purchasing power. Irving Fisher's 1911 book *The Purchasing Power of Money* was used as a source by Henry W. Sweeney in his 1936 book *Stabilized Accounting*, which was about Constant Purchasing Power Accounting. During the Great Depression, some corporations restated their financial statements to reflect inflation. At times during the past 50 years, standard-setting organizations have encouraged companies to supplement cost-based financial statements with price-level adjusted statements[①].

In their response to the inflation of 1973-1974, there was general price level accounting. Because GPLA merely converted historical cost financial statements to a current dollar unit of measurement however, it failed to come to grips with the effects of inflation on specific corporate assets. The publication of Great Britain's Sandilands Report in September 1975 starts English-speaking countries down the road toward current value accounting, phase Two of inflation accounting history. In recommending current value accounting without monetary adjustments, the Sandilands Report failed to recognize the transfer of real purchasing power between lenders and borrowers caused by inflation. At the end of 1970s, English speaking countries seemed to enter Phase Three—a retreat away from full current value financial statements and toward limited supplementary disclosure. In British, the Hyde Committee has recommended income statement that charge depreciation and cost of sales on a current value basis, but contain a monetary adjustment by which companies can add back to current value profits purchasing power gain on their borrowings. In the United States, the SEC has restricted its current value requirements to supplementary reporting of replacement costs by companies with more than $100 million of fixed assets and inventory (Hale, 1978).

Studies have found little if any utilization of inflation accounting. In the earlier

---

① Data comes from the following website: https://en.wikipedia.org/wiki/Inflation_accounting.

surveys, a majority of respondents indicated that they would use inflation accounting if it were available. In more recent surveys, however, a majority of respondents have indicated that they did not use these available data. Rosenzweig (1985) found that 90 percent of respondents indicated that they seldom if ever used their inflation adjusted data, in a survey of controllers. In another survey of controllers, Govindarajan and Anthony (1983) found that 90 percent of respondents used historical costs rather than replacement cost in pricing. The lack of utilization of inflation accounting by preparers and users of financial statements may have been disappointing. The inflation induced biases of historical cost accounting tended to increase reported earnings and compensation under various incentive plans, both of which benefited incumbent managers. Another factor is that historical cost accounting is used for taxes, bankruptcy, and financial covenants. Finally, inflation accounting disclosures were not audited and were available only for large firms (Thies and Sturrock, 1987).

Terms of the Chapter

accounting for changing price 物价变动会计

budget 预算

comparability 可比性

continuing operation 持续经营

conventional accounting 传统会计

current cost adjustments 现行成本调整

current cost-nominal dollar accounting 现行成本名义购买力模式

current cost-constant dollar accounting 现行成本不变购买力模式

depletion 折耗

double dipping 双重舀取

financial information 财务信息

financial trend 财务趋势

foreign operation 外国经营

foreign currency translation adjustment 外币折算调整

gearing adjustment 资本搭配调整

general price level change 一般价格水平调整

general purchasing power equivalents 一般购买力等值

historical cost-constant dollar accounting 历史成本—不变购买力模式

historical cost measurement 历史成本计量

historical cost-nominal dollar accounting 历史成本—名义购买力模式

host government 东道国政府

holding gain or loss 持产利得或损益

hyperinflation 恶性通货膨胀

inflation adjustment 通货膨胀调整

inflation rate 通货膨胀率

monetary gain or loss 货币性项目的损益

monetary asset or liability 货币性资产或负债

mark up 加成

minority interest 少数股东权益

monetary items 货币性项目

monetary gain or loss 货币性利得或者损失

monetary unit 货币单位

monetary working capital adjustment 货币性营运资本调整

net realizable value 可实现净值

nominal amounts 名义货币

operating revenue 经营收入

operating performance 经营收益

overstatement 高估

overstated income 高估的盈余

performance 业绩

permanent asset 永久性资产

physical capital 实物资本

price index 价格指数

price level adjustment 价格水平调整

productive capacity 生产能力

purchasing power 购买力

replacement cost 重置成本

reported income 报告盈余

restate-translate method 重新表述—折算方法

specific price change 特殊价格变动

translate-restate method 折算—重新表述方法

unrealized gain or loss 未实现利得或损失

understatement 低估

Discussion Questions

1. Taking some examples to explain how price change affect the financial position and performance results.

2. Distinguish general price level index (GPL) and specific price index (SPL).

3. Where could we find the misleading financial statement if historical cost is used?

4. From a user's perspective, what is the inherent problem in analyzing historical cost-based financial statements when a company operated in an inflationary, or

devaluation-prone environment.

5. Explain the reasons for recognizing inflation's effect.

6. At what point do price-level-adjusted financial statements become more meaningful? Or at what point do price-level adjustment financial statements make no sense?

7. How does you evaluate the benefits and cost of price-level-adjusted accounting information?

8. Describe the historical cost-constant dollar model and its process.

9. Describe the current cost model and its process.

10. Distinguish the feature of historical cost-constant dollar model and current cost model.

11. Explain the nature of the current cost accounting experiments in the United States and the United Kingdom. Why did these experiments come to nothing?

12. Under what circumstances are companies likely to voluntarily disclose the impact of price changes and inflation? Under what circumstances is there necessary for a company to disclose inflation effect?

13. In China in recent years, there is a relatively high inflation. Yet no inflation accounting systems have been introduced. Should inflation accounting be required, and, if so, which approach would you recommend be used in China?

14. Explain briefly the history and development process of inflation accounting, then look ahead of inflation accounting in the future.

15. Inflation accounting has a popular practice around the world.

16. Current cost-nominal purchasing power model is better than historical cost-constant purchasing power model.

True or False

1. Mexico has had a hyperinflation problem, but has never used inflation accounting.

2. The effect of inflation can cause inefficient and misleading operation decisions by management.

3. General purchasing power accounting includes constant dollar accounting with historical cost.

4. Both cash and accounts receivables do not lose purchasing power during an inflationary period.

5. While current value accounting is applied, holding gains and losses occur when nonmonetary assets are revalued, but there is no holding gains and losses when monetary assets are revalued.

6. Current US GAAP requires SFAS No.33 to regulate inflation accounting.

7. For a hyperinflationary environment, the IAS 29 requires that restatement of primary financial statement information.

8. Replacement value accounting is well developed for many years in Netherlands.

9. In U.K, current company law requires a general indexation approach to restate historical costs in terms of current purchasing power at the balance sheet date.

10. Current UK GAAP does not require current value accounting reporting, and company could choose voluntary disclosure.

Multiple Choice

1. In high inflation economies financial assets are
   a. poor choices for MNEs to have on the balance sheet.
   b. good choices for MNEs to have on the balance sheet.
   c. prohibited by MNEs.
   d. restrictive for MNEs.
2. Inflation or price changes is
   a. only experienced in developing countries.
   b. only experienced in a country's recession.
   c. only experienced in developed countries.
   d. a worldwide phenomenon.
3. General purchasing power accounting
   a. is required for U.K. companies if the inflation rate exceeds 5 percent three years in a row.
   b. is designed to keep the same purchasing power for assets and liabilities.
   c. is not permitted by the IAS 29.
   d. is not permitted by the SFAS 89.
4. Current value accounting
   a. assumes that the prices of specific assets have not changed.
   b. assumes that the prices of specific assets have changed.
   c. assumes that the purchasing power of money go down.
   d. assumes that the purchasing power of money fluctuate.
5. Assume that Cloth Corporation purchases equipment with acquired cost of $200,000 in 2010 when the general price index is 150. At the end of 2013, the index has risen to 210 and the current cost of the machine is $300,000. What would be the unrealized holding gain in constant purchasing power terms?
   a. $100,000.
   b. $230,000.
   c. $110,000.

d. $ 80,000.

e. $ 24,000.

6. Assume that Cloth Corporation purchases equipment with acquired cost of $200,000 in 2010 when the general price index is 150. At the end of 2013, the index has risen to 210 and the current cost of the machine is $300,000. What is the unrealized holding gain in current cost accounting?

a. $100,000.

b. $230,000.

c. $110,000.

d. $ 80,000.

e. $ 24,000.

7. Which of the following countries experience substantially inflation accounting today?

a. The U.S.A.

b. The U.K.

c. The Netherlands.

d. Spain.

e. Mexico.

8. A major difference between the British and the U.S. approach to inflation accounting is that

a. Both of the countries do not mandate inflation accounting, but company could voluntarily disclose.

b. the British did not permit inflation adjustment.

c. the U.S. allowed general purchasing power adjustments but not current cost adjustments.

d. the U.S requires company disclose inflation information .

9. What has been the trend in inflation accounting in Britain and the U.S.?

a. change to current cost accounting.

b. change to general purchasing power adjustments.

c. require both of the current cost accounting and general purchasing power adjustments.

d. dropping of inflation accounting.

10. In Britain,

a. companies must use general purchasing power accounting.

b. many companies have periodic revaluations of their land, equipment and buildings to current market values or fair market value.

c. companies must use both of the general purchasing power accounting and current cost accounting.

d. only historical cost measurement is used by company.

Chapter 9   International Financial Statement Analysis

Learning objective

After careful study of this chapter, students will be able to:

1. Explain the challenges and opportunities in cross-board analysis of financial statements.

2. Discuss what is international business strategy analysis and why it is difficult compared with domestic strategy analysis.

3. Understand the difficulties in cross-border business strategy analysis.

4. Argue the logical approach to analyzing foreign financial statements.

5. Depict the difference between international accounting analysis and international financial analysis.

6. Explain the difficulties in cross-border accounting and financial analysis and find the ways to solve the problems.

7. Apply the ratio analysis and cash analysis method in cross board analysis.

8. Explain the pitfalls in conducting international ratio analysis and cash analysis and coping mechanism for dealing with these pitfalls.

9. Explain the prospective analysis and its pitfalls, and ways to figure out for these pitfalls.

9.1   Introduction

Analysis is employed in a number of functional areas. From accounting point of view, analysts evaluate an investment in some type of security that has characteristics of equity or debt. In arriving at investment decisions or recommendations, analysts need to evaluate the performance, financial position, and value of the company issuing the securities. Company financial reports, which include financial statements and other data, provide the information necessary to evaluate the company and its securities. Consequently, the analyst must have a firm understanding of the information provided in each company's financial reports, including the financial notes and other forms of supplementary information (Thomas et al, 2009).

Before we begin to analyze financial statements, we should know that analysis works in a variety of positions. Some are equity analysts whose main objective is to evaluate potential equity investment to determine whether a prospective investment is attractive and what an appropriate purchase price might be. Others are credit analysts who evaluate the creditworthiness of a company to decide whether a loan should be made or what credit rating should be assigned. Analysts may also be involved in a variety of other tasks, such as evaluating the performance of a subsidiary company, evaluating a private equity investment, or finding stocks that are overvalued for purposes of taking a short position (Thomas et al, 2009).

Financial statements are prepared with the intention or supervision of managers under the national accounting standards, which is affected by a country's institutional factors. Effective institutional factors could help to increase quality of financial statements. A good country-level governance should lead to a transparent economic and business environment, being at the same time a promoter of free market policies, justice and rule of law. It is widely accepted that the effects of good governance are felt by the business and economic environment, because a strong national governance should imply fair regulatory frameworks, accountability and transparent policymaking, all these proxies being significant for the country level economic activity. Therefore, a good governance framework should be able to provide a good predictability of economic interactions among various players within the economic environment. The relationship between the quality of country-level governance and audit and financial reporting requirements is highly debated because governance has a significant impact on the information environment of a country. Therefore, good governance should generate an increasing demand for high-quality information in a country.

High-quality information within the economic environment is provided by high-quality audits(Avram, Grosanu and Rachisan, 2015).

9.2 Challenges and Opportunities in Cross-Board Analysis

9.2.1 The need of international financial statement analysis

Company from different countries has a differential effect of internationalization variety degree. Large company experienced much more in international capital market, with little effect from accounting variety. When a company is affected much more, the company has to pay much more addition to disclose its information. These additional requirements include consolidated financial statements, more disclosure to different sectors or agencies, explain to different investors in detail. Different users of financial statements have their own dealing methods, depending on how they understand source level for financial information of foreign operation. To some extent, small investor may cancel investment for a foreign business without providing information, while institutional investors trend to invest a foreign business with being familiar with its operation environment, being able to analyze its financial statements for foreign operation. Institutional investors have enough sources for them to forecast profitability.

In recent decades, more and more companies list their shares in international capital markets with the internationalism development and appearance of "world village". For example, there are about 526 non-U.S. companies in the NYSE. As of June, 2012, there are about 900 companies listed outside the China Mainland. Among outside raiser or registrants, about 80 companies raised capital in NYSE. Users of financial statements find it necessary to analyze foreign financial statements. The common reasons are diversified.

First of all, investors, equity research analysts, bankers, and other users have a growing need to read and analyze non-domestic financial statements and make cross border financial comparisons. Investors, in order to reduce portfolio risks, often diversify their investments. In international capital market, with more and more foreign companies listing shares, there is a growing need to understand non-domestic financial statements.

Secondly, merger and acquisition activities have become more international. Some of the largest mergers in recent years have involved foreign companies acquiring U.S firms. The Daimter-Chrysler, and BP-Amoco mergers are two examples. Both before and after the merger and acquisition of cross board, financial statements are the basic information source, which could help merger and acquisition process go smoothly.

Thirdly, as business becomes more global, financial statements become more important than ever as a basis for competitive analysis, credit decisions, and business negotiations. Foreign operation is more complex than domestic operation with more uncertain factor, which is beyond the national level. Under the situation, managers, competitor, business partners are more reliable on financial statements before they make decisions.

Fourthly, other reasons include making credit decision about foreign customers, evaluating the financial health of foreign suppliers and benchmarking against global competitions.

International financial statement analysis provides an in-depth understanding of the discipline compared with domestic analysis. It helps readers understand the mechanics of the accounting process, comprehend the differences and similarities in income statements, balance sheets, and cash flow statements, assess the implications for securities valuation of any financial statement element or transaction, and become familiar with different financial analysis techniques that provide valuable insight into a company's operations, risk characteristics, and valuation.

9.2.2 Challenges and opportunities

Challenges of cross-board analysis indicate that hard questions will occur when analysis is conducted. It should be noted that analysis tools that are effective in one jurisdiction might be ineffective in a different jurisdiction. For example, criteria for current ratio could be 2:1 in the United States, while it may not be appropriate for 2:1 criteria in Japan. In practice, international financial analysis and valuation are characterized by many contradictions. In many countries there continues to be a great gulf between expectations based on these advances and reality. Moreover, accounting quality and disclosure credibility has recently been criticized by senior regulators in countries such as the United States, with traditions of full disclosure, quality financial reporting, and relatively stringent regulation.

Surely, there are many opportunities. The barriers to international financial analysis and valuation are falling, and the overall trend for the analysis is positive. Incentives for company to voluntarily improve their external reporting practices include the globalization of capital markets, advances in information technology, and increasing competition by national governments, stock exchanges, and companies for investors and trading activity.

The distinctions between cross-border and within-border financial analysis will blur, with continuing globalization and improvements in international accounting and disclosure. Globalization means that strictly domestic analysis becomes less relevant. In other words, international financial statements analysis is more important than ever.

9.3 Business Analysis Framework

Business analysis covers a variety issues. Users of financial statements concern the firm in different ways. A security analyst may interest how well the firm is performing, whether the firm could meet performance expectation, what is the value given assessment of the firm's current and future performance. A loan officer may want to know what is the credit risk involved in lending a certain amount of money to the firm, how well the firm is managing its liquidity and solvency, what is the firm's business risk, and what is the additional risk created by the firm's financing and dividend policies. A management consultant may concern what is the structure of the industry in which the firm is operating, what are the strategies pursued by various players in the industry, and what is the relative performance of different firms in the industry. A corporate manager could care about how firm be properly valued by investors, and whether investor communication program is adequate to facilitate the process. Furthermore, top managers of a firm may concern whether the firm is a potential takeover target, how much value could be added if the firm is acquired, and how to raise money for acquisition. As independent auditor, he may take care about whether accounting policies and accrual estimates in this company's financial statements are consistent with understanding of business and its recent performance. Financial statements analysis is a valuable activity when managers have complete information on a firm's strategies and a variety of institutional factors make it unlikely that they fully disclose the information. It is obvious that business analysis could help security analyst, loan officer, managers, company consultant and auditor to deeply explore what happen to the firm and how to change decision strategy (Palepu and Healy, 2012).

Palepu, Bernard, and Healy (1996) developed a framework for business analysis and valuation using financial statements data. The framework has four stages that there are business strategy analysis, accounting analysis, financial analysis and prospective analysis.

The logical approach to analyzing foreign financial statements is to undertake a business strategy analysis, conduct an analysis of a firm's financial reporting practices, conduct a financial analysis using ratio and cash flow data and do a prospective analysis.

9.3.1 International business strategy analysis

The first step in foreign financial statement analysis is international business strategy analysis. Strategy analysis allows the analyst to probe the economics of the firm at a qualitative level so that the subsequent accounting and financial analysis is grounded in business reality. Also strategy analysis provides the identification of the firm's profit drivers and key risks. In return, this enables the analyst to assess the sustainability of the firm's current performance and make realistic forecasts of future performance. A firm's value is determined by its ability to earn a return on its capital in excess of the cost of capital. While a firm's cost of capital is determined by the capital markets, its profit potential is determined by its own strategic choices. These strategic choices include the choice of an industry or a set of industries in which the firm operates, the manner in which the firm intends to compete with other firms in its chosen industry or industries, the way in which the firm expects to create and exploit synergies across the range of businesses in which it operate. Industry analysis consists of identifying the economic factors which drive the industry profitability. Competitive strategy analysis involves identifying the basis on which the firm intends to compete in its industry. Corporate strategy analysis concerns about examining whether a company is able to create value by being in multiple business at the same time. A well equipped corporate strategy reduces costs of increases revenues from running several businesses in one firm relative to operating the same businesses independently and transacting with each other in the marketplace (Palepu and Healy, 2012).

A qualitative understanding of a company, its competitors, and its economic environment that ensures that quantitative analysis is based on reality. By identifying key profit drivers and business risks, business strategy analysis helps the analyst make realistic forecasts. However, it is very hard for MNEs to identify key profit drivers and business risks because MNEs operate worldwide and uncontrollable factors such as foreign currency rate, interest rate, political and economic risks contribute the profit drivers and risk analysis complicated. When most MNEs operate involved diversified fields, complicated business activities also increase risk of identifying key profit drivers. When analyzing a multibusiness organization, an analyst has to not only evaluate the industries and strategies of the individual business units but also the economic consequences-either positive or negative- of managing all the different businesses under one corporate umbrella. For example, General Electric has been very successful in creating significant value by managing a highly diversified set of businesses ranging from aircraft engines to light bulbs, but Sears has not been very successful in managing retailing together with financial services.

Business strategy analysis is very difficult in some countries due to a lack of reliable information about macroeconomic development, industry situation, and realistic company situation. Even in some developed countries such as the United States, information quality and reliability are often criticized by capital markets regulators. In some developing or emerging market countries, available information is more difficult than those in developed countries. Business and legal environments and corporate objectives vary around the world. Many risks (such as regulatory risk, foreign exchange risk, and credit risk) need to be evaluated and brought together coherently. In some countries, sources of information are limited and may not be accurate.

Recommendations for analysis is to travel, surf on internet, and search "International Briefings" publications. Generally speaking, standard procedures for gathering information for business strategy analysis includes following ways.

Exhibit 9.1   Ways for business strategy analysis

No.	Ways	Ways in details
1	examining annual reports	
2	other company publications	
3	speaking with company staff, analysts, and other financial professionals	
4	other information resources	World Wide Web trade groups competitors customers reporters lobbyists regulators trade press

The insights gained from strategy analysis could be useful in performing the other analysis of financial statements. In accounting analysis, the analyst could examine whether a firm's accounting policy and estimates are consistent with its stated strategy. Strategy analysis could guide financial analysis. For example, in a term series analysis, the analyst should closely monitor any increases in expense ratios and asset turnover ratios for low cost firms, and any decreases in investments critical to differentiation for firms that follow differentiation strategy. Business strategy analysis could help in prospective analysis and valuation. It allows the analyst to assess whether differences between the firm's performance and its industry performance are likely to persist. Also strategy analysis facilitates forecasting investment outlays the firm has to make to maintain its competitive advantage ((Palepu and Healy, 2012).

9.3.2 Accounting analysis

In a globalized business world it is often necessary to compare companies across national boundaries. This comparison often includes an examination of financial statements. While the harmonization of accounting standards continues to progress, there still remain differences in how accounting information is reported between companies located in different countries, especially with regard to the accounting policies, accounting strategy, quality of disclosure used in the financial statements. It is consequently important that students be able to both identify these differences, and have a method for coping with them (Ding, Gary and Herve,2007).

The purpose of accounting analysis is to assess the extent to which a firm's accounting amounts reflect economic reality. Sequence for evaluating a firm's accounting quality include to identify key accounting policies, assess accounting flexibility, evaluate accounting strategy, evaluate the quality of disclosure, identify potential red flags and adjust for accounting distortions. A firm's industry characteristics and its own competitive strategy determine its key success factors and risks. One of the goals of financial statement analysis is to evaluated how well these success factors and risks are being managed by the firm. Therefore, in accounting analysis, the analyst should identify and evaluate the policies and the estimates the firm uses to measure its critical factors and risks. As for assessing accounting flexibility, if managers have little flexibility in choosing accounting policies and estimates related to their key success factors, accounting data is likely to be less informative for understanding the firm's economics. In contrast, if managers have considerable flexibility in choosing the policies and estimates, accounting numbers have the potential to be informative, depending upon how managers exercise this flexibility. Regardless of the degree of accounting flexibility a firm's managers have in measuring their key success factors and risks, they will have some flexibility with respect to several other accounting policies. When managers have accounting flexibility, they could use it either to communicate their firm's economic situation or to hide true performance. Some of the strategy questions one could ask in examining how managers exercise their accounting flexibility. The questions include how the firm's accounting policies do comparing to the norms in the industry, whether managers face strong incentives to use accounting discretion for earnings management or firm has changed its accounting policies or estimate, and firm's accounting policies or estimate have been realistic in the past, and if the firm structure its any significant business transactions so that it can achieve certain accounting objectives. Managers could make it more or less easy for an analyst to assess the firm's accounting quality and to use its financial statements to understand business reality (Palepu and Healy, 2012). High accounting quality means the gap between accounting amounts and economic reality is small. Because it is hard to evaluate economic reality, the gap between reported income and cash flow from operating could be used to represent accounting quality. For example, unusually large asset write-offs, unexplained transactions that boost profits and an increasing gap between company reported income and its cash flow from operations are evidence of all red flags.

One of the fundamental features of corporate financial reports is that they are prepared using accrual rather than cash basis accounting. Accrual basis accounting distinguishes between the recording of costs and benefits associated with economic activities and the actual payment and receipt of cash. Net income is the primary periodic performance index under accrual basis accounting. To compute net income, the effects of economic transactions are recorded on the basis of expected, not necessarily actual, cash receipts and payments. Expected cash receipts from the delivery of products or services are recognized as revenues, and expected cash outflows associated with these revenues are recognized as expenses. While there are many rules and convention that govern a firm's preparation of financial statements, there are only a few conceptual building blocks that form the foundation of accrual accounting. Under the principle of accrual accounting, managers are entrusted with the primary task of making the appropriate judgment in portraying myriad business. The accounting discretion granted to managers is potentially valuable because it allows them to reflect inside information in reported financial statements. However, since investors take profits as a measure of managers' performance, managers have an incentive to use their accounting discretion to distort accounting numbers by making biased assumption. Earnings management is a way for manager to distort financial statements. Perhaps accounting rules and auditing are mechanisms designed to reduce the cost and preserve the benefit of delegating financial reporting to corporate managers (Palepu and Healy, 2012).

When company extends its operating activities to foreign countries, transaction or events may be more complicated. Complicated transactions add difficulty of preparation and communication of financial statements. National difference of accounting and auditing standards makes analysis more challenged. Many differences including measurement, corporate transparency, and auditing differences impact foreign financial statement analysis. Measurement differences within and between countries make performance comparisons difficult. Measurement differences may relate to measurement options permitted by GAAP. Measurement differences may be due to differences in management discretion, and financial statement orientation; i.e., creditor vs. shareholder protection. Measurement differences may relate to the objectives of financial statements; i.e., oriented toward more macro decisions vs. micro decisions.

Differences in corporate transparency make it difficult to comprehend what measurement rules are being followed. Also transparency differences could make future performance metrics estimating hard. When there is transparency differences, valuing forecasted numbers will be no so easy because of large variances of these subjective probability distributions.

Auditing differences affect the credibility of reported numbers owing to many differences, which include the information content of the auditor report, the source of auditing standards, the enforcement of auditing standards, auditor liability to third parties, auditor qualifications, auditor certification procedures and auditor independence.

Therefore, difficulties in accounting analysis involve two important issues. The first is cross-country variation in accounting measurement quality, disclosure quality, and audit quality. National characteristics that cause this variation include required and generally accepted practices, monitoring and enforcement, and extent in managerial discretion in financial reporting. The second issue concerns the difficulty in obtaining information needed to conduct accounting analysis. The level of credibility and rigor of financial reporting in Anglo-American countries generally is much higher than that found elsewhere. In fact, many evidences indicate financial reporting quality can be surprisingly low in both developed and emerging-market countries.

In order to solve these problems, it is suggested that analyst should meet with management to evaluate their reporting incentives and accounting policies. At the same time, new communications technology needs to be facilitated for analyst to apply.

Moreover, there are some limitations for accounting analysis. Since the mechanisms that limit managers' ability to distort accounting data themselves add noise, it is not optimal to use accounting regulation to eliminate managerial flexibility completely. Therefore, real world accounting systems leave considerable room for managers to influence financial statement data. The net result is that information in corporate financial reporting is noisy and biased, even in the presence of accounting regulation and external auditing. The objective of accounting analysis is to evaluate the degree to which a firm's accounting captures its underlying business reality and to undo any accounting distortions. When potential distortions are large, accounting analysis could add considerable value (Palepu and Healy, 2012).

9.3.3 International financial analysis

The assessment of a firm's financial health is recognized as an important decision task. An incorrect evaluation of financial risks can result in serious losses to creditors or investors. As world business activities become more internationalized, it is increasingly important to understand the financial characteristic of corporations in different countries in order to develop a global risk assessment process. Such an understanding would be particularly important for auditors, investors, and bankers in evaluating different risk characteristic of a firm, either foreign or domestic (Tessmer, Shaw, and Gentry, 1993).

The goal of international financial analysis is to evaluate a firm's current and past performance, and to judge whether its performance can be sustained. There are two important tools for international financial analysis. One is ratio analysis, while the other is cash flow analysis.

Ratio analysis involves comparison of a firm's ratios between the firm and other firms in the same industry, comparison of a firm's ratios across years or other fiscal periods, and comparison of ratios to some absolute benchmark. Ratio analysis is also to help evaluate the effectiveness of managers' policies in operating management, investment management, financing strategy and dividend policies.

All of the difficulties mentioned previously in conducting business strategy, accounting, and financial analysis are pitfalls in conducting international ratio analysis. A lack of understanding of the political, legal and business environment that affects the analysis of financial ratios generated in that environment is another pitfall.

Examples of environmental differences include government systems, legal systems, fiscal system, and capital markets. As regard to government systems, UK and U.S. governments are more laissez-faire; i.e., ensure free markets. In these two countries, self-regulation is encouraged. German and Japanese governments are more active in orchestrating growth. For legal systems, UK and U.S. governments are common law countries where standard-setting is delegated to professional bodies and standards oriented toward investor decisions. Germany and Japan are code law countries. Government activity in standard setting with pronouncements is oriented toward societal rights. For fiscal systems, UK and U.S. make a distinction between financial reporting and tax reporting and emphasize on consolidated reporting, while Germany and Japan exhibit a degree of tax-book conformity, and parent company financial statements are important. For capital markets, UK and U.S. markets oriented more toward equity investors. They're more equity-oriented with significant individual ownership. Earnings tend to have an optimistic bias. German and Japanese markets traditionally oriented toward creditors. Earnings tend to have a more conservative bias with more smoothing opportunities.

In order to conduct ratio analysis, analyst should design a coping mechanism, which deal with differences. For measurement differences, it is appropriate for analyst to adopt a mutual fund (passive) approach to investing, restate foreign GAAP to domestic GAAP, restate foreign GAAP to IFRS, rely on non-accounting data using a dividend discount model or cash flow data, and immerse yourself in the language, currency and GAAP of the country you are investing in; i.e., develop a multiple-principles capability. For disclosure differences, undertaking company visitations, attending company road shows, altering investment classifications from speculative grade (poor disclosure) to investment grade (good disclosure), and altering investment strategies from active investing (good disclosure) to passive or non-investing (poor disclosure) are all the ways to facilitate analysis. For audit differences, researching the auditing environment in the country being analyzed, and assessing a higher risk premium for audit risk could help. Institutional investors ask for a second audit opinion or engage a recognized audit firm when confidence in the integrity of the attest function is in doubt.

Comparing financial ratios is merely one way of conducting financial analysis. There are several theoretical challenges for ratio analysis. One challenge is that it is little about the firm's prospects in an absolute sense. The insight about relative performance requires a reference point from other time periods or similar firms. The second challenge is that one ratio holds little meaning. Ratio as indicators could be logically interpreted in at least two ways. One can partially overcome this problem by combining several related ratios to paint a more comprehensive picture of the firm's performance. The third challenge is that seasonal factors may prevent year end values from being representative. The fourth challenge is that financial ratios are no more objective than the accounting methods employed. Changes in accounting policies or choices could yield drastically different ratio values. Therefore, financial analyst could use percentage analysis which involves reducing a series of figures as a percentage of some base amount. Comparative method could provide a better way to determine trends[1].

Besides ratio analysis, cash flow analysis is another tool. A firm's cash inflows and outflows are usually classified into operating, investing and financing activities. Using cash flow analysis could address many questions about the firm's performance and management. To some extent, for foreign analyst or users, cash flow analysis is more helpful or useful than ratio analysis for decision making.

---

[1] Data comes from the following website: https://en.wikipedia.org/wiki/Financial_analysis

9.3.4 Prospective analysis

Forecasting is a task of uncertainty and great risk, based on historical or current information. Generally speaking, forecasting covers most items from financial statements. Forecasting financial statements is imperative for the management because it can provide a rough guide to the future performance of the firm. It is very important to do some prospective analysis for the long term in order to develop strategies for meeting the challenges that will surely arise. Moreover, for most firms, it is vital to have a financial model that allows management to control value creation. This can be done by constructing cash flows from the financial statements and having a permanent assessment of the firm value (Ignacio and Joseph, 2008).

Under the business analysis framework, prospective analysis is the last step for foreign financial statements analysis. Prospective analysis involves into forecasting a firm's prospects based on an assessment of a firm's business strategy, accounting policy, and its financial analysis, and arriving at an estimate of the firm's value.

Prospective analysis concerns forecast future financial performance with using appropriate valuation models to produce an estimate of firm value. As valuing a publicly traded company for the common shareholders, analyst should focus on the value of a share of common stock in that company and compare your own valuation to the market valuation, providing possible explanation for any differences. Analyst also should comment on the extent to which management is adding value, at the same time providing remedies for these concerns.

There are many complicating factors that affect prospective analysis. For example, institutional variation including technological development level, institutional design or system, and culture, is the basic element to be considered. Before the prospective analysis is made, analyst should understand there variations. Fluctuating exchange rates make it difficult to forecast a firm's future costs and revenues when sales/purchases are invoiced in foreign currencies. National variations in measurement, disclosure, and auditing practices including national enforcement regimes add to the difficulty of achieving forecast accuracy. National variations in pricing risk make it difficult to select an appropriate discount rate for valuation purposes. Valuation multiples such as P/E ratios also vary from country to country complicating appropriate corporate valuations.

Terms of the Chapter

accounting analysis　会计分析
accounting policy　会计政策

accounting flexibility 会计灵活性

analyst 分析师

asset turnover 资产周转率

auditors' report 审计报告

auditor opinion 审计意见

book value per share 每股账面值

business analysis framework 商业分析框架

business strategy 商业策略

cash flow analysis 现金流量分析

cash flow from operating activity 来自经营活动的现金流

coping mechanism 应对机制

credit analysis 信用分析

credit decision 信用决策

cross country variation 跨国差异

cross border analysis 跨国分析

current ratio 流动比率

current cash debt ratio 现金比率

deferred tax 递延税

disclosure credibility 披露的可信度

dividend 股利

dividend discount model 股利折现模型

earning per share 每股收益

financial statement analysis 财务报表分析

financial analysis 财务分析

forecasting 预测

foreign financial statements 外国财务报表

gross profit margin 毛利

information availability 资料可获得性

information access 信息渠道

institutional variation 制度差异

international business strategy analysis 国际商业战略分析

inventory turnover 存货周转率

liquidity 流动性

merger and acquisition analysis 兼并与收购分析

market hypothesis 市场假设

material difference 主要差异

opportunity 机会

payout ratio 股利率

P/E ratio 市盈率

pension 抚恤金
portfolio risk 投资组合风险
prospective analysis 前景分析
profitability 盈利能力
quick ratio 速动比率
ratio analysis 比率分析
recommendation 推荐，建议
receivable turnover 应收账款周转率
registrant 注册者
reporting practice 报告实务
reporting income 报告盈余
return on asset 资产回报率
return on equity 权益回报率
risk premium 风险溢价
securities analysis 证券分析
self-regulation 自律
statement format 报表格式
stock exchange 股票交易
solvency 偿债能力
times interest earned 利息倍数
timeliness 及时性
terminology barriers 术语障碍
valuation 评估
quick ratio 速动比率

Discussion Questions

1. Which groups such as banks or creditors, investor, government agency, market regulators, and trade union do concern about foreign financial statements? Why or why not?

2. Why is foreign financial statement analysis more difficult than domestic one?

3. What is challenge and opportunity for foreign financial statement analysis?

4. What is logical procedure for foreign financial statement?

5. What are four steps for business analysis using financial statements? In each step, analysis is more difficult in cross-board situation than a single-country analysis, why or why not?

6. Explain both advantage and disadvantage of raising fund in international capital markets.

7. Do you think how investor conduct ratio analysis and create coping mechanism?

8. You are asked to provide the five most important recommendations you could think of analyzing nondomestic financial statements.

9. What are the factors that must be taken into account when comparing the reported profitability of companies in different countries?

10. What are the factors that must be taken into account when comparing cash flow in different countries?

11. The quick ratio is frequently used to assess the short term debt-paying ability of a business enterprise. As a rule of thumb, U.S commercial lenders often consider a ratio of at least 1 to 1 to be satisfactory. Why might it be inappropriate to apply this standard when evaluating the liquidity of a non-U.S. company such as Chinese company?

12. Explain the difference between accounting analysis and financial analysis.

13. Explain the difficult issues for prospective analysis.

14. Taking some examples to describe accounting analysis.

15. Taking some examples to state significance for business strategy analysis.

True or False

1. A key international financial analysis question is to what extent that accounting differences affect on earnings assessments.

2. In dissimilar economic environments, accounting diversity could lead to non-comparable results.

3. Measurement of accounting income is strongly influenced by tax rules in France, Germany and Switzerland.

4. R&D costs are usually capitalized and amortized in Germanic countries.

5. If IAS or IFRS is the benchmark in a conservatism comparison with a company in a foreign country, then more conservative mean that index is greater that 1.

6. Earnings tend to be more conservative in France, Italy and Germany than in the United Kingdom, and the United States.

7. Higher accounting quality means a small gap between accounting amount and economic reality.

8. Financial analysis is to evaluate or judge whether the company performance could be sustained in the future.

9. Ratio analysis is the easiest way to conduct international financial statement analysis.

10. International business strategy analysis is the first step for conducting foreign financial statements.

11. The purpose of accounting analysis is to evaluate to which extent a company could earn profit.

12. Large unusually written off that boost profits mean a poor accounting quality.

13. One of easily solved problems for accounting analysis is information availability.

14. Using cash flow analysis could address many questions about a firm's performance and management.

15. Prospective analysis involve estimate of a firm's value.

Multiple Choice

1. Accounting analysis involves into
   a. evaluating company's sustainable performance.
   b. assessing the extent to which a company's accounting amounts reflect economic reality.
   c. earning much net income.
   d. earning much more cash flow.
2. International accounting diversity results in many problems and costs.
   a. the ides is not real.
   b. the idea is bad.
   c. the ides is very real.
   d. the idea is wrong.
3. Historical cost is frequently modified by revaluations in
   a. Germany.
   b. French.
   c. the United Kingdom and the Netherlands.
   d. some Asian countries.
4. R&D costs are required to be expensed immediately in
   a. in China.
   b. in the United States.
   c. in the Germany.
   d. the United Kingdom.
5. Goodwill
   a. is capitalized and amortized in the United States.
   b. is immediately expensed in British.
   c. is amortized in Japan.
   d. is subject to an impairment test in China.
6. One of factors that affect prospective analysis is
   a. investor's expectation.
   b. governmental policy.
   c. fluctuating exchange rate.
   d. financial situation of a company.

7. In order to conduct ratio analysis, analyst should design a coping mechanism,
    a. which deal with performance change.
    b. which deal with inflation.
    c. which deal with measurement, disclosure and auditing difference.
    d. which deal with accounting standard setting sector.
8. Which of the following possibly has a low accounting quality?
    a. large asset write-offs that boost profits and increasing gap between reported income and its cash flow from operation.
    b. great decrease in sales due to recession economy .
    c. increased cost because of inflation.
    d. lower market price of company share.
9. It is hard for MNEs to identify key profit driver and business risk,
    a. because MNEs has many subsidiaries and branch offices.
    b. because MNEs increase sales dramatically.
    c. because MNEs want to consolidate financial statements.
    d. because MNEs operate worldwide and uncontrollable factors such as foreign currency rate, interest rate, political and economic risk make things complicated.
10. Conducting foreign financial statements analysis
    a. makes no sense.
    b. is easier than domestic financial statement analysis.
    c. need to design an analytical framework and do it step by step.
    d. is impossible due to facing many challenges.
11. Business strategy analysis is very difficult due to
    a. a lack of reliable information about macroeconomic development, industries situation and realistic company situation.
    b. a lack of analysis tool.
    c. fluctuation of foreign currency.
    d. difference in corporate transparency.
12. The purpose of financial analysis is to
    a. make sure a firm earn more profit.
    b. evaluate performance and judge whether performance could be sustained.
    c. increase firms' s ratio.
    d. increase firm's cash flow from operating activities.

Case Analysis

Case 9   Accounting Quality Analysis

Accounting quality varies substantially among countries. Companies' financial statements, notes, and auditor reports often yield important clues about accounting quality.

Required question solution:

1. Based on general information given in the text about financial reporting and economic and business environments in China, what is your overall assessment of accounting quality in that country?

2. Study the financial statements, notes, and auditor's report of China Petroleum & Chemical Corporation (Sinopec Corp.) for 2014 fiscal year. Is the accounting quality reflected in these materials consistent with your expectations? Critically evaluate China Petroleum & Chemical Corporation, including a discussion of factors that led to your conclusions.

3. Find the way to assess accounting quality for China Petroleum & Chemical Corporation (Sinopec Corp.).

4. Is Chinese GAAP more conservative than the IAS or IFRS, based on the report of China Petroleum & Chemical Corporation (Sinopec Corp.) for 2014 fiscal year?

Chapter 10　The Governance of Multinational Enterprises

Learning objective

After careful study of this chapter, students will be able to:

1. Define the governance and corporate governance.

2. Understand the importance of corporate governance.

3. Take an example to explain the corporate governance model.

4. Describe the corporate governance mechanism.

5. Distinguish between internal and external corporate governance mechanisms.

6. Learn about the benefit of good multinational governance practice.

7. Describe the use of corporate governance scorecards.

8. Gain an understanding of the challenges faced by MNEs in maintaining effective internal control.

10.1　Corporate Governance

A multinational enterprise is an organization that owns or controls production of goods or services in one or more countries other than their home country.[①] It can also be referred as an international corporation, a "transnational corporation", or a stateless corporation.

A multinational enterprise is usually a large corporation which produces or sells goods or services in various countries (Christopher, 2013). It has operating subsidiaries, branches or affiliates located in foreign countries. Thus MNEs are owned by a mixture of domestic and foreign shareholders. In recent years, MNEs have extended their presence all over the globe, conducting a multitude of activities for a multitude of purposes. Governing these activities requires a well-prepared plan that strategically plots which governance mechanisms ought to be employed.

Corporate governance is the way a corporation polices itself. It is a method of governing the company like a sovereign state, instating its own customs, policies and laws to its employees from the highest to the lowest levels.

---

① http://www2.econ.iastate.edu/classes/econ355/choi/mul.htm

10.1.1 Corporate governance model

The following model is one of the most common models that are used. The model clearly spells the position of every person in society. Every person should know his or her hierarchy, every member of the firm has a role, to play within the organization. A shareholder has no capacity to dictate the way chief executive officer of the firm should work. The shareholder will have to give his or her views in the general meeting to senior management official, issue instruction to the board of directors. Given that this is a publicly traded company, there must be a board of directors who will be monitoring the operations of the firm on behalf of the shareholders. The board of directors is answerable to the general assembly. The chief executive will be answerable to the board of directors. The strategic policies of the organization will always be developed by the general assembly with guidance from the board of directors. The chief executive officer is responsible for the general operations of the firm. The departmental heads are the immediate subordinates of the chief executive. At the lowest end, of the ladder are the junior employees who are not in a senior managerial position. The models show that communication will be flowing from the upper part of the ladder to the junior officers.

Exhibit 10.1 Corporate Governance Model

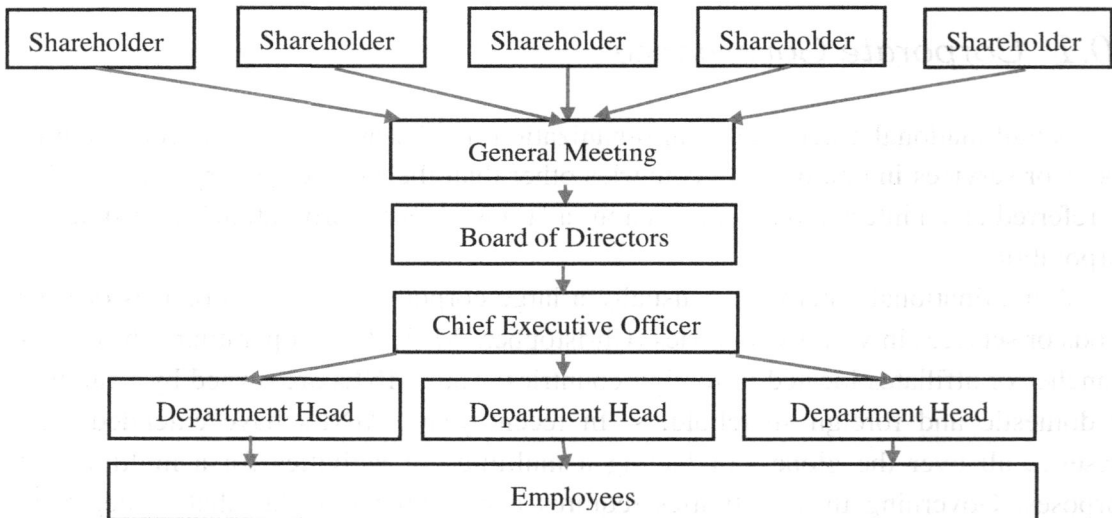

Source: Free Case Study on Employees Corporate Governance Participation in Abu Dhabi Commercial Bank[1]

---

[1] https://livepaperhelp.com/blog/essay-examples/free-case-study-on-employees-corporate-governance-participation-in-adcb

10.1.2 Corporate governance mechanism

Corporate governance is intended to increase the accountability of the company and to avoid massive disasters before they occur. Failed energy giant Enron, and MCI Inc. (formerly WorldCom) is a prime argument for the importance of solid corporate governance. Their demise is associated with the U.S. federal government passing the Sarbanes-Oxley Act 2002, intending to restore public confidence in corporate governance.

Effective corporate governance is essential if a business wants to set and meet its strategic goals. A corporate governance structure includes controls, policies and guidelines that drive the organization toward its objectives while also satisfying stakeholders' needs. A corporate governance structure is a combination of internal and external governance mechanisms.

Exhibit 10.2　Corporate governance mechanism

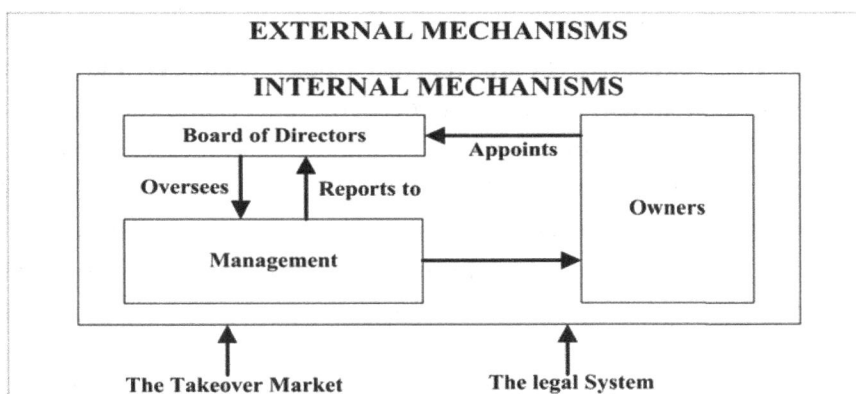

Note: the exhibit comes from Radebaugh, Gray and Black (2006), page 314

1. Internal governance mechanisms

Internal corporate governance encompasses the controlling mechanisms between various actors inside the firm: the company's management, its board and the shareholders. Internal governance mechanisms (see Exhibit 10.2) are mechanisms controlled directly by the owner, in order to achieve the best interest of the themselves. Internal governance mechanism includes the board of directors and the ownership structure (Denis & McConnell, 2003).

① Boards of directors

According to agency theory[①], there are two problems would arise between principals (such as shareholders) and agents of the principals (for example, managers).

---

① http://www.investopedia.com/terms/a/agencytheory.asp

First of all, when their desires or goals are in conflict, the agent is motivated to act in his own best interests rather than those of the principal. Secondly, because of different risk tolerances and different attitudes towards risk, the principal and agent may each be inclined to take different actions. In order to make sure managers will use firm's resources most efficiently and act best interest of the shareholders, most corporations have a boards of directors, whose job is to represent the best interest of owners. And best practices in governance suggest that boards should have a large proportion of outside, independent board members. And the CEO and the chairman of the board should be separate individuals.

Boards of directors' duties not only include governing the organization by establishing broad policies and objectives, selecting, appointing, supporting and reviewing the performance of the chief executive, and ensuring the availability of adequate financial resources, but also cover approving annual budgets, accounting to the stakeholders for the organization's performance and setting the salaries and compensation of company management.[1]

In some European and Asian countries, there are two separate boards, called "two-tier system"[2], an executive board for day-to-day business and a supervisory board (elected by the shareholders and employees) for supervising the executive board. In these countries, the CEO (chief executive or managing director) presides over the executive board and the chairman presides over the supervisory board, and these two roles will always be held by different people. This ensures a distinction between management by the executive board and governance by the supervisory board and allows for clear lines of authority. The aim is to prevent a conflict of interest and too much power being concentrated in the hands of one person.

In the United States, the board of directors (elected by the shareholders) is often equivalent to the supervisory board, while the executive board may often be known as the executive committee (operating committee or executive council), composed of the CEO and their direct reports (other C-level officers, division/subsidiary heads).

② Ownership structure

From a firms' perspective, ownership structure is a strategic decision that determines how capital will be infused into the firm and how wealth will be distributed around the various parties (Radebaugh, Gray and Black, 2006). In particular, ownership structure is an incentive device for reducing the agency costs associated with the separation of ownership and management, which can be used to protect property rights of the firm (Barbosa and Louri, 2002). With the development of corporate governance, many corporations owned by disperse shareholders and are controlled by hire manager. As a results incorporated firms whose owners are dispersed

---

① "Basic Role of the Board". Governance Basics. Institute on Governance (Canada)

② https://en.wikipedia.org/wiki/Board_of_directors

and each of them owns a small fraction of total outstanding shares, tend to underperform as indicated by Berle and Means (1932).

In the developed countries with open financial market, such as United States and United Kingdom, public traded corporations sell shares of stocks to shareholders all over the world, the ownership will be dispersed. While in other countries, family business, state-owned enterprises and listed companies with institutional investors usually have the ownership more concentrated.

Different ownership structure will form difference corporate governance. Fama (1980) and Fama and Jensen (1983a,1983b,1985) maintain that there are efficiencies to separating ownership and control into decision-making and risk-bearing functions which make dispersed ownership advantageous because the efficiency gains outweigh the agency costs. While the empirical evidence on corporate governance suggests that large owners have stronger incentive and better opportunities to exercise control over manager than small shareholders, Claessen (1999) also find evidence of a positive relation between shareholding concentration and firm performance. Kuznetsov and Muravyev (2001) argue that concentrated ownership has its costs when large shareholders, capable to influence corporate decision directly, maximize value for themselves and deprive small owners of their part of residual income. Other negative consequences of ownership concentration includes raised cost of capital due to lower market liquidity or decrease diversification opportunities on the part of the investors (Fama and Jensen, 1983), prevents additional monitoring of managers by the stock market available under dispersed ownership with high liquidity of shares (Holmstrom and Tirole, 1993).

③ Other examples of internal corporate governance mechanisms:

A. The corporate charter of the firm

It is a written document filed by the founders of a corporation detailing the major components of a company such as its objectives, its structure, its planned operations, voting rights and restrictions, preferred stock, anti-takeover mechanisms,staggered board of directors, etc. It is also called "Articles of Association", "Articles of Association". If the charter is approved by the state government, the company becomes a legal corporation.

B. Special Committees

According to the largest multinational energy enterprise Exxonmobil, its board of directors has 5 committees: Audit Committee, Board Affairs Committee, Finance Committee, Public Issues and Contributions Committee, Executive Committee[①]. Most large MNEs have boards with similar committees.

C. (Other) internal control procedures

Other internal control procedures cover whistle-blowers, Sarbanes-Oxley Act 404,

① http://corporate.exxonmobil.com/en/investors/corporate-governance/board-committees/overview

COSO, Code of conduct, and so on. Details will provide in 10.5 of this chapter.

D. Employee participation

Employees play an important role in contributing to the long-term success and performance of the corporation. Under normal operations, there is an upward communication. As the shareholders are not taking part in the daily operations of the firm, there are some facts that he/she may be unclear, he/she would need the information from the employees to enact policies or make decisions relevant to the firm.

2. External governance mechanisms

External governance encompasses the influences from outside the firm on the governance of the firm. These mainly include the takeover market and the legal system (see Exhibit 10.2).

① Takeover market

Corporate takeover market, in which a third party (a raider) can take control of the firm and replace inefficient managers (Jensen and Scharfstein,1988). Takeovers are expected to occur when the target firm performs poorly and its internal corporate governance mechanisms fail to discipline managers. Thus the takeover market serves as an important source of protection for investors In countries with highly developed securities markets, such as the United States and United Kingdom, anyone with sufficient capital can buy a majority shares of a company and take over its operation.

Numerous studies found that takeovers create value (positive stock price changes) for target companies. Empirical Test found bid premium (% of pre-bid stock price) ranges from 99.6% (Japan) to 227% (Indonesia) (Rossi & Volpin , 2004).

② Legal system

According to Anne Anderson (2009)[1], the legal system of a country or the quality of legal protection afforded to minority shareholders is often viewed as being made up of two elements that are statutory provisions and the degree to which the statues are enforced. In some countries like United States and United Kingdom, law systems offer good protection to small and individual shareholders. Countries like Germany and France offer better protection to large institutional shareholders. Yet other countries may offer almost no protection to either type of the owner.

③ Other examples of external corporate governance mechanisms

Other examples indicate markets and media (watchdog, guard dog). There exist market such as labor market (for executives and for employees), product / services markets in which the firm operates, and capital market (either debt or equity).

3. Both internal and external governance mechanisms

Depending on the country, the focus on the two mechanisms can differ. For

---

① Anne Anderson, 2009. A Cross-Country Comparison of Corporate Governance and Firm Performance, http://martindale.cc.lehigh.edu/sites/martindale.cc.lehigh.edu/files/CrossCountryGovernance.pdf example, in the US and other Anglo-Saxon countries we can generally see a bigger trust in markets/shareholders (shareholder value perspective) with a resulting focus on external corporate governance. Europe and Japan generally rely more on relations/networks/stakeholders (stakeholder value perspective) and consider internal corporate governance mechanisms as more important.

10.2 International Importance of Corporate Governance

The importance of corporate governance and accountability in multinational enterprises (MNEs) has never been more evident than today, following the debacles of some large MNEs, corporate accounting scandals, and drastic deflation of market values in the U.S. and elsewhere in the world. Current attempts at legislative and organizational reforms to achieve better governance in many MNEs seem to be a precursor to companies worldwide looking beyond the "earning game". MNEs now have to deal with more demanding global shareholders and stakeholder groups who seek greater disclosure and more transparent explanation for major decisions, escalating pressure to run global businesses in the best interests of these highly demanding international stakeholders.

10.2.1 The features of poor corporate governance

The scandals over the last 25 years have highlighted the need for guidance to solve the various risks and problems that can arise in organizational systems of governance.

1. Domination by a single individual/ small group

A feature of many corporate governance scandals has been boards dominated by a single senior executive with other board members merely acting as a rubber stamp. Sometimes the single individual may bypass the board to action his own interests. Even if an organization is not dominated by a single individual, there may be other weaknesses. The organization may be run by a small group centered round the chief executive and chief financial officer, and appointments may be made by personal recommendation rather than a formal, objective process.

2. Lack of involvement of board

Boards that meet irregularly or fail to consider systematically the organization's activities and risks are clearly weak. Sometimes the failure to carry out proper oversight is due to a lack of information being provided.

3. Lack of adequate control function

An obvious weakness is a lack of internal audit. Another important control is lack of adequate technical knowledge in key roles, for example in the audit committee or in senior compliance positions. A rapid turnover of staff involved in accounting or control may suggest inadequate resourcing, and will make control more difficult because of lack of continuity.

4. Lack of supervision

Employees who are not properly supervised can create large losses for the organization through their own incompetence, negligence or fraudulent activity. The behavior of Nick Leeson, the employee who caused the collapse of Barings bank was not challenged because he appeared to be successful, whereas he was using unauthorised accounts to cover up his large trading losses. Leeson was able to do this because he was in charge of dealing and settlement, a systems weakness or lack of segregation of key roles that was featured in other financial frauds.

5. Lack of independent scrutiny

External auditors may not carry out the necessary questioning of senior management because of fears of losing the audit, and internal audit do not ask awkward questions because the chief financial officer determines their employment prospects. Often corporate collapses are followed by criticisms of external auditors, such as the Barlow Clowes affair where poorly planned and focused audit work failed to identify illegal use of client monies.

6. Lack of contact with shareholders

Often board members may have grown up with the company but lose touch with the interests and views of shareholders. One possible symptom of this is the payment of remuneration packages that do not appear to be warranted by results.

7. Emphasis on short-term profitability

Emphasis on success or getting results can lead to the concealment of problems or errors, or manipulation of accounts to achieve desired results.

10.2.2 Need for corporate governance

Corporate governance issues came to prominence in the USA during the 1970s and in the UK and Europe from late 1980s. The main, but not the only, drivers associated with the increasing demand for the development of corporate governance include the following aspects.

Increasing internationalization and globalization meant that investors, and institutional investors in particular, began to invest outside their home countries. The differential treatment of domestic and foreign investors, both in terms of reporting and associated rights/dividends caused many investors to call for parity of treatment.

Issues concerning financial reporting were raised by many investors and were the focus of much debate and litigation. Shareholder confidence in many instances was eroded and, while focus solely on accounting and reporting issues is inadequate, the regulation of practices such as off-balance sheet financing has led to greater transparency and a reduction in risks faced by investors.

The characteristics of individual countries may have a significant influence in the way corporate governance has developed.

An increasing number of high profile corporate scandals and collapses including Enron, WorldCom, Paramalat, Xerox, Shell, Ahold, Polly Peck International, BCCI, and Maxwell. Communications Corporation prompted the development of governance codes in the early 1990s. However the scandals since then have raised questions about further measures that may be necessary.

10.2.3 Development of governance codes

The lack of board accountability in many of these company collapses demonstrated the need for code of best practice in corporate governance all over the world. United Kingdom set up the Cadbury committee in May 1991 because of the lack of confidence which was perceived in financial reporting and in the ability of external auditors to provide the assurances required by the users of financial statements. The main difficulties were considered to be in the relationship between external auditors and boards of directors (Cadbury Commission, 1992).

One section of the Cadbury report (The financial aspect of corporate governance), named "The Code of Best Practice". Now the Code of Best Practice are found in countries all over the world, most major stock exchanges require listed companies to comply with Code of Best Practice. Companies also take initiative to provide information regarding their governance practices on their websites and annual reports.

10.3 Multinational Enterprises (MNEs) Governance Practice

MNE governance is important in every aspect of society whether it be the corporate environment or general society or the political environment. Good MNE governance can improve public faith and confidence in the political environment.

10.3.1 Good MNE governance practice

MNE governance procedures determine every aspect of the role for management of the firm and try to keep in balance and to develop control mechanisms in order to increase both shareholder value and the satisfaction of other stakeholders. In other words MNE governance is concerned with creating a balance between the economic and social goals of a company including such aspects as the efficient use of resources, accountability in the use of its power, and the behavior of the corporation in its social environment. The definition and measurement of good MNE governance is still subject to debate. However, good corporate governance will address all these main points expressed in the Exhibit 10.3.

Exhibit 10.3   Main points addressed in corporate governance

No.	Main points
1	Creating sustainable value
2	Ways of achieving the firm's goals
3	Increasing shareholders' satisfaction
4	Efficient and effective management
5	Increasing credibility
6	Ensuring efficient risk management
7	Providing an early warning system against all risk
8	Ensuring a responsive and accountable corporation
9	Describing the role of a firm's units
10	Developing control and internal auditing
11	Keeping a balance between economic and social benefit
12	Ensuring efficient use of resources
13	Controlling performance
14	Distributing responsibility fairly
15	Producing all necessary information for stakeholders
16	Keeping the board independent from management
17	Facilitating sustainable performance

10.3.2 Benefit of good governance practice

As can be seen, all of these issues have many ramifications and ensuring their compliance must be thought of as a long term procedure. However firms naturally expect some tangible benefit from good governance. So good governance could offer some long term benefits for firms. These benefits include increasing the firm's market value, increasing the firm's rating, increasing competitive power, attracting new investors, shareholders and more equity, more or higher credibility, and enhancing flexible borrowing condition from financial institutions. At the same time, decreasing credit interest rate and cost of capital, new investment opportunities, attracting better employees, reaching new markets, enhanced company image and staff morale are also the advantages for efficient governance.

10.3.3 Corporate governance scorecards

Companies with strong governance practices achieve higher market valuations.

However, once good practices have been adopted, how can a board know whether its company remains on track? Corporate governance scorecards are used to assist boards, investors, financial analysts, regulators, and other stakeholders to systematically assess the level of corporate governance that individual companies have achieved[1]. With the use of scorecards, companies can easily assess the quality of their own governance, and points to opportunities for improvement. There is no "one size fits all" for a scorecard's content and structure, because local adaptation is key to the tool's overall effectiveness. Exhibit 10.4 is an example of German corporate governance scorecard.

Exhibit 10.4   German corporate governance scorecard

Criteria	Weighting
Supervisory Board	45%
Management Board	20%
Transparency	16%
Shareholders	12%
Internal Controls	7%
Total corporate governance score	100%

Note: the exhibit comes from Corporate Governance Scorecard[8]

10.4 Multinational Enterprises(MNEs) Internal Control

The world has undergone a tremendous shift since 1992 that has led to dramatic business and operating environment changes. Markets continue to globalize. Business models have changed significantly, including greater use of shared services and outsourced service providers. The complexity and pace of change in rules, regulations, and standards have intensified demands on companies. Regulators and other stakeholders have higher expectations regarding governance oversight, risk management, and the detection and prevention of fraud. While advances have been made in better connecting risk management and internal control practices in pursuit of organizational strategic goals, the many changes since 1992 have significantly increased business risk, resulting in a much greater need for competence and accountability than ever before.

The Committee of Sponsoring Organizations of the Treadway Commission (COSO) is a joint initiative of the five private sector organizations listed on the left and is dedicated to providing thought leadership through the development of frameworks and guidance on enterprise risk management, internal control and fraud deterrence. COSO framework helps the enterprise achieve its objectives and to optimize the

① Corporate Governance Scorecard—Versatile Tool for Companies, Investors, and Regulators. Experiences from Southeast Europe and East Asia. 2011. International Financial Corporation & Global Corporate Forum inevitable tension between the enterprise's value creation and value protection activities. The internal control is defined as: a process, effected by an entity's board of directors, management and other personnel, designed to provide reasonable assurance regarding the achievement of objectives in many categories (Radebaugh, Gray and Black, 2006). The categories include effectiveness and efficiency of operations, reliability of financial reporting, and compliance with applicable laws and regulations.

Sarbanes-Oxley Act (SOX) Section 404[1] requires management at public companies to select an internal control framework and then assess and report on the design and operating effectiveness of their internal controls annually. The majority of U.S. publicly traded companies have adopted COSO's 1992 Framework to do this. Most MNE boards of directors have an Audit Committee, which manages the internal and external audit, including the monitoring of internal controls.

Here are the titles of the 17 internal control principles by internal control components as presented in COSO's 2013 Framework (Stephen, 2013).

Exhibit 10.5   internal control components

No.	Internal Control Components	Internal Control Principles
1	Control environment	Demonstrates commitment to integrity and ethical values
		Exercises oversight responsibility
		Establishes structure, authority, and responsibility
		Demonstrates commitment to competence
		Enforces accountability
2	Risk assessment	Specifies suitable objectives
		Identifies and analyzes risk
		Assesses fraud risk
		Identifies and analyzes significant change
3	Control activities	Selects and develops control activities
		Selects and develops general controls over technology
		Deploys through policies and procedures
4	Information & communication	Uses relevant information
		Communicates internally
		Communicates externally
5	Monitoring	Conducts ongoing and/or separate evaluations
		Evaluates and communicates deficiencies

These internal controls components apply to both local and multinational entities. While MNEs face challenges of globalization complex operation. It is difficult to

---

[1] KPMG Internal Control-Sarbanes Oxley 404, Available from
   http://www.kpmg.com/Ca/en/services/Audit/InternalControl/Pages/InternalControl%E2%80%93SarbanesOxley 404.aspx

establish a good control environment when integrating different philosophies, operating styles and ethical values among cultures. The risk assessment activities are more complex as MNEs not only face domestic risks, but also oversea markets combine. Establishing adequate control activities, providing clear and constant information and communication, and constantly monitoring large and geographically dispersed firms are also much harder than these functions for a local firm.

Terms of the Chapter

accountability 问责
Affairs Committee 事务委员会
affiliates 分支机构
agency theory 代理理论
anti-takeover 反收购
board of director 董事会
cadbury committee 凯伯里委员会
chief executive officer 首席执行官
code of conduct 行为准则
Committee of Sponsoring Organizations (COSO) of the Treadway Commission 反虚假财务报告委员会下属的发起人委员会
concentrated ownership structure 集中的股权结构
corporate charter 公司章程
corporate governance mechanism 公司治理机制
corporate governance model 公司治理模式
executive board 执行董事会
executive committee 执行委员会
departmental heads 部门领导
dispersed ownership structure 分散的股权结构
drastic deflation 剧烈通货紧缩
general assembly 大会
hierarchy 层次结构
immediate subordinates 直接下属
independent scrutiny 独立审查
multinational enterprise (MNE) 跨国企业
outsourced service 外包服务
ownership structure 股权结构
Public Issues and Contributions Committee 公共问题及捐款委员会
remuneration packages 薪酬方案
risk-bearing functions 风险承担功能

risk tolerance 风险承受能力
Sarbanes-Oxley Act 萨班斯-奥克斯利法案
senior management official 高级管理人员
sovereign state 主权国家
state-owned enterprises 国有企业
strategic goals 战略目标
strategically plots 战略图
stateless corporation 无国界公司
statutory provisions 法定规定
subsidiaries 子公司
supervisory board 监事会
The Code of Best Practice 最佳实践守则
transnational corporation 跨国公司
two-tier system 双级系统
whistle-blowers 告密者

Discussion Questions

1. Explain how takeover market, legal system affect corporate governance.

2. Compare the dispersed and concentrated ownership structure, what are their advantages and disadvantages?

3. The Cadbury Report on corporate governance contains the following statement: Had a Code such as ours been in existence in the past, we believe that a number of the recent examples of unexpected company failures and cases of fraud would have received attention earlier. In must, however, be recognized that no system of control can eliminate the risk of fraud without shackling companies as to impede their ability to compete in the market place. Do you agree with this statement? If good governance won't completely prevent fraudulent behavior, what would happen?

4. Code of Best Practice in governance has surfaced worldwide in great degree as a response to fraud and corporate failures. Although compliance with some Code of Best Practice is required by some stock exchanges, they remain mostly as guiding principles to improve governance practices. On the other hand, the Sarbanes-Oxley Act of 2002 is a U.S. Law that imposes criminal penalties for noncompliance. Which of these approaches is more effective? Can you think of a third approach to improve government practices?

5. The COSO framework on internal controls identifies five components of an internal control system: control environment, risk assessment, control activities, information & communication and monitoring. What challenges do MNEs face in trying to establish each of these components?

True or False

1. Multinational Enterprises are usually corporation which produces subsidiaries overseas.
2. External governance mechanism includes the board of directors and the ownership structure.
3. Boards of directors represent the interest of shareholders.
4. In European countries, supervisory board members' job is running the company.
5. In China, the state-owned enterprises usually have dispersed ownership.
6. Upward communication means employees can give information all the way to the executive.
7. Normally, companies' chairman of the board is presented by CEO.
8. Target companies would always benefit from the takeover as takeover would drive up share price.
9. Cadbury committee was initially founded as the need for code of best practice in corporate governance.
10. Monitoring is a internal control process that assess the quality of the system's performance afterwards.

Multiple Choice

1. Which one is not the component of external governance mechanisms?
   a. Legal systems.
   b. Capital market.
   c. Takeover market.
   d. Special Committees.
2. According to agency theory, what's the main problem between shareholders and managers?
   a. Shareholders are afraid of managers paying themselves too much.
   b. Shareholders and managers have different self interest and attitudes towards risk.
   c. Shareholders are afraid that managers are not qualified enough to run the company.
   d. Shareholders are afraid of managers wasting money on operation.
3. Which one is not the duty of board of directors?
   a. Selecting and reviewing the performance of the chief executive.
   b. Accounting to the stakeholders for the organization's performance.

c. Governing the sales department and make business plans.

d. Making salaries and compensation plans for company executive managers.

4. Which one is not the feature of good MNE governance?

a. Overlap all the board members with managers.

b. Have adequate risk management.

c. Facilitating sustainable performance.

d. Creating sustainable value.

5. Which one would not be a criteria of corporate governance scorecard?

a. Internal Controls.

b. Transparency.

c. Market share.

d. Management board.

6. Which one is not a component of internal control?

a. Executive board supervising supervisory board.

b. Control environment.

c. Information & communication.

d. Control activities.

Exercises

1. Bayer, the United State pharmaceutical firm has the following ownership structure: Banks and insurance companies (15%), individuals (50%), investment funds (20%), trade and industry (9%), others (6%). The other Chinese firm Sam have ownership structure of state (55%), individuals (24%), investment funds (12%), trade and industry (3%), others (6%).

What differences do you notice between Bayer and Sam?

2. Find information about Chinese Code of Best Practice, and answer the following questions:

a. What does the code suggest any specific committees for the board of directors?

b. Does it require that the role of chairman of the board and CEO be separate?

c. What areas of governance does the code cover?

Chapter 11　International auditing

Learning objective

After careful study of this chapter, students will be able to:.

1. Explain the feature of auditing profession.

2. Understand important factors influencing the quality of the accounting and auditing profession.

3. Distinguish between auditing and corporate governance.

4. Discuss the nature of global audit services and examine the challenges of auditing across borders.

5. Describe the difference between internal auditing and external auditing.

6. Show the development history of global accounting firms.

7. Know the structure of the audit industry and strategies of the global public accounting firms in servicing clients worldwide.

8. Provide a comparative international analysis of audit standards.

11.1　The Accounting and Auditing Profession

Auditing refers to a systematic and independent examination of books, accounts, documents and vouchers of an organization to ascertain how far the financial statements present a true and fair view of the concern. It also attempts to ensure that the books of accounts are properly maintained by the concern as required by law[①]. Auditing has become such an ubiquitous phenomenon in the corporate and the public sector that academics started identifying an "Audit Society". The auditor perceives and recognizes the propositions before him for examination, obtains evidence, evaluates the same and formulates an opinion on the basis of his judgment which is communicated through his audit report.

Auditing has been internationalized because of the demand for international auditing from international capital markets. Audited information helps lower the cost of debt offerings and contributes to greater investor confidence in the information provided. International auditing refers to the rules for auditing of financial statements

---

① https://en.wikipedia.org/wiki/Audit

to be applied internationally and the processes associated with auditing financial statements prepared by MNEs. With the increasing trend toward globalization of markets and rapid growth in international transactions, the issues associated with providing reliable, high-quality information have become crucial for MNEs in their efforts to succeed in increasingly competitive global markets.

In most nations, an audit must adhere to generally accepted standards established by governing bodies. These standards assure third parties or external users that they can rely upon the auditor's opinion on the fairness of financial statements, or other subjects on which the auditor expresses an opinion. The quality of the auditing profession in each country is a function of several factors, such as reputation of the accounting and auditing profession, the quality of the education system, and the certification process. Reputation is important because it determines whether or not the profession is able to attract competent people. In United State, the states vary in terms of educational and experience requirements, and each state is empowered to certify a candidate. However the National Uniform CPA exam is prepared by Board of Examiners of the American Institute of CPAs (AICPA), a private-sector organization.

Auditing issues concerning both external and internal auditing are directly linked to corporate governance. External auditing provides assurance to financial statement users that the information contained in those statements is of high quality. Monitoring risks and providing assurance regarding controls are two main internal auditing functions. Monitoring risks involves identifying risks, assessing their potential effect on the organization, determining the strategy to minimize them, and monitoring the possibility for new risks. As a result of recent credit market conditions, the risks to confidence in corporate reporting and governance are higher than they have been for some years. Companies may find that their precise circumstances are not expressly provided for in the standards. In fact, this is one of the strengths of principles-based standards. In a multinational context, the linkages between auditing and corporate governance can be explained in terms of a set of relationships, as depicted in Exhibit 11.1.

Exhibit 11.1   International Auditing and Corporate Governance

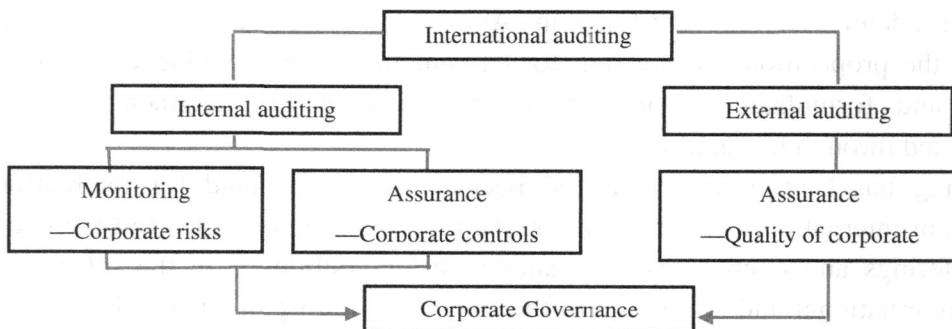

Source: Timothy Doupnik, Hector Perera, International Accounting, fourth edition, P679

11.2 Global Audit Services and the International Auditing Challenge

11.2.1 Global audit services

The services generally provided by global audit firms are (see exhibit 11.2) audit and assurance service, tax advisory and compliance service and consulting advisory service.

1. Audit/attestation and assurance service

Audit and Assurance is an independent service that enhances the reliability of information used by investors and other stakeholders.

2. Tax advisory and compliance service

Attitudes to tax are changing. Organizations of all sizes are ever more exposed to new trends in tax regulation, not just locally but globally.

3. Consulting/management advisory service

Advisory works are to create and protect the sustainable value of their business.

Exhibit 11.2 Attestation, Assurance, Consulting/Tax

	Attestation	Assurance	Consulting/Tax
Result	Written conclusion about the reliability of the written assertion of another party	Better information for decision-makers Recommendations might be a by-product	Recommendations based on the objectives of the engagement Tax documents for the government Tax advice
Objective	Reliable information	Better decision making	Better outcomes
Independence	Required by standards	Included in definition	Not required
Substance of Auditor Output	Conformity with established or stated criteria	Assurance about reliability or relevance of information. Criteria might be established, stated or unstated	Recommendations; not measured against formal criteria
Form of auditor output	written	Some form of communication	Written or oral

Note: the exhibit comes from Radebaugh, Gray and Black (2006), page 423

11.2.2 International auditing challenge

There are many problems common to both American and British firms practicing on a world-wide basis. Differences in tax laws and legal systems in general, language barriers, different currencies, finding and training personnel, strong nationalistic feelings in many countries, differences in accounting principles and auditing standards, are illustrations of some of the common problems.

1. Accounting practices

Regardless of the desirability of some international uniformity, there are differences in accounting practices (James, 1982).

(1) The revaluation of property

The revaluation of property in the United States is not generally accepted as proper accounting, but it has become accepted practice in many Latin American countries, such as Argentina, Brazil, Chile, and Panama. In other countries, such as Mexico, Germany and, to a certain extent, Canada, revaluation is permitted or accepted but is not very widely applied. It is accepted practice in Japan and common in France and Italy. Australia, Great Britain, and the Republic of South Africa accept the theory, but write-ups are generally made only in connection with reorganizations. From these few examples, we see that there are many and varied viewpoints concerning the revaluation of property throughout the world.

(2) Depreciation

In practically all countries mentioned where revaluation of property is accepted practice, depreciation is based on the restated property accounts for financial statement purposes and is an allowable deduction in determining taxable income. There are a few other differences between depreciation practices in some foreign countries and in the United States. In the Netherlands, for example, depreciation is provided on construction work in progress and it is considered permissible to continue to provide depreciation on fully depreciated assets. In Brazil, depreciation is not always provided on buildings because it is not deductible for tax purposes. In Japan, in addition to normal depreciation, companies may set up arbitrary additional amounts when such amounts are allowable deductions for income tax purposes. It seems that tax law has a significant influence on depreciation policy in many countries.

(3) Secret reserve

The European businessman, and businessmen in some other parts of the world, believes very strongly that it is good business to set aside a part of profits in a good year for use in bolstering profits in a bad year, with the concurrence of the accounting profession in those countries. They cannot understand why the American businessman does not do the same thing. Without doubt, inventories present the most fertile area for creating secret reserves. Except for the fact that LIFO is rarely used in other countries, there appears to be no major difference in the method of valuation of inventories between the United States and most other countries.

(4) The lower of cost or market

The lower of cost or market is generally used. However, most European businessmen are quite ingenious when it comes to finding ways and means of writing down perfectly good inventories. Furthermore, several countries have permitted inventory reserves for income tax purposes. In addition to the undervaluation of inventories, secret reserves are created by the arbitrary write-down of other assets, the unnecessary accrual of liabilities, and the creation of unneeded general reserves.

(5) Accrual of Liability for Income Taxes

Accrual of Liability for Income Taxes In a few countries, it is the practice to record income taxes when paid rather than to accrue them in the year in which the related income is earned. Brazil, Italy, Japan, and Switzerland follow this practice.

(6) Stock Dividends

The United States require only that the par value of the shares be transferred to capital stock, and in many countries the offsetting charge can be made to earned surplus or to capital surplus arising from any source. In many countries of the world, however, a stock dividend is regarded as income to the recipient, it need to record as income and pay taxes on it.

2. Local business practices and customs

Local business practices and customs can create challenges in simply confirming what has happened, as well as in assessing future risks.

(1) Predominance of cash

Although paying expense by cash rather than check is accepted in many countries (particular in developing countries), it makes record keeping of expenses and revenue control difficult.

(2) Inability to confirm accounts receivable

In most cases, the confirmation letter itself must be translated into another language. Relying on the customer to return the conformation is another challenge as foreign customers lack experience with conformation. It may not be customary for local auditors to send conformations for accounts receivable or even to confirm year-end bank balance. The mail service may also be inefficient and unreliable, and it may take weeks before the customer receives the letter. In emerging markets where qualified staff are rare, audit confirmations are often seem as an intrusion and are responded to with caution.

3. Currency, language and law

(1) Foreign currency

Auditors need to know the foreign currency restrictions as well as corporate procedures for translating financial statements and recording foreign currency translations so that reports sent to the parent in its own currency are prepared properly.

(2) Language and culture

In many countries, the financial statements must be kept in the local language and currency, so knowledge of local language is essential. And knowing the language can help auditors visiting the suppliers and retails, interviewing customers.

(3) Interaction of home country and local law

Home countries occasionally have laws that extend to subsidiaries of their domestic companies that operate abroad. This law may contradict or conflict with laws in the host country. Examples include boycotts on doing business with certain countries or anti-boycott legislation where the auditor must certify that no country is being discriminated against. Other examples like human rights or social disclosure.

4. Distance and organization for providing audit services

The auditor of a large multinational corporation has a very difficult time organizing the firm's services properly. A major challenge of auditing outside the home base is distance. It's often impossible to conduct pre-audit and post-audit visits, so most communication has to be by telephone, e-mail, fax or mail. When post-audit problems arise, it may be impossible to get the answer quickly or communicate adequately. In this case, the auditor might need to travel from home office to service a client abroad. However, in the long run, this traveling auditor method is unsatisfactory due to the complexity of the international audit and tax environment.

A stronger presence abroad is to be part of a global alliance of firms that share technology, clients, and sometimes staff. These alliances may be separate legal entities that use the parent firm's name or a derivative thereof. The partnership in individual countries retains its separate identity, allow for local knowledge plus global clients, but without the tight control of a single firm.

The strongest presence for any global firm would be a single entity with common equity holdings. Local firms can be acquired or newly established.

5. Audit impediments from international diversity, availability and training of auditors

If the audit firm chooses to open a branch rather than rely on correspondents, it faces the challenge of getting satisfactory staff on the ground. These challenges include problems of lack of local audit staff, a variety of training models for preparing staff for the audit function.

(1) The supply of auditors

The number of accountants depends on barriers to entry to the profession, such as strict educational and testing requirements. Countries have the big number of accountants per thousand in sequences are Canada, Australia, United Kingdom and United States. While some emerging market countries such as India, Bulgaria, Mexico, China have relatively small number of accountants per thousand.

(2) International differences in training of practicing auditors

The education system has influence on the quality of an accountant. There are essential three different models of accounting education leading to certification. The first model is the apprenticeship approach, patterned after the British experience, which does not require specific university training in accounting. The second is the

University-base model for certification, similar to the approaches used in the United States and Germany. The third model is the dual-track model, found in the Netherlands and France, which permits either approach.

Each model has its strength. But auditors may be unfamiliar with the competence level of staff in all countries. In the apprenticeship approach, even after years of study, staff with significant experience may still not yet be qualified. In the University-base model, staff may be qualified but not that experienced. One solution for the global firm is to concentrate on developing a stronger human capital base through common global training and internship or foreign residency programs. It's common to find accountants in various stages of their careers, usually from the manager level up, working in foreign offices to learn the challenges of audits in those countries and to train local accountant in the ways of international firm.

11.3 Global Accounting Firms

The largest international accounting firms were called the Big Eight for most of the 20th century, they were the eight largest international professional services networks, offering audit, assurance, tax, consulting, advisory, actuarial, corporate finance, and legal services. These firms are presented in alphabetical order.[①]

1. Arthur Andersen (until its closure in 2002 for a conviction related to the Enron scandal which was later overturned by the US Supreme Court).

2. Arthur Young & Co.

3. Coopers & Lybrand (until 1973 Cooper Brothers in the UK and Lybrand, Ross Bros, &Montgomery in the United States).

4. Ernst & Whinney (until 1979 Ernst & Ernst in the United States and Whinney Murray in the UK).

5. Deloitte Haskins & Sells (until 1978 Haskins & Sells in the United States and Deloitte & Co. in the UK).

6. Peat Marwick Mitchell (later Peat Marwick, then KPMG).

7. Price Waterhouse.

8. Touche Ross.

Most of the Big Eight originated in alliances formed between British and U.S. audit firms in the 19th or early 20th centuries. The firms' initial international expansion was driven by the needs of British and U.S.-based multinationals for worldwide service. They expanded by forming local partnerships or by forming alliances with local firms.

This group was once known as the "Big Eight", adopted modern marketing and grew rapidly, and was reduced to the "Big Six" and then "Big Five" by a series

---

① http://student.purduecal.edu/~wang786/anchor%20text/Big_Four_(audit_firms).htm

of mergers. The Big Five became the Big Four after the demise of Arthur Andersen in 2002, following its involvement in the Enron scandal.

Currently, the Big Four are Deloitte, PwC, EY and KPMG. They handle the vast majority of audits for publicly traded companies as well as many private companies, creating an oligopoly in auditing large companies. It is reported that the Big Four audit 99% of the companies in the FTSE 100, and 96% of the companies in the FTSE 250 Index, an index of the leading mid-cap listing companies.

Exhibit 11.3   Top International Accounting Firms by Revenue(2014)

Firm	Revenues	Employees	Revenue/per employee	Fiscal year	Headquarters
Deloitte	$34.2 billion	210,000	$162,857	2014	United States
PwC	$34.0 billion	195,000	$174,359	2014	United Kingdom
EY	$27.4 billion	190,000	$144,211	2014	United Kingdom
KPMG	$24.8 billion	162,000	$153,209	2014	Netherlands

Note: the exhibit comes from the website: www.bauer.uh.edu

11.4 International Auditing Standard

Although multinationals, audit firms, and governments attempt to standardize their practices and permit the cross-national transfer of audit services, obstacles to auditing will still exist. Efforts to "harmonize" accounting around the world began even before the creation of the International Accounting Standards Committee (IASC) in 1973.

High-quality auditing standards are necessary to ensure that accounting standards are rigorously interpreted and applied. Auditors validate and add credibility to external financial reports. Credible financial reporting is at the core of the efficient functioning of capital markets. International accounting and auditing standards are interrelated. It therefore makes sense that the development of international accounting and auditing standards should be aligned.

To accomplish its objectives, IFAC's boards and committees set standards in the following areas such as international standards on auditing assurance engagements, and related services, international standards on quality control, international code of ethics, international education standards and international public sector accounting standards. Yet the following points about (independent, external) auditing may be discerned from country to country.

1. The main purpose of an external audit varies around the world

(1) In the United States, auditors attest to whether financial statements "present

fairly" a company's financial position and results. The test of fair presentation is compliance with U.S. GAAP.

(2) In the United Kingdom, auditors attest to whether financial statements present a "true and fair view" of a company's financial position and results. There is a "true and fair override" of U.K. GAAP.

(3) In Germany, auditors primarily attest to whether financial statements comply with the law.

2. Auditor responsibility varies around the world

(1) In France, auditors must report criminal acts they become aware of to the state prosecutor, in addition to their other responsibilities.

(2) In Germany, auditors must provide a private report to the company's managing board of directors and supervisory board on the company's future prospects, in addition to their other responsibilities.

3. Who can conduct an audit varies around the world

(1) In the United States, only certified public accountants may do so.

(2) In the United Kingdom, members of four professional associations are allowed to do so. The four associations are chartered accountants in England and Wales, chartered accountants in Scotland, chartered accountants in Ireland, and chartered certified accountants.

(3) In the Netherlands, administrative accountants may audit smaller companies, while register accountants may audit all companies.

(4) In Germany, sworn book examiners audit small and medium-sized companies, while wirtschaftsprüfer may audit all companies.

4. Oversight bodies

Nations have taken steps to tighten control over the auditing profession. Recently established oversight bodies show as follows.

(1) The Public Company Accounting Oversight Board in the United States. It is a government agency established as a result of the Sarbanes-Oxley Act.

(2) The Haut Counseil du Commissariat aux Comptes (High Council of External Auditors) in France. It is overseen by the Ministry of Justice.

(3) The Professional Oversight Board in the United Kingdom. It is overseen by the Financial Reporting Council, an independent private-sector body.

(4) The Certified Public Accountant and Auditing Oversight Board in Japan. It is overseen by the Financial Services Agency, a government agency.

5. Auditors are facing increasing responsibility for improving corporate governance

(1) In the United States, auditors express an opinion on internal controls (for listed companies).

(2) In Japan, auditors express an opinion on management's assessment of the internal controls (for listed companies).

Despite the there are differences in international auditing standards, international convergence of financial reporting are driven toward international harmonization. As it will ensures the international capital markets that the audit process be consistent across.

11.5 International Audit Reports

There are significant differences in the audit reports across different countries and sometimes across different companies within the same country. Here are the comparisons of corporations' audit reports from China, Germany, UK and Japan (Doupnik and Perera, 2015).

1. China Southern Airlines' audit report states that an audit has been conducted in accordance with Hong Kong Standards on Auditing issued by the Hong Kong Institute of Certified Public Accountants.

2. China Eastern Airlines' audit report is in both English and Chinese. It states that the audit has been conducted in accordance with International Standards on Auditing. The audit opinion refers to IFRS and Hong Kong company ordinance (see appendix "Examples of Audit Reports from China Eastern Airlines").

3. The audit report of Bayer states that the audit has been conducted in accordance with German Commercial Code requirements and German generally accepted standards for the audit of financial statements promulgated by the Institute of Public Auditors in Germany. The audit opinion refers to IFRS as adopted by the EU and the German Commercial Code.

4. Toshiba's audit report has been prepared in accordance with auditing standards generally accepted in the United States. The audit report covers two years.

5. The audit report of Unilever PLC has been prepared in accordance with International Standards on Auditing (UK and Ireland).

Exhibit 11.4 provides an illustration of an unqualified opinion that incorporates the basic requirements.

Exhibit 11.4 Auditor's report

Auditor's report

(Appropriate Address)

We have audited the accompanying (the reference can be by page numbers) balance sheet of the ABC Company as of December 31, 201x, and the related statements on income, and cash flows for the year then ended. These financial statements are the responsibility of the company's management. Our responsibility is to express an opinion on these financial statements based on our audit.

We conducted our audit in accordance with International Standards on Auditing (or refer to relevant national standards or practices). Those standards require that we plan and perform the audit to obtain reasonable assurance about whether the financial statements are free of material misstatement. An audit includes examining, on a test basis, evidence supporting the amounts and disclosures in the financial statements. An audit also includes assessing the accounting principles used and significant estimates made by management, as well as evaluating the overall financial statements presentation. We believe that our audit provides a reasonable basis for our opinion.

In our opinion, the financial statements give a true and fair view of (or "present fairly" in all material respects) the financial position of the company as of December 31, 201x, and of the results of its operations and its cash flows for the year then ended in accordance with International Accounting Standards (or [title of financial reporting framework with reference to the country of origin]*) (and comply with. . . .†)

*In some circumstances it also may be necessary to refer to a particular jurisdiction within the country of origin to identify clearly the financial reporting framework used.

Refer to relevant statutes or law.

Source: ISA 700, Forming an Opinion and Reporting on Financial Statements.

Terms of the Chapter

Accrual of Liability for Income Taxes 所得税负债的权责发生制
advisory service 咨询服务
assurance 担保
apprenticeship approach 学徒制
attestation 认证
audit opinion 审计意见
auditor's report 审计报告
audit services 审计服务
Audit and Assurance 审计和保险
auditing profession 审计职业
consulting 咨询
corporate finance 公司财务
depreciation 折旧
global accounting firm 全球会计师事务所
enron scandal 安然丑闻
external auditing 外部审计
fairness of financial statements 财务报表的公平性
financial statements presentation 财务报表呈报

internal auditing　内部审计

international auditing standards　国际审计准则

material misstatement.　重要误报

management's assessment　管理层评估

Ministry of Justice　司法部

predominance of cash　现金优势

revaluation of property　财产重估

relevance　相关性

reliability　可靠性

secret reserve　秘密储备

supervisory board　监事会

state prosecutor　国家检察官

stock dividends　股票股利

taxable income　应税收入

the lower of cost or market　成本与市价的孰低

true and fair value　真实和公允的价值

ubiquitous phenomenon　普遍现象

Discusses Questions

1. Why is it necessary to have international auditing standards?

2. Why do auditing standards differ internationally?

3. What are the main differences between internal auditing and external auditing within an MNE?

4. What are the main factors that complicate the issue of auditor independence?

5. Why are the audits of most of the largest global companies done by the Big Four accounting firms? How do these large firms provide value to their customers?

6. If you have the opportunity to work as an internship in a foreign country for an audit firm with an office in that country. What would be the advantage and challenges of such an experience? What would you do to prepare for the experience?

7. What's the nature of global audit services?

8. With the increase of multinational enterprises, what's the effect on audit firms?

9. What will affect auditor's independence?

True or False

1. The barrier of geographic distance for international auditing has been eliminated by the email, telephone etc.

2. True and fair is the most basic criteria when audit financial reports in UK.

3. International auditing focus more on external auditing than the internal part.

4. Global audit's main job is providing services of attestation, assurance and consulting.

5. Having the BIG4 rather than small accounting firms to write independent auditors' report makes the financial statement more reliable.

6. International auditing standard indicates that auditors need express an opinion on internal controls for listed companies.

7. Auditors are facing increasing responsibility for improving corporate governance.

8. Auditors validate and add credibility to external financial reports.

9. Credible financial reporting is at the core of the efficient functioning of capital markets.

10. The revaluation of property in the United States is generally accepted as proper accounting, but it does not become accepted practice in many Latin American countries.

Multiple Choice

1. Which one of the following is not difficult for international auditing?
    a. Language and culture.
    b. Auditing standards.
    c. Tax and regulation.
    d. Human resource.
2. Which one is not the standards set by IFAC's boards and committees?
    a. International Standards on Auditing Assurance Engagements.
    b. International Code of Best Practice.
    c. International Standards on Quality Control.
    d. International Code of Ethics.
3. Different countries have different policies towards "who can conduct an audit varies around the world", which of the following statement is not true?
    a. In Germany, wirtschaftsprüfer audit small and medium-sized companies, while sworn book examiners all companies.
    b. In the United States, only certified public accountants may allowed to audit firms.
    c. In the Netherlands, administrative accountants may audit smaller companies, while register accountants may audit all companies.
    d. In the United Kingdom, members of four professional associations are allowed to conduct an audit.

4. As regard to main purpose of an external audit, which of the following is correct?

    a. In the United States, auditors attest to whether financial statements "present fairly" a company's financial position and results.

    b. In the United Kingdom, auditors attest to whether financial statements present a "reliability" of a company's financial position and results.

    c. In Germany, auditors primarily attest to whether financial statements comply with the economic reality.

    d. In Germany, auditors primarily attest to whether financial statements comply with microeconomics idea.

Exercises

Ernst & Young (EY) is one of the Big Four audit firms. Visit http://www.ey.com/ to learn more about this firm.

(1) Where does the firm have offices? What are the benefits of having a presence in so many locations? What are the challenges of providing accounting services in such a dispersed set of location?

(2) What industries does Ernst & Young (EY) cover?

(3) What is the issue faced by audit profession today?

(4) Find Ernst & Young (EY) most recent Annual Review, what does the review contain? Choose an area that interests you and learn more about it.

Case Analysis

Case 11　Internal control and auditing

1. Sarbanes-Oxley legislation

Major corporate scandals such as Enron in the United States triggered the establishment of "Sarbanes-Oxley legislation" (SOX Act).The Sarbanes–Oxley Act of 2002, also known as the "Public Company Accounting Reform and Investor Protection Act" and "Corporate and Auditing Accountability and Responsibility Act" and more commonly called Sarbanes-Oxley, Sarbox or SOX, is a United States federal law, which strengthened the external auditing of companies, information disclosure system and other relevant corporate governance stipulations (from wikipedia).

Section 302 of the SOX Act requires companies to establish a financial reporting disclosure internal control; Section 404 stipulates the requirements of the internal control system: (1) Management publishes an annual report on the internal control system; (2) Management of listed companies evaluate the effectiveness of the internal control system; (3) The accounting firm in charge of auditing the annual financial report will also test and evaluate the internal control system, and also issue an evaluation report.

2. Internal Control and Audit Risk in China

In China, "Internal Control and Audit Risk" was promulgated in 1997 to implement auditing standards. Also, the Bank of China promulgated "The Guiding Principles of Strengthening the Internal Controls of Financial Institutions" in May 1997. In 1999, Section 27 of the revised "Accounting Law" put forward certain requirements of the internal control system, such as position separation, authorization approval, property control and internal auditing. In 2006, the Ministry of Finance, the State-owned Assets Supervision and Administration Commission, China Securities Regulatory Commission, China Insurance Regulatory Commission, China Banking Regulatory Commission, and the Audit Commission, established the National Internal Control Standards Committee. In March 2007, they promulgated the basic guidelines of internal control. In June 2008, the Ministry of Finance and four other ministries and committees, promulgated "Basic Norms of Internal Control". These norms were implemented among listed companies on July 1, 2009 to encourage its implementation in non-listed medium-sized enterprises (Zhu, 2009, p. 9). On April 26, 2010, the Ministry of Finance, China Securities Regulatory Commission, Audit Commission, China Banking Regulatory Commission, and China Insurance Regulatory Commission established "The Guidelines for the Internal Control of Companies", which contains: "Application Guidelines for the Internal Control of Companies", "Evaluation Guidelines for the Internal Control of companies", and "Auditing Guidelines for the Internal Control of Companies". The promulgation of "Basic Norms of Internal Control" and "The Guidelines for the Internal Control of Companies" marked the establishment of internal controls in companies in China. To improve the seting up of the internal control system in listed companies, the Ministry of Finance and four other commissions established a timetable for the internal control systems implementation. The internal control system will first be implemented in listed companies on January 1, 2011, and will expand to listed companies on the Shanghai Stock Exchange and Shenzhen Stock Exchange on January 1, 2012 (Sato and pan, 2012).

Based on this, it will be carried out in the companies randomly. Meanwhile, the advance implementation of the large and medium enterprises will be encouraged (White Paper, 2010)

3. Chinese subsidiary

Suppose you are the engagement partner for the audit of Morgan Inc., a U.S.-based MNE with a subsidiary in China. In the past several years, you have relied on the work of local auditors for the Chinese subsidiary. However, this year you are unsure about how much to rely on the work of local auditors to comply with Section

404, since China is not subject to SOX and auditors there have little experience auditing internal controls in such a rigorous manner. You are also concerned that management of the Chinese subsidiary is unaware of SOX and its requirements under Section 404. Based on above scenario, answer the following questions.

(1) Explain how SOX Act affects internal control report in China.

(2) Describe the development of internal control report in China for public company, and forecast its future development trend.

(3) Should you rely on the work of the local auditors to comply with Section 404? Justify your answer.

(4) How can you make up for the lack of training of the local auditors?

(5) How would you coordinate the internal controls audit in the Chinese subsidiary?

Appendix

**Examples of Audit Reports from China Eastern Airlines
Independent auditors' report 2014**
China Eastern Airlines Corp. Ltd
To the Shareholders of China Eastern Airlines Corporation Limited
(incorporated in the People's Republic of China with limited liability)

We have audited the consolidated financial statements of China Eastern Airlines Corporation Limited (the "Company") and its subsidiaries (together, the "Group") set out on pages 78 to 197, which comprise the consolidated and company balance sheets as at 31 December 2014, and the consolidated statement of comprehensive income, the consolidated statement of changes in equity and the consolidated cash flow statement for the year then ended, and a summary of significant accounting policies and other explanatory information.

Directors' Responsibility for the Consolidated Financial Statements

The directors of the Company are responsible for the preparation of consolidated financial statements that give a true and fair view in accordance with International Financial Reporting Standards and the disclosure requirements of the Hong Kong Companies Ordinance, and for such internal control as the directors determine is necessary to enable the preparation of consolidated financial statements that are free from material misstatement, whether due to fraud or error.

Auditor's Responsibility

Our responsibility is to express an opinion on these consolidated financial statements based on our audit. We conducted our audit in accordance with International Standards on Auditing. Those standards require that we comply with ethical requirements and plan and perform the audit to obtain reasonable assurance about whether the consolidated financial statements are free from material misstatement. An audit involves performing procedures to obtain audit evidence about the amounts and disclosures in the consolidated financial statements. The procedures selected depend on the auditor's judgment, including the assessment of the risks of material misstatement of the consolidated financial statements, whether due to fraud or error. In making those risk assessments, the auditor considers internal control relevant to the entity's preparation of the consolidated financial statements that give a true and fair view in order to design audit procedures that are appropriate in the circumstances, but not for the purpose of expressing an opinion on the effectiveness of the entity's internal control. An audit also includes evaluating the appropriateness of accounting policies used and the reasonableness of accounting estimates made by the directors, as well as evaluating the overall presentation of the consolidated financial statements. We believe that the audit evidence we have obtained is sufficient and appropriate to provide a basis for our audit opinion.

Independent Auditor's Report Opinion

In our opinion, the consolidated financial statements give a true and fair view of the state of affairs of the Company and the Group as at 31 December 2014, and of the Group's profit and cash flows for the year then ended in accordance with International Financial Reporting Standards and have been properly prepared in accordance with the disclosure requirements of the Hong Kong Companies Ordinance.

Other Matters

This report, including the opinion, has been prepared for and only for you, as a body, and for no other purpose. We do not assume responsibility towards or accept liability to any other person for the contents of this report.

Pricewaterhouse Coopers
Certified Public Accountants
Hong Kong, 23 March 2015

Chapter 12 International Management Accounting

Learning objective

After careful study of this chapter, students will be able to:

1. Understand the significance of international management accounting for a MNE.

2. Explain the differences between traditional costing system and activity based costing.

3. Describe when the MNE could use activity based costing system.

4. Use different capital investment techniques to make capital investment decisions.

5. Describe the differences of management control, tactical control and transactional control.

6. Demonstrate an understanding of culture influence on management control.

7. Discuss the effect of Currency fluctuation on MNEs.

8. Explain performance evaluation system within a multinational corporation.

9. Distinguish performance valuation methods between economic value added and balanced scorecard.

12.1 International Management Accounting

Management accounting is a profession that involves partnering in management decision making, devising planning and performance management systems, and providing expertise in financial reporting and control to assist management in the formulation and implementation of an organization's strategy. [①] Management accounting serves both to provide information to management and to be used by management as a tool for ensuring that employees' actions and objectives are aligned with those of the firm. With the trend of globalization, management accounting provides managers of MNE useful operating management information so that they can make full use of firm's resources to gain the maximal economic profit.

---

① Definition of Management Accounting. Institute of Management Accountants. 2008.

12.2 Costing System

12.2.1 Traditional costing system

In traditional costing system, allocation of indirect costs is made based on some common allocation bases such as labor hour, machine hour. The main drawback of this method is that, it pools all the indirect costs and allocates them using the allocation bases to departments. In most of the cases, this allocation method does not make sense as it pools the indirect costs of all products of different stages. In the traditional method, it allocates overheads first to the individual departments then reallocates the costs to products. Especially in the modern world, traditional method loses its applicability as a single company produces larger number of different types of product without using all departments.[1] As a result, cost experts came up with a new concept call activity based costing (ABC), which was simply reinforced the existing traditional costing method.

12.2.2 Activity based costing (ABC)

Activity-based costing (ABC) is a costing methodology that identifies activities in an organization and assigns the cost of each activity with resources to all products and services according to the actual consumption by each. This model assigns more indirect costs (overhead) into direct costs compared to conventional costing[2]. ABC is an approach to the costing and monitoring of activities which involves tracing resource consumption and costing final outputs. Resources are assigned to activities, and activities to cost objects based on consumption estimates[3].

It is obvious that ABC has many benefits. First, ABC leads to more activity cost pools with more relevant cost drivers. Second, ABC leads to enhanced control of overhead costs since overhead costs can be more often traced directly to activities. Third, ABC helps management decisions by providing more accurate product costs, which contributes to setting selling prices that will achieve desired product profitability levels. Last, ABC provides more accurate product costing helps in setting selling prices and in deciding to whether make or buy components.

12.3 Capital Investment Techniques

There are four techniques often used in evaluating and making capital investment

---

① http://www.differencebetween.com/difference-between-activity-based-costing-and-vs-traditional-costing.

② https://en.wikipedia.org/wiki/Activity-based_costing.

③ CIMA official Terminology, 2005 (PDF).

decisions: (1) payback period, (2) return on investment, (3) net present value, and (4) internal rate of return.

12.3.1 Payback period

The payback period of a project is the length of time required to recoup the initial investment. Calculation of payback period requires knowledge of the amount to be invested and an estimate of the after-tax cash flows to be received from the investment for each year of the project's life. For example, with an initial outlay of $600,000 and annual after-tax net cash inflows of $100,000, the payback period would be six years. If the decision rule is to accept only those projects with a payback period of five years or less, the company would reject an investment proposal with a payback period of six years. This is simple and straightforward. The length of the payback period can be viewed as a measure of the investment's risk—the longer the payback period, the riskier the investment. The major limitations of this technique are its failure to consider the time value of money and an investment's total profitability. The use of payback period could lead to inappropriate investment decisions by rejecting investment proposals that provide larger cash inflows in the latter part of their useful lives. Payback period only considers the length of time required to recoup the initial investment, regardless of the investment's total profitability.

12.3.2 Return on Investment (ROI)

Calculation of return on investment (ROI) requires knowledge of the amount to be invested and an estimate of the average annual net income to be earned from an investment:

$$ROI = \frac{Average\ annual\ net\ income}{Book\ value\ of\ investment}$$

In using ROI for making capital budgeting decisions, a company must determine the minimum rate of return that makes an investment project worthwhile. Assume that a company requires ROI of at least 10% and has the following investment opportunities available.

Exhibit 12.1   Calculation of ROI

Project	Required Investment	Average Annual Net Income
A	$800,000	$96,000
B	500,000	30,000
C	300,000	54,000

Project	ROI
A	12% ($96,000/$800,000)
B	6% ($30,000/$500,000)
C	18% ($54,000/$300,000)

Exhibit 12.2　ROI for the three projects

Based on the company's decision rule, only projects A and C would be accepted because their ROI exceeds the 10% rate of return hurdle. ROI is easy to compute using data from financial reports. Unlike payback period, it considers the entire period of an investment. However, it also ignores the time value of money. Further, it does not consider the possibility that a project may require other outlays such as working capital commitments in addition to the initial investment.

12.3.3　Discounted cash flow techniques

Two discounted cash flow techniques are in common use in capital budgeting. They are (1) the net present value (NPV) method and (2) the internal rate of return (IRR) method. These techniques use present values of future cash flows in evaluating potential capital investments, using a discount rate. Usually the discount rate used is the firm's cost of capital or some other minimum rate of return. The cost of capital is a composite of the cost of various sources of funds comprising a firm's capital structure. A minimum rate of return is often determined by referring to the strategic plan, the industry average rate of return, or other investment opportunities.

If foreign investments are evaluated with this discounted cash flow model, an appropriate discount rate must be developed. Capital budgeting theory typically uses a firm's cost of capital as its discount rate, which is related to the proportions of debt and equity in a firm's financial structure as follows (Choi and Meek, 2010).

$$ka = ke(E/S) + ki(1 - t)(DT/S)$$

where:

ka = weighted average (after tax) cost of capital

ke = cost of equity

ki = cost of debt before tax

E = value of a firm's equity

D = value of a firm's debt

S = value of a firm's capital structure (E + D)

t = marginal tax rate

1.　Net Present Value (NPV)

The NPV of an investment is the difference between the initial investment and the sum of the present values of all future net cash inflows from the investment, calculated as follows:

Present value of future net cash flows – Initial investment = Net present value (NPV)

The amount of NPV can be positive, negative, or zero. A positive NPV means that the investment is expected to provide a rate of return on the initial investment greater than the discount rate, whereas a negative NPV means that the return provided would be less than the discount rate. If the NPV is zero, the project is expected to provide a rate of return exactly equal to the discount rate. The decision rule is to accept positive (or zero) NPV investment projects. Calculation of NPV requires knowledge of the amount of initial investment; estimation of future cash flows to be derived from the investment, including cash flows to be received upon the investment's liquidation (known as terminal value); and an appropriate discount rate based on the desired rate of return on investment.

2. Internal Rate of Return

A positive NPV implies that an investment's return exceeds the desired rate of return (discount rate), but it does not indicate the exact rate of return provided by the investment. This can be determined by calculating the internal rate of return (IRR). IRR is the discount rate that equates the present value of future net cash inflows to the initial investment. Essentially, a project's IRR is the discount rate at which NPV is equal to zero. The following example illustrates how IRR is determined.

Assume that a company is considering a potential investment with a four-year life, no terminal value, and the following estimated cash flows:

Total initial investment : $5,000

Net cash inflows for each of four years: $1,750

We solve the following equation to determine the present value (PV) of an annuity factor that equates the present value of the net cash inflows to the initial investment:

$5,000 =$1,750×Present value of annuity factor (4 periods)

$$\text{PV annuity factor 4 periods} = \frac{\$5000}{\$1750} = 2.857$$

From a present value of annuity table, where number of periods is equal to 4, we find 2.857 to be the present value factor at a discount rate of 15 percent. Thus, the IRR for this investment project is 15%, which will be compared with the firm's desired rate of return in deciding whether to invest in this particular project.

Regardless of the technique used, the quality of the capital budgeting decision rests on the accuracy with which future cash flows can be estimated. Forecasting future income to be generated by a project is often the starting point for determining future cash flows.

12.4 Management Control

There are various methods of classification of management control in MNEs. By levels of control here it is meant whether the parent/corporate level managers or subsidiary/country-level managers are involved. The former might be called higher level and the later lower level control. Depending on the sphere of focus we have two types of control called "Strategic control and operational control". In the MNE's context, strategic control is the responsibility of parent and operational control is the preserve of the subsidiary.

Another way puts "management control, tactical control and transactional control" as the 3 levels of control respectively carried out by the corporate top management, collectively by corporate & subsidiary management and subsidiary management in the case of MNEs. Of course, whether an MNE's structure is ethno-centric, geo-centric, multi-domestic/poly-centric or region-centric is another factor that influences the exact distribution of responsibility.

The forward looking information is provided by strategic control systems. It is "external response" oriented. It gives managers timely "quantitative and qualitative" information they need to "drive into the future" with confidence and success. In dynamic and uncertain business environment with extended competitive challenges this system functions well. Sensing and responding to change, detecting changes in assumptions and coping with a dynamic environment are the specific issues in strategic control. Operational control is "internal response" oriented to ensure targets are achieved. Managers use performance measurement and operational control measures to ensure fulfillment of targets.

Management controls keep a company's Goals or Strategy on track. Strategic control adapts an organization over time to forces in its environment, such as changes in society, advances in technology, development of the economy, and shifts in policy. MNE managers must know that, although cost and innovation are important, the company's major competitive advantage lies in the marketing of differentiated/ undifferentiated consumer products. As such, it is better subsidiary's managers concentrate on marketing-such as branding, advertising, and distribution-rather while corporate managers concentrate on capacity building through acquiring capital or business units or pursuing R&D. Corporate managers must have a clear-cut understanding of competitive entry strategies. They should look to acquire first-in advantages or companies with an established brand and significant market share. Corporate managers allocate resources to emphasize those product and geographic markets in which they prefer to grow more rapidly. It would be almost inconceivable for a subsidiary manager to launch a new product in his area or build a plant there without considerable scrutiny and approval from corporate management in the headquarters. But it is needed that country-level managers adjust to specific environmental and competitive conditions in their countries of operation. At the same time, the subsidiaries share information, fixed costs from new product development, and spillover advantages, which make it easier for the parent to sell to global distributors.

Tactical controls involve control with field reality in mind while acting within a set of policy and budgetary allocations. They cannot compromise on key results, but depending on the exigencies follow a different priority from the planned one. Tactical controls are budgetary control, authority/responsibility changes, procurement control, production control etc. Speed of execution, balancing diverse claims and the like involve. Sensitivity to the situation rather than strict adherence to rules and procedures, making navigational changes as circumstances warrant, etc are involved. The corporate and subsidiary level managers collectively do this, though the role of subsidiary level is more.

Transactional controls deal with individual tasks and processes within the envelope of available resources. While primarily aimed at ensuring that these individual efforts are efficient, operational control also maps these to the overall control goals. Inventory control, action against delinquent customers, procurement procedures, etc come here. These are the preserve of the subsidiary managers.

For MNEs, a successful performance evaluation system must be sensitive to the national cultures to which local managers belong. Indeed, cultural factors should be considered in the entire strategy implementation process.

Implementing a corporate strategy that will influence human behavior in the desired manner requires cultural awareness, as a given method of implementation may not produce the desired outcome across all cultures. Noerreklit and Schoenfeld (2000) explain how differences in culturally determined value systems may lead to different managerial decisions across countries:

Different background knowledge and culturally determined value systems exist in all MNEs, because employees grow up and are educated in different national environments and thus have non-congruent value systems. Such different values may (at a minimum) place a different emphasis on specific issues. Different emphasis and values are typically placed on specific subjects during the educational process (e.g., ethics, family relationships, work, sports, art, moral contained in children stories, songs, and proverbs). Each of these influences (individually or jointly) will evoke slightly or substantially different reactions in people. This applies for day-to-day life as well as for management decisions as a special dimension of life. It suggests different actions to resolve similar problems (e.g., under-utilisation of capacity may suggest lay-offs in the US, however, in Europe, due to the existing labor law and tradition, a lay-off is too costly or unacceptable socially) (Noerreklit and Schoenfeld, 2000).

Due to cultural differences, MNEs may find that changes are necessary to the manner in which strategies are implemented in different countries. For example, Japanese companies assign responsibility to the group rather than to the individual, and every group member is partially responsible for the group's performance (Kelley, Whatley and Worthley, 2001).

This notion of group responsibility conflicts with the way standard costs and budgets are used in the United States, in which responsibility is assigned to specific individuals within an organization. This also calls into question the universal acceptability of one of the fundamental assumptions of the Western concept of management control—that the responsibility for specific tasks lies with the individual to whom the task is traceable. Research also has found differences between the United States and Japan in their use of budgets. U.S. managers tend to be more involved in the budgeting process, and budget variances are used as the basis for evaluating performance and determining rewards. Japanese managers, in contrast, tend to view budget variances as providing information that can be used to improve performance (Bailes and Assada, 1991).

Local managers' attitudes toward budgets also can be influenced by environmental factors. Researchers have discovered, for example, that managers in Central American countries view budgets as less critical than U.S. managers do (Mandoza, Collins and Holzmann, 1997).

Central American managers are more likely to see budgets as a source of certainty and security and as a means to protect resources amid turbulence, rather than as a performance evaluation and planning tool. The researchers argue that the differing attitudes toward budgets are due partly to the widely varying levels of environmental turbulence between the United States and Central America. Culture also can affect management styles. Researchers have found that Mexican executives tend to use an authoritarian leadership style, do not see the need to share information with subordinates, and have little faith in participative management styles. This will have direct implications for the manner in which budgeting is applied within Mexican organizations. In particular, the idea of participative budgeting is not likely to be well received (Kelley, Whatley and Worthley, 1987).

Finally, cultural differences can influence capital budgeting decisions. For example, strong uncertainty avoidance (intolerance of uncertainty) can lead managers to require short payback periods for capital investments, because once the investment is recouped, the level of uncertainty associated with the investment is reduced significantly. This makes projects with shorter payback periods the preferred choice for some managers, even though projects with longer payback periods may produce greater longer-term benefits.

12.5 Currency Effect on MNEs

For MNEs, exchange rate changes have impact on consolidated financial statement conversion as well as enterprise's performance. For example, Argos, a MNE's main business is in Europe, the standard currency is British pound. The company needs to buy oil and oil-related products, which are dollar denominated, so the oil costs are dollar denominated and their revenues are denominated in other European currencies. If the pound appreciates against all other currencies, then revenues arising from foreign sales, and even those from U.K. sales subject to competitive pressures, will be reduced. As partial compensation, raw material costs (dollar-denominated oil) will be lower, but on Argos's consolidated financial statement is worse off because the decrease in raw material costs is less than the decrease in sales revenue in absolute terms. The figure can be significant because Argos is the U.K.'s largest single exporter (Choi, Meek, 2010).

Exchange rate variation also affects firm's asset, liability and expenses if company borrows foreign currency. For example, Argos subsidiary in United States borrowed 10 years long term loan of $1,000,000, and the exchange rate was GBP/USD=2, which means the parent company has British pound liability of GBP500,000. However, in the year end, British pound depreciated and the exchange rate became GBP/USD=1.4, the long term debt suddenly become GBP714,286.

12.6 Multinational Performance Evaluation

12.6.1 Economic value added (EVA)

Economic value added (EVA) is an estimate of a firm's economic profit, which is the value created in excess of the required return of the company's shareholders and debt holders.

ROIC: return on invested capital (operating profit minutes cash taxes paid dividend by average invested capital)

WACC: weighted average cost of capital (net cost of debt × percentage of debt used) + (net cost of equity × percentage of equity used)

AIC: average invested capital (average shareholder equity+ average debt)

EVA= (ROIC-WACC)×AIC

Exhibit 12.3   Economic value added

Total revenues	$10000(million)	Total costs	$5000(million)
Total operating expenses	2000	Cash tax paid	100
Shareholders' equity(average)	3000	Debt(average)	5000
After tax cost of debt	6%	Percentage of debt used	62.5%(5000/(5000+3000))
Cost of equity	15%	Percentage of equity used	37.5%(3000/(5000+3000))

Then the operating profit = 10000 − 5000 − 2000 − 100 = 2900

AIC = 3000 + 5000 = 8000

ROIC = 2900/8000 = 35.3%

WACC = (6% × 62.5) + (15% × 37.5) = 9.4%

EVA = (35.3% − 9.4%) × 8000 = 2072

From this example, we found EVA is positive as ROIC is larger than WACC, which means the company is adding value to the shareholder. The former CEO of Coca-Cola Roberto Goizueta said: "we raise capital to make concentrate, and sell it at an operating profit. Then we pay the cost of that capital. Shareholders pocket the difference." While in the real world, multinational enterprises' EVA computation might be influenced by currency fluctuation.

12.6.2 Balanced scorecard (BSC)

One of the most important achievements in the design of performance evaluation systems in recent years was the introduction of the balanced scorecard (BSC) in the early 1990s. Kaplan and Norton (1996) were awarded a prize by the American Accounting Association as the best theoretical contribution in 1997. In the business world, the balanced scorecard engendered great interest internationally. By 2004, about 57 percent of global companies were working with the balanced scorecard (Nerrelit, 2003). A balanced scorecard combines financial measures of past performance with nonfinancial measures of the drivers of future performance to provide management with a road map for creating shareholder value.

The balanced scorecard provides a framework to look at the strategies giving rise to value creation from the following perspectives (see Exhibit 12.4):

1. Financial perspective—growth, profitability, and risk from the perspective of shareholders.

2. Customer perspective—value and differentiation from the customer perspective.

3. Internal business perspective—the priorities for various business processes that create customer and shareholder satisfaction.

4 . Learning and innovation perspective—the priorities to create a climate supporting organizational change, innovation, and growth.

EXHIBIT 12.4 Basic Model of a Balanced Scorecard Performance System

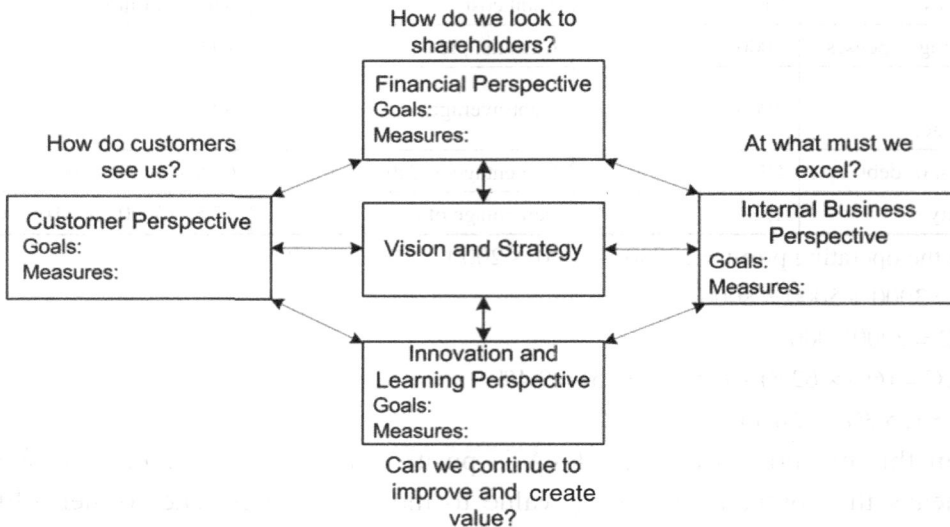

How do we look to shareholders?

Financial Perspective
Goals:
Measures:

How do customers see us?

Customer Perspective
Goals:
Measures:

Vision and Strategy

At what must we excel?

Internal Business Perspective
Goals:
Measures:

Innovation and Learning Perspective
Goals:
Measures:

Can we continue to improve and create value?

Source: Robert S. Kaplan and David P. Norton, "The Balanced Scorecard: measures That Drive Performance" Harvard Business Review, January–February 1992, p72.

BSC approach reveals the drives of long-term competitive performance. Although a firm's BSC is a proprietary strategy tool and is generally not available to general public, its principles are evident in strategic decisions made by MNEs. For example, IKEA, the Swedish firm, with Swedish culture and a centralized operation style, has become the world's largest furniture retailer. IKEA spread a simple concept: offer the broadest range of furniture at the lowest price possible. IKEA's success begins with internal learning and growth by insuring that all employees are trained in the cost-saving, hands-on, customer focused mentality. This enables employees to focus on creating efficient processes that keep costs down. For example, the design team is constantly looking for new materials and suppliers to lower the cost of furniture without sacrificing quality. Since its founding, IKEA identifies a customer base that would find value in low cost, innovative furniture: young couples looking to furnish their first apartment. This strategy contributes tremendous profit to the firm.

While establish a coherent BSC for an MNE still have some challenges. For example, as IKEA grows, it faces different customer bases in different countries. IKEA must also ensure that its product line appeal in various markets of operation. The cultural, geographical, and financial complexity of an MNE makes it challenging to establish a set of interrelated, cause-and-effect performance measures. Adequate use of BSC helps managers avoid using only one measure of performance (such as ROI), and forces them to link financial measure with non-financial factors.

Terms of this Chapter

activity based costing (abc) 作业成本法
average invested capital 平均投入资本
balanced scorecard (bsc) 平衡计分卡
capital investment techniques 资本投资技术
costing system 成本系统
consumption estimates 消费估计
currency fluctuation 货币波动
Discounted Cash Flow 贴现现金流
economic profit 经济利润
economic value added (eva) 经济增加值
environmental turbulence 环境波动
exchange rate variation 汇率变动
internal business perspective 内部业务视角
Internal Rate of Return 内部收益率
management accounting 管理会计
management control 管理控制
Net Present Value (NPV) 净现值
overheads 管理费用
Payback Period 投资回收期
performance evaluation 绩效评价
return on invested capital(ROI) 投资资本回报率
Return on Investment (ROI) 投资回报率
tactical control 战术控制
transactional control 事务控制
weighted average cost of capital(WACC) 加权平均资本成本

Discussion Questions

1. Explain the differences between traditional costing system and activity based costing.

2. When and how a MNE use Activity Based Costing system?

3. What's the disadvantage if we make capital investment decisions just by using ROI method?

4. Describe the differences of management control, tactical control and transactional control.

5. Demonstrate an understanding of culture influence on management control.

6. Discuss the effect of Currency fluctuation on MNEs.

7. Explain difference of the two performance evaluation system within a multinational corporation.

8. Describe the procedure of balanced scorecard.

9. Describe the calculation procedure of economic value added.

True or False

1. Management accounting provides information to shareholder to make investment decisions.

2. Activity-based costing method allocates overheads first to the individual departments then reallocates the costs to products.

3. Management controls keep a company's goals or strategy on track.

4. Tactical controls involve control like inventory control.

5. Cultural differences can also influence capital budgeting decisions.

6. If firm's net profit is positive, it means the company created in excess of the required return of the company's shareholders.

7. Balance scorecard approach reveals the drives of short-term competitive performance.

8. One of the most important achievements in the design of performance evaluation systems in recent years was the introduction of the balanced scorecard (BSC) in the early 1990s.

9. Economic value added (EVA) is the value created in excess of the required return of the company's shareholders and debt holders.

10. Exchange rate changes do not have impact on consolidated financial statement conversion as well as enterprise's performance.

Multiple Choice

1. Which one is not right about of activity-based costing method?
    a. It provides more accurate product costs.
    b. It helps managers setting selling prices and in deciding to whether make or buy components.
    c. It enhances control of overhead costs.
    d. It allocates overheads directly to the individual departments.

2. Which one is not the technique used for capital investment decision?
    a. Internal rate of return.
    b. Return on investment.

c. Payback period.

d. Balanced scorecard.

3. Which one is not a perspective for balanced scorecard?

a. Financial perspective.

b. Supply perspective.

c. Learning and innovation perspective.

d. Internal business perspective.

4. A Chinese multinational enterprise's main business is in China, the standard currency is RMB, if the U.S. subsidiary borrowed long term US Dollar and at the end of the year Dollar appreciates, what would be the effect of currency change on consolidated financial statement?

a. More liability.

b. More revenue.

c. Less expense.

d. More shareholders equity.

5. In order to calculate a project's IRR, what information do you need?

a. Opportunity cost.

b. Discount rate.

c. Probability of success.

d. Initial investment.

6. Which one is not true about balanced scorecard?

a. BSC aligns business activities to the vision and strategy of the organization.

b. BSC is a universal strategic planning and management system.

c. BSC improves internal and external communications.

d. BSC monitors organization performance against strategic goals.

Exercises

1. If a firm have ¥100,000 funds, including bond (WB) of RMB30,000, preferred stock (WP) of RMB10,000, ordinary shares (WS) of RMB40,000, retained earnings of RMB20,000, the cost of funds respectively are 6%, 12%, 15.5% and 15%.

Calculate the weighted average cost of capital of the enterprise.

2. If the firm have an opportunity to invest a 5 year's project for $10,000, and get $1,000, $2,000, $3,000, $5,000, $5,000 revenue respectively for the next 5 years.

Using the WACC calculated from the last question as discount rate, calculate the NPV, and discuss whether the company should invest in this project.

3. If a firm have 3 potential investment opportunities, Which one would be the best investing opportunity?

Exhibit 12.5　Potential investment opportunities

Project	Required Investment	Average Annual Net Income
A	$100,000	$12,000
B	800,000	80,000
C	200,000	4,000

4. Using the data provided below,

Exhibit 12.6　Data provided

Total revenues	$30,000(million)	Total costs	$9000(million)
Total operating expenses	7,000	Cash tax paid	1,000
Shareholders' equity(average)	10,000	Debt(average)	20,000
After tax cost of debt	8%	Cost of equity	20%

(1) Calculate the percentage of equity used.

(2) Calculate the percentage of debt used.

(3) Calculate operating profit.

(4) Calculate ROIC(return on invested capital).

(5) Calculate WACC(weighted average cost of capital).

(6) Calculate AIC(average invested capital).

(7) Calculate EVA.

(8) Please identify whether the firm actually bring value to shareholders.

Chapter 13　International Taxation and Transfer price

![Learning objective icon] *Learning objective*

After careful study of this chapter, students will be able to:

1. Describe differences in corporate income tax and withholding tax regimes across countries

2. Explain how overlapping tax jurisdictions cause double taxation

3. Show how foreign tax credits reduce the incidence of double taxation

4. Demonstrate how rules related to controlled foreign corporations, subpart F income, and foreign tax credit baskets affect U.S. taxation of foreign source income

5. Describe the importance of transfer pricing

6. Discuss the transfer pricing methods used in sales of tangible property.

7. Show how discretionary transfer pricing can be used to achieve specific cost minimization objectives.

Tax is a huge expense for most businesses, as it reduces net profits as well as cash flow. It is important for enterprises to minimize international taxes whenever possible. It is essential to have the knowledge of how the domestic country taxes the profits earned in foreign countries. Multinational enterprises (MNEs) make a number of very important decisions in which taxation is an important variable. Financial managers must contend with special rules regarding the taxation of foreign-source income. Besides, international tax agreements, laws, and regulations are not constant. Changes in one country's tax provisions have complex and wide-ranging effects in a multinational tax-planning system. In order to do tax planning for MNEs, there are some major variables that managers should be aware of, which are differences in national tax systems (i.e., how countries tax businesses operating in their jurisdictions), national attempts to address the issue of double taxation (i.e., how countries tax the foreign-source income of their business entities), and arbitrage opportunities between national tax jurisdictions for multinational firms.

13.1　Differences in National Tax System

A corporation conducts international trade by exporting goods and services or by making direct or indirect foreign investments. Exports seldom trigger a tax exposure in the importing country, as it is difficult for importing countries to enforce taxes levied on foreign exporters. besides, a company that operates in another country through a branch or an incorporated affiliate subjects itself to that country's taxes. Different tax systems (types of taxes, tax burdens, tax assessment and collection philosophies) will affect the effective management of tax exposure.

13.1.1 Types of taxes and tax rates

Corporations are subject to many different types of taxes, including property taxes, payroll taxes, and excise taxes. While it is important for managers of MNEs to be knowledgeable about these taxes, we focus on taxes on profit. The two major types of taxes imposed on profits earned by companies engaged in international business are corporate income taxes and withholding taxes, others indirect taxes such as Value-added tax, border taxes and transfer tax.

1．Income Taxes

Exhibit 13.1   International Corporate Tax Rates, 2012

Country	Effective Tax Rate (%)	Country	Effective Tax Rate (%)
Argentina	35	Italy	31.4
Australia	30	Japan	28[4]
Austria	25	Korea (South)	24.2
Belgium	34	Malaysia	25
Brazil	34[1]	Mexico	30
Canada	26[2]	Netherlands	25.5
Chile	18.5	New Zealand	28
China	25	Russia	20
Czech Republic	19	Singapore	17
Denmark	25	Spain	30
France	33.33	Sweden	26.3
Germany	29.48[3]	Switzerland	21.17[5]
Greece	30	Taiwan	17
Hong Kong	16.5	Thailand	23
Hungary	19	Turkey	20
Indonesia	25	United Kingdom	24
Ireland	12.5	United States	35[6]
Israel	25	Venezuela	34

Sources: KPMG, Corporate and Indirect Tax Rate Survey 2012, available at www.kpmg.comx

Notes:

① The effective tax rate on corporate profits in Brazil is the sum of a corporation income tax (25%) and a social contribution tax (9%).

② The Canadian effective tax rate is comprised of a federal corporate income tax rate of 19% plus a provincial corporate income tax rate, which varies by province. Depending on the province, the combined general corporate income tax rate ranges from 25−31%.

③ This is an approximate rate consisting of a 15% federal corporate income tax, a 0.825% solidarity tax, and an additional trade tax, which varies by locality.

④ The effective tax rate in Japan varies by locality. The rate presented relates to a company located in Tokyo.

⑤ The Swiss federal tax rate is 8.5%. Individual cantons levy an additional corporate income tax. The rate presented is for the canton of Zurich.

⑥ The U.S. federal tax rate is 35%. Individual states assess different levels of local tax, ranging from 0~12%.

Most, but not all, national governments impose a direct tax on business income. Exhibit 13.1 shows that national corporate income tax rates vary substantially across countries. The corporate income tax rate in most countries is between 20 and 35 percent. Differences in corporate tax rates across countries provide MNEs with a tax-planning opportunity as they decide where to locate foreign operations. In making this decision, MNEs must be careful to consider both national and local taxes in their analysis. In some countries, local governments impose a separate tax on business income in addition to that levied by the national government. For example, the national tax rate in Switzerland is 8.5 percent, but additional local taxes range anywhere from 6 percent to 33 percent. A company located in Zurich can expect to pay an effective tax rate of 21.17 percent to local and federal governments. Corporate income tax rates imposed by individual states in the United States vary from 0 percent (e.g., South Dakota) to as high as 12 percent (Iowa). In a few countries, corporate income taxes can vary according to the type of activity in which a company is engaged or the nationality of the company's owners. As examples, the rate of national income tax in France is reduced to 15 percent on income generated from certain intellectual property rights, in Malaysia a special 5 percent rate applies to corporations involved in qualified insurance businesses, and India taxes foreign companies at a 10 percent higher rate than domestic companies. In making foreign investment decisions, MNEs often engage in a capital budgeting process in which the future cash flows to be generated by the foreign investment are forecast, discounted to their present value, and then compared with the amount to be invested to determine a net present value. Taxes paid to the foreign government will have a negative impact on future cash flows and might affect the location decision. For example, assume that a Japanese musical instrument manufacturer is deciding whether to locate a new factory in Hungary or in Switzerland. Although the national tax rate in Hungary is much higher than in Switzerland, the effective tax rate in some parts of Switzerland would be higher than in Hungary because of the high local taxes that would have to be paid.

Apparently, the amount of taxes paid to a government is not determined solely by the corporate tax rate. The manner in which taxable income is calculated also will greatly affect a company's tax liability. Just as tax rates vary from country to country, so does the way in which taxable income is calculated. Expenses that can be deducted for tax purposes can vary greatly from country to country. For example, in the United States, only the first $1 million of the chief executive officer's salary is tax deductible. Most other countries do not have a similar rule.

The United States allows companies to use the last-in, first-out (LIFO) method for inventory valuation and accelerated depreciation methods for fixed assets in determining taxable income, whereas Brazil and China does not. All else being equal, a company with increasing inventory prices that is replacing or expanding its fixed assets will have smaller taxable income in the United States than in Brazil and China. The United States has a higher corporate income tax rate than Brazil, but because taxable income is smaller, a company in the United States may actually have a smaller amount of taxes to pay.

There has been a recent and continuing international trend to reduce corporate tax rates. The United States appears to have led the way in 1986 when the corporate tax rate was reduced from 46 percent to 34 percent (it was subsequently raised to 35 percent in 1994). The United Kingdom quickly followed suit by reducing its rate from 50 percent to 35 percent, Canada from 34 percent to 29 percent, and so on. More recently, Belgium lowered its rate from 40.17 percent in 2002 to 33.99 percent in 2003, and Austria lowered its rate from 34 percent to 25 percent in 2005. Israel has gradually lowered its tax rate from 36 percent in 2004 to 25 percent in 2012[1]. This follow-the-leader effect is explained by the fact that countries compete against one another in attracting foreign investment.

One way to compete for foreign investment is to offer a so-called tax holiday. For example, to attract foreign investment, the prime minister of the Czech Republic announced in March 2000 that foreign enterprises that invest at least $10 million may be entitled to a 10-year exemption from income taxation and customs duties. Following the financial crisis in Asia in the late 1990s, several countries in that region adopted various measures including tax incentives to help their economies recover. More recently, in 2011, Indonesia established holidays ranging from five to ten years for new projects in six categories of industries, including base metals, oil refining, petrochemicals, renewable energy, machinery, and telecommunications equipment.

2. Withholding Taxes

When a foreign citizen who invests in the shares of a U.S. company receives a dividend payment, theoretically he or she should file a tax return with the U.S. Internal Revenue Service and pay taxes on the dividend income. If the foreign investor does not file this tax return, the U.S. government has no recourse for collecting the tax. To avoid this possibility, the United States (like most other countries) will require the payer of

---

[1] World Bank and PricewaterhouseCoopers. Paying Taxes 2010: The Global Picture, available at www.doingbusiness.org

the dividend (the U.S. company) to withhold some amount of taxes and remit that amount to the U.S. government. This type of tax is referred to as a withholding tax. The withholding tax rate on dividends in the United States is 30 percent. To see how the withholding tax works, assume that International Business Machines Corporation (IBM), a U.S.-based company, pays a $100 dividend to a stockholder in Brazil. Under U.S. withholding tax rules, IBM would withhold $30 from the payment (which is sent to the U.S. Internal Revenue Service) and the Brazilian stockholder would be issued a check in the amount of $70. Withholding taxes are also imposed on payments made to foreign parent companies or foreign affiliated companies. There are three types of payments typically subject to withholding tax: dividends, interest, and royalties. Withholding tax rates vary across countries, and in some countries withholding rates vary by type of payment or recipient. Exhibit 13.2 provides withholding rates generally applicable in selected countries. In many cases, the rate listed will be different for some subset of activity. For example, although the U.S. withholding rate on interest payments is generally 30 percent, interest on bank deposits and on certain registered debt instruments (bonds) is exempt (0 percent tax).

Exhibit 13.2   Nontreaty Withholding Rates in Selected Countries and Areas

Country	Dividends(%)	Interest(%)	Royalties(%)
Australia	30	10	30
Austria	25	0	20
Brazil	0	15	15
Canada	25	25	25
France	30	0	33.3
Germany	25	0	15
Indonesia	20	20	20
Italy	20	12.5 or 20	30
Japan	20.42	15.31 or 20.42	20.42
Korea (South)	20	20	20
Malaysia	0	15	10
Mexico	0	4.9-30	25 or 30
New Zealand	30	15	15
Philippines	30	30	30
Singapore	0	15	10
Spain	21	21	24.75
Sweden	30	0	0
Switzerland	35	35	0
Taiwan	20	15 or 20	20
Thailand	10	15	15
United Kingdom	0	20	20
United States	30	30	30

Source: Deloitte, Withholding Tax Rates Matrix, available at:

3. Value-added tax

The value-added tax is a consumption tax found in Europe and Canada. This tax is typically levied on the value added at each stage of production or distribution. It applies to total sales less purchases from any intermediate sales unit. Thus, if an American merchant buys $500,000 of merchandise from an American wholesaler and then sells it for $600,000, the value added is $100,000, and a tax is assessed on this amount. Companies that pay the tax in their own costs can reclaim them later from the tax authorities. Consumers ultimately bear the cost of the value added tax.

Value-added taxes as well as other *indirect taxes* (such as sales and payroll taxes) need to be considered in determining the total rate of taxation to be paid in a country. A study conducted by the World Bank and PricewaterhouseCoopers in 2010 determined the total tax rate paid on business income in 183 countries[1]. Total tax rates in selected other countries were shown in Exhibit 13.3.

Exhibit 13.3   Total rate of taxation

Country	Tax rates	Country	Tax rates	Country	Tax rates
Brazil	69.20%	Hong Kong	24.20%	New Zealand	32.80%
Canada	43.60%	India	64.70%	Poland	42.50%
Chile	25.30%	Italy	68.40%	Saudi Arabia	14.50%
China	63.80%	Japan	55.70%	Switzerland	29.70%
France	65.80%	Mexico	51.00%	United Kingdom	35.90%
Germany	44.90%	Namibia	9.60%	United States	46.30%

Source: The World Bank and PricewaterhouseCoopers, Paying Taxes 2010

4. Border taxes

Border taxes like customs or import duties aim to protect domestic goods competing with imports. Border taxes assessed on imports typically parallel excise and other *indirect taxes* paid by domestic producers of similar goods.

5. Transfer tax

The transfer tax is another *indirect tax*. It is imposed on transfers of items between taxpayers and can have important effects on such business decisions as the structure of acquisitions, it is a transaction fee imposed on the transfer of title to property. This kind of tax is typically imposed where there is a legal requirement for registration of the transfer, such as transfers of real estate, shares, or bond. For example, business acquisitions in Europe are often made through the purchase of shares rather than the underlying net assets. More variations in structure are found in U.S. acquisitions

---

[1] The World Bank and PricewaterhouseCoopers, Paying Taxes 2010: The Global Picture, available at
www.doingbusiness.org/documents/fullreport/2010/paying-taxes-2010.pdf.

because transfer taxes are less important in the United States.

13.1.2 Tax burdens

In the real world, effective tax rates seldom equal nominal tax rates. A low tax rate does not necessarily mean a low tax burden. Tax burdens should always be determined by examining effective tax rates, which associate with tax rates and taxable income.

In theory, a portion of the cost of an asset is said to expire as the asset is used up to produce revenue. In keeping with the matching principle, this expired cost is recognized as an expense and deducted from its related revenue. Where the asset is consumed equally in each reporting period, an equal portion of its cost is commonly expensed each period for external financial reporting purposes. In the United States, however, a distinction is generally made between depreciation for external reporting and depreciation for tax purposes. As an incentive to invest in capital assets, including commercial buildings, companies in the United States are allowed to use accelerated depreciation methods. In Germany, tax law specifies depreciation rates, and buildings are depreciated in straight-line fashion. Tax law also determines depreciation rates in France, with most assets depreciated on a straight-line basis. However, antipollution and energy-saving assets may be depreciated on an accelerated basis.

Another item that accounts for inter-country differences in effective tax burdens relates to the host country's social overhead. To attract foreign investments, less industrialized countries often reduce marginal corporate tax rates, or broad corporate tax base. However, countries with low direct taxes need to fund government and other social services just like any other country. Therefore, lower direct corporate tax rates usually result in higher indirect taxes or in fewer and lower quality public services. Indirect taxes reduce purchasing power in the local market. Fewer and lower quality public services may impose a higher cost structure on multinational operations. Examples include poor transportation networks, inadequate postal services, ineffective telephone and telecommunications systems, and power shortages.

13.1.3 Tax havens

There are a number of tax jurisdictions with abnormally low corporate income tax rates (or no corporate income tax at all) that companies and individuals have found useful in minimizing their worldwide income taxes. These tax jurisdictions, known as tax havens, include the Bahamas and the Isle of Man, which have no corporate income tax, and Liechtenstein, which has tax rates ranging from 7.5%to 15%[1]. The worldwide trend toward both lowering and converging corporate income tax rates is a direct result of tax competition. Is tax competition harmful? Certainly it is beneficial if it makes

---

[1] https://en.wikipedia.org/wiki/Tax_haven

governments more efficient. On the other hand, it is harmful when it shifts tax revenues away from governments that need them to provide services on which businesses rely. The OECD's main concern has been about tax havens that allow businesses to avoid or evade another country's taxes. So-called brass plate subsidiaries have no real work or employment attached to them: They lack substantial activities and merely funnel financial transactions through the tax-haven country to avoid another country's taxes. The OECD lists four factors for identifying a tax haven[1], which are no or low taxes on income, lack of effective exchange of information, lack of transparency and no substantial activities.

In 2000, the OECD identified over 40 countries as tax havens. These countries often advertise their no or low tax rates to lure foreign money and had a "don't ask, don't tell" policy regarding foreign income. They often stonewalled requests from other countries who were hunting tax evaders. The Organization for Economic Cooperation and Development (OECD) has established guidelines for tax regimes to ensure that they cannot be used to avoid taxation in other countries. Uncooperative tax havens were pressured to adopt practices on the effective exchange of information and transparency. The pressure worked. By 2009, all uncooperative tax havens were removed from the original list. Now tax haven countries with 0% corporate tax rate are: Bahamas, Bahrain, Cayman Islands, Isle of Man, Jersey, Sark, Saudi Arabia, United Arab Emirates, British Virgin Islands.[2]

A company involved in international business might find it beneficial to establish an operation in a tax haven to avoid paying taxes in one or more countries in which the company operates. For example, assume a Brazilian company manufactures a product for $70 per unit that it exports to a customer in Mexico at a sales price of $100 per unit. The $30 of profit earned on each unit is subject to the Brazilian corporate tax rate of 34 percent. The Brazilian manufacturer could take advantage of the fact that there is no corporate income tax in the Bahamas by establishing a sales subsidiary there that it uses as a conduit for export sales. The Brazilian parent company would then sell the product to its Bahamian sales subsidiary at a price of, say, $80 per unit, and the Bahamian sales subsidiary would turn around and sell the product to the customer in Mexico at $100 per unit. In this way, only $10 of the total profit is earned in Brazil and subject to Brazilian income tax; $20 of the $30 total profit is recorded in the Bahamas and is therefore not taxed.

13.1.4 International harmonization

International tax reform and global harmonization of tax policies are needed as

---

① OECD, overview of the OECD's work on Countering International Tax Evasion (June 17, 2009)
② Deloitte & Touche. Taxation and Investment Guides: BVI Highlights 2013,

multinational companies are burdened by the disparities of national taxes. The European Union spare no effort in this direction as it works to create a single market. The EU's introduction of a single currency, the euro, highlights the tax disparities among its members.

13.2 Double Taxation

The combination of a worldwide approach to taxation and the various bases for taxation can lead to overlapping tax jurisdictions that can in turn lead to double or even triple taxation. For example, a U.S. citizen residing in Germany with investment income in Austria might be expected to pay taxes on the investment income to the United States (on the basis of citizenship), Germany (on the basis of residence), and Austria (on the basis of source).

The same is true for corporate taxpayers with foreign source income. The most common overlap of jurisdictions for corporations is where the home country taxes on the basis of residence and the country where the foreign branch or subsidiary is located taxes on the basis of source. Without some relief, this could result in a tremendous tax burden for the parent company. For example, income earned by the Japanese branch of a U.S. company would be taxed at the effective Japanese corporate income tax rate of 41% and at the rate of 35% in the United States, for an aggregate tax rate of 76%. The U.S. parent has only 24% of the profit after income taxes. At that rate, there is a disincentive to establish operations overseas. Without any relief from double taxation, all investment by the U.S. company would remain at home in the United States, where income would be taxed only at the rate of 35%.

An important goal of most national tax systems is neutrality; that is, the tax system should remain in the background, and business, investment, and consumption decisions should be made for non-tax reasons. In an international context, there are three standards for neutrality, one of which is capital-export neutrality. A tax system meets this standard if a taxpayer's decision whether to invest at home or overseas is not affected by taxation. Double taxation from overlapping tax jurisdictions precludes a tax system from achieving capital-export neutrality; all investment will remain at home. In order to achieve capital-export neutrality, most countries have one or more mechanisms for eliminating the problem of double taxation. One mechanism is a provision in bilateral tax treaties between countries in which foreign source income is exempt. Another major source of relief from double taxation is the foreign tax credit. For U.S. citizens and residents, including domestic corporations, perhaps the most important international tax provisions are those dealing with the foreign tax credit (Doernberg, 1999).

13.2.1 Foreign tax credit

Double taxation of income earned by foreign operations generally arises because the country where the foreign operation is located taxes the income at its source and the parent company's home country taxes worldwide income on the basis of residence. To relieve the double taxation, the question is, Which country should give up its right to tax the income? The international norm is that source should take precedence over residence in determining tax jurisdiction. In that case, it will be up to the parent company's home country to eliminate the double taxation. In keeping with the concept of foreign neutrality, a parent company's domicile (country of residence) can elect to treat foreign taxes paid as a credit against the parent's domestic tax liability or as a deduction from taxable income. Companies generally choose the credit, because it yields a one-for-one reduction of domestic taxes payable (limited to the amount of income taxes actually paid), whereas a deduction is only worth the product of the foreign tax expense multiplied by the domestic marginal tax rate. Foreign tax credits may be calculated as a straightforward credit against income taxes paid on branch or subsidiary earnings and any taxes withheld at the source, such as dividends, interest, and royalties remitted to a domestic investor.

The tax credit can also be estimated when the amount of foreign income tax paid is not clearly evident (e.g., when a foreign subsidiary remits a fraction of its foreign source earnings to its domestic parent). Reported dividend on the parent company's tax return would be grossed up to include the amount of the tax (deemed paid), plus any applicable foreign withholding taxes. It is as if the domestic parent received a dividend including the tax due the foreign government and then paid the tax.

The allowable foreign indirect tax credit (foreign income tax deemed paid) is determined as follows:

$$\frac{\text{Dividend payout(including any withholding tax)}}{\text{Earnings net of foreign income tax}} * \text{Creditable foreign taxes}$$

To illustrate how foreign tax credits apply in a variety of situations, assume that a U.S. parent company receives royalties from Country A, foreign-branch earnings from Country B, and dividends from subsidiaries in Countries C and D. Withholding taxes on royalty and dividend payments are assumed to be 15% in Countries A, C, and D; income tax rates are assumed to be 30 percent in Country B and 40% in Country C. Country D assesses a 40% indirect sales tax as opposed to a direct tax on earnings within its jurisdiction.

The key variables in this illustration, as shown in Exhibit 13.4 are the organizational form of the foreign activity (e.g., branch vs. subsidiary) and relative corporate income and withholding tax rates. In the first column, the royalty payment of

$20.00 is subject to a 15% withholding tax in the host country (netting a $17.00 payment to the parent). For U.S. tax purposes, the net royalty is grossed up to include the withholding tax, which then forms the base for the U.S. domestic tax of 35%. The U.S. tax of $7.00 is offset by the credit for the foreign tax paid to yield a net U.S. tax liability of $4.00.

In the second column of Exhibit 13.4, the foreign branch earnings of the U.S. parent are grossed up to include foreign income taxes paid of $30.00. U.S. taxes payable on this amount of $35.00 are offset by a foreign tax credit of $30.00, to yield a net U.S. Tax payable of $5.00. As with the royalty payment, the effect of the foreign tax credit is to limit the total tax on foreign-source income to the higher of the two countries' taxes. In this example, the U.S. tax rate of 35% was higher than the foreign tax rate of 30%, yielding a total tax on royalty and branch earnings of 35%.

Exhibit 13.4   U.S. Taxation of Foreign-Source Income

	Royalties from Operation in Country A	Earnings from Branch in Country B	Dividend from Subsidiary in Country C	Dividend from Subsidiary in Country D
Branch/subsidiary				
Before-tax earnings		100	100	60
Foreign income taxes(30%/40%)		30	40	0
After tax earnings		70	60	60
Dividend paid (50% of after-tax earnings)			30	30
Other foreign income	20			
Foreign withholding taxes (15%)	3		4.5	4.5
Net payment to parent	17		25.5	25.5
U.S. income	20	100	30	30
Dividend gross-up(30/60*40)			20	0
Taxable income	20	100	50	30
U.S. Tax (35%)	7	35	17.5	10.5
Foreign tax credit				
Paid	(3)	(30)	(4.5)	(4.5)
Deemed paid(30/60*40)			(20)	0
Total	(3)	(30)	(24.5)	(4.5)
U.S. Tax (net)	4	5	7	6
Foreign taxes	3	30	24.5	40
Total taxes of U.S. taxpayer	7	35	17.5	46

Note: the exhibit comes from Frederick D.D. Choi, Gary K. Meek (2011), page 441

Further scrutiny of Exhibit 13.4 is instructive. A comparison of columns 2 and 3 suggests the importance of organizational form on international taxes. A branch operation, viewed as an extension of the parent company, is subject to the full tax rate of the home country. In our example, the foreign branch pays a total tax of $35: $30 of foreign income taxes and $5 of U.S. taxes. Thus, the foreign branch bears the full burden of the U.S. income tax rate. However, it is spared any withholding taxes on earnings distributions to the parent because only a foreign subsidiary can distribute its earnings. On the other hand, a foreign operation organized as a subsidiary is taxed only on earnings that it remits to the parent company. It can defer taxes on retained income, and thus compete on an equal tax footing with local companies. Columns 3 and 4 illustrate how a system of worldwide taxation places a subsidiary at a competitive disadvantage when it is located in a country that relies primarily on an indirect tax for revenue. Note that the subsidiary in Country D has a higher total tax burden because the tax credit only relieves direct taxes, not indirect taxes. Similarly, the benefits of tax incentives granted by host governments may also be nullified.

13.2.2　Limits to tax credits

Home countries can tax foreign-source income in many ways. A country may elect to tax income from each separate national source. At the other extreme, all foreign-source income from any foreign source may be combined and taxed once. Some countries tax foreign-source income on a source-by-source basis, with the tax credit for foreign source income limited to the corresponding domestic tax applicable to that income. As illustrated in columns 2 and 3 of Exhibit 13.4, the maximum tax liability will always be the higher of the tax rates in the host or home country. Other countries allow parent companies to pool income from many country sources by income type (e.g., dividends vs. interest vs. royalties). Excess tax credits from countries with high tax rates (column 3 of Exhibit 13.4) can offset taxes on income received from low-tax-rate countries (column 2 of Exhibit 13.4).

To prevent foreign tax credits from offsetting taxes on domestic-source income, many countries impose an overall limit on the amount of foreign taxes creditable in any year. The United States, for instance, limits the tax credit to the proportion of the U.S. tax that equals the ratio of the taxpayer's foreign-source taxable income to its worldwide taxable income for the year. Assume that Alpha Company earned $2,000 of foreign-source income and $3,000 of U.S.-source taxable income. Its foreign tax credit would be the lesser of the foreign income taxes paid or the foreign tax credit limitation computed as follows:

$$\text{Foreign tax credit limeit} = \frac{\text{Foreign source taxable income}}{\text{Worldwide taxble income}} * \text{U.S. tax before credits}$$

$$= (\$2000/\$5000) * (\$5000 * 35\%) = \$700$$

Thus, only $700 would be allowed as a tax credit, even if foreign taxes paid exceeded $700. Excess foreign taxes paid can be carried back one year and forward 10 years.

A separate foreign tax credit limitation applies to U.S. taxes on the foreign-source taxable income of each of the two types of income (or baskets), which are passive income (e.g., investment-type income, such as dividends, interest, royalties, and rents), and general income (all other types).

Foreign-source taxable income is foreign-source gross income less expenses, losses, and deductions allocable to the foreign-source income, plus a ratable share of expenses, losses, and deductions that cannot be allocated definitely to any item or class of gross income. The interpretation of this provision is reportedly one of the major areas of dispute between taxpayers and the IRS.

13.3 International Tax Planning

International tax planning should be integrally woven into corporate activities. International tax planning is very complex but can contribute to multinational companies' overall profit. Multinationals will be trying to move profits from high-tax countries to lower-tax countries, avoid the taxation of the same income in two countries(double taxation), get tax deductions twice for the same expenses, and arrange for some income to be taxed nowhere.

In tax planning, multinational companies have a distinct advantage over purely domestic companies because they have more geographical flexibility in locating their production and distribution systems. This flexibility provides unique opportunities to exploit differences among national tax jurisdictions so as to lower the overall tax burden for the corporation. The shifting of revenues and expenses through intracompany ties also gives MNEs additional opportunities to minimize the global taxes paid.

1. Organizational Considerations

In taxing foreign-source income, many taxing jurisdictions focus on the organizational form of a foreign operation. A branch is usually considered an extension of the parent company. Accordingly, its income is immediately consolidated with that of the parent (an option not available to a subsidiary) and fully taxed in the year earned whether remitted to the parent company or not. Earnings of a foreign subsidiary are not generally taxed until repatriated. Exceptions to this general rule are described in the next section.

If initial operations abroad are forecast to generate losses, it may be tax-advantageous to organize initially as a branch. Once foreign operations turn profitable, operating them as subsidiaries may be attractive. For one thing, the corporate overhead of the parent company cannot be allocated to a branch, because the branch is viewed as part of the parent. Moreover, if taxes on foreign profits are lower in the host country than in the parent country, profits of a subsidiary are not taxed by the parent country until repatriated (see columns 2 and 3 of Exhibit 13.4). If the subsidiary were organized in a tax-haven country that imposes no taxes at all, tax deferral would be even more attractive. National governments know this phenomenon, and many have taken steps to minimize corporate abuse of it. One example is the U.S. treatment of Subpart F income.

2. Controlled Foreign Corporations and Subpart F Income

In the United States, like many other countries adopting the worldwide principle of taxation, income of foreign subsidiaries is not taxable to the parent until it is repatriated as a dividend — the so-called deferral principle. Tax havens give multinationals an opportunity to avoid repatriation—and home-country taxes—by locating transactions and accumulating profits in "brass plate" subsidiaries. These transactions have no real work or employment attached to them. The income earned on these transactions is passive rather than active.

The United States closed this loophole with the Controlled Foreign Corporation (CFC) and Subpart F Income provisions. A CFC is a corporation in which U.S. shareholders (U.S. corporations, citizens, or residents) directly or indirectly own more than 50 percent of its combined voting power or fair market value. Only shareholders holding more than a 10 percent voting interest are counted in determining the 50 percent requirement. Shareholders of a CFC are taxed on certain income of the CFC (referred to as tainted income) even before the income is distributed.

Subpart F income includes certain related-party sales and services income. For example, if a Bahamian subsidiary of a U.S. corporation "buys" inventory from its U.S. parent and sells the inventory to the European Union, the profits booked by the Bahamian subsidiary are Subpart F income. On the other hand, if the Bahamian subsidiary sells the imported inventory in the Bahamas, income from the local sales is not Subpart F income. Subpart F income also includes passive income, such as dividends, interest, rents, and royalties; net gains on certain foreign exchange or commodities transactions; gains from the sale of certain investment property including securities; and certain insurance income.

3. Offshore Holding Companies

In some circumstances, a U.S.-based multinational parent company with operations in several foreign countries may find it advantageous to own its various foreign investments through a third-country holding company. The essential features of this structure are that the U.S. parent directly owns the shares of a holding company set up in one foreign jurisdiction, and the holding company, in turn, owns the shares of one or more operating subsidiaries set up in other foreign jurisdictions. The tax-related advantages of this holding company organizational form could include securing beneficial withholding tax rates on dividends, interest, royalties, and similar payments, deferring U.S. tax on foreign earnings until they are repatriated to the U.S. Parent company, and deferring U.S. tax on gains from the sale of the shares of the foreign operating subsidiaries.

Realizing these advantages depends in large part on proper planning under complex U.S. tax rules (such as the Subpart F and foreign tax credit rules) and avoiding anti treaty shopping rules found in many tax treaties.

4. Financing Decisions

The manner in which foreign operations are financed can also be shaped by tax considerations. Other things equal, the tax deductibility of debt, which increases the after-tax returns on equity, increases the attractiveness of debt financing in high-tax countries.

Where local-currency borrowing is constrained by local governments that mandate minimum levels of equity infusion by the foreign parent, parent-company borrowing to finance this capital infusion could achieve similar end, provided the taxing jurisdiction of the parent allows the interest to be deductible.

In other instances, offshore financing subsidiaries domiciled in a low-tax or tax haven country also could be used as a financing vehicle. At one time, U.S. Companies wishing to borrow funds in the euro dollar market were constrained from doing so because the U.S. government imposed a withholding tax on interest paid to foreign lenders. To lower the cost of financing, they formed offshore financing subsidiaries in the Netherlands Antilles, a country that has no withholding tax on interest to nonresidents.

In general, an offshore financing subsidiary, located in a low-or no-tax country, will issue securities and then lend money to an operating subsidiary (or the parent) located in a country with higher taxes. This intracompany loan results in interest income for the (low-/no-tax) financing subsidiary and deductible interest expense for the (higher tax) operating subsidiary. The result is higher after-tax consolidated profits.

5. Location and Transfer Pricing

The locations of production and distribution systems also offer tax advantages. Thus, final sales of goods or services can be channeled through affiliates located in jurisdictions that offer tax shelter or deferral. Alternatively, a manufacturer in a high-tax country can obtain components from affiliates located in low-tax countries to minimize corporate taxes for the group as a whole. A necessary element of such a strategy is the prices at which goods and services are transferred between group companies. Profits for the corporate system as a whole can be increased by setting high transfer prices on components shipped from subsidiaries in relatively low-tax countries, and low transfer prices on components shipped from subsidiaries in relatively high-tax countries.

Transfer pricing has attracted increasing worldwide attention. The significance of the issue is obvious when we recognize that transfer pricing (1) is conducted on a relatively larger scale internationally than domestically, (2) is affected by more variables than are found in a strictly domestic setting, (3) varies from company to company, industry to industry, and country to country, and (4) affects social, economic, and political relationships in multinational business entities and, sometimes, entire countries (Frederick, Gary, 2010).

13.4 International Transfer Pricing

Transfer pricing refers to the determination of the price at which transactions between related parties will be carried out. Transfers can be from a subsidiary to its parent (upstream), from the parent to a subsidiary (downstream), or from one subsidiary to another of the same parent. Transfers between related parties are also known as intercompany transactions. Intercompany transactions represent a significant portion of international trade. In 2012, intercompany transactions comprised 42 percent of U.S. total goods trade: $1,132 billion (50 percent) of the $2,251 billion in U.S. imports, and $450 billion (29 percent) of the $1,547 billion in U.S. exports[①]. There is a wide range of types of intercompany transactions, each of which has a price associated with it. The basic question that must be addressed is, at what price should intercompany transfers be made?

Two factors heavily influence the manner in which international transfer prices are determined. The first factor is the objective that headquarters management wishes to achieve through its transfer pricing practices. One possible objective relates to management control and performance evaluation. Another objective relates to the minimization of one or more types of costs. These two types of objectives often conflict.

The second factor affecting international transfer pricing is the law that exists in most countries governing the manner in which intercompany transactions crossing their borders may be priced. These laws were established to make sure that MNEs are not able to avoid paying their fair share of taxes, import duties, and so on by virtue of the fact that they operate in multiple jurisdictions. In establishing international transfer prices, MNEs often must walk a fine line between achieving corporate objectives and

---

① U.S. Goods Trade: Imports and Exports by Related Parties, 2012. U.S. Census Bureau News, May 2, 2013, p1.

complying with applicable rules and regulations. In a recent survey, more respondents (30%) identified transfer pricing as the most important issue they face compared to all other international tax issues.

The methods used in setting transfer prices in an international context are essentially the same as those used in a purely domestic context. The following cost-based transfer price, market-based transfer price, and negotiated price methods are commonly used:

1. Cost-based transfer price

The transfer price is based on the cost to produce a good or service. Cost can be determined as variable production cost, variable plus fixed production cost, or full cost, based on either actual or budgeted amounts (standard costs). The transfer price often includes a profit margin for the seller (a "cost-plus" price). Cost-based systems are simple to use, but there are at least two problems associated with them. The first problem relates to the issue of which measure of cost to use. The other problem is that inefficiencies in one unit may be transferred to other units, as there is no incentive for selling divisions to control costs. The use of standard, rather than actual, costs alleviates this problem.

2. Market-based transfer price

The transfer price charged a related party is either based on the price that would be charged to an unrelated customer or determined by reference to sales of similar products or services by other companies to unrelated parties. Market-based systems avoid the problem associated with cost-based systems of transferring the inefficiencies of one division or subsidiary to others. They help ensure divisional autonomy and provide a good basis for evaluating subsidiary performance. However, market-based pricing systems also have problems. The efficient working of a market-based system depends on the existence of competitive markets and dependable market quotations. For certain items, such as unfinished products, there may not be any buyers outside the organization and hence no external market price.

3. Negotiated price

The transfer price is the result of negotiation between buyer and seller and may be unrelated to either cost or market value. A negotiated pricing system can be useful, as it allows subsidiary managers the freedom to bargain with one another, thereby preserving the autonomy of subsidiary managers. However, for this system to work efficiently, it is important that there are external markets for the items being transferred so that the negotiating parties can have objective information as the basis for negotiation. One disadvantage of negotiated pricing is that negotiation can take a long time, particularly if the process deteriorates and the parties involved become more interested in winning arguments than in considering the issues from the corporate perspective. Another disadvantage is that the price agreed on and therefore a manager's measure of performance may be more a function of a manager's ability to negotiate than of his or her ability to control costs and generate profit.

Management accounting theory suggests that different pricing methods are appropriate in different situations. Market-based transfer prices lead to optimal decisions when ① the market for the product is perfectly competitive, ② interdependencies between the related parties are minimal, and ③ there is no advantage or disadvantage to buying and selling the product internally rather than externally. Prices based on full cost can approximate market-based prices when the determination of market price is not feasible. Prices that have been negotiated by buyer and seller rather than being mandated by upper management have the advantage of allowing the related parties to maintain their decentralized authority. A 1990 survey of Fortune 500 companies in the United States found that 41% of respondent companies relied on cost-based methods in determining international transfer prices, 46% used market-based methods, and 13% allowed transfer prices to be determined through negotiation. The most widely used approach was full production cost plus a markup. Slightly less than half of the respondents reported using more than one method to determine transfer prices.

13.5 Transfer Pricing Methodology

13.5.1 Comparable uncontrolled price method

The comparable uncontrolled price method is generally considered to provide the most reliable measure of an arm's-length price when a comparable uncontrolled transaction exists. Assume that a U.S.-based parent company (Parentco) makes sales of tangible property to a foreign subsidiary (Subco). Under this method, the price for tax purposes is determined by reference to sales by Parentco of the same or similar product to unrelated customers, or purchases by Subco of the same or similar product from unrelated suppliers. Also, sales of the same product between two unrelated parties could be used to determine the transfer price.

To determine whether the comparable uncontrolled price method results in the most reliable measure of arm's-length price, a company must consider each of the factors. Section 1.482-3 of the Treasury Regulations indicates specific factors that may be particularly relevant in determining whether an uncontrolled transaction is comparable.[①] These specific factors include quality of the product, contractual terms, level of the market, geographic market in which the transaction takes place, date of the

---

① https://en.wikipedia.org/wiki/Treasury_regulations

transaction, intangible property associated with the sale, foreign currency risks, and alternatives realistically available to the buyer and seller.

If the uncontrolled transaction is not exactly comparable, some adjustment to the uncontrolled price is permitted in order to make the transactions more comparable. For example, assume that Sorensen Company, a U.S. manufacturer, sells the same product to both controlled and uncontrolled distributors in Mexico. The price to uncontrolled distributors is $40 per unit. Sorensen affixes its trademark to the products sold to its Mexican subsidiary but not to the products sold to the uncontrolled distributor. The trademark is considered to add approximately $10 of value to the product. The transactions are not strictly comparable because the products sold to the controlled and uncontrolled parties are different (one has a trademark and the other does not). Adjusting the uncontrolled price of $40 by $10 would result in a more comparable price, and $50 would be an acceptable transfer price under the comparable uncontrolled price method. If the value of the trademark could not be reasonably determined, the comparable uncontrolled price method might not result in the most reliable arm's-length price in this scenario.

13.5.2 Resale price method

The resale price method determines the transfer price by subtracting an appropriate gross profit from the price at which the controlled buyer resells the tangible property. In order to use this method, a company must know the final selling price to uncontrolled parties and be able to determine an appropriate gross profit for the reseller. An appropriate gross profit is determined by reference to the gross profit margin earned in comparable uncontrolled transactions. For example, assume that Odom Company manufactures and sells automobile batteries to its Canadian affiliate, which in turn sells the batteries to local retailers at a resale price of $50 per unit. Other Canadian distributors of automobile batteries earn an average gross profit margin of 25 percent on similar sales. Applying the resale price method, Odom Company would establish an arm's-length price of $37.50 per unit for its sale of batteries to its Canadian affiliate (resale price of $50 less an appropriate gross profit of $12.50 [25 percent] to be earned by the Canadian affiliate).

In determining an appropriate gross profit, the degree of comparability between the sale made by the Canadian affiliate and sales made by uncontrolled Canadian distributors need not be as great as under the comparable uncontrolled price method. The decisive factor is the similarity of functions performed by the affiliate and uncontrolled distributors in making sales. For example, if the functions performed by the Canadian affiliate in selling batteries are similar to the functions performed by Canadian distributors of automobile parts in general, the company could use the gross profit earned by uncontrolled sellers of automobile parts in Canada in determining an acceptable transfer price. Other important factors affecting comparability might include inventory levels and turnover rates, contractual terms, sales, marketing, and advertising programs and services, and level of the market (e.g., wholesale, retail).

The resale price method is typically used when the buyer/reseller is merely a distributor of finished goods—a so-called sales subsidiary. The method is acceptable only when the buyer/reseller does not add a substantial amount of value to the product. The resale price method is not feasible in cases where the reseller adds substantial value to the goods or where the goods become part of a larger product, because there is no "final selling price to uncontrolled parties" for the goods that were transferred. Continuing with our example, if Odom Company's Canadian affiliate operates an auto assembly plant and places the batteries purchased from Odom in automobiles that are then sold for $20,000 per unit, the company cannot use the resale price method for determining an appropriate transfer price for the batteries.

13.5.3 Cost-plus method

The cost-plus method is most appropriate when there are no comparable uncontrolled sales and the related buyer does more than simply distribute the goods it purchases. Whereas the resale price method subtracts an appropriate gross profit from the resale price to establish the transfer price, the cost-plus method adds an appropriate gross profit to the cost of producing a product to establish an arm's length price. This method is normally used in cases involving manufacturing, assembly, or other production of goods that are sold to related parties. Once again, the appropriate gross profit markup is determined by reference to comparable uncontrolled transactions. Physical similarity between the products transferred is not as important in determining comparability under this method as it is under the comparable uncontrolled price method. Factors to be included in determining whether an uncontrolled transaction is comparable include similarity of functions performed, risks borne, and contractual terms. Factors that may be particularly relevant in determining comparability under this method include Complexity of the manufacturing or assembly process, manufacturing, production, and process engineering, procurement, purchasing, and inventory control activities, and testing functions.

To illustrate use of the cost-plus method, assume that Pruitt Company has a subsidiary in Taiwan that acquires materials locally to produce an electronic component. The component, which costs $4 per unit to produce, is sold only to Pruitt Company. Because the Taiwanese subsidiary does not sell this component to other, unrelated parties, the comparable uncontrolled price method is not applicable. Pruitt Company combines the electronic component imported from Taiwan with other parts to assemble electronic switches that are sold in the United States. Because Pruitt does not simply resell the electronic components in the United States, the resale price method is not available. Therefore, Pruitt must look for a comparable transaction between unrelated parties in Taiwan to determine whether the cost-plus method can be used. Assume that an otherwise comparable company in Taiwan manufactures similar electronic components from its inventory of materials and sells them to unrelated buyers at an average gross profit markup on cost of 25 percent. In this case, application of the cost-plus method results in a transfer price of $5 ($4 + [$4 × 25%]) for the electronic component that Pruitt purchases from its Taiwanese subsidiary.

Now assume that Pruitt's Taiwanese subsidiary manufactures electronic components using materials provided by Pruitt on a consignment basis. To apply the cost-plus method, Pruitt would have to make a downward adjustment to the otherwise comparable gross profit markup of 25 percent, because the inventory risk assumed by the manufacturer in the comparable transaction justifies a higher gross profit markup than is appropriate for Pruit's foreign subsidiary. If Pruitt cannot reasonably ascertain the effect of inventory procurement and handling on gross profit, the cost-plus method might not result in a reliable transfer price.

13.5.4 Comparable profits method

The comparable profits method is based on the assumption that similarly situated taxpayers will tend to earn similar returns over a given period. Under this method, one of the two parties in a related transaction is chosen for examination. An arm's length price is determined by referring to an objective measure of profitability earned by uncontrolled taxpayers on comparable, uncontrolled sales. Profit indicators that might be considered in applying this method include the ratio of operating income to operating assets, the ratio of gross profit to operating expenses, or the ratio of operating profit to sales. If the transfer price used results in ratios for the party being examined that are in line with those ratios for similar businesses, then the transfer price will not be challenged.

To demonstrate the comparable profits method, assume that Glassco, a U.S. manufacturer, distributes its products in a foreign country through its foreign sales subsidiary, Vidroco. Assume that Vidroco has sales of $1,000,000 and operating expenses (other than cost of goods sold) of $200,000. Over the past several years, comparable distributors in the foreign country have earned operating profits equal to 5 percent of sales. Under the comparable profi ts method, a transfer price that provides Vidroco an operating profit equal to 5 percent of sales would be considered arm's length. An acceptable operating profit for Vidroco is $50,000 ($1,000,000 × 5%). To achieve this amount of operating profit, cost of goods sold must be $750,000 ($1,000,000 − $200,000 − $50,000); this is the amount that Glassco would be allowed to charge as a transfer price for its sales to Vidroco. This example demonstrates use of the ratio of operating profit to sales as the profit level indicator under the comparable profits method. The Treasury Regulations also specifically mention use of the ratio of operating profit to operating assets and the ratio of gross profit to operating expenses as acceptable profit-level indicators in applying this method.

13.5.5 Profit split method

The profit split method assumes that the buyer and seller are one economic unit. The total profit earned by the economic unit from sales to uncontrolled parties is allocated to the members of the economic unit based on their relative contributions in earning the profit. The relative value of each party's contribution in earning the profit is based on the functions performed, risks assumed, and resources employed in the business activity that generates the profit. There are in fact two versions of the profit split method, which are comparable profit split method and residual profit split method.

Under the comparable profit split method, the profit split between two related parties is determined through reference to the operating profit earned by each party in a comparable uncontrolled transaction. Each of the factors must be considered in determining the degree of comparability between the intercompany transaction and the comparable uncontrolled transaction. The degree of similarity in the contractual terms between the controlled and comparable uncontrolled transaction is especially critical in determining whether this is the "best method." In addition, Treasury Regulations specifically state that this method "may not be used if the combined operating profit (as a percentage of the combined assets) of the uncontrolled comparables varies significantly from that earned by the controlled taxpayers." When controlled parties possess intangible assets that allow them to generate profits in excess of what is earned in otherwise comparable uncontrolled transactions, the residual profit split method should be used. Under this method, the combined profit is allocated to each of the controlled parties following a two-step process. In the first step, profit is allocated to each party to provide a market return for its routine contributions to the relevant business activity. This step will not allocate all of the combined profit earned by the controlled parties, because it will not include a return for the intangible assets that they possess. In the second step, the residual profit attributable to intangibles is allocated to each of the controlled parties on the basis of the relative value of intangibles that each contributes to the relevant business activity. The reliability of this method hinges on the ability to measure the value of the intangibles reliably. The transfer pricing methods allowed for tangible property transfers under U.S. regulations also are used in other countries. In a survey of 877 MNEs located in 25 different countries, Ernst & Young found the percentages of companies using various transfer pricing methods for transfers of tangible goods were.[①] These percentages show cost-plus method (30%), comparable uncontrolled price method (27%), comparable profits method (23%), resale price method (12%), profit split method (3%), and other methods (6%).

Terms of the Chapter

accelerated depreciation 加速折旧
affiliated companies 关联公司
anti treaty 反协议
arbitrage opportunities 套利机会
arm's-length price 公平交易价格
bear the cost 承担费用
bilateral tax treaties 双边税收协定
border taxes 边境税
business acquisition 企业收购
Comparable Profits Method 可比利润法
consolidated profits 合并利润
consumption tax 消费税
contractual terms 合同条款
corporate income taxes 企业所得税
cost-based transfer price 成本为基础的转移价格
direct foreign investments(FDI) 外商直接投资
direct tax 直接税
double taxation 双重课税
effective tax rates 有效税率
excise taxes 消费税
foreign tax credit 外国税收抵免
global harmonization 全球协调
indirect tax 间接税
market-based transfer price 以市场为基础的转移价格
matching principle 匹配原则
negotiated price 协商价格
nominal tax rates 名义税率
nontreaty 非条约
Offshore Holding Companies 远洋控股公司
Organization for Economic Cooperation and Development (OECD) 经济合作与发展组织

---

① Ernst & Young, 2010 Global Transfer Pricing Survey, p13.

payroll taxes 工资税

Profit Split Method 利润分割法

property taxes 财产税

ratable share 按比例分享

resale price method 转售价格法

retained income 留存收益

Subpart F Income 基于外国公司收入

substantial activities 实质性活动

tax assessment 纳税评估

tax burdens 税收负担

tax collection philosophies 税收征管理念

tax deductible 免税额

tax deferral 延期纳税

tax evader 逃税

tax haven 避税港

tax jurisdictions 税务司法管辖区

tax neutral 税收中性

tax shelter 税收庇护

tax treaties 税收协定

taxes levied on 征收税款

tax-planning dimensions 税收筹划维度

tax-planning system 税收筹划系统

transfer tax 交易税

value-added tax 增值税

withholding tax 预扣税

Discussion Questions

1. How can a country's tax system affect the manner in which an operation in that country is financed by a foreign investor?

2. Why might the effective tax rate paid on income earned within a country be different from that country's national corporate income tax rate?

3. What is a tax haven? How might a company use a tax haven to reduce income taxes?

4. Why do effective tax rates seldom equal nominal tax rates?

5. What are the different ways in which income earned in one country becomes subject to double taxation?

6. What are the mechanisms used by countries to provide relief from double taxation?

7. How can transfer pricing be used to reduce the amount of withholding taxes paid to a government on dividends remitted to a foreign stockholder?

8. According to U.S. tax regulations, what are the five methods to determine the arm's-length price in a sale of tangible property? How does the best-method rule affect the selection of a transfer pricing method?

9. What is the arm's-length range of transfer pricing, and how does it affect the selection of a transfer pricing method?

True or False

1. Corporate objectives and national tax laws heavily influence the manner of international transfer prices.

2. Tax burden means the tax rate.

3. Effective tax rates rarely equal nominal tax rates.

4. Withholding taxes are direct taxes imposed on payments made to foreigners, especially in the form of dividends, interest, and royalties.

5. Most countries provide relief from double taxation through foreign tax credits (FTCs).

6. Cost-minimization objectives that can be achieved through discretionary transfer pricing include minimization of worldwide income tax, minimization of import duties, circumvention of repatriation restrictions, and improvement of the competitive position of foreign subsidiaries.

7. Tax havens are jurisdictions that tend to have abnormally low corporate income tax rates.

8. Tax havens never tax corporate income.

9. In deciding whether to establish a foreign operation, multinational corporation might consider after-tax returns from competing investment locations.

10. The existence of overlapping bases leads to double taxation.

Multiple Choice

1. In deciding whether to establish a foreign operation, which factor(s) might a multinational enterprise (MNE) consider?

    a. After-tax returns from competing investment locations.

    b. The tax treatments of branches versus subsidiaries.

    c. Withholding rates on dividend and interest payments.

    d. All of the above.

2. Why might a company involved in international business find it beneficial to

establish an operation in a tax haven?

    a. The OECD recommends the use of tax havens for corporate income tax avoidance.

    b. Tax havens never tax corporate income.

    c. Tax havens are jurisdictions that tend to have abnormally low corporate income tax rates.

    d. Tax havens' banking systems are less secretive.

3. Which of the following item(s) might provide an MNE with a tax-planning opportunity as it decides where to locate a foreign operation?

    a. Differences in corporate tax rates across countries.

    b. Differences in local tax rates across countries.

    c. Whether a country offers a tax holiday.

    d. All of the above.

4. Why might companies have an incentive to finance their foreign operations with as much debt as possible?

    a. Interest payments are generally tax deductible.

    b. Withholding rates are lower for dividends.

    c. Withholding rates are lower for interest.

    d. Both (a) and (c).

5. Kerry is a U.S. citizen residing in Portugal. Kerry receives some investment income from Spain. Why might Kerry be expected to pay taxes on the investment income to the United States?

    a. The United States taxes its citizens on their worldwide income.

    b. The United States taxes its citizens on the basis of residency.

    c. Portugal requires all of its residents to pay taxes to the United States.

    d. None of the above.

6. What are the two most common methods of eliminating the double taxation of income earned by foreign corporations?

    a. Exempting foreign source income and deducting all foreign taxes paid.

    b. Deducting all foreign taxes paid and providing a foreign tax credit.

    c. Exempting foreign source income and providing a foreign tax credit.

    d. Deducting all foreign taxes paid and tax havens.

7. Bush Inc. has total income of $500,000. Bush's Polish branch has foreign source income of $200,000 and paid taxes of $38,000 to the Polish government. The U.S. corporate tax rate is 35 percent. What is Bush's overall foreign tax credit limitation?

    a. $70,000.

    b. $175,000.

    c. $150,000.

d. $38,000.

8. Which of the following objectives is not achieved through the use of lower transfer prices?

    a. Improving the competitive position of a foreign operation.

    b. Minimizing import duties.

    c. Protecting foreign currency cash flows from currency devaluation.

    d. Minimizing income taxes when transferring to a lower-tax country.

9. Which of the following methods does U.S. tax law always require to be used in pricing intercompany transfers of tangible property?

    a. Comparable uncontrolled price method.

    b. Comparable profits method.

    c. Cost-plus method.

    d. Best method.

10. Which of the following is not a method commonly used for establishing transfer prices?

    a. Cost-based transfer price.

    b. Negotiated price.

    c. Market-based transfer price.

    d. Industry wide transfer price.

11. Market-based transfer prices lead to optimal decisions in which of the following situations?

    a. When inter dependencies between the related parties are minimal.

    b. When there is no advantage or disadvantage to buying and selling the product internally rather than externally.

    c. When the market for the product is perfectly competitive.

    d. All of the above.

12. U.S. Treasury Regulations require the use of one of five specified methods to determine the arm's-length price in a sale of tangible property. Which of the following is not one of those methods?

    a. Cost-plus method.   b. Market-based method.

    c. Profit split method.   d. Resale price method.

Exercises

1. The partial income statement of the Future Manufacturing Company, a Italian-based concern producing electric products, is presented below: During the year, short-term interest rates in Italy averaged 5%, while net operating assets averaged €50,000,000. The company is entitled to a government subsidy of 3%. Its required margin to provide a profit and cover other expenses is 10%. All affiliates receive credit

terms of 60 days.

Required: Based on this information, at what price would the Future Manufacturing Company invoice its distribution affiliate in Germany?

Sales	170,000,000
Cost of goods manufactured and sold:	
Finished goods, beginning inventory	0
Cost of goods manufactured: (100,000 units)	
Direct materials used	50,000,000
Direct labor	15,000,000
Overhead	17,000,000
Cost of goods available for sale	72,000,000
Finished goods, ending inventory	17,000,000
Cost of goods sold	55,000,000
Gross Margin	115,000,000

2. A Chinese manufacturing subsidiary produces items sold in United States. The sales price is $10 and the cost is $6. A Cayman Islands subsidiary buys the items from the Chinese subsidiary for $6 and sells them to the United States parent for $10.

Required: What's the income taxes paid to these transactions. What are the implications for the company and the taxing authorities involved?

3. A steelworks manufacturer domiciled in UK purchases raw materials from a dealer for GBP 30,000, then makes these raw material into steel and sell it to a French retailer for GBP40,000.

Required: What's the value-added tax from the steelworks manufacturer's activities if the French value-added tax rate is 17.5 percent.

4. Nash, a U.S. multinational, receives royalties from Country A, foreign-branch earnings from Country B, and dividends equal to 45% of net income from subsidiaries in Countries C and D. There is a 10% withholding tax on the royalty from Country A and a 10% withholding tax on the dividend from Country C. Income tax rates are 10% in Country B and 25% in Country C. Country D assesses indirect taxes of 40% instead of direct taxes on income. Selected data are as follows:

	Country A	Country B	Country C	Country D
Royalty from Country A operations	$50			
Pretax income		$200	$200	$100
Income taxes (10%/25%)		20	50	0
Net income		$180	$150	$100

Required: Calculate the foreign and U.S. Taxes paid on each foreign-source income.

Reference

[1]   Ahrens T, Chapman C S. New measures in performance management. Oxford: Oxford University Press, 2006.

[2]   Akwasi A, Ampofo, Sellani R J. Examining the differences between United States Generally Accepted Accounting Principles (U.S. GAAP) and International Accounting Standards (IAS): implications for the harmonization of accounting standards. Accounting Forum, June 2005, Vol. 29 Issue 2: 219-231.

[3]   American Accounting Association. Report of the Committee on international accounting operations and education. Accounting Review Supplement, 1977: 65-132.

[4]   Avik D. Apache sells Egyptian oil stake to Sinopec for $3.1 billion, forms global JV. Reuters. 30 August 2013. https://en.wikipedia.org/wiki/Sinopec.

[5]   Avram, Cristina Bota, Grosanu, Adrian, et al. Does country-level governance influence auditing and financial reporting standards? Evidence from a cross-country analysis. Current Science. 2015, Vol. 108 Issue 7: 1222-1227.

[6]   Bailes J C, Assada T. Empirical differences between Japanese and American budget and performance evaluation systems. International Journal of Accounting, 1991, Vol. 26 Issue 2: 131-142.

[7]   Baker C R A. Critique of the concepts of measurement in financial accounting. Working paper. Adelphi University, 2013.

[8]   Barbosa N, Louri H. On the determinants of multinationals' ownership preferences: Evidence from Greece and Portugal. International Journal of Industrial Economics, 2002(20): 493–515.

[9]   Baydoun N, Willett R J. Cultural relevance of western accounting systems to developing countries. Abacus, 1995(31): 67-92.

[10] Burkart M. Large shareholders, monitoring, and the value of the firm. The Quarterly Journal of Economics, 1997,112 (3): 693–729.

[11] Benjamin J J, Grossman S D, Wiggins C E. The Impact of foreign currency translation on reporting during the phase-in of SFAS No. 52. Journal of Accounting, Auditing & Finance, June 1 1986:177-186.

[12] Berry I. The need to classify worldwide accountancy practices. Accountancy, October 1987: 90-91.

[13] Bertomeu J, Magee R P. Mandatory disclosure and asymmetry in financial reporting. Journal of Accounting & Economics, April 2015, Vol. 59 Issue 2: 284-299.

[14] Blanco B, Garcia L, Juan M, et al. Segment disclosure and cost of capital. Journal of Business Finance & Accounting. Apr 2015, Vol. 42: 367-411.

[15] Blanco B, García L, Juan M. et al. The relation between segment disclosure and earnings quality. Journal of Accounting & Public Policy, Sep 2014, Vol. 33 Issue 5: 449-469.

[16] Boritz J, Efrim, Timoshenko L M. Firm-specific characteristics of the participants in the SEC's XBRL voluntary filing program. Journal of Information Systems, Spring 2015, Vol. 29 Issue 1: 9-36.

[17] Bugeja M, Czernkowski R, Moran, et al. The impact of the management approach on segment reporting. Journal of Business Finance & Accounting, Apr 2015, Vol. 42: 310-366.

[18] Cadbury Commission. The financial aspects of corporate governance. London, 1992.

http://www.kaew.co.uk/viewer/index.cfm.

[19] Cairns D A. Guide to Applying International Accounting Standards. The Institute of Chartered Accountants in England and Wales: Central Milton Keynes, 1995.

[20] Cairns D. The future shape of harmonization: a reply. European Accounting Review, 1997, 6(2): 305-348.

[21] Carsberg B. The role and future plans of the international accounting standards committee. Essays in Accounting Thought: A Tribute to WT Baxter. Edinburgh: The Institute of Chartered Accountants of Scotland, 1996: 68-84.

[22] Chandra K, Rajdeep S, Andrew E S. Imprecision in accounting measurement: Can it be value enhancing? Journal of Accounting Research, June 2005, Vol. 43 No. 3: 487-521.

[23] Zhu C. Sinopec to pay $1.5 billion for parent's oil, gas assets. Reuters, 25 March 2013.
http://www.chinadaily.com.cn/business/2013-03/26/content_16347036.htm.

[24] Christopher N, Robert P. Comparative international accounting. Dalian: Dongbei University of Finance & Economics Press, 2010.

[25] Christopher N, Robert P. Comparative International Accounting. London: Pearson Education Limited, 2012.

[25] Claessens S, Djankov S. Ownership Concentration and Corporate Performance in the Czech Republic. CEPR Discussion Paper, 1999: 2145.

[27] Cooke T F, Kikuya M. Financial Reporting in Japan. Blackwell, Oxford, 1992.28.

[23] Da Costa R C, Bourgeois J C, Lawson V M. A classification of international financial accounting practices. International Journal of Accounting, Spring 1978: 73-85.

[29] De Albuquerque F, Almeida M do Ceu, Quiros J. The culture and the accounting values: an empirical study in view of Portuguese preparers. Journal of International Business and Economics, May, 2011, Volume 11 Issue 2.
http://www.freepatentsonline.com/article/Journal-International-Business-Economics/272616512.html

[30] Del Core, Tom, Barbagallo J. FASB's fair value update. Mergers & Acquisitions Report, 2010, Vol. 23 Issue 19: 9.

[31] Denis D K, McConnell J J. International corporate governance. Journal of Financial and Quantitative Analysis, 2003,38(1): 1-36.

[32] Ding Y, Gary M E, Hervé, et al. Identifying and coping with balance sheet differences: a comparative analysis of U.S, Chinese, and French oil and gas firms using the statement of financial structure. Issues in Accounting Education, Nov 2007, Vol. 22 Issue 4: 591-606.

[33] Donna L S, Kimberley A S. The evolution of the G4 + 1 and its impact on international harmonization of accounting standards. Journal of International Accounting, Auditing & Taxation, 1998, Vol. 7 Issue 2: 131-162.

[34] Doob C M. Social inequality and social stratification in US society. London: Pearson Education Inc, 2013.

[35] Doshi A R, Dowell G W S, Toffel M W. How firms respond to mandatory information disclosure. Strategic Management Journal, Oct 2013, Vol. 34 Issue 10: 1209-1231.

[36] Doupnik, Timothy S, Salter. An empirical test of a judgmental international classification of financial reporting practices. Journal of International Business Studies, 1993, Volume 24, Issue 1.

[37] Drobetz W, Merikas A, Merika A, et al. Corporate social responsibility disclosure: The case of international

shipping. Transportation Research: Part E, Nov 2014, Vol. 71: 18-44.

[38]   Elizabeth C C. Economic consequences of mandated accounting disclosures: evidence from pension accounting standards. The Accounting Review, 2013, Vol. 88, No. 2: 395-427.

[39]   Epstein B J, Mirza A A. IAS 97: Interpretation and Application of International   Accounting Standards. New York: Wiley,1997.

[40]   Ernst, Young. Worldwide corporate tax Guide, 2012. https://www.ey.com.

[41]   Eti E. The nature of the interaction between mandatory and voluntary disclosure. Journal of Accounting Research, September 2015, Vol.43 No.4: 593-623.

[42]   Fama E. Agency problems and the theory of the firm. Journal of Political Economy, 1980, 88: 288-307.

[43]   Fama E, Jensen M C. Agency problems and residual claims. Journal of Law and Economics,1983, 26 (2): 327–349.

[44]   Fama E, Jensen M C. Separation of ownership and control. Journal of Law and Economics, 1983, 26: 301–325.

[45]   Feng J. Accounting service market: a big cake for foreign giants. Beijing Review (May 2003). http://www.bjreview.com.cn/200305/Business-200305(C).htm.

[46]   Frederick D S, Choi, Carol A F, et, al. International Accounting (the 4th edition), 北京：北京大学出版社, 2002.

[47]   Frederick D S, Choi, Gary K. International Accounting (the 5th edition). 方红星, 改编. 大连：东北财经大学出版社, 2005.

[48]   Frederick D S, Choi, Gary K. International Accounting (the 6th edition) . 任明川, 改编. 北京：中国人民大学出版社, 2008.

[49]   Frederick D S, Choi, Gary K. International Accounting(the 7th Edition). Upper Saddle River: Prentice Hall, 2010.

[50]   Gary S J, Campbell L G, Shaw J C. International Financial Reporting. London: Macmillan, 1984.

[51]   Govindarajan V, Robert N A. How firms use cost data in price decisions. Management Accounting. July 1983: 30-36.

[52]   Gray S. International accounting: a case approach. New York: McGraw-Hill Inc., 1994.

[53]   Gray S. Towards a theory of cultural influence on the development of accounting systems internationally. Abacus, 1988, 24: 1-15.

[54]   Grundfest J A, Perino M A. Ten things we know and ten things we don't know about the Private Securities Litigation Reform Act of 1995: testimony before subcommittee on securities of the committee on banking, housing and urban affairs of the United States Senate. 1997.
        http://securities.standord.edu/research/articles/19970723sen1.html.

[55]   Gujarathi, Mahendra R S. Corporation: a case in international financial statement analysis. Issues in Accounting Education. Feb 2008, Vol. 23 Issue 1: 77-101.

[56]   Habib A. The role of accruals and cash flows in explaining security returns: Evidence from New Zealand. Journal of International Accounting, Auditing & Taxation, Jun 2008, Vol. 17 Issue 1: 51-66.

[57]   Hale D. Inflation accounting in the 1970s. Financial Analysts Journal, Sep/Oct 1978, Vol. 34 Issue 5：59.

[58]   Hatfield H R. Some Variations in Accounting Practices in England, France, Germany and the US. Journal of

Accounting Research, Autumn1966, Vol. 4 Issue 2: 169-182.

[59] Healy P M, Palepu K G. Information asymmetry, corporate disclosure, and the capital markets: a review of the empirical disclosure literature. Journal of Accounting and Economics, Sep 2001, Vol. 31 Issue 1-3: 405-440.

[60] Hofstede G. Culture's consequences: international differences in work related values. London: Sage Publications,1980.

[61] Hofstede G, Gert J H, Michael M. Cultures and organizations: software of the mind (the 3rd edition). New York: McGraw-Hill, 2010.

[62] Holmström B, Tirole J. Market liquidity and performance monitoring. Journal of Political Economy. Aug1993, Vol. 101 Issue 4: 678-710.

[63] Horngren C T, Datar S M, Rajan M V. Cost accounting: a managerial emphasis(the fourteenth edition). Harlow: Pearson Education, 2012.

[64] Ignacio, Joseph. Prospective analysis: guidelines for forecasting financial statements. Working paper, May 4, 2008. http://papers.ssrn.com/sol3/papers.cfm?abstract_id=1026210

[65] James H P. A brief history of property and depreciation accounting in municipal accounting. The Accounting Historians Journal, 1982, 9: 25-37.

[66] Jocelynhusser, Evraert-Bardinet, Frederique. The effect of social and environmental disclosure on companies' market value Management International / International Management / Gestión Internacional. 2014, Vol. 19 Issue 1: 61-84.

[67] Jones T C, Luther R. Anticipating the impact of IFRS on the management of German manufacturing companies: some observations from a British perspective. Accounting in Europe, 2005, 2: 165-193.

[68] Karmel R S. IOSCO's response to the financial crisis. Journal of Corporation Law, Summer 2012, Vol. 37 Issue 4: 849-901.

[69] Kelley L, Whatley A, Worthley R. Assessing the effects of culture on managerial attitudes: a three-culture test. Journal of International Business Studies, 1987,18:17-31.

[70] KPMG. Corporate and Indirect Tax Rate Survey-2012. www.kpmg.com.

[71] László K. The sustainability of the current account in the Czech Republic, Hungary and Slovenia. Empirical Economy , 2009, 36: 367–384.

[72] Lee H R, Sidney J G, Ervin L B. International Accounting and Multinational Enterprise (6th edition). Beijing: China Machine Press, 2007.

[73] Lee H R, Sidney J G, Ervin L B.   International Accounting and Multinational Enterprise (6th edition). 王全喜，张晓农,译. 北京：机械工业出版社, 2008.

[74] Leuz C, Verrecchia R. The economic consequences of increased disclosure. Journal of Accounting Research, 2000, 38(Suppl.): 91-124.

[75] Li Feng. The information content of forward looking statements in corporate filings- a naïve Bayesian machine learning approach. Journal of Accounting Research, December 2010, Vol.48 No.5: 1049-1104.

[76] Lu, J, Jean B P. Public accounting in China: decades of uncertainy. Working paper, 2005.

[77] Lu J, Gary S. Public accounting in China: 1900s to present. Journal of Accounting and Finance Research. March 2006, Vol.12 No.1: 1-11.

[78] Lúcia L, R, Russell C. Assessing international accounting harmonization using Hegelian dialectic, isomorphism and Foucault. Critical Perspectives on Accounting, Sep 2007, Vol. 18 Issue 6：739-757.

[79] Mandoza R, Collins F, Holzmann O J. Central American budgeting scorecard: cross cultural insights. Journal of International Accounting, Auditing and Taxation, 1997, 6: 192－209.

[80] Mary E B. Measurement in financial reporting: the need for concepts. Accounting Horizons, 2014, Vol. 28 No. 2: 331–352.

[81] Meek G K, Gray S J. Globalization of stock markets and foreign listing requirements: voluntary disclosure by continental European companies listed on the London Stock Exchange. Journal of International Business Studies, Summer1989 20(2): 315-336.

[82] Melissa R. Statistics of income bulletin. Spring 2008. http://www.irs.gov/uac/SOI-Tax-Stats-SOI-Bulletins.

[83] Michael H G, Gerhard G M. Father of international accounting education. Bingley: Emerald Group Publishing Limited, 2010.

[84] Mike N. The feature of standard setting. The CPA Journal, 2004,1: 18-21.

[85] Mongiello M. International financial reporting（the first edition）. Marco Monglello & Ventus Publishing APS, 2009.

[86] Mueller G. G. Whys and Hows of International Accounting. Accounting Review. Apr 1965, Vol. 40 Issue 2: 386-394.

[87] Mueller G G. The dimensions of the international accounting problem. Accounting Review. Jan1963, Vol. 38 Issue 1：142-148.

[88] Zafar I, Trini U, Melcher, et, al. International Accounting: A Global Perspective. 大连：东北财经大学出版社，1998.

[89] Mueller G G. International Accounting. Macmillan, 1967.

[90] Nair R D, Werner G F. The impact of disclosure and measurement practices on international accounting classification. The Accounting Review, July 1980, Vol.LV No.3:426-452.

[91] Nerrelit H. The Balanced Scorecard: what is the score? a rhetorical analysis of the Balanced Scorecard. Accounting. Organizations and Society, Aug2003, Vol. 28 Issue 6: 591-619.

[92] Nobes C W. A judgmental international classification of financial reporting practices. Journal of Business Finance & Accounting. Spring1983, Vol. 10 Issue 1：1-19.

[93] Nobes C. Towards a general model of the reasons for international differences in financial reporting. Abacus, Sep1998, Vol. 34 Issue 2: 162-187.

[94] Nobes C. International accounting harmonization: a commentary. The European Accounting Review, 1995, Vol.4 Issue 2: 249-254.

[95] Noerreklit H, Schoenfeld H W. Controlling multinational corporations: an attempt to analyze some unresolved issues, International Journal of Accounting, 2000, Vol.35 No. 3: 418.

[96] OECD Principles of Corporate Governance, 2004

[97] Organization for Economic Cooperation and Development. The OECD's Project on Harmful Tax Practices: The 2004 Progress Report. www.oecd.org.

[98] Palepu K, Bernard V L, Healy P M. Business analysis and valuation using financial statements. Cincinnati：South-Western College Publishing, 1996.

[99]   Pankaj M M. Corporate governance and disclosure practices of Indian firms: an industry perspective. The IUP Journal of corporate governance, 2014, Vol. XIII, No.2:27-41.

[100]   Palepu K G, Healy P M. Business analysis valuation: using financial statements. South Western Educational publishing, 2012.

[101]   Paton W A. Observations on inflation from an accounting stance. Journal of Accounting Research, Spring 1968, Vol. 6 Issue 1: 72-85.

[102]   Paul R. Accounting for foreign operations. Journal of Accountancy, Aug1987, Vol. 164 Issue 2: 102-112.

[103]   Peter C, Sue H. Voluntary disclosure of corporate governance practices by listed Australian companies corporate governance: An International Review, Mar 2005, Vol. 13 Issue 2: 188-196.

[104]   Pinto J A. How comprehensive is comprehensive income? The value relevance of foreign currency translation adjustment. Journal of International Financial Management & Accounting. Summer 2005, Vol. 16 Issue 2: 97-122.

[105]   Pinto S, DE Villiers C, Samkin G. Corporate social responsibility disclosures during the global financial crisis: New Zealand evidence. New Zealand Journal of Applied Business Research, 2014, Vol. 12 Issue 2: 33-49.

[106]   Richard L D. International Taxation In a Nutshell (the 4th edition). St. Paul: West, 1999.

[107]   Robert S K, David P N. The Balanced Scorecard: measures that drive performance. Harvard Business Review, Jan/Feb1992, Vol. 70 Issue 1: 71-79.

[108]   Robson K. The discourse of inflation accounting. European Accounting Review, July1994, Vol. 3 Issue 2: 195-214.

[109]   Zhao R, Benedicte M. Ownership structure and accounting information content: evidence from France. Journal of International Financial Management and Auditing , 2007, Vol.18 Issue 3: 223-248.

[110]   Rosenzweig K. Companies are not using FAS 33 data. Management accounting, April 1985: 51-57.

[111]   Rossi S, Volpin P F. Cross-country determinants of mergers and acquisitions. Journal of Financial Economics, 2004, Vol.74 Issue 2: 277-304.

[112]   Rowan J, Evelyne L, Klaus L, et al. A comparison of budgeting and accounting reforms in the national governments of France, Germany, the UK and the US. Financial Accountability & Management, November 2013, 29(4): 0267-4424

[113]   Ruland R G, Doupnik T S. Foreign Currency Translation and the Behavior of Exchange Rates. Journal of International Business Studies, Fall 1988, Vol.19 Issue 3: 461-537.

[114]   Simon A, Pascale D, Stuart M. A statistical model of international accounting harmonization. Abacus. Mar 1996, Vol. 32 Issue 1: 1-29.

[115]   Stephen D M, Brian B S. Foreign currency translation under the temporal rate method. International Advances in Economic Research, Nov 1996, Vol. 2 Issue 4: 444-455.

[116]   McNally S J. The 2013 COSO Framework & SOX Compliance. 2013.

[117]   Stephen S, Sean. Forward looking voluntary disclosure in proxy contest. Contemporary Accounting Research, 2013,Vol.31 No.4:1008-1046.

[118]   Sato T, Pan J. Comparison of internal control systems in Japan and China. International Journal of Business Administration, January 2012, Vol.3, No.1: 66-75 .

[119] Susan M S, Donald L K. Currency Translation Adjustments. Journal of Accountancy, Jul 2008, Vol. 206 Issue 1: 42-47.

[120] Tang Y. Bumpy road leading to internationalization: a review of accounting development in China. Accounting Horizons, March 2000, 14(1)：93-103.

[121] Tessmer A C, Shaw M J, Gentry J A. Inductive learning for international financial analysis: a layered approach. Journal of Management Information Systems, Spring 1993, Vol. 9 Issue 4: 17-36.

[122] Thies C F, Sturrock T. What did inflation accounting tell us? Journal of Accounting, Auditing & Finance, Fall1987, Vol. 2 Issue 4: 375-391.

[123] Thomas R R, Hennie van G, Elaine H, et, al. International financial statement analysis. Hoboken: John Wiley & Sons, Inc, 2009.

[124] Timothy D, Hector P. International Accounting. McGraw- Hill/Irwin, 2007.

[125] Timothy D, Hector P. International Accounting (the Fourth edition). McGraw Hill Higher Education, 2015.

[126] Tricker A. Essentials for Board Directors: an a–z guide. New York: Bloomberg Press, 2009.

[127] U.S. Internal Revenue Service. Publication 901, U.S. Tax Treaties. www.irs.gov.

[128] Velinger J. World Bank Marks Czech Republic's graduation to 'developed' status. Radio Prague. 28 February 2006. http://www.radio.cz/en/article/76314.

[129] Wang T, Seng J. Mandatory adoption of XBRL and foreign institutional investors' holdings: evidence from China. Journal of Information Systems. Fall 2014, Vol. 28 Issue 2：127-147.

[130] Webster F JR, Largay III J A, Stickney C P. The impact of inflation accounting on marketing decisions. Journal of Marketing, October 1, 1980: 9-20

[131] Weetman, Pauline, Gray S J. International financial analysis and comparative corporate performance: the impact of UK versus US accounting principles on earnings. Journal of International Financial Management & Accounting. Summer/Autumn 1990, Vol. 2 Issue 2/3：111-130.

[132] White Paper on Internal Control in Chinese Listed Companies, 2010. http://news.163.com/10/0902/00/6FHNUBQ100014AED.html.

[133] Xu Z, Xie R, Hu C. Due professional care of Certified Public Accountants in the People's Republic of China. Managerial Auditing Journal, 1997.12(4)：214-218.

[134] Yang J, Yang J. Accounting firms and Certified Public Accountants, Chapter XVII. Handbook of Chinese Accounting. Oxford University Press, 1997.

[135] Yousuf K, Craig D. Corporate social and environment-related governance disclosure practices in the textile and garment industry: evidence from a developing country. Australian Accounting Review, Jun 2013, Vol. 23 Issue 2: 117-134.

[136] Zhu   R. International control standards and cases. Beijing: China Economic Times Press, 2009.

[137] 常勋, 常亮. 国际会计.6 版. 厦门：厦门大学出版社，2008.

[138] 克里斯托弗·诺比斯，罗伯特·帕克. 比较国际会计.8 版. 薛清海，译. 大连：东北财经大学出版社，2005.

[139] 徐经长, 杜胜利, 陈轲. 国际会计学. 北京：中国人民大学出版社，2007.

Some Helpful Websites

http://www.nyse.com

http://www.nasdaq.com

http://www.londonstockexchange.com

http://www.hkex.com.hk

http://www.iasc.org.uk

http://www.iasplus.com

http://www.ifac.org

http://www.sec.gov

http://www2.iosco.org

http://www.fibv.com

http://www.oecd.org

http://www.aaa-edu.org

http://rutgers.edu/Accounting/raw

http://www.imf.org

http://www.aicpa.org

http://www.europa.eu.int

http://www.fasb.org

http://www.wsj.com

http://www.eia.doe.gov/emeu/cabs/newint.html

http://www.ameinfo.com/